Correlation of

EFFECTIVE

Speech

Second Edition

with
Texas Essential Elements for
Introduction to Speech Communication
and
Texas Educational Assessment
of Minimal Skills (TEAMS)
for English Language Arts

Glencoe Publishing Company
220 East Danieldale Road
DeSoto, Texas 75115
(214) 224-1562

Contents

Correlation between
Texas Essential Elements for Introduction to Speech Communication
and
EFFECTIVE SPEECH

The following pages present a correlation between EFFECTIVE SPEECH and the essential elements for Introduction to Speech Communication. Cross-references for these essential elements appear as notations in the Teacher's Resource Binder.

(1) Communication as process. The student shall be provided opportunities to:

(A) develop awareness of the importance of communication;

Lesson pages: 4, 5, 6–9, 11, 12, 21, 22, 49, 50, 53–55, 59, 61, 76, 81, 88, 95, 105, 107, 113, 119, 144, 145, 175, 178–180, 222–224, 261, 262, 273–275, 278, 279, 349, 359

Chapter Review Pages: 44, 45, 76, 100, 101, 109, 171, 207, 245, 281, 354

Communicating on the Job pages: 46, 78, 102, 110, 208, 218, 320, 356

Communicating as a Citizen pages: 47, 79, 103, 111, 173, 219, 245, 271, 283, 321, 357, 375, 387

Teacher's Resource Binder pages: LP1, 7, 8, 9, 13, 14, 18, 19, 21, 22, 32, 33, 39, 40, 42, 43, 47, 48, 52, 53, 55, 56, 61, 62, 68, 69, 72, 73, 75, 76; T1–2

(B) demonstrate an understanding of the elements of the communication process.

Page 7 of EFFECTIVE SPEECH states: "The speech communication process is the sending and receiving of oral messages in order to share meaning. Setting, commonality or lack of commonality of knowledge and language as well as nonverbal signals, and ability of those communicating to interpret feedback affect whether the participants achieve understanding."

Students will learn about the elements of communication as they pertain to the individual—attitudes, thoughts and knowledge, language, voice, and bodily movement—throughout the book. (In Chapter 1 there is a lesson devoted to each.) Students will learn about the anatomy of speaking (resonators and articulators) and how to improve articulation and pronunciation. They will learn of the importance of listening for meaning in messages and techniques to improve their listening skills (by analyzing, discriminating, judging, and evaluating messages for knowledge as well as for relaxation, enjoyment, or inspiration). They will learn the art of successful interpersonal communication and the art of establishing lasting relationships built on communication.

3

Lesson pages: 5–8, 11, 13–16, 18–20, 21–23, 25, 26, 29–31, 33–37, 39–42, 49, 53, 54, 61, 66, 74, 88, 89, 93–95, 98, 105, 107, 113, 114–117, 119, 122, 123, 130, 131, 133, 136, 141, 151, 152, 154, 156, 161, 163, 175, 178–181, 188, 192, 211, 214–216, 222–227, 256, 259, 273–275, 286, 291, 296, 316, 323, 338, 342, 359, 362, 364, 377–381

Chapter Review pages: 44, 45, 76, 77, 100, 101, 109, 170, 171, 206, 207, 217, 281, 318, 319, 354, 355, 372, 373, 383

Communicating on the Job pages: 46, 78, 102, 110, 208, 218, 274, 282, 320, 384

Communicating as a Citizen pages: 47, 79, 111, 173, 209, 283, 321, 385

Teacher's Resource Binder pages: LP1–8, 9, 13, 14, 18, 19, 21, 22, 32, 39, 40, 42; 43, 47, 48, 52, 53, 55, 56, 61, 62, 69, 72, 73, 75, 76; CT4, 7; LW1–4; EC1–13; EF1–6; T/TW1–5; C1–3; T1–2

(2) Self as communicator. The student shall be provided opportunities to:

(A) analyze and assess the role of self and participation in communication effectiveness;

Students will examine themselves in two roles, in that of the communicator and in that of the responder. They will learn the appropriate verbal and nonverbal styles to convey certain messages and learn how to analyze situations and make needed decisions. They will learn to recognize context clues, to take notes (interviews), and to be open-minded in their listening. A myriad of activities to support fulfillment of these objectives appear in the text.

Lesson pages: 10–14, 16–19, 21, 22, 27 (#4), 29–35, 39, 42, 55, 56, 61, 69, 75, 105–107, 113, 139, 141, 144, 164, 175, 179, 188, 211, 214, 225, 227, 253, 256, 273–275, 291, 296, 323, 338, 364, 370, 381

Chapter Review pages: 44, 45, 76, 77, 109, 170, 171, 206, 207, 217, 268, 281, 318, 319, 354, 355, 372, 373, 383

Communicating on the Job pages: 46, 78, 102, 110, 208, 282, 320, 374, 384

Communicating as a Citizen pages: 47, 79, 103, 111, 173, 209, 283, 321, 375, 385

Teacher's Resource Binder pages: LP1–8; LW1–2; CT1; EC1–5; SJ1–2; EF1–3; T/TW1; C1

(B) recognize ethical and social responsibilities of a communicator.

Students using EFFECTIVE SPEECH rapidly become aware of their individual responsibilities as communicators, especially as citizens. Every chapter in the text provides, after the Chapter Review, a one-page lesson entitled "Communicating as a Citizen," which affords students an opportunity to broaden their ethical horizons. Students will further learn methodologies of resolving conflicts, the role of the mediator and that of a group leader, and will learn to examine generalizations and faulty cause-effect relationships. They will further learn to distinguish between fact and opinion and to avoid misleading comparisons, personal attacks, and half-truths.

Lesson pages: 25, 35, 36, 39, 40, 41, 49, 50, 53, 54, 79, 88–89, 93, 105, 107, 115, 163, 164, 167, 168, 175, 179, 180, 188, 207 (#2), 221, 222–227, 229–231, 235–237, 243, 249–267, 273–275, 279, 280, 296, 301

Chapter Review pages: 44, 45, 76, 77, 100, 101, 109, 171, 206, 207, 244–245, 268, 269, 281

Communicating on the Job pages: 78, 110, 246, 282, 356

Communicating as a Citizen pages: 79, 103, 111, 173, 209, 219, 247, 271, 283, 321, 357, 375, 385

Teacher's Resource Binder pages: LP8, 9, 14, 16, 17, 19, 20, 22, 23, 34, 36–38, 40–43, 54, 56, 62, 69, 73; LW11; EC11, 12, 13, 22, 24–26, 33; SJ4, 5, 7; CT4, 6; EF6, 11; T/TW6

(3) Communication in interaction. The student will be provided opportunities to:

(A) use appropriate nonverbal symbols;

Students will learn the definition of nonverbal communication and will understand that the acceptance of these messages is dependent upon one's alertness, past experiences and training, and on the acuteness of one's senses. Students will learn various ways of expressing and receiving nonverbal messages and will learn the elements common to those messages.

Lesson pages: 7–9, 11, 16–20, 25, 26, 39, 40, 41, 42, 43, 55, 74, 102, 105–107, 111, 138–143, 144, 151, 156, 188, 192, 193, 205, 286, 287, 291, 295, 316, 317, 345–348, 359–364, 370, 371

Chapter Review pages: 44, 45, 109, 170, 318, 319, 372, 373

Communicating on the Job pages: 46, 102, 172, 374

Communicating as a Citizen pages: 47, 111

Teacher's Resource Binder pages: LP1, 2, 4, 66, 70, 71; LW1; EC1, 5, 42, 43; SJ2; EF3

(B) recognize and select appropriate oral verbal symbols;

Students will learn the acceptable standards for verbal messages and learn to differentiate between formal and informal usage. Students will further learn to develop an oral style suitable to projecting themselves well in a variety of speaking situations.

Lesson pages: 8, 11, 13, 16–20, 21–26, 35, 36, 49, 53, 66, 95, 97, 98, 107, 113–132, 136, 137, 144–150, 151–157, 161, 192, 193, 205, 211, 212, 221, 222–224, 253, 259, 265, 273, 291, 295, 296, 299–301, 316, 317, 323–330, 337, 338, 341–344, 353, 364, 370, 371

Chapter Review pages: 44, 45, 170, 171, 207, 268, 318, 319, 354, 355, 372, 373

Communicating on the Job pages: 46, 78, 110, 172, 208, 282, 320, 374

Communicating as a Citizen pages: 79, 173, 209, 219, 247, 321, 357, 375

Teacher's Resource Binder pages: LP4; EC3; EF2; Correct Usage (all pages)

(C) listen;

Students will learn the purposes for listening, such as information gathering, relaxation, enjoyment, analysis, discrimination, judgment, evaluation, or critical analysis. Students will examine conflicting messages and learn some of the reasons for poor habits; students will work on improving their skills through related activities.

Lesson pages: 3, 5, 6, 7, 8, 9, 21, 22, 26, 27, 33–35, 37, 38, 49, 53, 73, 74, 89, 92, 95, 97, 98, 104–108, 151–152, 154, 158, 178, 210–216, 223, 256, 259, 265, 273–280, 286, 316, 327, 328, 337, 363, 376–382

Chapter Review pages: 44, 45, 76, 77, 100, 101, 109, 207, 216, 217, 268, 281, 372, 373, 383

Communicating on the Job pages: 78, 110, 208, 218, 282, 384

Communicating as a Citizen pages: 79, 111, 173, 219, 247, 283, 385

Teacher's Resource Binder pages: LP1, 12, 16, 17, 20, 41, 54, 74; T/TW1; LW4, 12, 17, 26; EC1–44; L1–4; EF1–17; CW1–8; T8, 14, 20, 28

(D) give, receive, and evaluate feedback.

Students will learn positive ways to provide peers with feedback as well as how to build lasting peer relationships based on effective communication.

Lesson pages: 7, 15, 33(B), 36, 37, 42, 43, 68, 74, 75, 87, 94, 99, 117, 125, 132, 143, 150, 157, 169, 180, 187, 198, 205, 286, 287, 295, 312, 316, 317, 363, 369, 371

Chapter Review pages: 44, 45, 77, 170, 171, 217, 372, 373

Communicating on the Job pages: 78, 102, 172, 208, 218, 282, 320, 374

Communicating as a Citizen pages: 103, 209, 219, 375

Teacher's Resource Binder pages: EC1–44, EF1–17

(4) Communication in democratic group processes. The student shall be provided opportunities to:

(A) develop awareness of the importance of the group process;

Students will study the factors influencing group process. They will learn the types of leadership roles that may be used and the responsibilities of the group leader and the discussants.

Lesson pages: 49–54, 81–99, 108, 131, 158–162, 224–227, 229–230, 235–245

Chapter Review pages: 100, 101, 109, 244, 245, 269

Communicating on the Job pages: 110, 216, 246, 270

Communicating as a Citizen pages: 103, 173 (Activity), 271

Teacher's Resource Binder pages: LP15–17, 45, 46, 49–51; LW4, 13, 14–16; CT3, 8, 9; SJ4, 9, 10; EC10–12, 28–32; EF5, 6, 13; CW5–8; T5, 16, 17

(B) analyze the purposes, functions and roles of members for a variety of formal and informal groups;

Students learn that group discussion is a cooperative, critical exchange of information, opinions, and ideas about one general subject. They will learn to establish a framework for orderly discussion and will learn to be responsible discussants. They will understand how to be ready to deal with two types of objectives: human relations objectives and task objectives. They will learn to be well prepared, to evaluate facts and opinions, and to accept their share of responsibility for effective communication.

Lesson pages: 49–54, 81–99, 108, 131, 158–162, 221–241

Chapter Review pages: 100, 101, 109, 244, 245, 269

Communicating on the Job pages: 216, 246, 270

Communicating as a Citizen pages: 103, 209, 247

Teacher's Resource Binder pages: LP16, 17, 44–46, 49–51; LW13–16; CT4, 9; SJ4, 9, 10; EC11, 12, 28–32; EF5, 6, 13; CW5–8; T5, 16, 17

(C) develop skill in conflict diagnosis and management in the group process;

Students using EFFECTIVE SPEECH will develop their situation analysis skills and be able to discern real issues and present those issues for group consideration. Unit 1, Chapter 2 "Communicating to Resolve a Conflict" provides students with a step-by-step approach to conflict resolution through motivation analysis and careful application of mediation techniques.

Lesson pages: 48–75

Chapter Review pages: 76, 77

Communicating on the Job pages: 78

Communicating as a Citizen pages: 79

Teacher's Resource Binder pages: LP9; EC6; T/TW2

(D) demonstrate competence in a variety of formal group discussion formats;

Students will be provided instruction in the most common types of group discussion, including problem-solving group discussion, parliamentary discussion, and debate. They will understand that the type of discussion will depend on such factors as the number of participants, the subject to be discussed, the time allowed for discussion, the degree of formality desired, and their own critical listening skills.

Lesson pages: 81–99, 105–108, 224–227, 229–236, 248–267, 273–279

Chapter Review pages: 109, 238, 268, 269, 281, 282

Communicating on the Job pages: 246, 270

Communicating as a Citizen pages: 103, 246, 271

Teacher's Resource Binder pages: LP15, 16, 17, 20, 45, 46, 49, 50, 51, 54; LW4, 13, 14–16, 17; EC10–13, 28–29, 30–33; T/TW3, 4, 8–10; SJ4, 5, 9–11; Correct Usage (all pages); CW5–8; Debate Tape; SA13; L3; EF5, 6, 13, 14; T5–8, 15–20

(E) demonstrate the use of parliamentary procedure for group effectiveness.

A complete study of parliamentary procedure and its purposes is provided in the student text. Students are expected to become familiar with all the terminology and basic principles of the procedure in order to protect their right to speak in social, political, or business settings.

Lesson pages: 221–242

Chapter Review pages: 243, 244

Communicating on the Job pages: 246

Communicating as a Citizen pages: 247

Teacher's Resource Binder pages: LP45–48; LW13, CT8; EC28, 29; SJ9; T/TW8; T15, 16

(5) Communication through public address—speech preparation.

EFFECTIVE SPEECH provides students with a complete background in the art of public speaking. Areas of instruction include:

- Purposes and Types of Public Speaking
- Finding Suitable Topics
- Researching and Structuring Speeches
- Techniques of Delivery
- Analyzing and Responding

The student will be provided opportunities to:

(A) select and limit appropriate topics for speaking;

Students will learn to consider various factors when selecting topics, such as time limits, the audience, the occasion, and use of stylistic variances to create interest. Secondary considerations such as universal significance, benefits to self, simplification of difficult topics and rare or exotic topics are also discussed. Students are taught a variety of sources for speech topics and are given assistance in selecting titles for their speeches.

Lesson pages: 114–117, 119–123, 126, 130, 131, 144, 181, 186

Chapter Review pages: 170–171

Communicating on the Job pages: 172, 270

Communicating as a Citizen pages: 173

Teacher's Resource Binder pages: LP23, 24, 25, 28, 35; LW5, 6, 7, 10; EF7, 10; EC14, 15, 18, 23

(B) choose a general purpose to meet the speaker's intent, such as informing, persuading, promoting social cohesion, or entertaining;

Students learn that every good speech has a purpose and a thesis, and that the purpose of a speech will determine the development of the speech.

Unit 2, Chapter 5 of the text is devoted to speaking to *explain* while Chapter 6 concentrates on speaking to *persuade*. Unit 3, Chapter 10 provides students with instruction in evaluating persuasive appeals. Unit 4, Chapters 11, 12, and 13 focus on telling stories, interpreting, entertaining radio and television audiences, and performing dramatic scenes.

Lesson pages: 113–169, 174–205, 272–280, 286–289, 291–317, 323–353, 359–371

Chapter Review pages: 170, 171, 206, 207, 281, 318, 319, 354, 355, 372, 373

Communicating on the Job pages: 172, 208

Communicating as a Citizen pages: 173, 209

Teacher's Resource Binder pages: LP23–40, 54–73, LW5–11, 17–25; EF7–11, 14–16; CT5, 6, 10–13; EC14–26, 33–43; O1–11; SA1–12, 13; Oral Report Section, Correct Usage (all pages), CW1–8; T/TW5, 6, 9–13; SJ6, 7, 11–14; T9–12, 19–26

(C) use effective research skills to gather information and support data;

Students using EFFECTIVE SPEECH will be instructed in note taking, audience observation, historical background references, outlining, organizing information cards, surveying known information, ordering information, and identifying the necessary steps in speech preparation. They are provided assistance in library research, effective note taking, and are taught the purposes and elements of effective outlining.

Lesson pages: 19, 20, 85, 114–119, 123, 126, 130, 131, 132, 133–137, 152, 153, 163, 164, 175, 181, 211–216

Chapter Review pages: 44, 45, 100, 101, 170, 171, 206, 217

Communicating on the Job pages: 172, 218, 246, 270, 374

Communicating as a Citizen pages: 79, 103, 321, 357

Teacher's Resource Binder pages: LP23, 26, 41, 42, 52; LW5, 8, 12; EF7, 12; EC16, 27; CT3, 7; SJ8; L2; T/TW7; T9, 13, 14, 18

(D) organize and outline speeches through the use of chronological, spatial, cause-effect, problem-solution, or topical patterns of organization;

Students learn that ideas in the body of a speech may be organized in many different ways, depending on the topic and the speaker's preference.

Lesson pages: 126, 127, 128–131, 132, 137

Chapter Review pages: 170, 171

Communicating on the Job pages: 172

Communicating as a Citizen pages: 173

Teacher's Resource Binder pages: LP25; LW7; EC15; O1-6; SA3; T9

(E) utilize logical, ethical, and emotional appeals for support and amplification of ideas;

Students will learn to control and utilize gestures, rhetorical devices, and audience interaction techniques to involve the responders. They will further learn that to be effective speakers, they need to develop their thinking skills, especially those of perceiving, arranging, inquiring, inferring, and reasoning.

Lesson pages: 16–20, 175–176, 178, 179, 181–187, 188–193, 194–205, 273–280

Chapter Review pages: 44, 45, 206–207, 281

Communicating on the Job pages: 110, 208, 218

Communicating as a Citizen pages: 209, 247, 283

Teacher's Resource Binder pages: LP3, 34–38, 54; LW11, 17; EC2, 22–26, 33; O7–11; CT6, 10; Correct Usage (all pages); CW3, 4; T/TW6, 10; SA6–13; SJ7, 11; L3; T1, 11, 12, 19, 20

(F) compose effective introductions, transitions, and conclusions for the speech.

Students will learn that the introduction to a speech creates the first impression and draws the listener's curiosity to the subject being discussed. They will learn that any good speech contains internal transitions and displays the speaker's fluency and ease of speaking. They will know that the conclusion to a speech may do three things—summarize, reinforce a specific purpose, and/or obtain audience acceptance of the specific purpose.

Lesson pages: 26, 69, 119–125, 132, 149, 181, 211, 250, 251

Chapter Review pages: 44, 76, 170–171, 206, 207, 217, 268, 269

Communicating on the Job pages: 172

Communicating as a Citizen pages: 209, 219, 247, 321, 357

Teacher's Resource Binder pages: O1–11

(6) Communication as public address—speech presentation. The student shall be provided opportunities to:

(A) develop competence in impromptu, extemporaneous, manuscript, and memorized modes of delivery;

EFFECTIVE SPEECH provides students with comprehensive guidelines and instruction in a variety of types of speeches from improvisational to story telling, from oral interpretation to introducing a speaker, from presenting an award to role playing.

Lesson pages: 151–157, 163–169, 290–317, 359–371, 390–400

Chapter Review pages: 170, 171, 288, 318, 319, 372, 373

Communicating on the Job pages: 172, 208, 320, 374

Communicating as a Citizen pages: 173, 321, 357, 375

Teacher's Resource Binder pages: LP23–39; LW5–11; CT11–13; EC14–26; O1–11; SJ6, 7; EF7–12; CW1–4; T/TW5–6; C5, 6; Correct Usage (all pages); Oral Report (all pages) T9, 11

(B) utilize effective vocal and nonverbal techniques in speech presentation;

Students are taught to concentrate on their pitch, volume, movement, gestures, and eye contact during speech giving; they are further taught to avoid giving distracting verbal and nonverbal messages.

The Guidelines sections set specific criteria for evaluating speech presentations and further serve to remind students to employ mastered techniques in their delivery of speeches.

Lesson pages: 21–43, 192, 193, 287–289, 291–295, 313–317, 323–328, 337, 359–371

Chapter Review pages: 44, 45, 206, 207, 318, 319, 354, 355, 372, 373

Communicating on the Job pages: 46, 320, 356, 374

Communicating as a Citizen pages: 209, 321, 357, 375

Teacher's Resource Binder pages: LP4–6, 26, 27, 29; EC3–5, 16, 17; SJ2, 6; EF2, 3; Correct Usage (all pages); T1, 3, 9

(C) refine skills of diction, enunciation, pronunciation, articulation, and grammar.

Students will study proper pronunciation and articulation techniques and language usage preparatory to giving their speeches. Students using EFFECTIVE SPEECH will further be expected to employ learned techniques in all speech presentations; these techniques will also be acknowledged in the Evaluation Checklists.

Lesson pages: 21–27, 31–38, 295, 316, 317, 323, 337

Chapter Review pages: 44, 45, 318, 319, 354, 355

Communicating on the Job pages: 46, 209, 320

Communicating as a Citizen pages: 47, 321, 387

Teacher's Resource Binder pages: LP5; EC4; EF; Correct Usage (all pages)

(7) Communication as public address—speech analysis. The student shall be provided opportunities to:

(A) develop skills of speech analysis through a study of written speech models;

Lesson pages: 23–25, 119–122, 127–130, 144–148, 175–177, 182–185, 189–192, 194–197, 199–203, 212–214, 257–259, 262–265, 275–278, 291–294, 297–301, 314–316

Appendix A of the text of EFFECTIVE SPEECH contains:

Historical Speeches

- "The Gettysburg Address" Abraham Lincoln, 404
- From "The Greatness of Lincoln" Richard S. Emrich, 405–406
- "Join Hands, Hearts, and Minds" Rosalyn S. Yalow, 406–407
- The Nobel Prize Acceptance Speech William Faulkner, 408–409
- "Blood, Toil, Tears, and Sweat" Sir Winston Churchill, 409–410
- From "A Glory Has Departed" Jawaharlal Nehru, 411

Appendix B of the text contains:

Contest Speeches
- From the 1986 Championship Team Debate   Brian Kramer, Robert Unikel, Holly Bartling, Steve Dvorske, 414–424
- 1985 Final Round U.S. Extemporaneous Speech   Cortney Sylvester, 424–427
- 1985 Final Round Original Oratory   Andy Thornton, 427–430

Teacher's Resource Binder pages: EC14–26; EF7–11; CW1–14; SA1–12

(B) acquire and utilize specific criteria for the evaluation of public speeches;

Students are taught post-speech audience analysis techniques, such as formal questionnaires and interviews.

Lesson pages: 116, 125, 132, 137, 143, 150, 157, 162, 169, 187, 193, 198, 205, 260, 267, 295

Chapter Review Pages: 170, 171, 206, 207, 281, 282

Communicating on the Job pages: 208, 218, 283

Communicating as a Citizen pages: 209, 219, 283

Teacher's Resource Binder pages: EC14–26; EF7–11; CW1–4; SA1–12

(C) identify and evaluate the speaker's use of logical, ethical, and emotional forms of proof;

Students will be expected to identify and to analyze the audience persuaders used by speakers and to be able to present valuable critical feedback.

Lesson pages: 175–205, 273–280

Chapter Review pages: 206, 207, 281

Communicating on the Job pages: 208

Communicating as a Citizen pages: 209

Teacher's Resource Binder pages: LP54; LW11, 17; CT6, 10; EC22–26, 33; SA6–13; EF10, 11, 14; CW3–4; T11–19

(D) present analytical critiques of speeches in both oral and written forms.

Instruction is provided for students to master these objectives. Evaluation sheets have been designed to assist students in their analysis of speeches as evidenced by response to Objective 7B.

Lesson pages: 116, 125, 132, 137, 143, 150, 157, 162, 169, 187, 193, 198, 205, 260, 267, 295

Chapter Review pages: 170, 171, 206, 207, 281, 282

Communicating on the Job pages: 208, 218, 283

Communicating as a Citizen pages: 209, 219, 283

Teacher's Resource Binder pages: EC14–26; EF7–11; CW1–4, SA1–13; T19

Correlation between
Texas Educational Assessment of Minimal Skills, Exit Level
and
EFFECTIVE SPEECH

The following pages present a correlation between EFFECTIVE SPEECH and the Texas Educational Assessment of Minimal Skills (TEAMS) in the areas of reading and writing. Cross-references for the TEAMS appear as marginal notations in the teacher lesson plans in the Teacher's Resource Binder.

Reading

Skill Area: Main Idea

Main Idea: Identify the main idea.

Lesson pages: 119–123, 125, 130–132, 133–137, 138, 144–149, 169, 181–187, 189–192, 199, 204, 205, 211–216, 249–255, 256–259, 261–265, 296–302, 312, 313–315, 317

Chapter Review pages: 170, 206, 207, 217, 268, 318, 319

Communicating on the Job pages: 218

Teacher's Resource Binder pages: LP50; O1-7; LW6, 7, 8, 9, 11, 12, 14–16, 18, 27; EF12

Skill Area: Word Meaning

Contextual Analysis: Uses context to understand the meaning of words.

Lesson pages: 21–25, 273, 278

Chapter Review pages: 44, 76, 100, 170, 206, 244, 268, 281, 318, 354, 372

Teacher's Resource Binder pages: LP4; EC3; EF1; LW18; Correct Usage (all pages)

Skill Area: Detail

Specifics: Identify specific details.

Lesson pages: 3, 11–12, 16–17, 23–25, 32–34, 50–52, 57–58, 61–66, 69–73, 82–85, 90–92, 95–98, 105–107, 119–122, 127–130, 134–136, 140, 144–148, 152–155, 158–160, 165–167, 175–177, 182–185, 189–192, 194–197, 199–203, 212–214, 238–240, 251–253, 257, 262–265, 275–278, 291–293, 297–301, 314–316, 324–326, 330–335, 338–342, 349–351, 359–361, 364–369

Teacher's Resource Binder pages. LW8, 18; SA1-13

Sequence: Identify the sequence of events.

Lesson pages: 69–73, 125, 126, 165–167, 175–177, 199–203, 211–214, 225, 291–295, 330–335, 349–351, 359–363

Chapter Review pages: 170, 171, 206, 207, 217, 318, 319

Communicating on the Job pages: 218, 356

Communicating as a Citizen pages: 47

Teacher's Resource Binder pages: LP41; EC27, 34; EF1, 15; T9, 21; O4

Skill Area: Inference

Conclusions: Draw logical conclusions.

Lesson pages: 39–41 (Activity C), 73, 81–87, 92, 95–99, 119–122, 127–131, 163–167, 175–180, 181–187, 197–198, 199–203, 225–227, 249–253, 256–259, 261–265, 273–279

Chapter Review pages: 100, 101, 206, 207, 268, 269, 281, 383

Communicating on the Job pages: 218

Communicating as a Citizen pages: 47, 103, 209, 247, 271, 283, 385

Teacher's Resource Binder pages: LP8, 15, 17, 19, 24, 25, 31, 34–48, 40, 44, 48–51, 53, 54, 56, 76; EC1–44; SA1, 2, 4–13; EF10–12; LW4, 11, 14–17; CT4–6,10; O5–8; T11

Fact and Opinion: Distinguish between fact and opinion.

Lesson pages: 53, 81, 85, 99, 130, 131, 163–168, 175–178, 179–180, 181–185, 187, 204, 223, 253, 257, 273–279

Chapter Review pages: 170, 171, 206, 207, 281, 383

Communicating as a Citizen pages: 209, 283, 385

Teacher's Resource Binder pages: LP31, 34, 54, 56, 76; LW17; SA4, 6, 12, 13; CT3; T9, 12, 20; O3, 4

Skill Area: Reference Usage

Selecting Reference Sources: Identify the appropriate reference sources.

Lesson pages: 26, 35, 55, 81, 85, 87, 138–142, 163–168, 235, 243, 296, 388, 390

Chapter Review pages: 101, 245, 281

Communicating on the Job pages: 270

Teacher's Resource Binder pages: LP4, 24, 34, 46, 52, 59, 71; LW11, 17; CT3; T15, 18

Using Reference Sources: Use reference sources to locate information.

Lesson pages: 134–136, 138–142

Communicating on the Job pages: 270

Teacher's Resource Binder pages: LP27, 52; LW9; O1, 2

Skill Area: Analysis of Literature

Analysis of Literature: Analyze literary selections.

Lesson pages: 21–26, 163–168, 175–177, 273–278, 291–294, 296–302, 312, 324–326, 364–371

Chapter Review pages: 44, 45, 170, 171, 281, 318, 319, 372, 373

Teacher's Resource Binder pages: LP4, 31, 58, 59, 71; LW18, 19, 25; CT11, 13; EF1; T21, 25

Writing

Skill Area: English Usage

English Usage: Demonstrate knowledge of correct English usage.

Teacher's Resource Binder pages: Correct Usage (all pages)

Skill Area: Organization

Organization: Demonstrate the ability to organize a written communication.

Lesson pages: 26, 69–75, 119–125, 126–132, 163–169, 175–177, 181–187, 188–192, 211–214, 250–255, 257–259, 261–266, 291–295, 296–302, 345–348

Chapter Review pages: 76, 170, 171, 206, 207, 217, 268, 269

Communicating on the Job pages: 172

Communicating as a Citizen pages: 219

Teacher's Resource Binder pages: LP12, 25, 28, 32, 41, 49, 50; LW6, 7, 9, 11, 12, 14–16, 18; CT5,7, 8, 9; SJ7; O3, 4

Henry Evans
West Texas/Panhandle

Jean Parmer
North Texas

Don Gore
Vice President

Mike Brawley
Regional Manager

Mary Corder
Southeast Texas

Jim Kaml
Southwest Texas

— Your GLENCOE Texas Staff —

MIKE BRAWLEY
Southwest Regional Manager
220 East Danieldale Rd.
DeSoto, TX 75115
(512) 426-5133

MARY CORDER
701 Bering, Unit #403
Houston, TX 77057
(713) 782-2303

HENRY EVANS
P.O. Box 50131
Denton, TX 76206
(817) 566-0307

JIM KAML
P.O. Box 4721
McAllen, TX 78502
(512) 585-6694

JEAN B. PARMER
7220 Harvey Lane
Plano, TX 75023
(214) 867-0336

GLENCOE PUBLISHING COMPANY
15319 Chatsworth Street, Mission Hills, California 91345

The activity-based program that involves your
students in *all* phases of communication —
speaking, listening, reading, and writing

EFFECTIVE

Speech

- self and audience
- democratic group process
- interactive communication
- the communication process
- public speaking: preparation,
  presentation, and analysis
- oral interpretation, television,
  and the performing arts

Logical organization and consistent lesson format make *Effective Speech* easy to use.

Photographs demonstrate effective communication techniques.

A chapter summary highlights main ideas.

Students apply speaking *and* listening skills immediately, often in other content areas.

Chapter objectives guide students' study.

Students check their understanding of key vocabulary terms from the chapter.

Review questions let students check their comprehension of facts and ideas.

Discussion questions spark creative thinking.

KEY FEATURES

Special features help students relate speech to real-life situations.
- Communicating on the Job
- Communicating as a Citizen

Important material is assembled in the back of the book for quick student reference
- Handbook of Contest Speaking
- Appendix A: Historical Speeches
- Appendix B: Contest Speeches
- Glossary

New vocabulary is introduced in boldface type and immediately defined in context to help students learn key terms.

Students always analyze a model before they prepare and present.

Speech assignments include a summary of main ideas from the lesson as well as helpful tips.

Students are given step-by-step guidance to ensure success.

Self- and peer-evaluation is built right into every lesson.

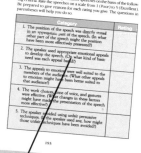

LESSON 3

Using Appeals to Emotion

Rather than appealing to the listeners' minds, as logical arguments do, some persuasive speeches appeal to the listeners' emotions. Emotional appeals are based upon the three kinds of basic needs all people have—physical needs, psychological needs, and social needs. **Physical needs** involve the life and health of an individual's body; examples of physical needs include the need for food and the need to avoid physical pain. **Psychological needs** involve an individual's inner life; examples of psychological needs include the need for love and the need for self-respect. **Social needs** involve an individual's relationship to a group; examples of social needs include the need for freedom and the need for acceptance by others. Appeals to emotion are intended to convince listeners that accepting the speaker's position will satisfy one or more of these basic needs.

When you plan to use appeals to emotion in a persuasive speech, you must constantly consider your position, the specific purpose of your speech. You should be sure that each appeal you choose will lead your listeners to accept that position.

Being able to make such judgments, of course, involves knowing your audience thoroughly. You must be familiar with your listeners' most important needs, with their interests, and with their fears. If you misjudge your audience, your appeals to their emotions will not be successfully persuasive.

In organizing a persuasive speech with appeals to emotions, you may want to develop your position before you state it. For example, you might begin by interesting listeners in the topic of your speech. Then you might present statements, examples, or short **anecdotes** (brief stories) that appeal to specific emotions and that will sway your listeners in favor of your position. By the time you reach the conclusion of your speech, you should have already succeeded in persuading your listeners to accept your position. This may be the most effective time to state that position directly to the audience.

When you present a persuasive speech developed through appeals to emotion, you should use particularly vivid language. You may also want to employ voice tones and gestures that depict greater intensity.

Working with the Model

In 1976, Representative Barbara Jordan of Texas was the keynote speaker at the Democratic National Convention. Read the following excerpt from the speech she made on that occasion. As you read, think about the specific purpose of Jordan's speech and about the appeals she uses to achieve that purpose.

From the Keynote Speech

There is something special about tonight. What is different? What is special? I, Barbara Jordan, am a keynote speaker.

A lot of years passed since 1832, and during that time it would have been most unusual for any national political party to ask that a Barbara Jordan deliver a keynote address . . . But tonight here I am. And I feel that, notwithstanding the past, my presence here is the additional bit of evidence that the American Dream need not forever be deferred.

Now that I have this grand distinction, what in the world am I supposed to say?

I could list the many problems which Americans have. I could list the problems which cause people to feel cynical, angry, frustrated:

Preparing and Presenting

Choose a product, real or imaginary, to use as the topic of a persuasive speech. Select a specific audience, such as preschool children or wealthy middle-aged adults, for your speech. Think about the emotional appeals that will most effectively convince the members of that audience of their need for your product. Plan a brief persuasive speech, developed with at least two specific appeals to emotion, that will persuade the people in your audience to use the product.

After you have planned and rehearsed your speech, select a partner. Have your partner listen as you give your persuasive speech. Then listen as your partner gives his or her persuasive speech.

Evaluation Checklist

Evaluate each other's persuasive speeches on the basis of the following criteria. Rate the speeches on a scale from 1 (Poor) to 5 (Excellent). Be prepared to give reasons for each rating you give. The questions in parentheses will help you do so.

Category	Rating
1. The position of the speech is directly stated in an appropriate part of the speech. (In what part of the speech might the position have been more effectively presented?)	
2. The speaker used appropriate emotional appeals to develop the speech. (On what kind of basic need was each appeal based?)	
3. The appeals to emotion were well suited to the members of the audience. (What other appeals to emotion might have been better suited to that audience?)	
4. The work choices, tone of voice, and gestures were effective. (What changes in these factors might have made the presentation of the speech more effective?)	
5. The speaker avoided using unfair persuasive techniques. (If the speaker used any, how might those unfair techniques have been avoided?)	

Guidelines

These guidelines will help you plan and present an effective persuasive speech developed with appeals to emotion.

1. Appeals to emotion are based on the three kinds of basic needs common to all people: physical needs, psychological needs, and social needs. When you select the specific appeals to use in your speech, you must think carefully about the needs, interests, and fears of the people in your audience.
2. Use vivid language, a forceful voice, and clear gestures when you present your speech.
3. Carefully avoid unfair persuasive techniques, such as lying, calling names, using obscenities, and making irrelevant personal attacks.

A. The specific purpose of Jordan's speech is to persuade her listeners that they must work together in forming a national community based on the principles of democracy. Think about how the speech is organized around that purpose.
1. Which single sentence in Jordan's speech do you consider the direct statement of her position?
2. How does the introduction of Jordan's speech capture the listeners' interest in her position?
3. How does the main portion of her speech develop that position?
4. How does the conclusion emphasize that position?
B. Think about the appeals to emotion which Jordan uses to develop her persuasive speech.
1. Read the following appeals to emotion from Jordan's speech. On which kind of basic need—physical, psychological, or social—is each appeal based?
   "to create and sustain a society in which all of us are equal"
   "the reality of material . . . poverty"
   "problems which cause people to feel cynical, angry, frustrated"
   "only if each of us remembers that we share a common destiny"
2. Find four other examples of appeals to emotion in Jordan's speech. On what kind of basic need is each appeal based?
C. Think about the audience to whom Jordan's speech is addressed.
1. Who are the people in the audience?
2. How do the appeals Jordan uses show her understanding of those people?

5 reasons to adopt *Effective Speech*

- **Comprehensive content,** specifically designed to integrate all communication skills, helps you meet your curriculum objectives.
- **Activity-based learning** gets your students excited about and involved in the processes of communication — speaking, listening, reading, and writing.
- **Consistent chapter and lesson formats,** including student learning objectives and extensive review materials, make *Effective Speech* easy to use.
- **Well-designed teaching materials,** including a Teacher's Edition and a Teacher's Resource Binder, review and extend important concepts. These supplements also help you better plan and utilize your valuable classroom time.
- **The Handbook of Contest Speaking** is an excellent reference tool for your more able students. It also provides additional speaking and listening activities appropriate for all ability levels.

Student Text   0-02-659880-9
Teacher's Edition   0-02-659881-7

Teacher's Resource Binder   0-02-659882-5
Speaking and Listening Cassettes 0-02-659883-3

Expand your teaching options with the *Effective Speech* Teacher's Resource Binder.

This comprehensive package includes

- reproducible lesson plans to save you preparation time
- a complete testing program
- overhead transparencies for greater flexibility
- follow-up worksheets for cassette tapes of speeches, debates, and oral interpretations (cassette tapes sold separately)

- reproducible evaluation checklists for each lesson for self- and peer-evaluation
- worksheets for specific speech preparation skills
- activities and worksheets to sharpen critical thinking and listening skills
- a special Speech Journal section for students to keep track of their own progress, jot down ideas for future presentations, and more
- reproducible Handbook of Contest Speaking pages for easy student reference

EFFECTIVE Speech

Teacher's Edition

Richard W. Clark

Consultants

Vivian C. Bryant
River Rouge High School, Michigan

Shirley Smith
Richardson High School, Texas

Thelma Pate
Mesquite High School, Texas

Glencoe Publishing Company
Mission Hills, California

Glencoe Publishing Company
15319 Chatsworth Street
Mission Hills, CA 91345

Printed in the United States of America

ISBN 0-02-659880-9 (Student Text)
ISBN 0-02-659881-7 (Teacher's Edition)
ISBN 0-02-659882-5 (Teacher's Resource Binder)

2 3 4 5 6   92 91 90 89 88

Contents

Introduction

EFFECTIVE SPEECH is a complete activity-based speech communication program that has been proven to help students become more competent speakers and more efficient listeners. The student text and the teaching aids present and thoroughly reinforce the concepts, skills, and techniques essential for effective speaking and interactive listening in both formal and informal situations. Throughout the program speaking and listening are integrated with the reading and writing to build a solid base of communication skills.

Key Concepts

Through clear step-by-step instruction and a variety of activities, EFFECTIVE SPEECH develops the key concepts of:

Communication as a process
The self as a communicator
Communication in interaction
Communication in democratic group process
Preparation of public speeches
Presentation of public speeches
Analysis of public speeches
Performance and media

Instructional Features

In EFFECTIVE SPEECH concepts and skills are organized and presented so that students can master them. The instructional features of the program help make such mastery possible.

Content Organization The student book is organized into four parts, each part covering a fundamental area of speech and listening: Communicating, Speaking to an Audience, Parliamentary Procedure and Debate, and Performing. This organization allows an in-depth sequential presentation of each area.

Consistent, Clearly-Constructed Lessons The lessons in the student book provide

—models to demonstrate the principles being taught
—step-by-step guidance in mastering and applying these principles
—Evaluation Checklists for self-, peer-, or teacher-evaluation

Communication Models Each lesson is built around a model demonstrating clear, effective communication. Questions in the text help students to analyze and learn from the model.

Career and Citizenship Skills Development   These one-page lessons, entitled Communicating as a Citizen and Communicating on the Job, are found after each chapter. The activities in these lessons guide the students in applying speaking skills to career and citizenship situations.

Listening Skills Development   The text presents a complete program of listening skills. These skills are integrated into each lesson.

Abundant Practice Activities   Appropriate, clearly explained activities, found throughout the program, help students master speaking and listening skills.

Flexibility   The organization of the program makes it readily adaptable to a wide variety of teaching and learning situations, enabling teachers to meet a broad range of student needs.

Handbook of Contest Speaking   This handbook introduces students to contest speaking and provides activities to help students develop the skills needed to participate successfully in speaking contests.

Appendix of Historical Speeches   These speeches of famous men and women provide additional models of how speaking skills have been used in real situations.

Appendix of Contest Speeches   This section provides examples of successful student speeches.

The Student Text

Overall Organization

The table of contents of EFFECTIVE SPEECH shows that not only the completeness of the content but also a logical organization promote student learning. The text is divided into four units:

Unit 1   Communicating   This unit deals with the nature of the communication process, the self as communicator, interactive communication, and democratic group discussion. Interactive listening is stressed.

Unit 2   Speaking to an Audience   This unit provides instruction and opportunities for preparation and presentation of expository and persuasive speeches and for the analysis of historical and contemporary speeches. The skills of listening to understand and learn are developed.

Unit 3   Parliamentary Procedure and Debate   Parliamentary procedure as a form of democratic group process is taught and the skills of debate and critical listening are presented.

Unit 4   Performing   This unit deals with a variety of aspects of performing, including oral interpretation, drama, radio drama, and television production. Skills for evaluating media presentations are developed.

Each unit begins with a Case Study and a Unit Introduction, which provide background and introduce fundamental concepts that will be developed in the unit. Three or four chapters follow, each dealing with a specific aspect of the unit topic.

The Chapter

Each chapter consists of a series of related, in-depth lessons, a Chapter Review, and one-page lessons on Communicating on the Job and on Communicating as a Citizen.

The Lesson

If students are to interview successfully, to participate satisfactorily in discussions and debates, and to speak effectively, they must do more than develop specific techniques and skills. They must also learn a process by which they can compose and evaluate their presentations. Each lesson in EFFECTIVE SPEECH is developed in a format that reflects such a process.

The Process	*The Lesson Plan*
Preparation	— An introduction briefly explains the concepts and skills to be taught in the lesson.
	— Working with the Model
	The model provides an example of a speaking situation.
	Questions help the student analyze the model.
	— Guidelines
	These statements summarize what the students have learned.
	— Preparing and Presenting
	Students are given step-by-step guidance in developing their own presentations.
Speaking	— Students give their talks to a partner, a small group, or the class.
Assessment	— Evaluation Checklist
	Questions encourage group- or self-evaluation.

The lesson format of EFFECTIVE SPEECH benefits both teacher and student. For the teacher, this consistent lesson plan greatly simplifies class management and reduces both preparation time and the time needed to evaluate student presentations. In addition, the logical development of the lessons allows the teacher to evaluate student progress at every step. For the students, the plan offers both consistent guidance and the security of knowing what is expected of them at every step. Thus, students will be able to approach new concepts and skills with the confidence necessary for mastery.

The Teacher's Edition

The Teacher's Edition of EFFECTIVE SPEECH provides a management tool that makes planning and teaching easier and more effective.

— Full-sized student pages
— Complete, detailed lesson plans, including cross-references to all support materials in the Teacher's Resource Binder
— An answer section for the Chapter Reviews

Using the Lesson Plans

The teacher's lesson plans are designed to help you plan efficiently and teach effectively by bringing together all the information and materials you need. The lesson plans consistently follow this easy-to-use format:

Teacher's Lesson Plan

To be used with
    This line gives the page numbers of the lesson in the student text.

Aids for Extension and Reinforcement
    This section gives page references to materials in your Teacher's Resource Binder and references to the EFFECTIVE SPEECH audiocassettes and videotape that you can use to support and extend the lesson.

Objective(s)
    A clear statement of the lesson's objective helps you focus the lesson for your students.

Vocabulary
    This list of terms introduced and defined within the context of the student text allows you to preview new vocabulary with your students.

Presentation of Subject Matter
    Here you will find suggestions for guiding the lesson.

Extension Activity
    This activity can be used to extend and enrich your students' learning.

Evaluation and Feedback
    The page numbers of the resources in the student text and in the Teacher's Resource Binder for evaluating student progress are listed.

The Teacher's Resource Binder

Your Teacher's Resource Binder provides a variety of reproducible support materials and transparencies to save you time, money, and effort. They make it easy for you to do the following for your students.

— Provide practice for all students
— Adjust and adapt the program to the needs of each student
— Enrich and expand the study of communication, group interaction, public speaking, and performing
— Monitor and evaluate student progress

The support materials are completely integrated with the material in the student text and the teacher's lesson plans. Each activity sheet, test, and transparency has been cross-referenced to the appropriate lesson plan. The Teacher's Resource Binder is divided into the following sixteen sections.

Lesson Plans

The reproducible lesson plans in your Teacher's Resource Binder contain all of the teaching aids and material in the lesson plans of the Teacher's Edition. (For a full description of these lesson plans, please see page viii of this introduction.)

Critical Thinking Work Sheets

These reproducible activity sheets guide students in applying higher level thinking skills to key communications activities.

Correct Usage

These work sheets provide reference material and practice on words that are easily confused as to meaning or pronunciation.

Lesson Work Sheets

These work sheets provide extra practice in lesson concepts.

Lesson Evaluation Checklists

The checklists, which match the ones at the end of each lesson, allow your students to actually write out their evaluations and, if you wish, hand them in.

Evaluation Forms
for Speeches, Debates,
and Discussions

These forms guide student listening and evaluation.

Speech Journal

These reproducible sheets form a personal journal in which students can record personal goals and achievements in communications.

Listening Work Sheets

These reproducible pages provide materials and response activities designed to improve student listening skills.

Speech Outlines

These outline formats are designed to help students plan and outline presentations in a variety of organizational patterns.

Speech Analysis

These reproducible pages offer a variety of speeches and exercises that build analytical skills.

Oral Report

If you wish your students to give oral reports, these pages will assist your students in planning, preparing, presenting, and evaluating these reports.

Related Composition Activities

The activities provide written follow-up to the students' oral presentations.

Cassettes Work Sheets

These reproducible pages assist your students in getting the most out of the EFFECTIVE SPEECH audiocassettes and videotape.

Handbook of Contest Speaking

These pages duplicate the material in the student text. Reproducing them will allow your students to have copies of their own of this useful material.

Tests

This section contains reproducible tests for each chapter and for each Communicating as a Citizen and Communicating on the Job page.

Transparencies and Work Sheets

To introduce each chapter there is a transparency and a reproducible follow-up work sheet.

Videotape and Audiocassettes

To supplement the textbook and to make public speaking, oral interpretation, and debate come alive for your students, the EFFECTIVE SPEECH program includes audiocassettes and a videotape of student presentations and teacher critiques.

To be used with:

Unit One (Communicating): A Case Study (page 3)

Objective
To understand the basic role speech communication plays in our daily lives

Presentation of Subject Matter
After the students have discussed the questions following the case study, have them work in pairs or in triads to develop their own cases. Encourage them to use actual events from their own lives. Have them focus their cases on communication interactions involving two or three persons and then role-play their case studies before the class. Follow the role playing with a discussion of questions similar to those in the student text, but now directed toward the student-originated cases.

Extension Activity
Have the class watch an excerpt from a current television program, e.g., *The Cosby Show*. After watching for five or ten minutes, turn off the TV and discuss the direct and indirect examples of speaking and listening. Students will pick up direct conversation quickly. You may have to ask some leading questions to help them spot indirect examples, such as a speech one character is going to have to give or a conflict between characters generated by previous instances of poor communication.

To be used with:

Unit Introduction: Analyzing the Communication Process (pages 4–9)

Objective
To understand the speech communication process and the essential elements of speech for individuals engaged in that process

Vocabulary
speech communication
   process (4,7)
speaker (5)
listener (5)

message (5)
setting (5)
body of knowledge (5)

language (5)
interference (7)
feedback (7)

Presentation of Subject Matter
As they think through the information in the introduction, lead the class in a discussion that asks them to give examples of the effects of various elements in the speech communication process. The interviews of adults suggested as an activity at the end of the introduction can be a valuable way of

helping students obtain a broader view of the speech communication process. It also requires students to engage in several speech activities: setting up an interview, interviewing, and reporting to the class.

As you discuss speech communication examples, you need to help students distinguish between the components of the speech communication *process* (setting, knowledge, language, speaker, listener, feedback, interference) and the elements of speech that are pertinent to the *individuals* taking part in the process (self-understanding and attitudes, thought process, language, voice, and bodily action). These aspects of process and individual behavior will be fundamental to the learnings that will be called for throughout the text. Also, understanding the basic nature of these elements will help students keep a broad perspective on speech communication rather than focus on such a narrow view of speech as addressing an audience.

Extension Activity

If you have not discussed the original case study before having the students read the introduction, do so after they have worked through the introductory session. You may also find it helpful to go back and review the case or the cases the students created on their own, even if you have talked with them prior to reading the introduction.

To be used with:

Chapter 1 Lesson 1 (pages 11–15) ·

Aids for Extension and Reinforcement

In the TRB: Lesson Work Sheets page LW1, Critical Thinking Work Sheets page CT1, Correct Usage Section, Speech Journal page SJ1, Transparencies page T1, Transparency Work Sheets page TW1

Objective

To become aware of one's own strengths and weaknesses as a communicator

Presentation of Subject Matter

After the students have read the introductory section of the lesson, have them suggest different ways in which people communicate (for example, clothes, gestures, body language) or fail to communicate. Emphasize that each person has both strengths and weaknesses as a communicator. You may wish to use examples from your own teaching experience to show how you learned to communicate effectively.

As you work through the Model questions, you can easily expand into a discussion of conversation, the area Susan has so much difficulty with. Encourage students to offer positive and practical suggestions for conversing with others.

The students should study the Guidelines thoroughly before beginning the Preparing and Presenting activity. You may wish to have them submit written answers to the Guidelines questions in order to show they have really thought about them. You may also wish to have students exchange written responses to each other's self-evaluations instead of, or in addition to, the oral discussion.

Extension Activities

In addition to writing a self-evaluation, students may watch a film or television drama (either broadcast or taped) and write an evaluation of one character's strengths and weaknesses as a communicator.

Evaluation and Feedback

In the text: Evaluation Checklist page 15, Chapter Review pages 44–45
In the TRB: Evaluation Checklists page EC1

To be used with:

Chapter 1 Lesson 2 (pages 16–20)

Objectives

To improve one's thinking abilities by sharpening one's senses
To understand how people attach meaning to experiences

Presentation of Subject Matter

The cartoons at the beginning of this lesson are intended to stimulate discussion. You may find that you get better student involvement by asking students to search for their own cartoons, demonstrating the role that the senses play in developing the mental images that each of us has for various words and phrases. As the students reflect on their own experiences and develop written statements calling on all five senses, you may find it helpful to have them develop a list of alternative situations to those suggested in the text. Generating their own list may lead them to more interest in the topic about which they are writing.

The Speaker's Journal called for in this lesson can be a valuable tool throughout the course. If you decide to have your students prepare one, you need to spend time making sure they understand your expectations concerning it. It will be most useful if you make references to it throughout the course. Once you have had students make entries on a daily basis for several weeks, you may want to set a pattern that calls for you to observe the condition of their journal every three or four weeks so that they know you are expecting them to maintain it. As you work with these journals and as individual students create good ones, make copies that can serve as models for subsequent students.

Extension Activities

There are a variety of related exercises that require students to sharpen their observational skills. For example, have two students leave the room for a brief time and rearrange some of the classroom furniture while they are gone. When they return, ask them to tell the class what is different. Debrief by discussing why some changes were picked up quickly while others were missed.

Evaluation and Feedback

In the text: Evaluation Checklist page 20, Chapter Review pages 44–45
In the TRB: Evaluation Checklists page EC2

To be used with:

Chapter 1 Lesson 3 (pages 21–28)

Aids for Extension and Reinforcement

In the TRB: Evaluation Forms page EF1

Objective

To understand the requirements for the appropriate and effective use of spoken language

Vocabulary

denotation (21)	figures of speech (22)	personification (23)
connotation (21)	simile (22)	analogy (23)
cliché (22)	metaphor (22)	transitions (26)
figurative language (22)		

Presentation of Subject Matter

Before the students consider the Model, have them read through the definitions. Take time to talk with the class about the different terms. Encourage them to create examples of each.

King's "I Have a Dream" speech has become one of the most quoted speeches of current times. Encourage students to seek out a copy of the full speech. Have them analyze the language in it with the same kind of questions as are included in the text serving to guide their exploration.

The Guidelines list "rules" for language usage that require discussion and elaboration useful for students seeking to improve their speaking. The activities associated with the Speaker's Journal are designed to help the students understand the Guidelines. Take time to discuss the materials the students enter in their journals. You may find that a good approach is to take one item a day for several days and use a few minutes at the beginning of class to discuss the materials the students have added to their journal and to make sure they are making correct interpretations.

Extension Activities

Encourage students to explore language in more depth. Books such as *Less than Words Can Say* by Richard Mitchell (Little Brown and Co., 1979) or *Strictly Speaking* by Edwin Newman (Bobbs-Merrill, 1974) provide many examples that can be used to get students involved in discussions about the way language is used.

Evaluation and Feedback

In the text: Evaluation Checklist page 28, Chapter Review pages 44–45
In the TRB: Evaluation Checklists page EC3

To be used with:

Chapter 1 Lesson 4 (pages 29–38)

Aids for Extension and Reinforcement

In the TRB: Evaluation Forms page EF2

Objective

To develop an effective speaking voice through an understanding of the way the voice works

Vocabulary

lungs (29)	nasal cavity (30)	articulation (31)
diaphragm (29)	pharynx (30)	pronunciation (31)
trachea (30)	coloration (30)	loudness (31)
larynx (30)	consonant (31)	rate (31)
vocal cords (30)	vowel (31)	
pitch (30)	diphthong (31)	

Presentation of Subject Matter

While working through the introductory section of this lesson, you may wish to supplement the diagrams in the text with a film or videocassette on the voice. You might also borrow three-dimensional models of the head and thorax from the biology department. Students should also be able to locate their own larynxes, hard palates, and soft palates. They should feel the air vibrating in their throats as they speak and experiment to see how different configurations of the mouth and tongue produce different vowel and consonant sounds.

The rules and exercises in Lesson 4 as well as the Voice Evaluation Checklist on page 38 will be useful throughout the course. You can assign Lesson 4 to individual students who need further practice. You can also have the entire class review the lesson before studying the lessons on public speaking.

Extension Activities

You can expand the treatment of speech sounds by bringing in tape recordings of the voices of friends, family members, or radio or television personalities for comparison. You may also wish to have students record a variety of voices and play them for the class. Have students listen for the five major characteristics of good speech listed in the Guidelines.

Evaluation and Feedback

In the text: Evaluation Checklist page 38, Chapter Review pages 44–45
In the TRB: Evaluation Checklists page EC4

To be used with:

Chapter 1 Lesson 5 (pages 39–43)

Aids for Extension and Reinforcement

In the TRB: Speech Journal page SJ2, Evaluation Forms page EF3

Objective

To use the body to enhance communication

Vocabulary

posture (42)	expression (42)
movement (42)	eye contact (42)
gesture (42)	

Presentation of Subject Matter

Begin this lesson with the students discussing the questions following the Model. Extend that conversation by playing sections of videotapes without any sound and discussing the communications being provided by bodily action. Some current videos of popular music provide material that could be used for this.

In addition to the five activities listed for the students to use to increase their awareness of the way movement communicates, have the students create other activities for each other.

The major class activity of this lesson is one that the students should find enjoyable. In order for the students to get the most benefit from it, you need to make sure they think through the planning stages and prepare the written description called for. In order for the students to be able to relate their group activity to a speaker's use of movement, you will need to take them through some thorough debriefing. Get them to think through the connection between their movements interpreting the music and the way an effective speaker uses bodily actions.

Extension Activity

Nonverbal responses from audiences are a major means of obtaining feedback during a communication occasion. Have the students observe other students in other classrooms and write a brief description of what they would understand about the students' responses if they were the teacher in those classrooms. Would they, for example, be able to tell if the students were interested? What were students doing that might tell the teacher that they understood or didn't understand what was being said?

Evaluation and Feedback

In the text: Evaluation Checklist page 43, Chapter Review pages 44–45
In the TRB: Evaluation Checklists page EC5, Chapter Tests page T1

To be used with:

Communicating on the Job: Analyzing Your Career Interests (page 46)

Aids for Extension and Reinforcement

Related Composition Activities page C1

Objective

To analyze one's interests and experience in terms of possible careers

Presentation of Subject Matter

You may wish to go over the questions during class, with a single student supplying the information and the rest of the students suggesting possible occupations. Then the other students can answer the questions at home and bring their career ideas to class for discussion.

Evaluation and Feedback

In the TRB: Chapter Tests page T2

To be used with:

Communicating as a Citizen: Reporting an Incident (page 47)

Objective

To report an incident accurately

Presentation of Subject Matter

As you work through the lesson, ask students to think of specific incidents—for example, fires, accidents, or altercations—that they have witnessed or read about. Have them practice reporting such incidents in two ways. First, ask a student to simply describe the incidents in order ("First A, then B, then C"). Then ask another student to relate the incidents according to cause and effect ("A caused B to happen, and C was caused by A and B"). Have the class discuss the similarities and differences between the two reports. You may also wish to have students describe incidents that they believe were misreported or misinterpreted and to suggest how such reports might be improved.

Evaluation and Feedback

In the TRB: Chapter Tests page T2

To be used with:

Chapter 2 Lesson 1 (pages 49–54)

Aids for Extension and Reinforcement

In the TRB: Critical Thinking Work Sheets page CT2, Correct Usage Section, Transparencies page T2, Transparency Work Sheets page TW2

Objectives

To recognize the causes of conflict
To communicate effectively in order to resolve conflict

Vocabulary

mediator (50)

Presentation of Subject Matter

Assign pairs of students to prepare and present brief skits illustrating each source of conflict. Ask the rest of the class to supply further examples (from their own experience or from movie or television dramatizations) of each kind of conflict.

Have students take turns playing Ken, Hugh, and Ervin as they act out the Model dialogue. As they discuss the Model questions, students should recognize that both Hugh and Ervin are at fault and that Ken has not found a way to bring them together.

Remind the class of the Model as you discuss the Guidelines. Also ask students to offer examples of successful mediation from their own experience. If you wish, you can expand the Guidelines discussion by having students describe examples of conflict resolution in current news stories.

You may wish to have two or more groups of students cooperate with each other in planning the stages of the resolution of the Model conflict. Then each group can write, rehearse, and present one stage in that resolution.

Extension Activities

You can expand this lesson by having groups of four to six students write, rehearse, and present their version of a conflict similar to that in the Model. The other members of the class can identify the sources of the conflict according to the guidelines in the lesson. The entire class can discuss possible approaches for resolving the conflict.

You also might have a specialist in conflict resolution, such as a counselor or community mediator, talk with your students about the techniques he or she has found helpful in resolving communication deadlocks.

Evaluation and Feedback

In the text: Evaluation Checklist page 54, Chapter Review pages 76–77
In the TRB: Evaluation Checklists page EC6

To be used with:

Chapter 2 Lesson 2 (pages 55–60)

Aids for Extension and Reinforcement

In the TRB: Lesson Work Sheets page LW2

Objective

To prepare for an interview

Presentation of Subject Matter

You may introduce this lesson by showing a film or tape of a recent interview with a famous person. Ask the students to identify the different kinds of preparation the interviewer must have done. As students may not readily think of making an appointment for a time when the interviewee is free, in a quiet setting, and unlikely to be interrupted, you should be prepared to suggest these things. Emphasize that these physical arrangements are important to the success of the interview.

As you work through the Model and the Model questions, have the class explain why each step in the preinterview checklist is important and discuss what might happen if the step were omitted. As you work through the Guidelines, suggest the names of different people in politics, sports, or entertainment and ask students to describe how the steps in the preinterview checklist would apply to each interviewee.

You may wish to have a starter list of celebrities ready to be used by students preparing their preinterview checklists. Or you may wish to have the entire class brainstorm such a list. After the students' checklists have been exchanged and corrected, select the three best examples to serve as models for general classroom discussion. You can duplicate and distribute these checklists or use an opaque projector to show them to the class.

Extension Activity

An excellent way to stimulate student interest in interviewing is to invite a television, radio, or newspaper reporter to talk to the class. The reporter should describe how he or she prepares for, conducts, and edits an interview. If a reporter cannot visit your class, you may wish to assign a group of three to five students to interview a reporter at work. The students' questions should focus on the techniques of interviewing, and they can report to the class on what they have learned.

Evaluation and Feedback

In the text: Evaluation Checklist page 60, Chapter Review pages 76–77
In the TRB: Evaluation Checklists page EC7

To be used with:

Chapter 2 Lesson 3 (pages 61–68)

Aids for Extension and Reinforcement

In the TRB: Lesson Work Sheets page LW3

Objective

To write and ask effective interview questions

Vocabulary

follow-up questions (61)

Presentation of Subject Matter

You may introduce this lesson by showing a film or videotape of a Woody Allen interview so that students will have a clearer idea of one of the personalities in the Model interview. Ask pairs of students to take turns acting out the Allen interview in the Model. As you work through the Model questions and the Guidelines, have students practice asking questions that will elicit useful information. Pick one student to ask a *Yes/No* question and then call on a second student to turn that into a question beginning with *who, what, how, where, when,* or *why.*

You can extend the Guidelines activity by having students bring in published interviews with celebrities and evaluate the interview questions according to the characteristics listed in the Guidelines.

As in Lesson 2, it may be useful to have a starter list of interviewees available for students when they do the Preparing and Presenting activity, or you may prefer to have students build on their earlier work by preparing interview questions for the same person they used for the preinterview checklist in Lesson 2. You may wish to assign groups of three to six students to work independently on questions for the same person, and then to compare their work. The Evaluation Checklist may be used by pairs of students or larger groups, or you may wish to have students read their questions aloud for evaluation by the entire class.

Extension Activity
As a follow-up activity for Lesson 3, have the class take notes on the questions asked by a television or radio talk-show host. Have the students note examples of questions that they think were particularly good or particularly bad and ask them to explain the reasons for their evaluations.

Evaluation and Feedback
In the text: Evaluation Checklist page 68, Chapter Review pages 76–77
In the TRB: Evaluation Checklists page EC8

To be used with:

Chapter 2 Lesson 4 (pages 69–75)

Aids for Extension and Reinforcement
In the TRB: Speech Journal page SJ3, Evaluation Forms page EF4

Objective
To conduct an effective interview

Presentation of Subject Matter
Begin the lesson by having pairs of students take turns acting out the Model interview. It may be possible to have two students from an advanced class make an audio or videotape recording of the interview and let the rest of the class listen to it as well as read it. When you have worked through the Model with the class, have the students identify the introduction, body, and conclusion of the interview. Then work through the Model questions, asking students to suggest both additional interview questions and ways in which questions could have been reworded by the interviewer.

After students have completed the Preparing and Presenting section and the Evaluation Checklist, you may wish to have them fill out the same Evaluation Checklist for a recorded or telecast interview. The class should evaluate the interview according to the Guidelines, and students should be prepared to explain their evaluations.

Extension Activities
Have students record or videotape interviews with teachers, members of student government, team members, or community figures. The rest of the class can listen to and evaluate these interviews. Such interviews can be conducted by teams of two or more students. You may also wish to have the entire class conduct interviews on a single theme (for example, educators, law enforcement, or senior citizens). You may wish to have students write up their interviews into brief narrative reports.

Evaluation and Feedback
In the text: Evaluation Checklist page 75, Chapter Review pages 76–77
In the TRB: Evaluation Checklists page EC9, Chapter Tests page T3

To be used with:

Communicating on the Job: Inquiring about a Job (page 78)

Objective
To make successful oral inquiries about advertised jobs

Presentation of Subject Matter
After working through the Guidelines in this lesson, you might distribute a selection of job advertisements (either real or made-up) to the class. Ask students to identify the jobs they might apply for and have them explain why they think they are qualified. This exercise can lead into the first Activity, in which students role-play a telephone inquiry about a job. You may also wish to have students role-play an in-person job inquiry.

Evaluation and Feedback
In the TRB: Chapter Tests page T4

To be used with:

Communicating as a Citizen: Interviewing Candidates and Public Officials (page 79)

Aids for Extension and Reinforcement
Related Composition Activities page C2

Objective
To obtain informative responses in interviews with candidates or public officials

Presentation of Subject Matter
You might introduce this lesson by having the students read the Guidelines; then listen to a candidate or public official being interviewed on a radio or television public affairs show. Work through the Guidelines with the class, asking the students to evaluate the interview they watched, according to the rules given in the lesson.

You may expand this lesson by inviting a reporter, radio or television journalist, or freelance writer to speak to the class. The speaker should describe his or her experiences in interviewing candidates and public officials and the techniques he or she uses in order to obtain full and informative responses.

Evaluation and Feedback
In the TRB: Chapter Tests page T4

To be used with:

Chapter 3 Lesson 1 (pages 81–87)

Aids for Extension and Reinforcement
In the TRB: Lesson Work Sheets page LW4, Critical Thinking Work Sheets page CT3, Correct Usage Section, Transparencies page T3, Transparency Work Sheets page TW3

Objective
To prepare a complete and well-organized prediscussion outline

Vocabulary
group discussion (81)   criteria (81)
problem-solving process (81)

Presentation of Subject Matter
Have the students read the Model outline carefully, noting that the organization of the outline reflects the four steps in the problem-solving process. As the students respond to the discussion questions in Working with the Model, they will identify and discuss the kinds of details included in a prediscussion outline.

Before the students form groups for the Preparing and Presenting assignment, you may wish to lead them in discussing possible problems to be considered in their group discussions. Then, if groups select problems that have not yet been discussed in class, check to be sure their selections are appropriate. As the students research the topics of their problems, provide as much guidance as necessary. You may wish to have each student submit a list of his or her sources and, later, his or her notes for your approval.

Remind the students that the purpose of the Evaluation Checklist activity is to help them improve their own outlines. They should not expect their outlines to be exactly like those of the other group members; in fact, some differences in these outlines will help the group members conduct an interesting and productive group discussion.

Extension Activity
In addition to the Evaluation Checklist activity, you might wish to have each student discuss his or her prediscussion outline with a partner from another group. Since the partners' outlines will be on different problems, they should be able to offer fresh perspectives and ask one another helpful questions.

Evaluation and Feedback
In the text: Evaluation Checklist page 87, Chapter Review pages 100–101
In the TRB: Evaluation Checklists page EC10

To be used with:

Chapter 3 Lesson 2 (pages 88–94)

Aids for Extension and Reinforcement
In the TRB: Evaluation Forms page EF5

Objective
To practice the formal and informal roles members play in group discussions

Presentation of Subject Matter
After the students have read the lesson introduction, you might have them discuss the informal roles presented in the chart on page 89. Encourage volunteers to suggest specific things that group members in each role might say or do. Have other volunteers describe the ways in which those words and actions would contribute to or detract from the development of the group discussion.

Ask seven volunteers to assume the roles of the example group discussion members and read the Model aloud to the rest of the class. Then encourage all the students to contribute to a discussion based on the questions about the Model.

You may wish to have all the groups role-play discussion simultaneously, or you may prefer to have a single group role-play a discussion while the rest of the class observes. If the groups role-play one at a time, have the observers identify and describe the roles assumed by each discussion group member.

Extension Activity
After the students have completed the Preparing and Presenting assignment and the Evaluation Checklist activity, you might have each student write a brief report on the roles he or she assumed during the role playing. These reports should include descriptions of how the students helped or hindered the discussion in each of their roles and of how other group members responded to the various roles.

Evaluation and Feedback
In the text: Evaluation Checklist page 94, Chapter Review pages 100–101
In the TRB: Evaluation Checklists page EC11

To be used with:

Chapter 3 Lesson 3 (pages 95–99)

Aids for Extension and Reinforcement
In the TRB: Speech Journal page SJ4, Evaluation Forms page EF6

Objective
To work effectively with other participants in a small problem-solving group

Presentation of Subject Matter
After the students have read the lesson introduction, you may wish to lead them in a brief discussion of differences of opinion within a problem-solving group. Help the students recognize that such differences can improve a discussion by leading the members to consider a variety of options, as long as the group members respect one another and agree to resolve their differences constructively.

Have volunteers assume roles and read aloud the transcript in Working with the Model. After a class discussion of the questions, you might let groups of students role-play revised versions of the group discussion.

You may have all the groups conduct their problem-solving discussions at one time, or you might have them conduct their discussions in turn before the rest of the class. If the groups work before an audience, have the students complete Evaluation Forms pages EF5 and EF6 (on Group Discussion) in the TRB for each group they observe. Then let the members of each group consider those completed forms as part of their own evaluating activity.

Extension Activity
You may wish to record the problem-solving discussion conducted by each group. Later you may play back part or all of each taped discussion for the consideration of the group members or of the entire class.

Evaluation and Feedback
In the text: Evaluation Checklist page 99, Chapter Review pages 100–101
In the TRB: Evaluation Checklists page EC12, Chapter Tests page T5

To be used with:

Communicating on the Job: Being Interviewed for a Job (page 102)

Objective
To prepare for a successful job interview

Presentation of Subject Matter

After working through the Guidelines for a good interview, you can assign two pairs of students to role-play an interview. Outline an interview situation for both pairs to role-play; for example, Todd, whose work experience is very limited, is applying for a part-time job packing electronic components for shipment. After ten or fifteen minutes' preparation, one pair of students should role-play a successful interview, and the other pair should enact an unsuccessful interview in which the applicant fails to follow most of the Guidelines. The class can then compare and discuss the two interviews. Encourage students to describe any interview experiences they have had.

If you teach this lesson immediately after Communicating on the Job: Inquiring about a Job (78), you can invite an interviewer or personnel officer to speak to the class both about job inquiries and about interview behavior. Your school's career counselor will also have many useful suggestions to give the students.

Evaluation and Feedback

In the TRB: Chapter Tests page T6

To be used with:

Communicating as a Citizen: Solving a Community Problem (page 103)

Aids for Extension and Reinforcement

Related Composition Activities page C3

Objective

To role-play a problem-solving session whose topic is a community problem

Presentation of Subject Matter

In preparation for this lesson, you might ask the students to gather news items about local community problems and the attempts citizens are making to solve those problems. Let the students discuss the examples they have found. Then, after reading the lesson introduction, the students should evaluate the approaches used by the citizens in the example news stories.

To help the students discuss and understand the problem-solving guidelines presented in the lesson introduction, you might suggest a common community problem to which the students might apply the guidelines. For example, you might suggest they consider a neighborhood intersection that seems dangerous to the residents or an increase in daytime burglaries in a large neighborhood area. As the students read about each guideline, have volunteers explain how it should affect the efforts of citizens trying to solve the example problem.

After the students have planned their problem-solving sessions, as instructed in the lesson Activity, you may have each group role-play its session either for the rest of the class or for the members of one other group.

Evaluation and Feedback
In the TRB: Chapter Tests page T6

To be used with:

Chapter 4 Lesson 1 (pages 105–108)

Aids for Extension and Reinforcement
In the TRB: Critical Thinking Work Sheets page CT4, Speech Journal page SJ5, Listening Work Sheets page L1, Transparencies page T4, Transparency Work Sheets page TW4

Objectives
To effectively use the techniques of active listening
To provide effective feedback to speakers in conversations and informal group discussions
To participate in an interesting, friendly conversation

Presentation of Subject Matter
You may wish to begin this lesson by having students look at Communicating as a Citizen: Role Playing to Understand Communication Problems (page 375). Then have five students read the Model dialogue, each student taking the parts of each of the speakers.

For Model question 3, ask a group of students to prepare briefly and then present a continuation of the dialogue by role playing. The rest of the class should observe the listening habits these students display and the nonverbal cues they give. In the discussion, students should compare the role-played dialogue with the one in the text.

You can make the class more aware of nonverbal cues by having two volunteers stand in front of the class and demonstrate the way they express different emotions, such as interest, boredom, anxiety, happiness, friendliness, caution. Ask students to describe and discuss other kinds of body language they have observed.

Some students may not be able to think readily of current events and issues to discuss during the Preparing and Presenting activity. You can have a starter list of topics ready for these students. Include in your starter list major events of the past few days and weeks on the local, state, national, and international levels.

Extension Activities

Extend the Evaluation Checklist activity by having students observe speeches, panels, or other discussions, either in person or on television. Ask them to evaluate the listening behavior of audience members in terms of the Guidelines in this lesson.

Evaluation and Feedback

In the text: Evaluation Checklist page 108, Chapter Review page 109
In the TRB: Evaluation Checklists page EC13, Chapter Tests page T7

To be used with:

Communicating on the Job: Exploring Careers in Communications (page 110)

Objective

To be aware of the range of possible careers that require good communication skills

Presentation of Subject Matter

This lesson can be integrated with Communicating on the Job: Analyzing Your Career Interests (46). As you go through either the careers in this list or those the students suggested for Communicating on the Job: Analyzing Your Career Interests, have the class discuss the ways good speaking and listening habits might help in each job. For example, you might ask the students to list the people a television director must speak to every day and to imagine the difficulties of a director who had trouble making himself or herself understood.

Having a guest speaker from one of the professions in the list (Activity 1) can make this a very stimulating discussion. If you assign Activity 2, you will find it helpful to work through Communicating as a Citizen: Role Playing to Understand Communication Problems (375) with the class first.

Evaluation and Feedback

In the TRB: Chapter Tests page T8

To be used with:

Communicating as a Citizen: Being Aware of Communication Methods Used by the Hearing-Impaired (page 111)

Aids for Extension and Reinforcement

Related Composition Activities page C4

Objective
To compare three methods of communication used by hearing-impaired people

Vocabulary

lip reading (111)
manual communication (111)
manual alphabet (111)
sign language (111)

signing (111)
captioned (111)
closed captioned (111)

Presentation of Subject Matter
As you work through this lesson, you may wish to show the students the symbols of the manual alphabet, either by passing out a copy of the symbols or by displaying them on a chart to the entire class. (The complete manual alphabet may be found in many dictionaries.) Have students practice saying their own names and common phrases using the manual alphabet. Encourage them to "speak" as rapidly and accurately as they can. Although this system is surprisingly easy to learn, students will realize that it is too slow a method for interpreting ordinary speech.

Students can practice reading passages, moving their mouths without making any sound. Other students should see whether they can read their lips. If possible, students should observe an interpreter signing a television program using a combination of lip movements, sign language, and manual alphabet. The class will realize that gaining information by such methods requires long practice. Nevertheless, you should emphasize, millions of hearing-impaired people have mastered these techniques.

Public television stations in your area may broadcast captioned programs, or you may have access to closed-caption decoding equipment. If possible, have the members of the class watch a captioned program, both with and without sound, and compare the information they receive by listening with what they receive while only reading the captions.

Evaluation and Feedback
In the TRB: Chapter Tests page T8

To be used with:

Unit Two (Speaking to an Audience): A Case Study (page 113)

Objective
To evaluate a message for clarity and appropriateness of language

Presentation of Subject Matter
Have one or more students read the BART message aloud while the rest of the class listens. Hearing the message, as well as reading it, will make

students realize how many times the key phrase "the opposite tunnel" is repeated. As you work through the Think and Discuss activity, have students identify the words and phrases that are especially designed to reassure passengers (for example, "for your own safety," "the instructions . . . will be repeated").

You can extend this lesson by having students write their own messages for use in emergencies (for example, fires, floods, earthquakes, or power blackouts). Before the students write their message, they should decide the location of the emergency and the kind of structure in which people will be listening to the message. Have them read these messages to the class. Have the other students evaluate the clearness, conciseness, and usefulness of the information in each message.

To be used with:

Unit Introduction: Your Audience and You
(pages 114–117)

Aids for Extension and Reinforcement
In the TRB: Lesson Work Sheets page LW5, Evaluation Forms page EF7

Objectives
To understand the relationship between public speaking and the elements of speech
To familiarize oneself with an audience

Vocabulary
   expository speech (114)
   persuasive speech (114)
   audience (114)

Presentation of Subject Matter
Divide the class into groups of three. Divide the introduction into thirds and have each student read one third and explain it to the other students. Encourage the students to discuss the explanation within their group until they are sure they understand it. Then, at random, call on a representative of each group to explain each of the sections of the introduction. After each explanation, stop and encourage others in the class to add to or modify the explanation. Enter your own remarks if you discover any confusion as a result of these student explanations.

Once the groups have discussed the narrative up to the Activities section, have them complete Activities 1 and 2 in the small groups. Debrief by having selected groups share with the rest of the class. Create new groups of three and have the students complete the final Activity.

Extension Activity

Have the students consider the basic model of the communication process introduced in Unit One and talk about the way the information in the introduction they have just read relates to that model. Help them see the need for awareness of the audience as it affects setting, language, knowledge, and feedback. Encourage them to consider the model in terms of specific examples of communications situations they have been a part of.

To be used with:

Chapter 5 Lesson 1 (pages 119–125)

Aids for Extension and Reinforcement

In the TRB: Lesson Work Sheets page LW6, Critical Thinking Work Sheets page CT5, Outlines page O1, Speech Analysis pages SA1 and SA2, Developing an Oral Report Section, Correct Usage Section, Cassettes Work Sheets page CW1 and CW2, Speeches/Oral Interpretation Tape, Transparencies page T5, Transparency Work Sheets page TW5

Objective

To explain a familiar process in an expository speech

Presentation of Subject Matter

You can introduce this lesson by asking the students to volunteer different processes that they have recently explained to someone or had explained to them. Write the students' lists on the board and emphasize that all these explanations were informal expository speeches. Tell the class that in this chapter they will study every step in preparing, practicing, and giving an expository speech.

As you work through the Model speech by Huxley, emphasize that induction and deduction are very common thought processes that students use all the time. Have students rephrase portions of Huxley's speech in their own words and ask them to supply other illustrative examples that could have been used to make the same point as the example in the Model.

Understanding the basic outline for expository speeches given in the Guidelines section is essential for understanding the lessons in Chapter 5. You may wish to review this outline with the students as you begin teaching each of the lessons in this chapter. When students begin the Preparing and Presenting activity, you may wish to have a starter list of topics available for them, in addition to the sample topics in the text. You may wish to have the Preparing and Presenting and Evaluation Checklist activities take place in several smaller groups (perhaps of eight to ten students) rather than before the entire class.

Extension Activities

You can extend the lesson by having students bring in brief articles (from magazines such as *Good Housekeeping* or *Popular Mechanics*) or selections from books that explain simple processes. Each student can rewrite his or her selection into a brief expository speech that follows the Guidelines in Lesson 1. Students may deliver their speeches either to small groups or before the entire class for evaluation.

Evaluation and Feedback

In the text: Evaluation Checklist page 125, Chapter Review pages 170–171
In the TRB: Evaluation Checklists page EC14

To be used with:

Chapter 5 Lesson 2 (pages 126–132)

Aids for Extension and Reinforcement

In the TRB: Lesson Work Sheets page LW7, Outlines pages O2–O6, Speech Analysis page SA3

Objective

To clearly and effectively arrange the information in an expository speech

Vocabulary

chronological pattern (126)
spatial pattern (126)
topical pattern (126)

Presentation of Subject Matter

As you work through the introductory section of this lesson, have students suggest further examples of topics for expository speeches that could be arranged according to each of the five kinds of organization. Have the class discuss why each pattern would be appropriate and what the purpose of each speech might be.

Although the Model speech by President Johnson is organized according to a topical expository pattern, students should recognize that the speaker is also trying to persuade his listeners that the program he is explaining is worthwhile. As you work through the Guidelines with the class, ask the students to suggest further examples of each method of development that President Johnson might have used to make his speech more effective.

You can have a starter list of topics ready to give to students before they begin the Preparing and Presenting activity. You may also wish to invite the school librarian to inform the class about reference resources and other research materials that are available to students. You may wish to duplicate several of the better student outlines (or show them using an opaque projector) for the students to keep in mind as they work on the later lessons in Chapter 5.

Extension Activity

You can expand the lesson by having students choose a second pattern of organization and rewrite their outlines using that pattern. If a student has written about the problems of American cities according to a topical pattern (for example, the major types of urban problems), he or she could rewrite the outline according to a spatial pattern (problems of the Northeast, the Southeast, the Midwest, and so forth), a chronological pattern (prewar problems, postwar problems, problems of the 1960s, and so forth), or using a cause-and-effect or problem-solution pattern. Duplicate two or three such rewritten outlines. Have the class discuss the differences between the patterns and evaluate which organization is more effective.

Evaluation and Feedback

In the text: Evaluation Checklist page 132, Chapter Review pages 170–171
In the TRB: Evaluation Checklists page EC15

To be used with:

Chapter 5 Lesson 3 (pages 133–137)

Aids for Extension and Reinforcement

In the TRB: Lesson Work Sheets page LW8,

Objective

To prepare clear speaking notes and use them effectively

Presentation of Subject Matter

As you work through the introductory section of this lesson, you might ask students to discuss the experiences they have had in speaking from notecards. Emphasize that notecards should contain neither too much nor too little information but should simply remind the speaker of what he or she has already decided to say.

As the class discusses the Model notecards, ask students to describe how they would rewrite the cards for their own use. For example, how, if at all, would they expand or shorten the information? Might they use symbols or color codes? Would they type or write the information on the cards?

Before the students do the Preparing and Presenting and Evaluation Checklist activities, you may wish to check their notes briefly for neatness and clarity. After they have given their speeches, you may wish to offer practical suggestions on using notecards. You may need to have the students practice holding their notes comfortably in one hand without dropping, twisting, or shuffling them. As students learn to speak with their notes in one hand, they will quickly discover the importance of writing on only one side of a notecard.

If your students generally use a podium while speaking, you may wish to have them practice without one. Many real-life speaking situations will not have a podium available, and students should be prepared to speak under those circumstances as well.

Extension Activities

You can provide further practice in using notecards by having students prepare brief expository speeches based on a magazine article or book chapter. Have the other members of the class follow the speakers, using their own copies of the article. Have the students compare the speakers' notecards with the article or chapter and then discuss how much essential information each speaker included on his or her notecards.

You may also wish to have one or more students practice giving a speech using another student's notes. Ask the speakers to discuss this experience and to describe what they have learned about the information they need in their speaking notes.

Evaluation and Feedback

In the text: Evaluation Checklist page 137, Chapter Review pages 170–171
In the TRB: Evaluation Checklists page EC16

To be used with:

Chapter 5 Lesson 4 (pages 138–143)

Aids for Extension and Reinforcement

In the TRB: Lesson Work Sheets page LW9

Objective

To prepare and use effective visual aids

Presentation of Subject Matter

As you work through the introductory section, the Model, and the Guidelines, you can show the class a variety of visual aids, including three-dimensional models, maps, charts, graphs, diagrams, and working models. Have the students discuss which types of visual aids would be most appropriate for the expository speeches they prepared and gave in Lessons 2 and 3. Also have them decide which types of aids would be too expensive, complicated, delicate, or unwieldy to use in their expository speeches. Emphasize that clarity and simplicity are the most important characteristics of a good visual aid and that if listeners are paying more attention to the aid than to the speech, the speaker needs to find an aid that is more appropriate.

As students do the Preparing and Presenting activity, you may wish to limit them to one or two visual aids. You may find it helpful to check over the proposals or sketches for visual aids before the students prepare them.

Lesson 4 builds on the material students developed during Lessons 2 and 3. Consequently, the presentation they make for this lesson will provide a second evaluation of their speaking notes and a third evaluation of their outlines.

Extension Activity

You can expand the lesson by having students present their speeches using different visual aids than the ones they first used. The change should be from one major type of aid to another, such as from slides to a flip chart, or from a working model to a two-dimensional diagram. When each student has completed a presentation, ask him or her to discuss the advantages and disadvantages of each type of visual aid. Have the other students evaluate which type of aid was the most effective and have them discuss the reasons for their evaluation.

Evaluation and Feedback

In the text: Evaluation Checklist page 143, Chapter Review pages 170–171
In the TRB: Evaluation Checklists page EC17

To be used with:

Chapter 5 Lesson 5 (pages 144–150)

Aids for Extension and Reinforcement

In the TRB: Lesson Work Sheets page LW10, Speech Analysis pages SA4 and SA5

Objective

To analyze an audience and adapt a speech accordingly

Presentation of Subject Matter

As you work through the Model and the Model questions, have the students identify all the places where Watson has used words, images, or ideas to appeal to his audience of graduating college students. You may wish to remind your students that this speech was given in 1964 and ask them in what ways each of the speaker's appeals to his audience might be changed to suit an audience of today.

As you work through the Guidelines, emphasize the importance of a strong introduction as part of a successful speech. Although introductions often include jokes or other humorous stories, such anecdotes must be relevant to the topic of the speech (as well as inoffensive to the audience). You may wish to have the class review these Guidelines when you teach Chapters 6, 8, and 9.

After students have evaluated the others' analyses and introductions while working in groups of three, you may wish to have them read their analyses and introductions to the entire class. Have the students discuss the various analyses of the class that have been prepared. Also ask the students to identify the introductions they find most interesting and to discuss the reasons for their response.

Extension Activities

Have students bring in examples of printed or recorded speeches that they believe contain effective introductions. Have them read or play these introductions for the class and have the other students evaluate them.

Ask students to find (or describe) examples of speeches that were not well adapted to their intended audience. Have them discuss the reasons for this poor adaptation and rewrite the speeches according to the Guidelines in this lesson and in the Audience Analysis Checklist found on page 116 of the student text.

Evaluation and Feedback

In the text: Evaluation Checklist page 150, Chapter Review pages 170–171
In the TRB: Evaluation Checklists page EC18

To be used with:

Chapter 5 Lesson 6 (pages 151–157)

Aids for Extension and Reinforcement
In the TRB: Evaluation Forms page EF8

Objectives
To develop confidence in speaking situations
To polish speaking skills

Presentation of Subject Matter
The amount of time you spend on the material in this lesson related to developing confidence should depend on the extent to which this issue concerns your students. If you only have one or two students who are seriously lacking in confidence, you may be better off helping them individually and not taking significant class time on the topic. If there is general concern in your class about speaking before an audience, you may want to expand on the lesson in the text. One way to do this would be to bring in some students who are well known in the school for their role as performers—musical, athletic, or dramatic (and in whom you have confidence). Have these students present a panel discussion talking about the ways they have developed their confidence for performing before an audience.

The practice record introduced in this lesson is a vital tool for assuring students perform effectively and for helping them build their confidence.

Before you have the students work through their own practice sessions, help them understand that this is a positive tool for building up their abilities, not a means of tearing them down. You can use a videotape model of a speech and work with the class using an overhead of the practice record to guide a discussion on the kinds of remarks that would be most helpful on the record.

As students practice with each other, make sure that they learn to use the response of others in a critical fashion—neither accepting nor rejecting everything they are told but giving it careful consideration.

Extension Activity

If you have advanced speech students in the school, use one of them to perform before the class. Then have everyone complete a practice record and discuss each other's remarks on the record to build students' ability to use this record. Emphasize specificity, positive response, and open-minded consideration of the feedback provided by the record.

Additional Teacher Assignments

In the text: Evaluation Checklist page 157, Chapter Review pages 170–171
In the TRB: Evaluation Checklists page EC19

To be used with:

Chapter 5 Lesson 7 (pages 158–162)

Aids for Extension and Reinforcement

In the TRB: Speech Journal page SJ6, Evaluation Forms page EF9

Objective

To respond effectively to questions from listeners

Presentation of Subject Matter

You can begin this lesson by having the class review the characteristics of good and bad interview questions outlined in Chapter 2, Lesson 3 (page 66). Have the students discuss how the same Guidelines apply to questions they might ask following an expository speech or other classroom presentation. Students should recognize that the purpose of questions is to obtain information from the speaker rather than to show off the questioner's knowledge. Emphasize that, whether a question is good or bad, the speaker should always answer directly, clearly, and politely. You may wish to use examples from your teaching experience to illustrate some of the questions a speaker must be prepared to deal with.

Tell the class to think about a general topic for an expository speech; for example, "Presidential Primaries." As you work through the Guidelines, have students suggest examples of questions on this topic that follow—or fail to follow—each of the rules. Ask other students to provide suitable responses that a speaker might make. Have the class discuss the characteristics of a good answer.

You may wish to have the students do the Preparing and Presenting and Evaluation Checklist activities in groups of five or six instead of before the entire class. You can monitor Preparing and Presenting and Evaluation Checklist sessions to see how well students have mastered question-answering techniques.

Extension Activity

If convenient, assign the class to watch a televised press conference or similar informal interview. Have the students evaluate the quality and relevance of the questions and of the speaker's responses to them. Ask the students to describe ways in which the questions and answers could have been improved.

Evaluation and Feedback

In the text: Evaluation Checklist page 162, Chapter Review pages 170–171
In the TRB: Evaluation Checklists pages EC20

To be used with:

Chapter 5 Lesson 8 (pages 163–169)

Objective

To prepare and present an expository speech that analyzes a work of literature or art

Vocabulary

analytical expository speech (163)

Presentation of Subject Matter

As you work through the introductory section of this lesson, you might have students think about a book, speech, story, or article they have read recently, and how each of the questions listed would apply to that work. Before the class reads the Model speech, you may wish to have the students read the Stevie Smith poem and briefly discuss the meanings they find in it. Then have them read Jewel's speech analyzing the poem. As you work through the Model speech and the Model questions, emphasize the importance of providing the kind of background that a specific audience will need in order to understand a work.

As you work through the Guidelines, you may wish to have students bring in book reviews that they believe follow—or fail to follow—the rules in the text. Have the class read or listen to reviews and discuss whether the authors have kept fact distinct from opinion and whether they have avoided sarcasm in their criticism.

You may wish to have the Preparing and Presenting and Evaluation Checklist activities conducted in groups of five or six students rather than before the entire class. Monitor the Evaluation Checklist sessions to see how well students have mastered the Guidelines for analytical expository speeches.

Extension Activity

The Stevie Smith poem, "Not Waving but Drowning," deals with some of the communication problems described in Chapters 1 and 2. You may wish to assign students to bring in other poems or stories that deal with the problems of communication. You might also ask the students to prepare analytical expository speeches on works with the general theme of communication and have the class discuss the ways in which different writers have dealt with it.

Evaluation and Feedback

In the text: Evaluation Checklist page 169, Chapter Review pages 170–171
In the TRB: Evaluation Checklists page EC21, Chapter Tests page T9

To be used with:

Communicating on the Job: Explaining a Work Process (page 172)

Objective

To explain a work process clearly and effectively

Vocabulary

introduction (172)
body (172)
conclusion (172)

Presentation of Subject Matter

After working through the Guidelines with the class, you may wish to have several students demonstrate both good and poor explanations they have listened to. Have the class discuss why the poor explanations were unsatisfactory and in what ways they could have been improved.

When your students begin the activities, you may wish to have the entire class brainstorm a list of occupations or other areas of life in which people might need to explain processes to others. Have the students list a number of different work processes and have each student select one process for a brief expository speech.

Evaluation and Feedback

In the TRB: Chapter Tests page T10

To be used with:

Communicating as a Citizen: Giving Testimony (page 173)

Aids for Extension and Reinforcement
Related Composition Activities page C5

Objective
To give accurate testimony in court or to a committee

Presentation of Subject Matter
Audio or videotape recordings of committee investigations are an excellent means of demonstrating how real witnesses respond to questions while testifying. After playing a portion of such a recording, ask the students how well the witnesses followed the principles given in the guidelines. You might ask students to contrast this authentic testimony with the dramatized courtroom scenes and committee investigations presented in movies and television plays.

Evaluation and Feedback
In the TRB: Chapter Tests page T10

To be used with:

Chapter 6 Lesson 1 (pages 175–180)

Aids for Extension and Reinforcement
In the TRB: Lesson Work Sheets page LW11, Critical Thinking Work Sheets page CT6, Outlines page O7, Correct Usage Section, Cassettes Work Sheets page CW3 and CW4, Speech/Oral Interpretation Tape, Transparencies page T6, Transparency Work Sheets page TW6

Objective
To develop awareness of the critical thinking skills needed in order to be an effective persuasive speaker

Vocabulary
oversimplify (179)	*post hoc ergo propter hoc* (179)
begging the question (179)	reasoning backward (179)
misleading statistics (179)	false analogy (180)

Presentation of Subject Matter
Have your students watch a congressional hearing videotaped from C-Span or some other activity in which they can observe critical thinking

taking place. Have them identify examples of each of the thinking skills listed as well as any logical fallacies presented in the Guidelines section.

Because students may be unfamiliar with the setting in which Susan B. Anthony spoke, you could provide them with some historical background or offer a challenge assignment for a student or for a small group of students. Have them prepare a report on the women's suffrage movement so that the thought processes in Anthony's speech can be discussed in a knowledgeable manner.

The logical fallacies identified in the text represent a common but incomplete list of such errors. Some students may accept the challenge of identifying other fallacies. Discuss the fallacies with the entire class and then in pairs to encourage students to cite specific examples of such errors in reasoning from their everyday experiences.

Extension Activity
Disinformation has been a much publicized tactic of Soviet bloc nations bent on influencing other nations of the world. Invite a social studies teacher or a community member who is familiar with these concepts and how they relate to the world of propaganda to talk with your class.

Evaluation and Feedback
In the text: Evaluation Checklist page 180, Chapter Review pages 206–207
In the TRB: Evaluation Checklists page EC22

To be used with:

Chapter 6 Lesson 2 (pages 181–187)

Aids for Extension and Reinforcement
In the TRB: Outlines page O8, Speech Analysis pages SA6, 7, and 8, Evaluation Forms page EF10

Objective
To plan a persuasive speech developed with logical arguments

Vocabulary
   position (181)
   logical argument (181)
   evidence (181)

Presentation of Subject Matter
Before the students begin reading the lesson, you might let them discuss persuasive speeches and sales presentations. Ask volunteers to identify the most effective persuasive speeches they have heard and to describe the qualities that made those speeches convincing. Then, as the students read the lesson introduction, focus their attention on the purpose of persuasive speeches and on the terms that are introduced.

The introduction to the Model will help the students understand the context of Macaulay's speech. If you want to provide further background, you might ask a volunteer to research and present a brief expository speech on the issue.

Read the speech aloud to the class or have one of the students practice and then read the speech aloud. As the students discuss the speech, you might want to help them consider it as a persuasive speech opposing all forms of bigotry. Ask the students to suggest logical arguments that a contemporary persuasive speaker might use in arguing against discrimination.

As the students begin the Preparing and Presenting section, you might want to help them extend the list of possible topics and check each statement of position before the students write their speech outlines

Extension Activities

Since the students will need to research their speech topics carefully before writing their outlines, you might wish to help them review their techniques of research. If necessary, take them on a tour of the school library or have the librarian make a brief presentation and answer the students' questions.

To provide additional speaking practice, have each student present his or her planned speech to the rest of the class. Have the listeners use Evaluation Forms page EF10 in the TRB to record their evaluations.

Evaluation and Feedback

In the text: Evaluation Checklist page 187, Chapter Review pages 206–207
In the TRB: Evaluation Checklists page EC23

To be used with:

Chapter 6 Lesson 3 (pages 188–193)

Aids for Extension and Reinforcement

In the TRB: Outlines page O9, Speech Analysis pages SA9 and SA10

Objective

To plan and deliver a persuasive speech developed with appeals to emotion

Vocabulary

physical needs (188)
psychological needs (188)
social needs (188)

Presentation of Subject Matter

As the students study the lesson introduction, you might help them discuss the three kinds of basic needs. Ask volunteers to give further examples of the basic needs and to suggest specific appeals directed to each kind of need.

In Working with the Model, play a tape of Jordan's speech, if possible, or have a student prepare the speech and then read it aloud to the class. You may also want to have a volunteer prepare a brief expository speech on Barbara Jordan as background for the Model.

If necessary, help the students think of specific topics for their persuasive speeches. After the Evaluation Checklist activity, you might have each student write a paragraph explaining how he or she could improve his or her persuasive speech.

Extension Activities

To provide further practice in speaking to larger audiences, you might have the students use the Preparing and Presenting activity and the Evaluation Checklist activity as practice sessions; then have them deliver their speeches to the entire class.

EFFECTIVE SPEECH contains excerpts from inaugural speeches by Presidents Roosevelt (Chapter 6, Lesson 4), Kennedy (Chapter 11, Lessons 2 and 3), and Reagan (Chapter 7, Lesson 1). You might have the students examine each of these Models for examples of emotional appeals. They can then contrast the specific needs each speaker appeals to and discuss the reasons behind the different appeals.

Evaluation and Feedback

In the text: Evaluation Checklist page 193, Chapter Review pages 206–207
In the TRB: Evaluation Checklists page EC24

To be used with:

Chapter 6 Lesson 4 (pages 194–198)

Aids for Extension and Reinforcement

In the TRB: Outlines page O10, Speech Analysis page SA11

Objective

To analyze techniques that encourage audience identification in a persuasive speech

Presentation of Subject Matter

After the students have studied the lesson introduction, you might have them review the speeches by Macaulay and Jordan in the previous two lessons. Ask them to identify the techniques each speaker used to encourage audience identification.

Ask one of the students to prepare and read aloud the selection from Roosevelt's speech. You may also wish to have a student research and deliver a short expository speech about the Great Depression as background for the Model.

If necessary, help the students select appropriate speeches for the Preparing and Presenting assignment. Encourage them to attend and analyze a campaign speech or sales presentation, if possible, rather than listening to a recording or broadcast.

After the students in each pair have compared and discussed their analyses, you might wish to have them prepare a brief report on the techniques used in the speech they heard. These reports may be written or presented orally to the rest of the class.

Extension Activity

If at all possible, introduce the Model by playing a recording of Roosevelt or by showing a film in which he speaks, since his confident delivery was an important factor in creating a sense of identification in his audience. Have the class discuss Roosevelt's speaking style, and let volunteers speculate on the effect a different kind of speaker might have had while delivering the same speeches.

Evaluation and Feedback

In the text: Evaluation Checklist page 198, Chapter Review pages 206–207
In the TRB: Evaluation Checklists page EC25

To be used with:

Chapter 6 Lesson 5 (pages 199–205)

Aids for Extension and Reinforcement

In the text: Handbook of Contest Speaking pages 393–395
In the TRB: Outlines page O11, Speech Analysis page SA12, Speech Journal page SJ7, Evaluation Forms page EF11

Objective

To plan and present a persuasive speech that effectively uses identification, appeals to logic, and appeals to emotion

Presentation of Subject Matter

This lesson gives the students an opportunity to recognize and practice using in combination the techniques of effective persuasive speaking. You might begin by having volunteers recall the most important points they have learned about using appeals to logic, appeals to emotion, and identification.

After the students have read the lesson introduction, have a prepared volunteer read aloud the excerpts from Zola's speech, or read the Model aloud yourself. The introduction to the Model provides important background information; in addition, you may want to have one of the students present more details in a brief expository speech.

For the Preparing and Presenting assignment, you may wish to help the students extend the list of possible speech topics. If necessary, provide specific guidance as the students research their topics. You might suggest that the students use Evaluation Forms page EF11 in the TRB in evaluating one another's practice sessions.

Extension Activity
You may wish to have the students study Chapter 10, "Evaluating Persuasive Appeals," in conjunction with this lesson. Ask the listeners to use the Guidelines presented in that lesson to evaluate the persuasive speeches of their classmates.

Evaluation and Feedback
In the text: Evaluation Checklist page 205, Chapter Review pages 206–207
In the TRB: Evaluation Checklists page EC26, Chapter Tests page T11

To be used with:

Communicating on the Job: Making a Sales Presentation (page 208)

Objective
To evaluate and practice making sales presentations

Presentation of Subject Matter
You might begin this lesson by letting a pair of volunteers role-play a meeting between a salesperson and a customer. Give the volunteers time to plan the situation they want to role-play and allow them to show either a pleasant and successful sales presentation or one in which the salesperson violates the principles presented in the lesson. After the role playing, let the students share their responses to the sales presentation. Then have the students study the principles in the lesson introduction and use them in analyzing the presentation.

For Activity 1, the group members may present their findings orally to the rest of the class, or they may work together to write a report of their findings.

For Activity 2, you might wish to have the students give their sales presentations to groups of other students rather than to the whole class. This procedure will save class time and will encourage the students to participate more actively in the discussions of each presentation.

Evaluation and Feedback
In the TRB: Chapter Tests page T12

To be used with:

Communicating as a Citizen: Evaluating Your Credibility as a Speaker (page 209)

Aids for Extension and Reinforcement
Related Composition Activities page C6

Objective
To evaluate the credibility of speakers

Presentation of Subject Matter
You might wish to have the students meet in groups to study and discuss the rating chart in the lesson introduction. They should examine the implications of each question, noting how a speaker's rating would affect his or her credibility. The students might also suggest examples of familiar speakers who rate especially well in each quality.

You might have the students work in the same groups for the lesson Activity. The members of each group should agree on the speakers whom they will rate. After the students complete the ratings independently, they should meet again to compare the rankings of the speakers.

Remind the students, too, that they should apply this rating chart to themselves as speakers. Each student should use the chart at least once during a practice session, discussing with a partner how his or her own credibility might be rated.

Evaluation and Feedback
In the TRB: Chapter Tests page T12

To be used with:

Chapter 7 Lesson 1 (pages 211–216)

Aids for Extension and Reinforcement
In the TRB: Lesson Work Sheets page LW12, Critical Thinking Work Sheets page CT7, Speech Journal page SJ8, Listening Work Sheets page L2, Evaluation Forms page EF12, Transparencies page T7, Transparency Work Sheets page TW7

Objectives
To recognize a speaker's signposts
To effectively record the essential information in a speech or lecture

Vocabulary
signposts (211)
informal outline (211)

Presenting the Subject Matter

You can begin this lesson by asking the students to suggest transitions and other words and phrases that speakers might use as signposts. Write these signpost words and phrases on the board and then have the students discuss what kind of signal each signpost gives to listeners and note-takers.

After working through the Model and the Model questions, you may wish to give the class further note-taking practice by having a student read a brief passage from a textbook or article while the other students take notes. You may wish to have half the class take notes in informal outline style and the other half use paragraph format. It may be helpful to use an opaque projector to compare the original text with various sets of notes.

As you work through the Guidelines, have the students discuss why each rule is important for taking good notes and what difficulties they might have if they failed to follow each of the Guidelines. You may wish to share some of the techniques you developed while taking notes in college.

You may wish to check the sets of notes taken by each pair of students for the Preparing and Presenting activities. You may wish to have the students work in groups of five or six, or even have the entire class listen to the same speech and compare notes.

Extension Activity

You can extend Lesson 1 by having students compare a set of listener's notes with speaking notes. One student can take notes as the members of the class listen to a speech. Then a second student, who has not heard the speech, can use those notes to present the speech to the class. The students who have heard both versions of the speech should identify the differences that result from the different sets of notes; then they should discuss any ways in which the notes might be improved.

Evaluation and Feedback

In the text: Evaluation Checklist page 216, Chapter Review page 217
In the TRB: Evaluation Checklists page EC27, Chapter Tests page T13

To be used with:

Communicating on the Job: Taking Notes on a Training Lecture (page 218)

Objective

To take useful notes on a training lecture

Presentation of Subject Matter

Ask the students to volunteer examples of training talks or lectures they have recently received (for example, in a shop or science class, in P.E., or as part of a team or club activity). Then, as you work through the Guidelines in the lesson, have the students discuss how each guideline applies to the training lectures they received. You can have a student give a training lecture (of five minutes or less) while the rest of the class takes notes on it. Topics might include minor repairs on automobiles or appliances; swimming or running techniques; conditioning exercises; use of the microscope or similar equipment. Encourage students to ask clarifying questions and ask questions yourself if the speaker has left some point unclear. Then have several students take turns explaining the procedure using their notes.

Evaluation and Feedback
In the TRB: Chapter Tests page T14

To be used with:

Communicating as a Citizen: Appealing to a Governmental Agency (page 219)

Aids for Extension and Reinforcement
In the TRB: Related Composition Activities page C7

Objective
To prepare a presentation appropriate for using as an appeal to a governmental agency

Presentation of Subject Matter
You might begin this lesson by having the students briefly discuss the kinds of appeals citizens may want to make to governmental agencies. If any of the students has participated in making such an appeal or has observed someone else making such an appeal, have the student share his or her experience and reaction with the rest of the class.

Then help the students study and discuss the guidelines. Encourage volunteers to explain how each guideline might help a person make an effective presentation.

For Activity 1, you might have the students form small groups and arrange to visit various public officials, or you might prefer to have the students select one official whom they can invite to visit the class.

Help the students select specific problems for consideration in Activity 2. If some of the groups decide to present their appeals, help those students practice and improve their presentations.

Evaluation and Feedback
In the TRB: Chapter Tests page T14

To be used with:

Unit Three (Parliamentary Procedure and Debate): A Case Study (page 221)

Objective
To evaluate the use of loaded language in a persuasive appeal

Presentation of Subject Matter
Begin by having students take turns reading the "perfect" foreign policy speech aloud. Have them try to adopt the emphasis and style of speaking that a presidential candidate might use. Then ask the other students to define the important words and phrases in the speech. Help the students see that the language is so vague that the speech can mean all things to all listeners, regardless of their political parties. Have the students discuss local, state, or national politicians of whom they are aware and evaluate how clearly or vaguely each politician's speeches express his or her ideas. Emphasize that in the following chapters the class will learn how to persuade through effective, well-planned arguments.

To be used with:

Unit Introduction: Communicating in a Democracy (pages 222–227)

Objectives
To understand the importance of effective and free speech to the functioning of our government
To reinforce the understanding of the basic speech communication model introduced in Unit One
To become aware of the basic models for decision making
To realize the importance of participating in our society's decision-making processes

Vocabulary
trial-and-error (225)   rational (225)
incremental (225)   scanning (225)

Presentation of Subject Matter
The relationship between free speech and active involvement in our governmental activities should be easy for students to understand. One reason for focusing on this relationship as it pertains to the basic speech communication model is that students who engage in debates and parliamentary activities often get so carried away with the formalities of the exercises that the students forget the underlying purposes of these activities. If you consider no other aspect of this introduction before dealing with debate and

parliamentary procedure, you should have a thorough discussion of these speech forms and how they relate to the communication process.

For the decision-making approaches to be useful to the students, you will need to spend some time talking about how the students and others they know make decisions. As they reflect on various decisions, encourage them to determine which approach (or some combination of them) identified in the text they used to reach each decision. The important thing is not what approaches were used but whether testing the approaches against their experience can help them understand the approaches and, therefore, gain a better perspective on the decision-making process itself.

Extension Activity

Several Supreme Court decisions concerning freedom of speech have been related directly to high school situations. Two cases, *Tinker V. Des Moines* and *Bethel School District V. Fraser*, provide somewhat different views of the extent to which a student's first amendment rights exist at school. Have some of your students research these cases and present a panel discussion on the subject of students' freedom of speech. They may find the Fraser case particularly relevant to this unit if they are aware that he was a member of a championship debate squad from his high school.

To be used with:

Chapter 8 Lesson 1 (pages 229–234)

Aids for Extension and Reinforcement

In the TRB: Lesson Work Sheets page LW13, Critical Thinking Work Sheets page CT8, Transparencies page T8, Transparency Work Sheets page TW8

Objectives

To understand the way a parliamentary body is organized
To know the nine events of a meeting conducted according to the rules of parliamentary procedure

Vocabulary

chairperson (229)	committee reports (230)
agenda (229)	old business (230)
call to order (230)	new business (230)
minutes (230)	announcements (230)
treasurer's report (230)	adjournment (231)
correspondence (230)	

Presentation of Subject Matter

You might want to introduce this lesson by playing a tape recording or showing a videotape of the beginning of a student council meeting (or of the meeting of another group that uses parliamentary procedure). In addition, you might let the students discuss their own experiences in attending and participating in meetings conducted according to parliamentary procedure. After the students have read the lesson introduction, encourage them to discuss the reasons underlying the wide use of parliamentary procedure. Be sure the class understands that the rules of parliamentary procedure help organization members use their meeting time constructively and guide them in reaching fair decisions.

Have the students carefully study the sample agenda in Working with the Model. If necessary, explain that, although most of them may not expect to assume the role of chairperson in a club or organization, understanding the preparation and use of a meeting agenda will help the students understand the plan and sequence of a meeting conducted according to parliamentary procedure.

Before the students write their own agendas as assigned in Preparing and Presenting, you might let them meet in pairs or small groups to discuss the specific plans to be made either for actual clubs in the school or for the imaginary clubs suggested in the text. Then have the students write their agendas independently. As they complete the Evaluation Checklist activity, be sure the students make changes after discussing their agendas.

Extension Activity

You might want to have the class develop a collection of actual agendas. Have volunteers bring in copies of the agendas used in school or civic clubs to which they or their parents belong. (You may also be able to contribute several examples of actual agendas.) Then let the students meet in groups to read and discuss the agendas.

Evaluation and Feedback

In the text: Evaluation Checklist page 234, Chapter Review pages 244–245
In the TRB: Evaluation Checklists page EC28

To be used with:

Chapter 8 Lesson 2 (pages 235–243)

Aids for Extension and Reinforcement

In the TRB: Correct Usage Section, Speech Journal page SJ9

Objectives

To participate effectively in a meeting conducted according to the rules of parliamentary procedure
To effectively introduce parliamentary motions

Vocabulary
  motion (235)
  amendments (235)

Presentation of Subject Matter
You may want to have volunteers read the lesson introduction aloud, giving special attention to the description of the most common parliamentary motions. Ask the students to give specific examples of each kind of motion.

You might have volunteers assume the roles of members of the Stevenson Service Club and read aloud the transcript in Working with the Model. Then have the same students or another group of students role-play a continuation of the meeting. The students may use the Model questions as a guide in role playing the meeting, or they may make up their own continuation.

For the Preparing and Presenting activity, you may wish to select one of the agendas written for Lesson 1, or you may prefer to have the students read the others' agendas and select the one to be used. All the students should know in advance what kind of meeting will be conducted, and each student—even if he or she does not have a specific role to play—should spend some time preparing for the meeting.

After the students have discussed the meeting in small groups, you might ask them to write brief evaluations of the meeting.

Extension Activities
To help the students become proficient in using parliamentary motions, you might have the class function according to the rules of parliamentary procedure for several weeks. The students may elect officers to serve during this time. Under the direction of the chairperson, the class may consider old and new business at the beginning of each session.

In addition, you may want to have some or all of the students become familiar with *Robert's Rules of Order (Revised)*. You might have each student read about a specific kind of motion and write a brief report on its use, or you might have several volunteers study the book and present brief oral reports on its content and format.

Evaluation and Feedback
In the text: Evaluation Checklist page 243, Chapter Review pages 244–245
In the TRB: Evaluation Checklists page EC29, Chapter Tests page T15

To be used with:

Communicating on the Job: Using an Agenda (page 246)

Objective
To write an agenda for the meeting of a class organization or student government committee

Presentation of Subject Matter

You might begin this lesson by having the students discuss their own experiences in attending and participating in meetings conducted according to parliamentary procedure. You may want to have volunteers respond to questions such as these: How did the meeting seem to be organized? How comfortable did the chairperson seem to feel about the organization of the meeting? How did he or she make the organization of the meeting clear to the other people participating in the meeting? As they discuss their experiences, help the students evaluate the importance of having a specific plan for organizing and planning a meeting in advance.

Then have the students study and discuss the lesson introduction. Encourage them to compare the listed order of events to the order of events in meetings they have attended.

You may want to have the students work in groups as they begin the lesson Activity. The members of each group should discuss the specific items of business to be included in the meeting they are planning. Then the group members might write one agenda together, or they might write their agendas individually and compare their completed work.

Evaluation and Feedback

In the TRB: Chapter Tests page T16

To be used with:

Communicating as a Citizen: Nominating a Candidate for Office (page 247)

Aids for Extension and Reinforcement

In the TRB: Related Composition Activities page C8

Objective

To prepare and evaluate nominating speeches

Presentation of Subject Matter

You may want to use Activity 1 as a lesson introduction. Play or read aloud to the students a famous nominating speech and let the students discuss their responses to the speech. Then help the students study and discuss the guidelines presented in the lesson introduction. When they are familiar with the guidelines, let the students listen to the speech again and evaluate it in terms of what they have learned.

You may also have the students complete Activity 1 as an independent assignment. Have each student find a nominating speech other than the one discussed in class. The students may write their reports about the nominating speeches, or they may present their reports orally.

For Activity 2, you might have the students form small groups and deliver their nominating speeches to the other group members. If you prefer to have the students write nominating speeches, the group members might read and discuss one another's work.

Evaluation and Feedback
In the TRB: Chapter Tests page T16

To be used with:

Chapter 9 Lesson 1 (pages 249–255)

Aids for Extension and Reinforcement
In the TRB: Lesson Work Sheets pages LW14–16, Critical Thinking Work Sheets page CT9, Correct Usage Section, Cassettes Work Sheets pages CW5 and CW6, Debate Tape, Transparencies page T9, Transparency Work Sheets page TW9

Objectives
To understand the terms used in debate
To effectively prepare a debate brief
To understand clearly how debate speeches are organized

Vocabulary

debate (249)	evidence (249)
proposition (249)	brief (249)
affirmative (249)	refutation (249)
negative (249)	constructive speech (249)
argument (249)	rebuttal speech (249–250)

Presentation of Subject Matter
Help the students study and discuss the listed debate terms. You might have volunteers paraphrase the explanations to demonstrate their own understanding and to help other students understand the terms.

Also guide the students in discussing the parts of a brief, as presented in the outline on pages 250–251. Have them carefully compare the outline with the beginning of the debate brief presented in Working with the Model. Be sure all the students understand that the Model presents only the first portion of a brief.

As the students begin the Preparing and Presenting assignment, you may wish to have them suggest and briefly discuss possible debate topics. Then divide the class into groups of four or allow the students to form their own groups. After each group has composed its debate proposition, you may wish to help the group members evaluate their proposition. If necessary, suggest specific changes the students should make to improve their proposition. Emphasize the importance of thorough research in preparation for a debate and allow the students as much research time as practical. You may wish to make regular checks of the students' sources, notes, and briefs.

Remind the students that they should not divide their groups into affirmative and negative teams until they have completed their briefs. Each student's brief should present both sides of the proposition. The group members should divide into teams, however, before they begin discussing and improving their briefs, as assigned in the Evaluation Checklist section.

Extension Activity

You might introduce this lesson by having two or more members of your school's debate team or debating club perform before the class. This presentation will develop student interest in debating and will provide a model you can use to illustrate the terms introduced in this lesson.

Evaluation and Feedback

In the text: Evaluation Checklist page 255, Chapter Review pages 268–269
In the TRB: Evaluation Checklists page EC30

To be used with:

Chapter 9 Lesson 2 (pages 256–260)

Aids for Extension and Reinforcement

In the text: Handbook of Contest Speaking pages 388–390
In the TRB: Speech Journal page SJ10, Evaluation Forms page EF13

Objective

To participate effectively in a debate by giving a constructive speech and a rebuttal speech

Presentation of Subject Matter

After the students have studied the lesson introduction and the Guidelines, you might let volunteers list the steps in preparing for and participating in a debate. You may also wish to have volunteers summarize the methods of planning and organizing a persuasive speech developed with logical arguments, as presented in Chapter 6, Lesson 2.

To help the students study and discuss the Model, you might have a volunteer read the rebuttal speech aloud. Be sure the students can identify the argument that the speaker is attempting to refute and guide them in analyzing and evaluating the effectiveness of the rebuttal.

As the students begin the Preparing and Presenting assignment, remind them that they have already thoroughly researched the issues of their debates; they should use the information they gathered for Lesson 1 rather than select a new issue and begin new research. The two members of each team should work together in evaluating and improving both the content and the delivery of their constructive speeches. They should also make specific plans for refuting the arguments they expect the other side to use.

During the presentation of each debate, the other class members should be actively involved as critical listeners. They should record their responses to the debate speeches using the Evaluation Checklists page EC31 or Evaluation Forms page EF13. After each debate, the participants may read and discuss their classmates' written evaluations, or the entire class may participate in a brief discussion of the debate.

Extension Activity
You might work with other teachers to help the students choose debate propositions that relate to the issues they are studying in other classes. Then the students in each group can conduct their debate as part of that related class. The students in each class can complete either Evaluation Checklists page EC31 or Evaluation Forms page EF13, and the teacher of the class can provide you with specific information on the performance of the debaters. In addition, you may wish to have the students make tape recordings so that you can listen to their debates and discuss their work with them.

Evaluation and Feedback
In the text: Evaluation Checklist page 260, Chapter Review pages 268–269
In the TRB: Evaluation Checklists page EC31

To be used with:

Chapter 9 Lesson 3 (pages 261–267)

Aids for Extension and Reinforcement
In the TRB: Lesson Work Sheets page LW16, Cassettes Work Sheets pages
       CW7 and CW8

Objective
To participate in a Lincoln-Douglas debate

Vocabulary
Lincoln–Douglas debate (261)
affirmative constructive speech (261)
negative cross–examination (261)
negative constructive speech (261)

affirmative cross–
   examination (261)
affirmative rebuttal (261)
negative rebuttal (261)

Presentation of Subject Matter
A live demonstration of a Lincoln-Douglas debate using members of your school's debate team would be a good introduction to this form of debate.

If such students cannot be scheduled into your class, the audiotape of a Lincoln-Douglas debate that has been prepared to accompany these resource materials provides another way of introducing your class to the give and take of this form of discourse.

Because Lincoln-Douglas debates bear a close relationship in form to the national and state debates of political candidates one often sees on television, students may be able to identify more easily with Lincoln-Douglas debates than with other debates. If you can obtain videotapes of some political debates, you may be able to use them to help develop student interest. Since none of them will follow the exact format used for academic L/D debates, you will want to engage students in discussions about the advantages and disadvantages of the differences in format.

They may also find Lincoln-Douglas debates more interesting because adolescents are particularly inclined to want to argue questions of "value" more than those of "policy."

Extension Activity
As a challenge to some of your students, have them dig into the history of Lincoln-Douglas debates. Undoubtedly your school librarian can help get the students started on their investigation. If you have some particularly able students, they may be able to track down enough information about the early debates to recreate one for the class.

Evaluation and Feedback
In the text: Evaluation Checklist page 267, Chapter Review pages 268–269
In the TRB: Evaluation Checklists page EC32, Chapter Tests page T17

To be used with:

Communicating on the Job: Avoiding Common Research Mistakes (page 270)

Objective
To avoid common mistakes in conducting research

Presentation of Subject Matter
You may wish to begin by having the students discuss their own experiences in doing research. Have volunteers recall the specific situations or assignments that have required research and describe the kinds of problems they may have had in finding, recording, and using information.

As the students read the lesson introduction, you may wish to have volunteers explain the purpose of the rules by answering the question: What specific kind of problem can a student avoid by following each rule?

If class time is available and the students need additional speaking practice, you might have them present oral reports based on the research they do for the lesson Activity. In this case, you may want to extend (or help the students extend) the list of possible research topics. If you do not wish to have the students make oral presentations, you might have them meet in groups to compare and discuss their notes. If you present this Communicating on the Job lesson with Lesson 1, you might prefer not to have the students do the Activity; instead, you may have them apply the lesson rules as they do research in preparation for their debates.

Evaluation and Feedback
In the TRB: Chapter Tests page T18

To be used with:

Communicating as a Citizen: Participating in a Candidate Debate (page 271)

Aids for Extension and Reinforcement
In the TRB: Related Composition Activities page C9

Objective
To role-play a candidate debate

Presentation of Subject Matter
Before the students begin studying this lesson, you may wish to have them discuss various candidate debates they have heard or read about. If possible, help the students recall (or become aware of) debates between candidates for local or state office as well as those between presidential candidates.

You might have the students read the lesson introduction independently and then contribute to a discussion of the procedure used in a candidate debate. During this discussion, the students may refer to the lesson if necessary, but they should explain each aspect of the debate in their own words. You might also wish to have the students compare the format of a candidate debate with the format of a competitive debate, as presented in Lessons 1, 2, and particularly 3.

For the lesson Activity, you may have the students form groups of six and let everyone participate in role playing one candidate debate. If class time is limited, you might prefer to have six students volunteer to prepare and role-play a candidate debate; the other students can participate by listening carefully and then discussing and evaluating the work of the volunteers.

Evaluation and Feedback
In the TRB: Chapter Tests page T18

To be used with:

Chapter 10 Lesson 1 (pages 273–280)

Aids for Extension and Reinforcement
In the TRB: Lesson Work Sheets page LW17, Critical Thinking Work Sheets page CT10, Speech Analysis page SA13, Speech Journal page SJ11, Listening Work Sheets page L3, Evaluation Forms page EF14, Transparencies page T10, Transparency Work Sheets page TW10

Objectives
To critically evaluate persuasive speeches and other appeals
To give a speech effectively analyzing a persuasive appeal
To correctly identify and analyze techniques of propaganda

Vocabulary
propaganda (273)
loaded words and phrases (273)
name calling (273)
faulty generalization (273)
hasty generalization (273)
glittering generalization (273)
bandwagon (274)
transference (274)

testimonial (274)
the big lie (275)
bias (275)
stereotyping (275)
suppressing (278)
distortion (278)
innuendo (279)

Presentation of Subject Matter
As you work through the eight propaganda techniques in the introductory section of the lesson, have the students give examples of each technique. They may be able to suggest examples from history or from recent political campaigns, or they can offer imaginary examples. Emphasize that some propaganda techniques, especially testimonials and the bandwagon technique, are sometimes used in advertising campaigns. You might have students bring in advertisements that make use of those appeals and have them discuss how they react to such advertising.

As the students study the Model speech, help them to see why Mussolini's oratory had great appeal to a nation just emerging from the Depression. You might have the students contrast Mussolini's self-confident emphasis on military conquest and the solution of problems by force with Roosevelt's sober evaluation of the problems facing America and his emphasis on the need for cooperation (Chapter 6, Lesson 4).

You may wish to have the students do the Preparing and Presenting and Evaluation Checklist activities in small groups rather than before the entire class. As the students analyze and discuss the speeches they have listened to, monitor their discussions.

Extension Activity
You might extend the lesson by having each student prepare two versions of a brief persuasive speech. One version should use straightforward appeals (as described in Chapter 6), and the other should use propaganda techniques. If possible, students should practice giving both speeches to an outside audience (for example, members of another class). Have the students report on the audience reaction to each version of the speech. Have them discuss which version was more effective and why.

Evaluation and Feedback
In the text: Evaluation Checklist page 280, Chapter Review page 281
In the TRB: Evaluation Checklists page EC33, Chapter Tests page T19

To be used with:

Communicating on the Job: Giving and Accepting Criticism (page 282)

Objective
To effectively give and accept constructive criticism

Presentation of Subject Matter
As you work through the introduction to this lesson, be sure the class understands that giving constructive criticism does not imply venting personal hostility. In work situations especially, it is important to provide a co-worker with praise and reassurance while criticizing specific aspects of his or her job performance. Ask students to volunteer examples of constructive criticism they have either given or received. (These responses can be particularly informative when a student has had a part-time job.) Have the class discuss why each example of constructive criticism was effective or how it might have been improved.

As the students read and discuss the guidelines for giving and accepting constructive criticism, encourage volunteers to suggest specific ways in which each guideline might be applied and guide the students in discussing the importance of accepting and learning from constructive criticism.

After the students have worked with partners for Activity 1, you may wish to have the teams report their findings to the class or even role–play their constructive criticisms of the interviewee they evaluated.

If time is limited, you might have the students complete Activity 2 by writing short essays about their experiences or by giving their speeches to small groups rather than to the entire class.

Evaluation and Feedback
In the TRB: Chapter Tests page T20

To be used with:

Communicating as a Citizen: Using Critical Listening (page 283)

Aids for Extension and Reinforcement
In the TRB: Related Composition Activities page C10

Objective
To use critical listening to evaluate persuasive appeals

Presentation of Subject Matter
After working through the guideline questions with the class, you might play a recording of a recent campaign speech or other persuasive speech by a public figure. Have the students listen critically and make a note of every point in the speech where the speaker may not be following the guidelines for responsible persuasive speaking. Afterwards, have the students discuss the speech and how they would go about checking the speaker's facts, promises, and previous positions.

Instead of having students listen to recorded speeches for Activity 1, you may wish to have students present persuasive speeches that they prepared for Chapter 6, Lessons 3 or 5.

Evaluation and Feedback
In the TRB: Chapter Tests page T20

To be used with:

Unit Four (Performing): A Case Study (page 285)

Objective
To evaluate the different appeals made by television

Presentation of Subject Matter
After looking at each of the cartoon panels with the class, have students explain what kinds of programs are represented and how most viewers are expected to react to them. Have the students discuss their own reactions to television: Do they enjoy it as much as they did when they were younger? Do they feel television viewing is time well spent? Would they like to watch better programs? Do they think that television programming is designed for their tastes and interests?

After they have discussed these questions, tell the students that in Unit Four they will learn more about the ways in which several forms of entertainment—including television—appeal to audiences.

To be used with:

Unit Introduction: Communicating as a Performer (pages 286–289)

Aids for Extension and Reinforcement
In the TRB: Speeches/Oral Interpretation Tape

Objectives
To realize that speaking as a performer is related to the elements of speech and to the speech communication process introduced in Unit One
To develop the ability to use memory effectively while performing

Presentation of Subject Matter
Before they are asked to read the entire introductory section, have students work in groups of four and discuss the initial four questions. Let the groups know that when they are satisfied that they have developed good answers to each of the questions, you will be calling on them to share their answers with the rest of the class. After they have talked with each other for 15–20 minutes, randomly select groups to report.

After the groups have reported, have the students read the remainder of the introduction individually. You may wish to separate the first part of the material and discuss it with the students before considering that portion having to do with memory.

The two activities listed at the end of the lesson can help students understand the concepts in this introduction. The memorization Activity is obviously intended to make sure they have read the suggestions carefully as well as to give them some material for practice.

Extension Activity
Some of your more able students may be interested in pursuing McLuhan's theories about the influence of the medium on the message being communicated. His basic exposition of this theory is in his *Understanding Media: The Extensions of Man* (McGraw-Hill Book Co., 1964). Encourage them to investigate it and report to the class.

Skill in memorizing is like any other skill. It requires practice. You may wish to establish short exercises for students to memorize and perform on a regular basis over a several week period. Since you won't have class time for each student to perform each week, have the students work in pairs and perform their material to each other. Call on students at random so that a few performances are shared with the whole class. Have the students work with poetry or with other materials that will help them develop greater language skills as they memorize.

To be used with:

Chapter 11 Lesson 1 (pages 291–295)

Aids for Extension and Reinforcement
In the TRB: Critical Thinking Work Sheets page CT11, Correct Usage Section, Evaluation Forms page EF15, Transparencies page T11, Transparency Work Sheets page TW11

Objectives
To identify the important elements of a story
To organize a story effectively, using specific details to make it clear
To deliver a story in the most effective manner to illustrate a point or entertain an audience

Vocabulary
narrative speaking (291)

Presentation of Subject Matter
As the students read the lesson introduction, be sure they recognize that a story usually has one of two purposes: to illustrate a specific point or to entertain an audience. You may wish to help the students recognize that an "entertaining" story is not necessarily humorous. Ask them to recall some entertaining stories that were simply interesting or unusual or even sad.

You might ask one of the students to read aloud the story in Working with the Model. The student's presentation will be more effective if he or she is given time to prepare the reading. You may wish to let the student practice reading for you so that you can offer specific suggestions.

As the students begin the Preparing and Presenting assignment, you might remind them of the four steps presented in the Guidelines. They should follow these steps in order as they plan and practice their stories.

When the students are ready to tell their stories, you might have them work in groups of four to six, or if the students need practice in formal speaking to larger groups, you might prefer to let each student tell his or her story to the entire class. If the students tell their stories to small groups, the group members can discuss each story, responding to the Evaluation Checklist. However, if the students tell their stories to the entire class, you might wish to have the listeners fill out Evaluation Forms page EF15 (Story Telling) for each speaker.

Extension Activities
You may wish to have the students discuss and even practice the use of anecdotes in expository and persuasive speeches. Stress the need for choosing a clear, brief story that relates directly to the topic of the speech.

As another extension, you might have the students prepare and tell stories to small groups of young children. Remind the students that their stories must be short, direct, and easy to understand.

Evaluation and Feedback
In the text: Evaluation Checklist page 295, Chapter Review pages 318–319
In the TRB: Evaluation Checklists page EC34

To be used with:

Chapter 11 Lesson 2 (pages 296–312)

Aids for Extension and Reinforcement
In the TRB: Lesson Work Sheets page LW18

Objectives
To recognize and record the major idea and major emotion expressed in a selection
To research and record background information on the author of a selection

Vocabulary
   oral interpretation (296)

Presentation of Subject Matter
Guide the students in carefully studying the lesson introduction, noting especially the purpose of oral readings and the specific steps in preparing oral readings. Encourage the students to discuss the importance of each suggested step and to mention specific ways in which the steps might be applied.

Unlike the Models in most lessons, Kennedy's speech and Adamé's poem are intended to be read silently rather than aloud. After the students have studied both selections, guide them in discussing their answers to the questions. This discussion will help the students understand the selections and guide them in practicing part of the preparation for an oral reading.

If necessary, provide literature anthologies or other sources in which the students might find selections and background information for use in the Preparing and Presenting assignment. After the students have compared and evaluated their outlines, encourage them to make improvements in their own work.

Extension Activity
You may wish to extend this lesson by having the students listen to one or more oral readings. You or one of the students might present an oral reading. Or you might play a recording of a writer reading his or her own work or of a famous actor or actress reading a popular work.

Evaluation and Feedback
In the text: Evaluation Checklist page 312, Chapter Review pages 318–319
In the TRB: Evaluation Checklists page EC35

To be used with:

Chapter 11 Lesson 3 (pages 313–317)

Aids for Extension and Reinforcement
In the text: Handbook of Contest Speaking pages 395–399
In the TRB: Speech Journal page SJ12

Objective
To prepare and deliver an effective oral reading of a selection

Vocabulary
  reading copy (313)

Presentation of Subject Matter
As the students read the lesson introduction, you may want to have them relate each step to a brief example selection. Then read the Model aloud while the students silently follow the reading copy. Discussing their responses to the questions will help the students understand the importance of preparing and using an effective reading copy of the selection for an oral reading.

    For the Preparing and Presenting assignment, you may wish to check each student's reading copy before he or she presents the oral reading. Discuss with each student any breaks or marks that are unclear to you, and make specific suggestions that will help each student improve the plan for his or her oral reading.

    If class time is limited, you might have the students conduct the Evaluation Checklist activity in small groups rather than with the entire class.

Extension Activity
Before the students begin the Preparing and Presenting assignment, you might wish to provide a practice activity in preparing a reading copy. Select a short prose or poetry selection and give each student a copy on which he or she can mark. Play a recording of that selection and have the students mark their copies as they think the performer might have marked it. You may then have the students listen to the recording again, comparing their markings with the pauses, emphases, and variations they hear the performer using.

Evaluation and Feedback
In the text: Evaluation Checklist page 317, Chapter Review pages 318–319
In the TRB: Evaluation Checklists page EC36, Chapter Tests page T21

To be used with:

Communicating on the Job: Using the Telephone Effectively (page 320)

Objective
To develop a polite and effective telephone manner for business calls

Presentation of Subject Matter
As you work through the guidelines, have the students act out the conversation that illustrates each guideline. Emphasize that a good telephone manner is practical as well as polite: it helps create goodwill in business dealings and saves both parties time and money.

Evaluation and Feedback
In the TRB: Chapter Tests page T22

To be used with:

Communicating as a Citizen: Introducing a Speaker (page 321)

Aids for Extension and Reinforcement
In the TRB: Related Composition Activities page C11

Objective
To give a brief, effective speech introducing a speaker

Presentation of Subject Matter
After working through the guidelines in this lesson, ask students to suggest names of famous living people, including politicians, writers, sports figures, and entertainers. Ask them to imagine what they would say when introducing a speech by each of these people. Have the students discuss the points they might include under each major category: background, accomplishments, qualifications.

You may wish to play audiotape or videotape recordings of political conventions or other events at which speakers are introduced. Ask students to evaluate each introduction and to discuss how each speaker could have been introduced more effectively.

Evaluation and Feedback
In the TRB: Chapter Tests page T22

To be used with:

Chapter 12 Lesson 1 (pages 323–328)

Aids for Extension and Reinforcement
In the TRB: Critical Thinking Work Sheets page CT12, Correct Usage Section, Transparencies page T12, Transparency Work Sheets page TW12

Objective
To use voice and sound effects to interpret ideas and emotions in a radio drama

Vocabulary
radio drama (323)

Presentation of Subject Matter
Guide the students in reading and discussing the lesson introduction. If necessary, help them review the steps in marking a reading copy (as presented in Chapter 11, Lesson 3).

You may want to have a group of students volunteer to practice and present the Model to the rest of the class. Help them prepare an effective reading of the scene and suggest methods for adding sound effects, if necessary. After the presentation, have all the students participate in discussing the questions in Working with the Model. Encourage the students to evaluate the volunteers' interpretation, praising specific aspects of their work and offering constructive criticism when appropriate.

As the groups begin working on the Preparing and Presenting assignment, be sure they understand that they may need to revise their scenes before they begin practicing. If the students select an excerpt from a novel or short story, they will have to rewrite the scene as a dramatic script. You may want to check each group's script before the students finish planning their presentations.

If the class time for this project is limited, you might have each group present its scene to the members of only one other group rather than to the rest of the class. The listening group can help evaluate the performance, responding to the questions in the Evaluation Checklist section of the lesson.

Extension Activity
You may wish to introduce this lesson by having the students listen to a recorded radio drama. You may choose a drama from radio's "golden age," many of which are available on record, or a current drama. Lead the students in comparing radio dramas to those of television and film and have volunteers discuss the success of the voices and sound effects used in the radio drama.

Evaluation and Feedback
In the text: Evaluation Checklist page 328, Chapter Review pages 354–355
In the TRB: Evaluation Checklists page EC37

To be used with:

Chapter 12 Lesson 2 (pages 329–337)

Objective
To participate in the creation, rehearsal, and presentation of a radio drama

Presentation of Subject Matter
After the students have read and discussed the lesson introduction, have a group of prepared volunteers read aloud the transcript in Working with the Model.

To help familiarize the students with the checklist presented in the Guidelines section, have the students note how the Model group followed each step. Then direct the students to follow the checklist steps as they work on their own radio dramas.

If the students were pleased with their work in Lesson 1, encourage them to stay in the same groups and to prepare expanded versions of those scenes for the Preparing and Presenting assignment. Allow the students to form new groups or to select new material if those changes will help the group members work more enthusiastically and effectively on their radio dramas.

You may wish to read each group's script and offer specific suggestions for improvement. Help the students develop scripts that include enough action to maintain the listeners' interest and that can be presented within the time limits established by the class.

Extension Activity
You may be able to arrange with a local radio station—perhaps a college station—to have the students use the station's equipment and facilities for their radio dramas. The students will benefit from exposure to professional working conditions, and the station may even wish to broadcast one or more of the better presentations.

Evaluation and Feedback
In the text: Evaluation Checklist page 337, Chapter Review pages 354–355
In the TRB: Evaluation Checklists page EC38

To be used with:

Chapter 12 Lesson 3 (pages 338–344)

Aids for Extension and Reinforcement
In the TRB: Lesson Work Sheets pages LW19–21

Objectives
To become familiar with basic television terminology
To write a six-minute television script

Vocabulary

close-up (339)   point of view (339)   fade (340)
medium shot (339)   over-the-shoulder   dissolve (340)
long shot (339)   shot (340)   wipe (340)
angle (339)   dolly (340)   videocassette
wide angle (339)   pan (340)   recorder (340)
reverse angle (339)   tilt (340)   edit (340)
establishing shot   zoom (340)   talent (340)
  (339)   cut (340)

Presentation of Subject Matter
With the time and equipment available, you are not likely to make television experts of your students. Your best hope is to increase their understanding of the communication process as a result of the experimenting they will do with the medium. New equipment and techniques are evolving rapidly. Do not hesitate to seek expert advice from audiovisual specialists at your school, from staff members at local access channels for cable television companies, or from local broadcast stations. Usually these experts are quite willing to share information and sample materials that will make your application of the material up-to-date and interesting for the students.

   To make the definitions at the beginning of the lesson meaningful, you might show videotapes of programs and have students identify examples of the different techniques. Pop music videos are a source of many examples of basic techniques that can be recorded and discussed in the classroom. If you lack confidence in your knowledge of what is happening in the contemporary music field, spend time previewing videos or work with some reliable students to find examples you will be comfortable using in class (that will not be scorned by students or attacked by parents).

Extension Activity
If the students are struggling for ideas for their script, have them prepare a script for a music video. Working back from the finished product may be just as useful in helping them understand the basic techniques as having

them create a program of their own. Because some of the music videos make extensive use of special effects that they will not know how to describe for a script, you may find it easier to take a portion of a newscast or a situation comedy and have them prepare a script of it.

Evaluation and Feedback
In the text: Evaluation Checklist page 344, Chapter Review pages 354–355
In the TRB: Evaluation Checklists page EC39

To be used with:

Chapter 12 Lesson 4 (pages 345–348)

Aids for Extension and Reinforcement
In the TRB: Lesson Work Sheets page LW23

Objective
To understand the basic camera techniques used in creating a television production

Vocabulary
   camera shot sheet (345)

Presentation of Subject Matter
Outside professionals may indicate that the highly planned shot sheet, which is the focus of this lesson, is more detailed than those they typically use in their productions. Nevertheless, you should find it a valuable instructional tool.

   As in the previous lesson, you may find that using a tape of a short segment of a television program and working back to a shot sheet will help you make the task clear. Another activity that can make the point more clearly than just having the students read through the Model would be to have them act out the model shot sheet. Have one student be the camera person, another Mary, another the lamb, another the narrator reading the audio portion of the shot sheet, and another the director signaling for the change in the shots using the time intervals indicated.

   After they have acted out the sheet, they should be in a better position to discuss the questions following the Model. When the small groups have completed their own shot sheet, have them act it out as well. Obviously they don't need a camera and other equipment for such a simulation.

Extension Activity
To understand the shots that the students are including in the scripts and in the shot sheets, they need to have an opportunity to experiment with the camera equipment and the different techniques described in the text. If

you have the equipment at the school, set up several class periods during which they simply try different kinds of shots and see how they turn out. If no equipment is available at the school, seek it out through a local public access cable channel. As the students experiment, help them see the problems of the too frequent use of panning, the advantages of using a tripod or a dolly, and the problems of too frequently changing shots. Such problems can really be understood only when they see the results as they experiment.

Evaluation and Feedback
In the text: Evaluation Checklist page 348, Chapter Review pages 354–355
In the TRB: Evaluation Checklist page EC40

To be used with:

Chapter 12 Lesson 5 (pages 349–353)

Aids for Extension and Reinforcement
In the TRB: Lesson Work Sheets page LW24, Speech Journal page SJ13

Objectives
To understand the complex, cooperative roles that a production team must play
To produce a six-minute videotape of a television script

Vocabulary

producer (349)	production assistant (349)	video tape recorder (350)
director (349)	mike boom (350)	preproduction planning (351)
associate director (349)	lavaliere (350)	rehearsal (351)
camera operator (349)	switcher (350)	production (351)
floor manager (349)	mixer (350)	postproduction (351)

Presentation of Subject Matter
If you have not done so previously, this is a lesson that should begin with a visit to a television production facility. If one isn't available, a film or videotape about such facilities may be available from your local supplier. If you can get a person who has production experience to visit your class, conduct a question-answer session about the realities of television production. The questions related to the Model in this lesson can serve as a guide for the students' questions.

As you discuss the guidelines with the students prior to their preparation of their own tapes, emphasize the communicative nature of their task.

Remind them that the program is being prepared for an audience—that what happens needs to be reasonable to the viewer, not just to the producers. If you have a public access channel in your community, examples of amateur productions can be taped from it and used as cases in point where the camera selections, shot sequence, or the audio is hard for the viewers to follow. These cases can serve as good grounds for discussion before the students begin their own creative efforts.

Extension Activity

An obvious extension of this lesson for those students who demonstrate they have mastered the basic techniques is the creation of a tape that can be publicly viewed. The school or public access channel on cable television is your best bet for an opportunity for "air time" for the students.

Another extension activity that may be possible is to arrange to have a local producer judge the student-produced tapes. You might be able to arrange for the winning students to shadow members of a local production team during the creation of a program and have them observe each step of the creation and production of a script. If they have such an experience, be sure to arrange for them to share it with the others in the class so that as many as possible benefit from what they learn.

Evaluation and Feedback

In the text: Evaluation Checklist page 353, Chapter Review pages 354–355
In the TRB: Evaluation Checklists page EC41, Chapter Tests page T23

To be used with:

Communicating on the Job: Problem Solving (page 356)

Objective
To participate effectively in a problem-solving group discussion

Presentation of Subject Matter
As the students discuss the lesson introduction, encourage volunteers to explain the reasons underlying each guideline. If necessary, help the students review the four steps of the problem-solving sequence (page 81).

You might wish to encourage the students to use the skills they gain in this lesson to work on solving one of the community problems they identified in Communicating as a Citizen: Solving a Community Problem (page 103).

Evaluation and Feedback
In the TRB: Chapter Tests page T24

To be used with:

Communicating as a Citizen: Presenting an Award (page 357)

Aids for Extension and Reinforcement
In the TRB: Related Composition Activities page C12

Objective
To make an effective speech while presenting an award

Presentation of Subject Matter
Bring in printed examples, tape recordings, or videotapes of award speeches. Have the class listen to these speeches and evaluate them according to the guidelines in this lesson. You may have the students rewrite and deliver any of the speeches they found inappropriate for the award, the occasion, or the recipient.

Evaluation and Feedback
In the TRB: Chapter Tests page T24

To be used with:

Chapter 13 Lesson 1 (pages 359–363)

Aids for Extension and Reinforcement
In the TRB: Critical Thinking Work Sheets page CT13, Correct Usage Section, Evaluation Forms page EF16, Transparencies page T13, Transparency Work Sheets page TW13

Objective
To develop basic acting skills by learning to improvise

Vocabulary
improvisation (359)
problem (359)
focus (359)

Presentation of Subject Matter
You may find it helpful to review some of the activities in Chapter 1, Lesson 5 before proceeding with this lesson. As the text suggests, have students enact the scenes in the Working with the Model section before you try discussing them. As you discuss the questions, have the students demon-

strate their answers. For example, in response to A-2, have them demonstrate those actions they might add to indicate the age of the person waiting. You may find it helpful to have several demonstrate their versions and then talk about which were most effective and why.

Improvisations should be fun for the students. As they perform, encourage other students to become involved in the scenes and to present problems for the performers' continuing responses. Emphasize the positive aspects of their performances as much as possible. You want them to be relaxed and to enjoy the experience of performing in front of others. As you create groups for such activities, mix and match students so that all are learning. If you are not careful, you will get all of the "hams" in one group and "wallflowers" in another. The "hams" can not only help the less forward students but also learn something themselves in the process of helping. Keep shifting groups as you observe interactions among the students.

Extension Activity

If your students respond well to improvisation, you may want to create opportunities for them to perform for others. Arrange for another class meeting, for a break during a lunch period, or even an evening program for parents and students. Have the improvisation teams ready to address a problem you present and then to adjust as members of the audience call out changes in the situation. Talk about how they should respond if someone calls out inappropriate actions. Usually if they simply ignore such comments and respond in an interesting fashion to someone else's more appropriate remark, the instigator of the out-of-line suggestions will give up.

Evaluation and Feedback

In the text: Evaluation Checklist page 363, Chapter Review pages 372–373
In the TRB: Evaluation Checklists page EC42

To be used with:

Chapter 13 Lesson 2 (pages 364–371)

Aids for Extension and Reinforcement

In the TRB: Lesson Work Sheets page LW25, Speech Journal page SJ14

Objective

To understand and communicate the essentials of a dramatic role

Vocabulary

characterization (364)
character (364)

Presentation of Subject Matter

Before considering the Model, take time to discuss the definitions in the introductory material. Help the students get an overview of what an actor does as he or she prepares for a role. As the text suggests, have the students perform the scene before you begin discussing the questions. This performance will probably be better if you first provide them with some background on the play. Or have a student or a small group read the entire play and prepare a background report for the class. The use of improvisation to continue the scene should enable you to reemphasize some of the ideas learned from the previous lesson and to continue to build on their understanding of characterization.

As the students begin preparing their own scenes, make sure that adequate copies of the plays are available. Check with your school librarian, the local public library, or the English department in your school to find multiple copies of a number of appropriate plays. Because the students really should be familiar with an entire play before trying to portray a character, you may want to give them the reading assignment several weeks in advance of starting the lesson. However, you will probably get more focused reading from them if you introduce the concepts of characterization to them before they start reading for their own play cuttings. While students are reading their plays, you might want to return to Chapter 1 and work on the elements of speech. The lessons and exercises on language, voice, and bodily movement will be particularly helpful for the students as they get ready to create dramatic roles.

Extension Activity

Young children are fascinated by dramatic productions. Your students may find presenting a cutting from a play, or a short one act, to an elementary classroom challenging and rewarding. Your students need not have elaborate costumes, and the props they use can be the bare minimum necessary to convey the action.

Evaluation and Feedback

In the text: Evaluation Checklist page 371, Chapter Review pages 372–373
In the TRB: Evaluation Checklists page EC43, Chapter Tests page T25

To be used with:

Communicating on the Job: Reading a Speech or Report Written by Someone Else (page 374)

Objective

To practice reading selections written by someone else, presenting them with clarity, variety, and interest

Presentation of Subject Matter

To introduce this lesson, you might have the students briefly discuss different situations in which they might be called upon to read a speech or report written by someone else. Also let the students mention the particular problems that such situations might involve.

Then guide the students in reading and discussing the lesson introduction. Have volunteers relate each set of guidelines to the various situations the class has discussed.

For the lesson Activity, you might have the students practice their readings with partners and then present the readings either to the whole class or to smaller groups.

Evaluation and Feedback

In the TRB: Chapter Tests page T26

To be used with:

Communicating as a Citizen: Role Playing to Understand Communication Problems
(page 375)

Aids for Extension and Reinforcement

In the TRB: Related Composition Activities page C13

Objectives

To define and develop a role-playing situation
To use role playing to understand communication problems

Vocabulary

role playing (375)

Presentation of Subject Matter

Role playing is an important technique for speech classes since it helps students realize dramatically how the communication process works or fails to work. Have two students read the dialogue aloud and then ask the class to suggest other situations in which role playing would help people understand both sides of an issue. You may wish to have a pair of students prepare and present a continuation of Rob and Etta's role-playing session. The continuation should demonstrate both the customer's frustration and the clerk's patience.

You may assign students to prepare the Activity in pairs or in groups of three or four and then to role-play the situation before the class. You might have the entire class brainstorm a number of problems and then assign two or three students to role-play each of them. Keep the sessions fast-moving in order to minimize awkwardness. When a role-playing session has lasted one or two minutes or when the students are beginning to repeat themselves, thank them and ask the rest of the students to describe what they have learned. Focus the discussion on the *content* of each role-playing session rather than on each individual student's technique.

You may wish to schedule regular role-playing sessions throughout the course. They are especially appropriate to Chapters 2, 3, 8, and 9.

Evaluation and Feedback
In the TRB: Chapter Tests page T26

To be used with:

Chapter 14 Lesson 1 (pages 377–382)

Aids for Extension and Reinforcement
In the TRB: Lesson Work Sheets page LW26, Critical Thinking Work Sheets page CT14, Speech Journal pages SJ15 and SJ16, Listening Work Sheets page L4, Evaluation Forms page EF17, Transparencies page T14, Transparency Work Sheets page TW14

Objectives
To measure the time spent on watching television and listening to the radio
To evaluate the effects of radio and television on one's life
To decide how one can benefit most from electronic media

Vocabulary
media diary (377)
media evaluation (380)

Presentation of Subject Matter
As you work through the lesson introduction and the Model, go over the two media diaries carefully with the students. Help the class recognize that the large amount of time someone like Craig spends listening to radio or watching television is made up of many brief amounts of time and that keeping a media diary can help a person become aware of his or her listening and viewing habits. Have the students draw up tentative media diaries in class, based on their own impressions of their radio and television time. Then have them keep actual media diaries for two or more days and compare their real habits with their impressions.

As you work through the Guidelines, encourage the students to discuss the programs they watch and listen to and those they actually enjoy. Students may find that much of what they watch and listen to bores them but that they have never considered alternative activities.

Instead of having the students do the Preparing and Presenting activities in groups, you may wish to have them report on their habits and resolutions individually to the entire class. During the Evaluation Checklist activity, guide the discussion to help students realize that worthwhile programs exist and are worth seeking out.

Extension Activity
Have students read articles by local or national television critics on current programs. Then have the class discuss and evaluate the critics' opinions in comparison with their own. If possible, assign a group of students to interview a local television critic and report on the interview to the class. (This assignment could be integrated with the interviewing lessons in Chapter 2.)

Evaluation and Feedback
In the text: Evaluation Checklist page 382, Chapter Review page 384
In the TRB: Evaluation Checklists page EC44, Chapter Tests page T27

To be used with:

Communicating on the Job: Using a Microphone (page 384)

Objective
To read a selection clearly and effectively, using a microphone

Presentation of Subject Matter
As an introduction to this lesson, you might have the students discuss the special problems speakers sometimes have when using microphones. Let volunteers describe situations in which a microphone system was a hindrance to a speaker or in which the speaker misused the microphone system. As the students study the lesson, they will learn how such problems can be avoided.

Guide the students in discussing the rules presented in the lesson introduction and encourage volunteers to explain how each rule might have helped the speakers mentioned in the example situations.

If most of the students have not used microphones, let them experiment with different kinds of systems in rooms of various sizes. If possible, conduct the lesson Activity in at least two stages, so that each student will have an opportunity to read over the microphone system again after his or her first reading has been evaluated.

Evaluation and Feedback
In the TRB: Chapter Tests page T28

To be used with:

Communicating as a Citizen: Listening Critically to Documentaries and Docudramas (page 385)

Aids for Extension and Reinforcement
In the TRB: Related Composition Activities page C14

Objective
To evaluate the accuracy and fairness of television documentaries and docudramas

Vocabulary
documentary (385)
docudrama (385)

Presentation of Subject Matter
As you work through the guidelines, have the students discuss documentaries and docudramas that they have watched on their own or have been assigned to watch for other classes. Emphasize that although a docudrama looks "fictional" and a documentary looks "real," it is possible for a documentary to suppress, distort, or oversimplify the facts—an accusation that critics sometimes make against docudramas. If you have access to videotapes of a documentary and a docudrama on the same subject, you might have the students watch both of them and compare their treatments of the subject.

If possible, organize this lesson around one or more television documentaries or docudramas that the entire class can be assigned to watch. Have the students do further reading or research on aspects of the program's subject and have them report to the class on the similarities and differences between the program and the facts they have learned. You might invite a history teacher or other authority to speak to the class on a specific subject or period on which he or she is an expert.

Evaluation and Feedback
In the TRB: Chapter Tests page T28

Chapter 1

Reviewing Vocabulary

1. n
2. o
3. j
4. h
5. i
6. b
7. a
8. q
9. p
10. f
11. g
12. d
13. e
14. k
15. r
16. c
17. l
18. m

Reviewing Facts and Ideas

1. By making you more aware of the strengths that can help you and the weaknesses that you need to overcome.
2. The means by which you learn what the listener understands of the message you are conveying./Being aware of reactions from listeners, whether verbal or simply facial expressions or gestures, helps you to judge the audience's interest and response, to be sure that the audience can hear and understand you, and to adjust your voice if necessary.
3. Answers will vary, but students might mention that a good imagination helps you better reflect and use your intuition to solve problems as well as look at things from another's perspective.
4. Answers will vary, but students should mention that the primary way we acquire information is through our senses and that skillful acquiring, analyzing, arranging, and remembering of this information is necessary for effective thinking.
5. Because people's backgrounds help determine their interpretation of the world and thus help determine meaning./Past experiences also help shape our present perceptions, both in the way we perceive and in the way we interpret our sensory impressions.
6. The art of speaking so that every sound is clear and distinct./By moving your lips and tongue, taking care in forming the beginnings and ending of words, rehearsing aloud, and watching for feedback.
7. The manner of producing speech sounds— specifically, saying words correctly and clearly./By studying and analyzing the pronunciation of words by those around us, looking up problem words in the dictionary, and practicing saying problem words correctly, either to a friend or to a tape recorder.
8. Answers will vary, but students might mention to make your voice more attractive and lively, to prevent boredom, or to emphasize the content of what you are saying.
9. They help the speaker clarify meaning and provide emphasis. Also they help give the speaker feedback.
10. They help clarify meaning and provide emphasis. Also they help give the speaker feedback.

Discussing Facts and Ideas
Discussions will vary.

Applying Your Knowledge
Responses will vary.

Chapter 2

Reviewing Vocabulary
Sentences will vary.

Reviewing Facts and Ideas

1. Prejudice, lack of information, verbal confusion, different values, misplaced emotion, and desire to dominate./Answers to remaining questions will vary.
2. A person who resolves a conflict between two parties./By encouraging people to discuss their true feelings and by separating the trivial issues from the important ones./Answers will vary.
3. Establish communication, exchange information, try to understand others, define your terms, define your values, get to the root of the problem, find common ground, and be willing to compromise./Answers to the remaining questions will vary.
4. To help you be well prepared for an interview./Confirm arrangements, arrange setting, become informed, examine attitudes, prepare opening remarks, and plan how to record interview./Answers will vary.
5. To help you save time during the interview and ask intelligent questions that will lead to interesting answers./Answers will vary.
6. It helps you obtain interesting, informative responses./Because they usually elicit dull and uninformative answers.
7. Answers will vary.
8. To obtain further information on an unexpected remark or to clarify something that has not been covered by the prepared questions./One kind asks for further information on the subject. Another kind asks for a brief explanation of an unfamiliar term or name.
9. The body.
10. To remind the interviewee of the purpose of the interview and to ask the opening (prepared) question./By asking a question that requires a brief, simple answer./Asks more general questions, summarizes the interview, clarifies any ambiguities, obtains permission to use the interview, and thanks the interviewee.

Discussing Facts and Ideas
Discussions will vary.

Applying Your Knowledge
Responses will vary.

Chapter 3
Reviewing Vocabulary
Definitions will vary.

Reviewing Facts and Ideas
1. Describe and understand the problem, identify criteria for evaluating possible solutions, identify and define possible solutions, and evaluate each possible solution according to the criteria.
2. Because group members share their ideas and build on one another's contributions to solve a problem.
3. The notes and outline act as a summary to help you remember your research material during the actual group discussion.
4. To make arrangements for the meeting, stimulate participation, resolve conflicts, and keep the discussion focused on the goal.
5. Answers will vary but should mention any of the various ways that members advance the discussion.
6. Answers will vary but should mention any of the various ways that members detract from the purpose of the discussion.
7. Because members need to be able to respond constructively to the comments of others and to take into consideration new facts and opinions. Thoughtful listening also helps prevent domination of the discussion, interruptions, one-track thinking, and other disruptive effects.
8. To help you be open to new facts, opinions, and solutions and to be ready to change your ideas or opinions in response to new ideas.
9. Because lack of consideration or any strain in the relationships between group members may detract from the accomplishment of the group's purpose.
10. Answers will vary but might mention the idea that the more complex the problem, the more the group needs each group member's contribution.

Discussing Facts and Ideas
Discussions will vary.

Applying Your Knowledge
Responses will vary.

Chapter 4
Reviewing Facts and Ideas
1. Giving active attention to what is being said./The active listener is alert and responsive to the remarks of others, whereas the passive listener is inattentive.

2. Response that lets the speaker know whether he or she has been understood./It helps the speaker know that he or she needs to clarify a remark or that the listener understands and/or is interested in what the speaker is saying./Asking the speaker to repeat what was said or expand on it as well as repeating what was said and asking the speaker whether or not you have understood correctly.
3. The listeners are alert and responsive, ask questions, or give other kinds of nonverbal feedback./Answers will vary but might mention not making eye contact with the speaker, reading, looking bored, etc.
4. Ask the speaker a question, paraphrase a comment to clear up the confusion, or ask the speaker to repeat a remark.
5. Answers will vary.

Discussing Facts and Ideas
Discussions will vary.

Applying Your Knowledge
Responses will vary.

Chapter 5
Reviewing Vocabulary
1. chronological pattern
2. analytical expository speech
3. topical pattern
4. spatial pattern

Reviewing Facts and Ideas
1. To explain or inform./The introduction.
2. Chronological.
3. The body./Using definitions, examples, comparison or contrast, narratives, testimony, or statistics.
4. Answers will vary but might mention to quote a source, to read complicated facts or figures, etc.
5. To help your listeners better understand your speech./By pointing out major features in the aid only briefly and then focusing your attention on the audience.
6. Because in order to be effective, the speech should be geared to the audience's knowledge and interests./Answers will vary but might mention the audience becoming bored, inattentive, or confused.
7. Answers will vary but might mention, among others, concentrating on the speech, breathing deeply, and relaxing the entire body as well as thoroughly preparing and practicing.
8. Asking a questioner to clarify his or her question, repeating a question to make sure everyone knows what the question is, or if someone asks a series of questions, answering them one at a time, repeating each question before you answer it./Because how well you answer questions strongly influences the audience's opinion of your speech as a whole.

9. To analyze the meaning of a speech, poem, novel, piece of music, or a short story for your audience./No, you are merely presenting one viewpoint of the subject.
10. Because you need to know whether or not the audience members are familiar with your subject to ensure they will understand your speech. If they are not, you will need to provide background information./The introduction./To capture the audience's attention and to provide a link to the topic.

Discussing Facts and Ideas
Discussions will vary.

Applying Your Knowledge
Responses will vary.

Chapter 6
Reviewing Vocabulary

1. e	8. f
2. d	9. a
3. i	10. k
4. b	11. j
5. n	12. m
6. g	13. h
7. c	14. l

Reviewing Facts and Ideas
1. Answers will vary.
2. Answers will vary but might include the superstitions about not walking under a ladder, avoiding a black cat crossing in front of you, or finding a four-leaf clover.
3. The sentence that states the specific purpose of your speech./In the introduction./Because drawing your audience's attention to the topic and the position you are taking on it before you actually begin supporting it usually makes the speech easier to follow and more persuasive./When you are developing your speech with appeals to emotion.
4. Logical arguments./They should be objective reasons, not personal preferences or opinions, that your listeners are likely to understand, accept, and be interested in.
5. Factual illustrations, statistics, expert testimony, and other such specific details.
6. Physical needs, psychological needs, and social needs./Because with some topics and some audiences, appealing to the audience's needs, interests, and fears is more convincing than appealing to their sense of logic.
7. Because in such a speech such uses of language, voice, and gesture are more important and more effective than they are in a speech developed through appeals to logic.

8. Thinking of the speaker as a person much like oneself, as a person who can be trusted and believed./It builds credibility and goodwill.
9. Establish a good reputation, demonstrate knowledge of the topic, be sincere, and appear trustworthy.
10. Stress interests in common with the audience, identify self with a person or cause that the audience admires, and compliment the audience on its positive qualities.

Discussing Facts and Ideas
Discussions will vary.

Applying Your Knowledge
Responses will vary.

Chapter 7
Reviewing Facts and Ideas
1. Words or phrases the speaker uses to enable the listener to follow the speech more easily./Those that tell what part of the speech you are listening to and those that emphasize important ideas./Examples will vary.
2. It is simple and brief, uses words and phrases instead of complete sentences, shows the relationship between topics and subtopics, uses as many abbreviations, symbols, and initials as possible, and includes signposts./Because a listener can take notes more easily and quickly with an informal outline than with a formal one, particularly if he or she doesn't know in advance the organization of the speech.
3. To help you identify and remember the relationships between topics, subtopics, and supporting details.
4. Because the listener will comprehend more as well as take better notes if he or she tries to understand the speech and to listen carefully to the speaker's actual words rather than tries to evaluate and anticipate.
5. Because doing so might make you miss another, perhaps even more important, piece of information.

Discussing Facts and Ideas
Discussions will vary.

Applying Your Knowledge
Responses will vary.

Chapter 8
Reviewing Vocabulary
1. old business
2. adjourned
3. motion to amend the proposal
4. chairperson

5. motion to delay action on the proposal
6. treasurer's report
7. motion to refer the proposal to the committee
8. agenda
9. motion to move the previous question
10. minutes of the previous meeting
11. motion

Reviewing Facts and Ideas

1. Clubs, civic groups, student councils, Congress, etc.
2. To help meetings proceed fairly and efficiently.
3. Writes the agenda and makes other preparations for the meeting, conducts the meeting impartially, and adjourns the meeting./Answers will vary but might mention a long, disorganized, and biased meeting./Because there would be no one to plan the meeting, prepare the agenda, call on members to speak, limit discussion, etc.
4. Discuss his or her plans with the chairperson and sometimes take notes or prepare a written report or proposal for distribution.
5. Other members should think about likely topics for consideration and, if necessary, review the rules of parliamentary procedure.
6. Call to order, minutes, treasurer's report, correspondence, committee reports, old business, new business, announcements, and adjournment./Answers will vary but new business or old business are probably the best answers./Because it is in these events that most of the discussion and voting take place.
7. Formal suggestions or proposals for action./Any member recognized by the chairperson makes the motion and any other member seconds it. Then it may be discussed by all members.
8. Answers will vary but should focus on the idea that such a procedure provides fair opportunity for members to express their opinions and makes available ample information on which to base a decision.
9. Answers will vary but should focus on the idea that such rules are precautionary in that they help prevent the chairperson from exercising too much control, monopolizing the time, or manipulating the motions or discussions toward his or her personal ends, and thus they ensure more fair, impartial proceedings that respect the will of the majority.
10. *Robert's Rules of Order (Revised)*.

Discussing Facts and Ideas
Discussions will vary.

Applying Your Knowledge
Responses will vary.

Chapter 9

Reviewing Vocabulary
1. Lincoln-Douglas debate
2. constructive speech
3. proposition
4. brief
5. evidence
6. refutation
7. negative cross-examination
8. debate
9. affirmative
10. argument
11. rebuttal speech
12. negative

Reviewing Facts and Ideas
1. A competition between persuasive speakers.
2. A complete debate outline of all the necessary definitions, arguments, and evidence on both sides of a proposition./The statement of the proposition, introduction, body, and conclusion./Answers will vary but should focus on enabling the debater to be better prepared and organized.
3. Facts, statistics, expert testimony, and the like.
4. The primary purpose of a constructive speech is to present arguments in support of the position, whereas the primary purpose of a rebuttal speech is to refute arguments presented by the other side and to rebuild the case of one's own team./Constructive speeches are traditionally six minutes each and rebuttal speeches are three minutes each.
5. The First Affirmative and First Negative speakers present their team's proposition and support it with arguments in the first constructive speech as well as give the first rebuttal speeches; the Second Affirmative and the Second Negative speakers provide the remaining arguments in the last two constructive speeches as well as summarize their team's case in the last two rebuttal speeches.
6. A format for a debate featuring one-on-one exchanges between two speakers debating a proposition of value./From the famous 1860 confrontations between Abraham Lincoln and Stephen Douglas.
7. Two.
8. Resolutions involving propositions of value rather than of policy. / They rely more on logical reasoning, philosophy, and theory and less on statistically based evidence (as in traditional arguments).
9. To persuade listeners that the values he or she is arguing for best suit the public.
10. To counter the affirmative speaker's arguments and supply listeners with a reasonable alternative.

Discussing Facts and Ideas
Discussions will vary.

Applying Your Knowledge
Responses will vary.

Chapter 10
Reviewing Vocabulary
1. loaded words and phrases—c
2. name calling—e
3. faulty generalizations—h
4. the bandwagon—f
5. transference—a
6. testimonials—d
7. the big lie—g
8. bias and stereotyping—b

Reviewing Facts and Ideas
1. A one-sided argument that tries to win people over to a cause, such as a political movement./By being alert and informed.
2. Because they produce in listeners instant, unthinking reactions. Even though they may be used in a meaningful way, some listeners react only to the good or bad associations of the words, not to the ideas behind them.
3. They both attack a person personally rather than on the basis of his or her ideas.
4. Urging listeners to support or "jump on" a movement, faction, or cause simply because everyone else is./Examples will vary.
5. Because celebrities are usually no more or less competent to judge issues outside their own fields than the rest of us are. And propagandists, knowing the lure of celebrities names, often use testimonials to gain support for causes they could get support for no other way.

Discussing Facts and Ideas
Discussions will vary.

Applying Your Knowledge
Responses will vary.

Chapter 11
Reviewing Vocabulary
1. c
2. f
3. a
4. d
5. e
6. b

Reviewing Facts and Ideas
1. The *who, when, where,* and *what* of the story.
2. Chronological./Because this order usually makes it easier for the listener to follow the story and allows for a dramatic buildup to the most exciting part.
3. Because details help make the story events clearer and more interesting to the listeners.
4. Adjusting your rate of speech, pausing, or using facial expressions and gestures.
5. The art of reading aloud a story, poem, or speech./To convey the ideas and emotions in a selection as completely as possible.
6. The denotation is a word's dictionary meaning, whereas the connotation is what it suggests, the emotional message it carries./The connotation.
7. Expressions that make ideas more vivid by comparing them to things people have seen, touched, or felt./By presenting ideas vividly through unusual comparisons and by heightening the emotional message of the words.
8. The skillful use of phrasing, repetition of sounds, words, or phrases, as well as contrast, rhythm, and rhyme.
9. It helps make your oral interpretation more smooth and more effective by reminding you how you want to deliver it.
10. Draw a vertical line after every punctuation mark, after an idea or emotion requiring a pause, and after any word at which it seems natural to pause; type or write the selection, ending a line at each vertical mark; mark any place you want to pause for emphasis with a double vertical line; underline any words or phrases you want to emphasize; draw brackets around the climax; and make notes in the margin where you want to alter volume or rate or where you want to suggest a particular emotional tone.

Discussing Facts and Ideas
Discussions will vary.

Applying Your Knowledge
Responses will vary.

Chapter 12
Reviewing Vocabulary
1. e
2. g
3. p
4. i
5. l
6. j
7. k
8. a
9. b
10. c
11. d
12. n
13. f
14. o
15. h
16. m

Reviewing Facts and Ideas

1. Answers will vary.
2. They help the audience understand the play and make the action seem more real.
3. Because it helps to remind the actors and the narrator how their roles have been interpreted, how they should deliver lines, and where changes in narration, dialogue, music, or sound effects have been made.
4. The director./Answers will vary but should focus on the necessity of a person whose task is to coordinate action and provide a unified interpretation of the selection.
5. Through visual images and nonverbal sounds./Words are used to supplement and clarify the visual images.
6. Informal, conversational language (including contractions, simple sentences written in the active voice, and common but exact words)./Because the language should be simple, direct, and easily understood in order to supplement, not detract from, the visual images.
7. The detailed instructions for a camera operator to follow during a taping./Because a thorough preplanning and organization of the shots to be taken helps the shooting to flow smoothly, efficiently, and quickly.
8. The producer.
9. The director.
10. Blocking, technical rehearsal, control room rehearsal, run-through, and dress rehearsal./Because carefully rehearsing and coordinating a program saves time and money during the actual shooting of a production.

Discussing Facts and Ideas
Discussions will vary.

Applying Your Knowledge
Responses will vary.

Chapter 13
Reviewing Vocabulary

1. e
2. c
3. d
4. b
5. a

Reviewing Facts and Ideas

1. Definitions will vary./Answers will vary.
2. The specific task addressed in an improvisation through which the actors reveal *who* they are, *where* they are, and *what* they are doing./By providing you with a given task to concentrate on, the problem gives your actions and reactions a framework and thus helps make them more natural and spontaneous.
3. The point of concentration in an improvisation./Directing your attention to a particular aspect of a scene helps make your actions and reactions more specific and clear to the audience; the concentration also helps you stay in character, reacting more spontaneously and naturally within the given framework (as the situation dictates).
4. Because much of a group improvisation's success depends on the natural and spontaneous interaction among the characters' words and actions, and such interaction, especially since nothing is scripted, requires careful listening.
5. Introduction: to make the problem apparent and begin to deal with it; Body: to develop the action; Conclusion: to end the action, making it clear how you have dealt with the problem.
6. A person, or a thing with human characteristics, faced with a problem and trying to resolve it./Through his or her actions and mannerisms, language and speech, and attitudes as well as those of the other characters.
7. Answers will vary.
8. What the character says and does as well as what the playwright might indicate about him or her in the directions. Also look for what the other characters say and do in relation to your character./Answers to remaining questions will vary.
9. What makes the character behave as he or she does, particularly in relation to his or her interaction with the other characters, to the essential problem of the play, and to the contributions he or she makes toward solving it.
10. Answers will vary but should focus on the idea that improvising helps you to develop and better understand a character's voice, mannerisms, and movements so that you can "stay in character" during the performance, i.e. behave and react naturally as that character in any situation.

Discussing Facts and Ideas
Discussions will vary.

Applying Your Knowledge
Responses will vary.

Chapter 14
Reviewing Facts and Ideas

1. A record of how much time radio listening and television viewing actually take out of each week./To help you become more aware of and better control the time you spend on radio and television.

2. A record of what programs you listen to or watch as well as how much you enjoyed them and whether or not you learned anything./It makes you more aware of how well (or poorly) you spend time on radio and television so that you can better manage that time and perhaps resolve to improve your listening and viewing habits.

3. Whether or not you enjoyed a program and whether or not you learned anything from it./Answers to remaining questions will vary.

4. Answers to these questions will vary.
5. Answers to these questions will vary.

Discussing Facts and Ideas
Discussions will vary.

Applying Your Knowledge
Responses will vary.

Supplementary Readings and Instructional Materials

The Speech Communication Teacher: Ideas and Strategies for Classroom and Activities. Speech Communication Association, 5105 Backlick Road, #E, Annandale, VA 22033. Issued periodically beginning with Vol. 1, No. 1 in the Fall of 1986.

Copeland, Lewis, and Lawrence Lamm, eds. *The World's Great Speeches*. 3rd ed. Garden City, NY: Garden City Publishing, 1958.

Chapter 1

Fast, Julius. *Body Language*. 1971. New York: M. Evans and Co., 1982.

Hall, Edward T. *The Silent Language*. 1959.

Krupar, Karen. *Communication Games*. New York: The Free Press, 1973.

Linklater, Kristin. *Freeing the Natural Voice*. New York: Drama Book Specialists, 1976.

Ross, Raymond, and Mark Ross. *Relating and Interacting: An Introduction to Interpersonal Communication*. New York: Prentice-Hall, 1981.

Chapter 2

Brady, John Joseph. *The Craft of Interviewing*. New York: Random, 1977.

Johnson, David. *Reaching Out*. 3rd ed. Englewood Cliffs, NJ: Prentice-Hall, 1986.

Walters, Barbara. *How to Talk with Practically Anybody about Practically Anything*. New York: Dell, 1971.

Chapter 3

Luft, Joseph. *Group Processes: An Introduction to Group Dynamics*. 3rd ed. Palo Alto, CA: Mayfield Publishing, 1984.

Millar, Dan P. *Introduction to Small Group Discussion*. Speech Communication Association, Annandale, VA: (ERIC/Speech Communication Module), 1987.

Scheidel, Thomas M., and Laura Crowell. *Discussing and Deciding*. New York: Macmillan, 1979.

Chapters 4 and 7

Adler, Mortimer J. *How to Speak—How to Listen*. New York: Macmillan, 1985.

Nichols, Ralph C., and Leonard Stevens. *Are You Listening?* New York: McGraw-Hill, 1957.

Chapter 5

The following list includes the most useful reference works for preparing expository speeches. Most of them are brought up to date periodically. Your reference librarian can direct you to the latest edition and to other sources.

General
Collier's Encyclopedia
Encyclopaedia Britannica
New Columbia Encyclopedia

Science
McGraw-Hill Encyclopedia of Science and Technology
Van Nostrand's Scientific Encyclopedia

Periodical Indexes
Access
Biography Index
Book Review Index
Readers' Guide to Periodical Literature

Biography and History
American Men and Women of Science
Contemporary Authors
Current Biography
Dictionary of American Biography
Dictionary of National Biography (British)
International Who's Who
Who's Who in the World (with editions for different countries and professions)

Statistics and Current Events
Facts on File
Hammond Almanac
World Almanac

Chapter 6   Boettinger, Henry M. *Moving Mountains: or the Art and Craft of Letting Others See Things Your Way*. 1969. New York: Macmillan, 1975.

O'Keeffe, Virginia P. *Affecting Critical Thinking through Speech*. Speech Communication Association, Annandale, VA: (ERIC/Speech Communication Module), 1986.

Ross, Raymond, and Mark Ross. *Understanding Persuasion*. 2nd ed. New York: Prentice-Hall, 1985.

Chapter 8   Robert, H. M. *Robert's Rules of Order, Newly Revised*. Ed. Rachel Vixman. New York: Jove Publications, 1984.

Sturgis, A. F. *Sturgis' Standard Code of Parliamentary Procedure*. 2nd ed. New York: McGraw-Hill, 1966.

Chapter 9   *The 1986 Championship Debates and Speeches*. By the American Forensic Association. Eds. John K. Boaz and James R. Bery. Annandale, VA: Speech Communication Association, 1986. (Includes transcripts of final rounds, winning speeches, and judges' critiques from major college tournaments, 170 pages.)

Freeley, Austin J. *Argumentation and Debate: Reasoned Decision Making*. 6th ed. Belmont, CA: Wadsworth Publishing, 1985.

"Nationals Via Videotape." By the National Forensic League. (Tapes available for Cross-Examination Debate, Original Oratory, Lincoln-Douglas Debate, Foreign Extemporaneous Speaking, Domestic Extemporaneous Speaking, Extemporaneous Commentary, and Impromptu Speaking.) Dale Publishing, P.O. Box 151, Grandview, MO 64030.

"Lincoln-Douglas Debate Packet." (Includes Adkins, Carl and J. E. Masters. *The Lincoln-Douglas Debate Handbook, 1986–87* and *Resources for Lincoln-Douglas Debate* (which includes American documents and historical speeches). University Interscholastic League of Texas, Box 8028, University Station, Austin, TX 78713.
(UIL also provides ballots and videocassettes on a variety of speech forms.)

Chapter 10   Hayakawa, S. I. *Language in Thought and Action*. 4th ed. New York: Harcourt Brace Jovanovich, 1978.

Howard, Phillip. *Weasel Words: The Art of Saying What You Don't Mean*. New York: Oxford UP, 1979.

Orwell, George. *Nineteen Eighty-Four*. 1949. New York: New American Library, 1983.

———————. "Politics and the English Language," in *A Collection of Essays by George Orwell*. New York: Harcourt Brace Jovanovich, 1970.

Chapter 11   Baker, Augusta, and Ellin Greene. *Storytelling: Art and Technique*. New York: Bowker, 1977.

Lee, Charlotte, and Timothy Gura. *Oral Interpretations*. 6th ed. Boston: Houghton Mifflin, 1982.

Chapter 12   Cheshire, David. *The Video Manual*. New York: Van Nostrand Reinhold Company, 1982.

Chester, Giraud, Garnet R. Garrison, and Edgar E. Willis. *Television and Radio*. 5th ed. Englewood Cliffs, NJ: Prentice-Hall, 1978.

Chapter 13   McGaw, Charles, and Gary Blake. *Acting Is Believing: A Basic Method*. 4th ed. New York: Holt, Rinehart, and Winston, 1980.

Schulman, Michael, and Eva Mekler. *Contemporary Scenes for Student Actors*. Baltimore: Penguin, 1980.

Spolin, Viola. *Improvisation for the Theatre: A Handbook of Teaching and Directing Techniques*. rev. ed. Evanston, IL: Northwestern UP, 1983.

White, Edwin, et al. *Acting and Stage Movement*. Colorado Springs, CO: Meriwether, 1985.

Chapter 14   Berger, Arthur A. *Media Analysis Techniques*. Beverly Hills: Sage Publications, 1982.

Newcomb, Horace. *Television: The Critical View*. 3rd ed. New York: Oxford UP, 1982.

E F F E C T I V E
Speech

Richard W. Clark

Consultants

Vivian C. Bryant
River Rouge High School, Michigan

Shirley Smith
Richardson High School, Texas

Thelma Pate
Mesquite High School, Texas

Glencoe Publishing Company
Mission Hills, California

PHOTOGRAPHS: Courtesy of ABC Radio page 56, 331; Associated Press/Wide World 24, 88, 189, 195, 220, 228, 240, 241, 252, 276, 298, 310; Ed Baker 40a; Bettmann Archives 183, 202; Charlie Borland 31; Courtesy of Fred Bressee 325; Cleo Freelance Photos 40b; Culver Pictures 266; Dan DeWilde 48, 80, 83, 120, 210; Alec Duncan 377; Tony Freeman 112; Susan Friedman 104, 124, 129, 287, 352; From the private collection of Linda Goss 290; Richard Hutchings 40c, 289, 350, 376; Courtesy of International Business Machines Corporation 146; Courtesy of LBJ Library 126; Library of Congress 176, 305; Robert Maust 27; National Archives 196; Roger Neal 91; Photo Agora/Blaire Saitz 35; Gene Plaisted 92; Karen Stafford Rantzman 2, 14, 118, 143, 174, 358, 361; James Shaffer 10, 41a, 41b, 51, 58, 70, 86, 94, 114, 148, 153, 156, 159, 161, 185, 215, 226, 233, 237, 248, 254, 258, 263, 272, 274, 279, 284, 294, 312, 336, 341, 343, 345, 347, 367, 381, 385; Peter Smolens 322; Strix Pix 37, 53, 96, 238, 333; Texas Stock/Mike Boroff 228; Texas Stock/Larry Kolvoord 241; Jim West 41c, 178, 280; Courtesy of the White House 213; Woodfin Camp/Dilip Mehta 106.

MARGIN PHOTOGRAPHS: David Iriguchi

ILLUSTRATIONS: Cyndie Clark-Huegel

Glencoe Publishing Company
15319 Chatsworth Street
Mission Hills, CA 91345

Printed in the United States of America

ISBN 0-02-659880-9 (Student Text)
ISBN 0-02-659881-7 (Teacher's Edition)
ISBN 0-02-659882-5 (Teacher's Resource Binder)

2 3 4 5 6   92 91 90 89 88

Table of Contents

UNIT 4   Performing

Communication Models

Evaluation Checklists

Communication Skills

EFFECTIVE

Speech

Communicating

A Case Study

Frowning, Jenna looked at her watch. It was 25 minutes since she had called for a taxi. She had been extra careful giving directions on how to get to her house, so she could not imagine what was taking so long. In the background the radio reported that the weather in Dallas, where she was headed, was warm and dry. Then she saw the cab pull up at the curb. She rushed out the door, hurriedly told the driver to take her to the airport, and let herself into the back seat, ignoring the offer to place her luggage in the trunk.

As the taxi sped to the airport, she went over in her mind again the presentation she was going to make. "Will the group from the West Coast be there?" she muttered under her breath. "If so, will that opinionated vice president from Seattle interrupt me before I get to my main point the way he did last year?" Vaguely she realized the driver was saying something to her. "What? Oh, yes. I'm flying Globe Airways."

The cab screeched to a halt. As quickly as he could say the amount, she counted out the cab fare and handed it to the driver. She ran into the airport and rushed to the ticket counter. "No, I don't want to take a later flight. I don't care if you are overbooked. I have to be in Dallas by one o'clock." Jenna began to feel her blood pressure rise as the agent continued to explain to her the advantages of waiting for a later flight.

Finally, the boarding call came, and she walked down the ramp and onto the plane. She found the flight attendant's assurances that they would arrive on time comforting and settled into her seat.

Think and Discuss

1. List all the examples of speaking and listening you can find in this case study.
2. We are told that people spend 80 percent of their waking hours communicating with others but use only about 25 percent of their ability to communicate at any one time. What are some instances in the case study in which there was less than full use of communication ability?
3. What are some instances you can think of when you have not listened as carefully as you should? When have your directions or other spoken communications been not as clear as you needed to make them?
4. What are some of the things you can learn about Jenna as you think about her communications? What does she seem to know about those with whom she must communicate? Think about the different instances of communication. Then describe what you imagine Jenna's voice would be like and what the others in the case study would sound like as they spoke.

In Unit One, "Communicating," you will learn more about how and why people communicate, and you will develop a better understanding of yourself and others in a communication setting.

Unit Introduction: Analyzing the Communication Process

Defining the Communication Process

FUNKY WINKERBEAN   **BY TOM BATIUK**

SPEECH I –

THIS COURSE IS OFFERED FOR THOSE STUDENTS WHO PLAN PROFESSIONS REQUIRING GOOD COMMUNICATION SKILLS SUCH AS RADIO, TELEVISION, TEACHING, AND WORKING AT A FAST FOOD DRIVE-THRU WINDOW!

News America Syndicate © News Group Chicago, Inc., 1985   2-14

Good communication skills, as the preceding cartoon suggests, are needed for many occupations. Engineers, for example, spend more of their time communicating than engaging in any other skill. Effective speech is needed for more than the performance of one's occupation. In a recent study, a major computer manufacturer determined that we spend 80 percent of our waking hours communicating with others.

What is speech communication? Why do we communicate? Why do we need to study speech communication? At first glance, the cartoonist may seem to be suggesting that the answers to such questions are very simple, but they are not.

> Before reading further, take a few minutes to create your own definition of the speech communication process. If possible, discuss your definition with another student. Then, as you read on, compare your original definition with what follows.

Think for a moment of the different uses you have made of speech communications during the past week. Who else was present? Were you satisfied with each of the experiences? Did you spend more time listening than speaking? What differences were there between when you were speaking with your friends and when you were speaking with your parents or with your teacher? One way to define **speech communication** is to consider a number of examples and then to list elements of each example.

4

Your list might have included some of the same items as those that follow.

Told a joke to a group of friends

Answered questions in class

Discussed a rock concert with a friend

Explained to a parent why I came home so late

Took notes during a lecture about the discovery of America by European explorers

Argued with my uncle who told me he believes all teenagers are lazy

Tried to persuade a neighbor to buy some candy to support the band

Asked a friend for a date

Turned down a person I did not know who asked me for a date

Interviewed for a job at a nearby supermarket

Gave a report in English about a book I read

Gave directions to a person who wanted to know how to get to the freeway from our school

Watched a program on television and then had to explain what happened for a friend who had missed the broadcast

In each of these situations, there are certain common elements. There was at least one **speaker** and one **listener**. In several instances there were several speakers and/or listeners. There was also a **message**. Recognizing that these elements are present might lead you to conclude that speech communication consists of a speaker conveying a message to a listener as suggested in the following diagram.

Components of the Communication Process (1)

With further thought, you will likely realize that there is more to the communication process than is contained in the above diagram. While it is true that speech communication requires interaction between speaker and listener, the **setting** for the communication, the **body of knowledge**, and the **language** shared by speakers and listeners help to determine the nature of any communication experience. When you were on your telephone, explaining the latest events in your favorite program to your friend, the setting was quite different than when you were giving your book report or interviewing for the job. Such differences in setting change the way in which you communicate. So does the extent to which you share a common body of knowledge with others in the communication setting. For example, if you had tried to explain what had just happened in one episode of a television series to someone who had never seen the series before, the task would have been much more difficult than it was when you were explaining the episode to your friend who had missed just that one.

Regardless of whether you have knowledge of similar things, if you lack a common language, communication will be almost impossible. But even when you both speak English, you may discover that there are some aspects of the language that you do not share. For example, as you talked with your uncle who believes all teenagers are lazy, you were surprised to discover that he did not consider being actively engaged in sports an indicator that a person was not lazy. Until you clarified the meaning of such an apparently simple term as *lazy*, you were talking at cross-purposes. Even when you agreed on the meaning of *lazy*, you discovered that there were a number of words you frequently use when talking with your friend that have either no meaning for your uncle or a much different meaning for him than for you.

The following diagram provides a more complete, but not final, picture of the communication process.

Components of the Communication Process (2)

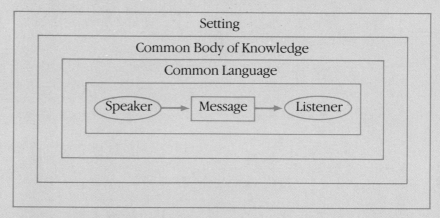

You can learn about two other vital elements of the communication process by examining another example on your list. You should realize that the message that the listener receives is not always the exact message that the speaker sends. For example, when you refused a date with the person you did not know, he heard you say "no" but also perceived that you did not like him or felt you were too good for him. He may have perceived such additional messages because of the tone of voice you used, your facial expressions, or something someone else had told him about you during an earlier conversation. Any or all of these factors could have caused **interference** with your message.

When you told this person "no," it did not take you long to realize that something other than what you had intended to communicate had been received. The anger on his face, the tone with which he said, "I thought so," and the way he looked away from you all told you he felt that you were rejecting him as a person, not just turning down a date with someone you did not know. The means by which you learn what the listener understands of the message is called **feedback**.

The following diagram adds concepts of interference and feedback to complete the depiction of the communication process.

The Communication Process

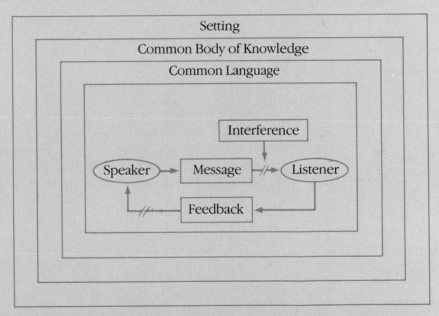

What, then, is the definition of the speech communication process?

The **speech communication process** is the sending and receiving of oral messages in order to share meaning. Setting, commonality or lack of commonality of knowledge and language as well as nonverbal signals, and the ability of those communicating to interpret feedback affect whether the participants achieve understanding.

Elements of Speech

It is important to understand the elements of speech communication and how they are important to both speaker and listener. These elements are:

Self-understanding. Both the speaker and the listener need to be aware of the motives and attitudes that influence their actions.

Thought processes. Depending on the nature of the material being communicated, both the speaker and the listener need to call upon a wide variety of thinking skills. The success of different communications may depend on the ability to imagine and empathize, or to analyze and organize information, or to solve problems.

Command of language. The speaker must be able to clearly express his or her thoughts. The listener must be able to understand the speaker's vocabulary.

Voice. The speaker's voice should be clear, distinct, and easily heard by the listener.

Bodily action. The speaker must provide nonverbal clues that reinforce the message and avoid nonverbal actions that confuse or contradict the message. The listener's nonverbal actions let the speaker know how the message is being received.

The Need to Communicate

Speech communication answers many human needs. Most obviously, it is used to share information and experiences, as when you give directions or a book report or describe a television program to a friend who has missed it. We also use speech communication to persuade, as when we attempt to sell something to others or to convince them that our views on a subject are correct. We develop our knowledge of ourselves through our communications with others. Also, we use speech communication to get to know one another better, whether it is in a formal interview or in a conversation about a rock concert. Sometimes we perform for others, as, for example, do the actors on our favorite program. For each purpose that can be identified by a speaker, there is one that describes the intentions of a listener. Listeners who are busy taking notes, for example, may be trying to understand what a speaker is seeking to explain.

The Need to Study Speech Communication

A number of authorities have noted that speech is a distinctly human activity. Mortimer Adler observes that "there is communication among brute animals in a wide variety of ways, but no conversation." In making this comment, he is trying to get us to understand the uniquely human nature of speech communication.

Effective speech is essential for effective participation in our society, both as citizens and workers. While we are able to make noises from the time we are born, speech is something we learn through interaction with others. With careful study we can improve this vital human ability. Most of us realize that we need to be able to explain, persuade, and occasionally even to perform. We know that if we are going to spend 80 percent of our time communicating, we ought to learn to do it well.

Activities

1. Compare your original definition of the speech communication process with those of your classmates. Note the elements that are common to most of them. Then reread the definition in this lesson and compare your definitions to it.
2. Interview several adults with whom you are acquainted. Ask them for examples of their use of speech communication. Obtain examples of incidents when they had difficulty with communications. Report to the class what they tell you about language problems, interference, lack of feedback, lack of a common body of knowledge, or other causes of their communication problems.
3. Colin Cherry said, "If I push a man in the lake, he goes in. If I tell him to go jump in, he is apt to do one of a 1,000 things." How does this statement relate to the definition of the communication process included in this introduction?

You the Communicator

After working through this chapter, you should be proficient at the following skills:

Lesson	Skills
Lesson 1	evaluating your strengths and weaknesses as a communicator
Lesson 2	using your mind and imagination to communicate more effectively
Lesson 3	using language accurately and vividly
Lesson 4	using your voice effectively
Lesson 5	using your body to enhance your communication
Communicating on the Job	analyzing your career interests
Communicating as a Citizen	reporting an incident

Knowing Yourself as a Communicator

Each communication experience is slightly different from the others. Sometimes you feel at ease with people, as when you are talking to your family or friends. With other people, such as teachers and acquaintances, you feel less comfortable. The way you feel toward people will be reflected in your voice, posture, and language, as well as in the information you communicate.

Every day, in hundreds of different ways, we use words and gestures to show other people how we feel about them and how we want them to feel about us. For example, when you say "Good morning" to a friend, you are not really giving that person useful information about the morning. Your words actually mean: "Because you're my friend, I'm glad to see you."

As a communicator, you have certain strengths and weaknesses. For example, your appearance and voice may cause people to pay attention to you. On the other hand, you may have nervous mannerisms that show others that you are uncomfortable when speaking. Such mannerisms can make you a less effective communicator. Before you begin to study speech and communication, evaluate both the strengths that can help you and the weaknesses that you can overcome.

Working with the Model

Read the following self-evaluation Susan wrote of her strengths and weaknesses as a communicator.

SELF-EVALUATION

Purpose: To identify my strong and weak points when I communicate with other people in conversation, so I can find ways of improving my communication skills.

Situations: Conversations with friends before and after school, between classes, on weekends; also, conversations with new acquaintances at friends' homes, at parties, or on Aerospace Club field trips.

Strong points: I dress neatly and always try to keep a friendly smile and attitude. This seems to make people interested in talking to me. Since I seldom talk about myself, I don't think I'm likely to bore anyone. In conversation with strangers, I always ask questions about their work and hobbies.

Weak points: I feel fairly comfortable with my friends, but conversations with strangers or people I know only slightly can be painfully embarrassing to me. Even though I ask polite questions, many people don't seem eager to answer. I don't have any "small talk," casual remarks about the weather, fashions, entertainment, and so forth that help people feel at their ease.

Evaluation: After thinking about it, I believe that my conversation shows a lack of self-confidence. Because I don't feel that *I* and *my* interests are worth talking about, I spend too much time trying to "draw out" other people. Many of them naturally resent being questioned so much, and they must feel that I am making them do all the work in the conversation. Being informed and having good manners are points in my favor, but I must be more willing to talk about myself.

Suggestions for improvement: The next time I have a conversation with a new acquaintance, I'll try to spend as much time talking as he or she does. Of course, I'll ask the usual polite questions, but I also resolve to tell that person about the Aerospace Club, about the last book I read, and about my plans for college. I want to make myself sound interesting, but not egotistical. I'll try the new system for a month. Then I'll reread this evaluation and see whether my conversation experience has changed in any way.

A. Think about the information Susan wrote under "Purpose," "Situations," "Strong Points," and "Weak Points."
   1. What type of communication causes Susan the most trouble?
   2. Which habits that Susan listed as "strong points" might actually be part of her problem? Explain your answer.
   3. Among her "weak points," Susan listed her inability to make small talk. Name at least one way in which she might be able to develop this talent.
   4. Imagine that you are having a conversation with Susan. Assuming that she has described her communication problems accurately, how do you think you would feel during the conversation? What would you do to make the experience more agreeable?
B. Think about the information Susan wrote under "Evaluation" and "Suggestions for Improvement."
   1. Briefly summarize Susan's evaluation of her communication problem.
   2. You have probably known at least one person who had as much difficulty in conversation as Susan has. How would you evaluate that person's communication problems?
   3. Briefly summarize Susan's suggestions for improvement.
   4. Name at least one suggestion that Susan could follow in order to become a better communicator.

Guidelines

In order to understand yourself better as a communicator, you should ask yourself the following questions.

Interests
What are my interests and enthusiasms?
What subjects do I know about that other people might be interested in?
How well do I convey information to others?
How successful am I in making other people share my enthusiasms?

Appearance and voice
How does my appearance either help or harm my ability to communicate?
How do people react to my posture, gestures, and way of speaking?
What effect does my voice have on people with whom I communicate?

Attitude toward myself
What is my attitude toward myself? Do I feel that I am an interesting person who is worth knowing?
What are my values? Do I believe in certain principles or goals? Are my values clear from what I say?
How consistent am I in what I believe and say to others? Do I change my ideas readily or reluctantly?

Attitude toward others
How do I treat people whom I know well? Do I show loyalty and respect toward my friends?
How do I react to people I have just met? Do new acquaintances feel that I find *them* interesting?
How good are my manners? Would a new acquaintance describe me as basically rude or basically polite?

By thinking about the answers to these questions, you can form an idea of the kind of communicator you are.

Preparing and Presenting

Although you will write your self-evaluation by yourself, you will later discuss it with another student. To begin, reread Susan's self-evaluation in the Working with the Model section of this lesson. Then evaluate your own skills as a communicator, using the outline on the following pages.

Purpose

Decide what type of communication causes you the greatest difficulties. Consider the following types of communication.

> discussion with family members
> conversation with friends
> conversation with acquaintances
> oral report before class or school organization
> job interview

Situations

List each occasion on which you must take part in this type of communication. Remember to list situations in school and after school, at home, on the job, and in an organization.

Strong points

List all the qualities that help you communicate well. Include your appearance, voice, manners, and attitude; your background, interests, and enthusiasms; and your ability to make other people feel interested in you.

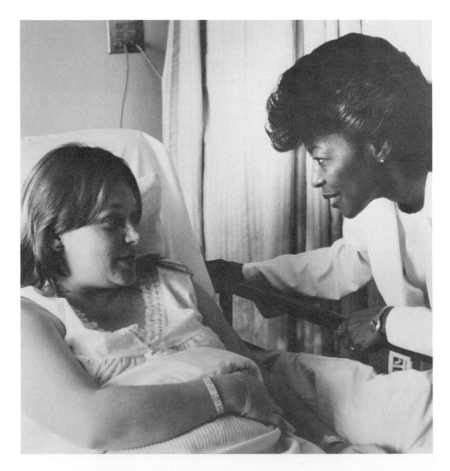

Weak points

List all the habits that keep you from communicating well. Include any problems you have with your appearance, voice, or manners; any difficulty in finding an interesting subject to talk about; any problems with attracting or holding other people's attention.

Evaluation

Decide what your principal problem as a communicator is and what the causes of the problem are.

Suggestions for improvement

Identify at least one way in which you could change your habits or attitudes in order to become a better communicator. Describe a specific plan you could follow in order to improve your performance.

After you have written your self-evaluation, read it over and make any changes you think are necessary.

Evaluation Checklist

Exchange self-evaluations with another student. Read the other person's self-evaluation and then evaluate it on the basis of the following criteria. Rate it on a scale from 1 (Poor) to 5 (Excellent). Be prepared to give reasons for each rating you give. The questions in parentheses will help you do so.

Category	Rating
The student . . . 1. Explained his or her communication problems clearly (How could the explanation be made clearer?)	
2. Listed strong and weak points that clearly illustrated the problems (What information, if any, could be added to these lists to better illustrate the problems?)	
3. Accurately evaluated his or her problems (In what ways, if any, could the evaluation be improved?)	
4. Made suggestions for improvement that are likely to work (What other suggestions, if any, could this person follow to become a better communicator?)	

Thinking and Imagining

Effective speaking requires effective thinking. If you are to think effectively, you will need to be skillful in acquiring, analyzing, arranging, and remembering information. To be an interesting communicator, you need information. Some of your information will come from books and other print and visual materials. Some will come from interacting with other people in formal and informal settings. The primary way you acquire information from whatever source is through the use of your senses: sight, hearing, smell, taste, and touch. Your perceptions of the world are shaped by how you apply your senses and by how you interpret the impressions collected through these senses. Like other people's, your interpretations are based on past experiences and the environment in which you operate.

In order to develop your potential for thinking, you need to sharpen your senses and to improve your understanding of the role experience and the environment play in determining meaning.

Working with the Model

Study the following cartoons.

A. Think about the sensory experiences that shaped the mental images of each person in the cartoons.
   1. Describe each mental image pictured in terms of each of the senses. Prepare a written list for each sense.
      a. What sounds could you hear in each scene?
      b. What sights could you see in each scene?
      c. What smells might be present in each scene?
      d. What could you feel by touching things in the scenes?
      e. What added knowledge could you gain through the sense of taste in each scene? For example, as the father thinks of his office, he might recall the taste of the bitter office coffee or the end of the pencil he chewed as he sought the answer to a problem.
   2. When you have finished compiling your list, compare it with that of another student in the class. Discuss why your lists included different items. What led to the different sensory images each of you called to mind?
B. Look at the second cartoon again. Think about the mental images the characters might have had if their experiences had been different.
   1. Imagine that the father was a commercial fisherman. Decide what his mental image might be. Write a list of sensory images that would be found in that scene.

17

2. Write a list of the "snow images" the children might have had if they lived all their lives on a pineapple plantation in Hawaii.
3. What mental image might the mother have had if she had an important business trip scheduled for the next day? List the sensory images in such a scene.
4. Compare each list with those of other students. Discuss why you included different experiences.

C. Think about your own experiences.
1. Choose one of the following. Write a description using all five senses.
   a. A great place to have fun
   b. An ocean beach on a cold, windy day
   c. The school cafeteria
   d. A city bus during rush hour
   e. Skiing on fresh powder
   f. Running up a steep hill
2. Compare your descriptions with others. How were they alike, how different? What experiences had each of you had that shaped your images?

Guidelines

1. One of the best ways to strengthen your skills in using your senses is to develop a pattern of regular exercise for them. Take walks and be alive to the world around you. Seek out people for conversations about subjects different than those you normally talk about with your friends. Help a handicapped person who is unable to use all senses. Describe scenes to people with impaired vision or help a hearing-impaired person have a feeling for the sounds of a scene.
2. Improve your understanding of the influence of your past experiences on new ones by imagining how something you have just observed might appear to someone with a different background than yours.
3. When communicating with others, be sensitive to their background and experiences in order to be able to estimate how they are interpreting what you are saying.
4. Think carefully about whether you have prejudged people, places, or ideas rather than used all your observational powers to understand them.
5. Develop your imagination. Engage in creative play. Give yourself time for fantasy and reflection. Be willing to use your intuition and feelings when solving problems. Practice putting yourself in someone else's place and looking at questions from his or her perspective.

Preparing and Presenting

In order to develop your skills in acquiring information and to help build that broad background of information that you need to communicate, you should keep a *Speaker's Journal.*

Use a three-ring binder for your journal. This will allow you to add material and to rearrange it. Try to make at least one entry each day.

Divide your notebook into major sections.

Section 1: **Record of sensory observations.** Try to record an entry in this section at least three times a week. Sometimes your entry should concentrate on one sense. For example, you could record all of the sights of a shopping trip to the mall. On other occasions you might want to record all of your sensory responses to a particular scene.

Section 2: **Record of interesting personalities.** This section might include information clipped from the paper about famous and obscure individuals whose activities are unusual. If you add such clippings, take a few minutes to record why you found the person interesting. You may also include descriptions of people you meet. Be sure to write enough about them so that you will be able to recall why you found the people interesting when you read about them later.

Section 3: **Record of humorous incidents.** Again, this section may include clippings of articles or cartoons from newspapers or magazines as well as firsthand experiences.

Section 4: **Record of strange events.** Clippings, pictures, and firsthand descriptions all have a place in such a section. When you include an item in this section, write why you found it strange. Write notes about it from the point of view of people with a different background than yours.

Section 5: **Record of questions for which you have no answers.** When someone asks you a question you cannot answer or you are faced with a problem that you cannot solve, take time to write about it in your journal. Make an intelligent guess about what the answer might be. Periodically take time to review this section of your journal. As you find answers to these questions, note how your guesses compare to your eventual answers.

Section 6:   **Record of information about future trends.** Include reports in the media about such items as breakthroughs in medicine, new technologies, advances in exploring the universe, new theories about how people learn, changes in the kinds of jobs people have, and changes in the ways people use their leisure time. Note any researchers' descriptions of their thought processes as they made their discoveries. As you place such items in your journal, take time to write some notes speculating on how the people who made the new discoveries felt about them.

You might include other sections, such as reviews of movies, videotapes, and concerts; descriptions of enjoyable recreational activities; definitions of new words and phrases you found to be helpful in communicating with others; or discussions of the ways particular events and settings may have changed your view of people or of ideas.

Evaluation Checklist

Use the following checklist as a basis for completing a self-evaluation. Rate yourself on a scale from 1 (Poor) to 5 (Excellent). Be prepared to give reasons for each rating you give.

Category	Rating
I . . . 1. Use all my senses as I try to learn through firsthand observation	
2. Am skillful in using the library and other learning resources	
3. Am able to analyze the logical, emotional, statistical, and testimonial information that I gather	
4. Can use a variety of patterns for arranging information when I talk with various groups	
5. Am able to recognize the contribution that my past experiences and my current surroundings make to my perceptions of words and events	
6. Make a regular practice of recording and reflecting on my observations	

Using Language

Effective use of language requires choosing appropriate words, that is, being accurate and correct in your choice of words, using vivid words and combinations of words, using words that are direct and familiar to those with whom you are speaking, and guiding listeners through effective use of transitional words. Whether you are having a conversation, conducting an interview, or giving a formal speech, you should be careful to use language that is appropriate to the setting, the subject, and the other people present.

While there are many similarities between good written language and good spoken language, there are also differences. Unlike written language, spoken language must be instantly understood. A listener cannot go back, as a reader can, and reread what has just been said. Spoken language is also more direct and personal than written language. Among specific differences between the spoken and written language are the following.

- Speakers use everyday language and familiar words more often than writers do.
- Speakers use shorter and simpler sentences than writers do.
- Speakers repeat key ideas more often than writers do.
- Speakers use transitional words and phrases more often than writers do.
- Speakers can more easily adapt their language to the specific audience than writers, who may have less precise knowledge of who will be reading their material.

You can think of words as a form of currency or money. You use words to help others understand ideas, just as you use money to buy groceries. Think what problems you would have if a $10 bill was worth $5 in one store and $25 in another. Words can have such varied meanings for people that it almost seems as if different people are responding to different words even though you are sure you are using the same words with all of them.

Many words and phrases have two levels of meaning. The first level of meaning, **denotation**, is the direct meaning, sometimes called the dictionary definition of the word. The second level, **connotation**, is what the word suggests to people because of associations they have with it from past experience. The word *bureaucracy* is a good example. The denotation of *bureaucracy* is a group of appointed government officials who help make policy and administer programs. To many people, however, *bureaucracy* has the connotation of unhelpful officials who waste taxpayers' money and complicate people's lives with governmental red tape. A politician need only to identify someone as a bureaucrat to make many people dislike that person. On the other hand, other words have positive connotations. Americans generally respond positively to such terms as *free enterprise, the American way,* or *democracy.*

Every word has its own history and associations for each listener. Abstract words have more varied associations, or connotations, than concrete ones. Thus, *bicycle* will call to mind relatively similar images for most people, while a word such as *justice* may have very different connotations for different people. Some words, such as *receiver,* may have several different denotations (for example, football receiver and stereo receiver). Unlike words with a variety of connotations, words with several denotations seldom cause confusion if the context in which they are used is clear. While readers can reread to clarify meaning, listeners must rely on the speaker to be precise in choosing words and combining them.

In addition to being accurate in your use of language, you need to have lively, interesting language. You know from listening to sportscasts and other television programming that some expressions that were once fresh and effective have become worn out. Overused words and phrases are called **clichés**. You should avoid their use. Here are some examples.

> As sharp as a tack
> Dead as a doornail
> As hungry as a bear
> In no uncertain terms
> Last but not least
> The depths of despair
> As Yogi said: "The game's not over until it's over."

Figurative language makes ideas more vivid by comparing them to things most people have seen, touched, or felt. Such techniques of comparison are called **figures of speech**. Using the following figures of speech appropriately can improve your communication.

A **simile** compares two unlike things, using the words *like* or *as.*

> Mike prowled the room like a cat looking for its rubber mouse.
> Her voice was as cold and sharp as an icicle.

A **metaphor** compares two unlike things by stating or implying one thing is another.

> Roger tiptoed downstairs through a jungle of shadows.
> This debate is a swamp of confusion and contradictions.

Personification is a type of metaphor in which an object is given the qualities of a human being. In the example below, the storm is given the human trait of behaving contemptuously.

The first winter storm contemptuously flattened the beach houses.

An **analogy** is an extended comparison based on the resemblance in some ways between two things ordinarily considered unlike.

A living cell is like a city under siege, letting food and other vital supplies enter its walls, but repelling hostile invaders—in this case, microbes.

Working with the Model

Dr. Martin Luther King, Jr. gave this speech in front of the Lincoln Memorial in Washington D.C., on August 28, 1963. He spoke before 200,000 people at a rally that was the culmination of the 1963 civil rights drive.

From "I Have a Dream"

. . . Five score years ago, a great American, in whose symbolic shadow we stand, signed the Emancipation Proclamation. This momentous decree came as a great beacon light of hope to millions of Negro slaves who had been seared in the flames of withering injustice. It came as a joyous daybreak to end the long night of captivity.

But one hundred years later, we must face the tragic fact that the Negro is still not free. One hundred years later, the life of the Negro is still sadly crippled by the manacles of segregation and the chains of discrimination. One hundred years later, the Negro lives on a lonely island of poverty in the midst of a vast ocean of material prosperity. One hundred years later, the Negro is still languished in the corners of American society and finds himself an exile in his own land. So we have come here today to dramatize an appalling condition.

In a sense we have come to our nation's capital to cash a check. When the architects of our Republic wrote the magnificent words of the Constitution and the Declaration of Independence, they were signing a promissory note to which every American was to fall heir. This note was a promise that all men would be guaranteed the unalienable rights of life, liberty, and the pursuit of happiness.

It is obvious today that America has defaulted on this promissory note insofar as her citizens of color are concerned. Instead of honoring this sacred obligation, America has given the Negro people a bad

check—a check which has come back marked "insufficient funds." But we refuse to believe that the bank of justice is bankrupt. We refuse to believe that there are insufficient funds in the great vaults of opportunity of this nation. So we have come to cash this check—a check that will give us upon demand the riches of freedom and the security of justice. We have also come to this hallowed spot to remind America of the fierce urgency of now. This is no time to engage in the luxury of cooling off or to take the tranquilizing drug of gradualism. Now is the time to make real the promises of Democracy. Now is the time to rise from the dark and desolate valley of segregation to the sunlit path of racial justice. Now is the time to open the doors of opportunity to all of God's children. Now is the time to lift our nation from the quicksands of racial injustice to the solid rock of brotherhood. . . .

A. Think about the appropriateness of the language for the occasion, audience, and setting.
   1. The rally at which Dr. King spoke was a major event in the campaign for civil rights. How does the language show that the speaker was aware of the importance of the occasion?

2. How does King connect the setting with the history of black people?
3. Take a paragraph and rephrase the language so that it would express the same ideas in language that would be more fitting for an informal conversation in a school hallway.

B. Look at the words and phrases with particular attention to their connotation and to the association that members of King's audience were apt to have with these words and phrases.
   1. Dr. King used several related metaphors based on banking. These metaphors center around the metaphor of the bad check. What are the connotations of a bad check? Why do you think the speaker wanted to associate the metaphor of a bad check with the status of black people?
   2. Look up the following terms in a dictionary or thesaurus. Then compare how the speech would have changed had King chosen other words with the same denotation but different connotations.

languished	brotherhood	island
hallowed	urgency	tranquilizing

C. Consider the way Dr. King made use of figurative language.
   1. Look again at the definitions of different figures of speech. Find examples of as many similes, metaphors, and analogies as you can in the model.
   2. Choose one of the figures of speech and discuss the ideas and feelings suggested by that phrase. For example, what does the idea of "great beacon light of hope" suggest? How would it differ from a flickering candle of hope or the constant sunshine of hope? What are the specific qualities of lighting that give this metaphor its strength?

Guidelines

1. Use language that is appropriate to the situation.

   a. Your language should be neither too formal nor too informal for the situation.
   b. Be cautious when using slang or colloquialisms.
   c. Avoid language that is too technical for those with whom you are speaking. If you must use specialized terms, define them.
   d. Be alert to nonverbal cues from your listeners that will tell you whether your language is appropriate.

2. Use the best word for the idea you are trying to express.
   a. Use a familiar word rather than an unusual one.
   b. Use a concrete word rather than an abstract one unless you are trying to stir emotions.
   c. Use verbs that express action rather than verbs such as *is* or *are*.
   d. Use adjectives sparingly.
   e. Whenever possible use one well-chosen word instead of a phrase.
3. Make use of figures of speech but keep in mind that comparisons are only useful if the audience understands the characteristics of the things being compared in the way you want these characteristics to be understood. For example, if you say someone is like an icicle to someone who has never seen or felt an icicle, they probably will not understand your point.
4. Use words that are grammatically correct. Be particularly alert to problems of subject-verb agreement and to the correct use of pronouns. Errors in grammar may cause your entire message to be discounted by some listeners.
5. Use **transitions**, words that connect ideas in one sentence or paragraph with the ideas in the next sentence or paragraph. Words and phrases such as the following serve as transitions.

first	in addition	by way of contrast
second	on the other hand	moreover
third	furthermore	therefore
next	in conclusion	however
finally	another point	similarly

Besides the language you select, your voice and body can also assist you in making transitions. Pauses, changes in loudness, and gestures all help your listeners know when you are moving on.

Preparing and Presenting

Create a special section for language in your Speaker's Journal and add to it the materials you develop from the following activities.

1. Listen to a recording of a well-known speech, from life or literature. If you cannot find a recording, use a speech published in *Vital Speeches* or a book of speeches. List all of the transitional words and phrases the speaker uses.
2. Listen to people from one age group or background talking with people from a different age group or background. For example, you might listen to a mechanic explaining something to a nonmechanic, children talking to adults, tourists talking with people in your town,

or a scientist explaining something to a nonscientist. Write a paragraph in your journal discussing the difficulties in communication you noted. If one of the parties did something during the conversation that improved the communications, be sure to note that also.

3. Invent figures of speech to make each of the following ideas or objects more understandable or vivid.

a jet plane	a rainy Sunday
a crowded street	a dark night
a mountain, lake, or	a political convention
some other natural feature	a nuclear explosion

    Record your figures of speech in your journal. Make a habit of adding other effective figures of speech to your journal as you hear them.

4. For one week, list the words and phrases you hear that have strong positive or negative connotations. Divide your list into two parts: positive and negative. Use language you hear on television and radio and in conversations and speeches. Pay particular attention to advertising as a source. As you become aware that certain loaded words are repeated, make a record of the different contexts in which they appear.

5. Make a list of clichés you hear in one weekend's television viewing. After having listed all the clichés you have heard, select the ten which you think are the most overused. Exchange your list with another student. Rewrite the ten expressions on the other student's list, stating them in fresh language. Place the original and rewritten material in your journal.

6. Prepare and place in your journal two examples of statements that could be used to complete the following similes in a fresh and vivid way.

As awkward as . . . .
As friendly as . . . .
As difficult as . . . .
As strange as . . . .
As big as . . . .
As quiet as . . . .

Evaluation Checklist

On the basis of the following criteria, evaluate the effectiveness with which you use language. Rate your effectiveness on a scale from 1 (Poor) to 5 (Excellent). Be prepared to give reasons for each rating you give.

Category	Rating
I . . . 1. Choose and combine words in a manner that is appropriate for the speaker, audience, subject, and occasion	
2. Select the specific and precise words that most effectively express my thoughts	
3. Use words familiar to the audience and combine them in direct, simple, yet varied patterns	
4. Use transitions and repetition to help guide the listener through my thought sequence	
5. Make use of active verbs, concrete nouns, and accurate adjectives and adverbs	
6. Use variety in word choice and combination and avoid trite phrases and clichés	
7. Make effective use of figurative language	

Using Your Voice

To learn how to use your voice, you need to know where your voice comes from and why it sounds the way it does. There are three stages in the physical process of speaking.

1. The first stage (as you can see in the diagram on this page) takes place in your chest. Your **lungs** rest on a powerful curved muscle called the **diaphragm**. As you inhale, your diaphragm moves downward, drawing air into the lungs. At the same time, your rib cage expands to make room for the air. As you exhale, or when you speak, the diaphragm moves upward, forcing air out of the lungs.

   Most people have more than enough lung capacity to speak comfortably. Nevertheless, many people feel short of breath when they must speak in public. This feeling is caused by nervousness and can be overcome. Instead of breathing rapidly and shallowly, practice breathing slowly and deeply. Use your abdominal muscles

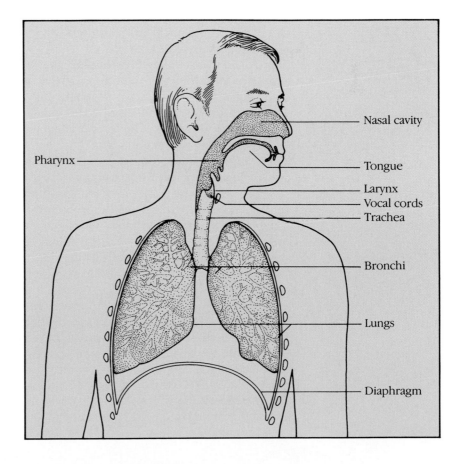

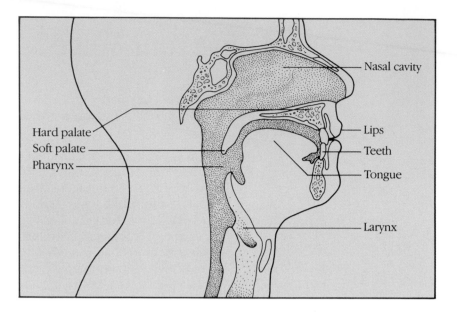

Nasal cavity

Hard palate
Soft palate
Pharynx

Lips
Teeth
Tongue

Larynx

to steadily push out the air as you exhale. (This is the method singers use to produce a great volume of sound.) Be sure that the muscles of your chest, neck, and shoulders are relaxed, so that your rib cage can move easily and freely.

2. The second stage of speech takes place in the throat. Air moves up and out of your lungs through the **trachea**, or windpipe. At the top of the trachea, the air passes through the **larynx** (also called the voice box or Adam's apple). The **vocal cords** are a pair of muscular folds across the center of the larynx. When you breathe freely, these folds are relaxed. When you speak, however, the folds tighten and vibrate rapidly as the air flows past them. The more rapid the vibration, the higher the **pitch**, or frequency, of your voice.

   You can vary the pitch of your voice voluntarily, as singers do. Tension, however, can also tighten your vocal cords and make your voice squeaky, grating, or harsh. To control the pitch of your voice, you need to relax the muscles that control your larynx. Before speaking, warm up by gently stretching your neck muscles, breathing deeply and calmly, and humming or singing to yourself.

3. After the air has passed your vocal cords, it enters your throat and mouth. Before leaving your mouth, the air resonates, or echoes, in your **nasal cavity** and **pharynx** (see the diagram on this page). The shape of these parts of your mouth gives your voice its personal **coloration**, the quality that distinguishes it from any other person's voice. Too much nasal resonance can make you sound as though you have a cold. Tense throat muscles can make your voice guttural, thin, or strident. Many unpleasant characteristics can be corrected by practice in relaxation and in reading aloud.

As you speak, you touch, or nearly touch, your tongue and other parts of your mouth together in order to form **consonants**. This list shows the parts of your mouth that produce each of these sounds:

lips only: b, m, p, w, wh
lips and teeth: f, v
tongue and hard palate: j, r, ch, sh, zh
tongue and soft palate: g, k, ng
tongue and gums: d, l, n, s, t, z
tongue and teeth: th
breath only: h

Unlike consonants, the **vowels** are produced by simply changing the shape of your mouth as you speak. The vowel sounds are represented by the letters *a, e, i, o,* and *u,* and by **diphthongs**, or pairs of letters, such as *au, oi,* and *ou.* American English has from thirteen to fifteen different vowel sounds. The way a person pronounces vowels shows which region of the country he or she comes from.

A speaker who has crisp, clear consonants and distinct vowels has good **articulation**. A speaker who pronounces words correctly, as well as clearly, has good **pronunciation**. Good articulation and pronunciation are characteristics of effective speakers. A good speaker also learns to vary the **pitch, loudness** (or volume), and **rate** (or speed) of his or her voice. Such vocal variety can make your speaking voice more attractive and will keep your listeners from becoming bored or irritated by its sameness.

Working with the Model

Each of the following groups of words will give you practice in articulating specific sounds. The first thirteen groups will help you practice consonants, and the last thirteen will help you practice vowels. As you read the words aloud, try to make each sound clear and distinct.

b/p	k/g	d/t	f/v	h
battle	cot	dame	few	ail
paddle	got	tame	view	hail
beat	hock	nod	strife	edge
peat	hog	not	strive	hedge
rib	kale	medal	fan	owe
rip	gale	metal	van	hoe
browse	hackle	daughter	fender	Euston
prows	haggle	totter	vendor	Houston

j/ch	l/r	m/n	ng/nk	s/z
junk	lack	mail	sinker	noose
chunk	rack	nail	singer	news
jaw	light	moon	hanker	cease
chaw	right	noon	hangar	seize
Jill	liver	doom	thinks	spice
chill	river	dune	things	spies
Madge	kneeler	dumber	pinging	conduce
match	nearer	dunner	pinking	contuse

sh/zh	t/th	w/wh
assure	threat	wail
adjure	thread	whale
azure	death	weigh
insure	debt	whey
injure	other	witch
issue	utter	which
censor	both	wile
censure	boat	while

ā	ă	ä	ē	ĕ
bait	bat	calm	breeze	den
cake	crack	cart	crease	fell
fail	flat	farther	lean	gem
hate	lap	father	niece	net
mail	pack	hot	peer	red
rake	rat	lock	reader	sell
tame	slap	stop	teach	speck
wave	track	wrought	wheel	tent

ī	ĭ	ō	ô	o͞o
bike	bit	bloat	bought	boom
dime	film	crow	cross	duke
height	kit	dough	horn	flew
line	knit	note	jaw	group
night	snip	slow	morgue	mule
style	split	soak	orb	rude
time	till	soak	stork	stew
vie	whip	though	talk	through
		throat		

o͝o	ûr	ŭ
bush	blurt	blood
could	further	enough
foot	germ	grunt
good	mercy	hut
nook	murder	pluck
pull	murmur	stub
rook	purge	thrush
wolf	turf	tough

A. Read each group of words aloud. As you pronounce each word, notice the shape of your mouth and the position of your tongue and teeth.

1. In the consonant practice, all the words in each group should be pronounced differently. What words, if any, in a given group did you pronounce the same? The letter or letters that appear before this group show which sounds you need to practice articulating. (For example, if you pronounced *death* and *debt* the same, you need to practice articulating the *th* sound.) Read aloud the words that gave you difficulty until you are able to articulate each consonant.

2. In the vowel practice, all the words in each group should have the same, or nearly the same, vowel sound. What words, if any, in a given group did you pronounce with a different vowel sound? The symbol before this group shows which vowel sound you need to practice. (For example, if the *o* in *hot* and the *a* in *father* sound very different, you are not pronouncing these words the way most public speakers do.) Look up the pronunciation of any problem words in a dictionary. Practice reading such words aloud until you are able to pronounce them correctly.

B. Read aloud the groups of words in the model to another student. Then listen carefully while the other student reads them to you.

1. What words, if any, were not clear to the person listening to you? Practice your pronunciation of those words.

2. What words, if any, were not clear when the other person read them aloud? Tell the person which words you had difficulty understanding and listen while he or she practices pronouncing them.

C. If possible, make a tape recording of yourself reading the groups of words in the model. Listen carefully to the recording.

1. In the consonant practice, which words, if any, sound alike? Practice articulating these words until you believe you are articulating them clearly. Then record the words again and listen to see whether they are clear.

2. In the vowel practice, which words, if any, sound different from the others in their group? Practice pronouncing these words correctly and then record them again. Listen to see whether the words in each group have the same vowel sound.

Guidelines

To make effective use of your voice, keep the following guidelines in mind.

Articulation and Pronunciation

1. Good articulation is the art of speaking so that every sound is clear and distinct. Articulation can be improved by:

   a. Moving your lips and tongue. Much indistinct articulation comes from lazy forming of sounds.
   b. Taking particular care in forming sounds at the beginning and ending of words.
   c. Rehearsing aloud. Tape record yourself and note any portions of your remarks that are difficult to understand.
   d. Watching for feedback from listeners that tells you they were not able to distinguish certain sounds.

2. Good pronunciation is achieved when the sounds that make up a word are uttered in a manner that meets the standards of the educated people in a community of which you are a part. Pronunciation can be improved by:

   a. Thoughtfully studying and analyzing the pronunciation of words by those around you, with particular attention to the way persons on radio and television pronounce words.

b. Looking up unfamiliar words and their pronunciations in a dictionary.
c. Making a list of words you have difficulty pronouncing and practicing saying them correctly, using a tape recorder. It will be helpful if you have a recording of each word pronounced correctly to compare with your pronunciation. You do not want to practice words incorrectly.

Rate and Pitch

1. The rate of speech is the number of syllables you speak per minute. Effective use of speaking rate can be achieved by:

   a. Striving to vary the rate with which you speak. While you are seeking variety, avoid speaking either so fast that your listeners cannot follow or so slowly that your audience becomes bored.
   b. Matching the variations in rate to the content of what you are saying.
   c. Practicing timely use of pauses to emphasize important points.

2. The pitch of your voice is the highness or lowness of the sounds you make based on the frequency of the vibration of your vocal cords. Effective use of pitch in speaking can be achieved by:

   a. Matching the pitch of your voice with the content of what you are saying. For example, you generally end a question by raising the pitch of your voice.
   b. Striving for variety in pitch to keep your voice lively and interesting. A monotone has no variation in pitch.
   c. Using variation in pitch as a means of providing emphasis.
   d. Supporting your voice with sufficient breath and remaining relaxed as you speak so that the general pitch of your voice is near its best, natural level.

Loudness

1. To speak effectively you need to control the volume or loudness of your voice so that it is appropriate for the setting and purpose of your speech. Effective control of loudness can be achieved by:

   a. Making sure that you are speaking loudly enough to be heard easily by all those you are addressing. Watch those with whom you are speaking for feedback that tells whether they are able to hear you.
   b. Using enough energy as you speak to form all the sounds clearly. Some of the breathing processes that help you achieve clear articulation help control loudness.
   c. Using sufficient variety in the degree of loudness to maintain interest and to match the content of what you are saying.
   d. Controlling the loudness of your voice by using the abdominal muscles to push air up out of your lungs. Keep your throat muscles relaxed and work with sufficient air in your lungs or your voice will become strained and the pitch will rise to an unpleasant level. You also risk the possible "loss" of your voice because of using improper techniques to speak loudly.

Preparing and Presenting

Choose a passage from a nonfiction book or article that you would like to read aloud. The passage should be 150 to 200 words long (about half a page). Practice reading this passage aloud, paying attention to the guidelines listed above.

First, practice the passage alone. Concentrate on reading the words with good articulation and correct pronunciation. After you have read the passage aloud two or three times, practice it in front of a mirror to see how your gestures and expressions will appear to your listeners.

If you have a tape recorder, you should record your reading of the passage. Listen carefully to the recording to see whether your articulation and pronunciation are as clear as they should be.

Next, work with another student and practice reading your passages to each other. At this stage you should concentrate on the quality, variety, and loudness of your voice as well as on your articulation and pronunciation.

Have the other person listen to your reading and try out any suggestions he or she makes on how to improve it. Also listen carefully to the other person's reading. Make any suggestion you think will make the reading more effective when he or she gives it before the class.

Finally, read in front of the class the passage you have chosen. Try to make it as clear and interesting as possible.

Evaluation Checklist

Ask the students in your class to evaluate your reading of the passage, following the standards described in the Guidelines section. They may use the Voice Evaluation Checklist below to evaluate your performance.

VOICE EVALUATION CHECKLIST				
Rating				
1. Articulation				
1 Poor	2	3	4	5 Excellent
2. Pronunciation				
1 Poor	2	3	4	5 Excellent
3. Rate				
1 Poor	2	3	4	5 Excellent
4. Pitch				
1 Poor	2	3	4	5 Excellent
5. Loudness				
1 Poor	2	3	4	5 Excellent

Using Your Body

When you speak, use your body to help clarify meaning and to provide emphasis. In old western movies a common line was "Smile when you say that, pardner." With these words, one cowboy was letting another know that as long as there was a smile, the words would be taken as friendly. A listener may often fail to understand the full intention of a speaker if words are not clarified by appropriate bodily actions. Your posture, movement, gestures, expressions, and eye contact all contribute to clarify and emphasize your message.

Bodily actions also promote interaction between speaker and listener. Although the messages of specific bodily actions vary from culture to culture, the actions themselves contribute to the closeness or distance that persons communicating feel. For example, many people believe that speaking with your arms crossed tightly across your chest—as opposed to relaxed by your side—reveals a defensive attitude. Thus, if you are speaking with someone whose arms are crossed, you might need to focus on communicating with open and warm gestures to encourage the listener to be more receptive to your message.

Bodily movement is especially important in providing the feedback that a speaker needs from a listener to help determine how what is being said is being interpreted. If your listener is staring blankly or quizzically, for example, you know you need to get his or her attention or to reword your last statement.

You should strive for bodily movement that is appropriate to the speaking situation. The movement you make should be suited to you as a person, to your subject, and to the occasion. You have seen individuals who tried to copy the motions of others as a means of making fun of them. The reason such acts are funny is often that these movements are clearly inappropriate for the person making them.

Movement is important in all kinds of speaking situations: conversations, discussions, interviews, public speaking, and performances. One of your tasks as a developing speaker is to learn to select the appropriate kinds of movement for different situations.

Working with the Model

The following pictures show various good and bad uses of bodily action in a communication setting. As you look at the pictures, think about how effective or ineffective the gesture, postures, and expressions are.

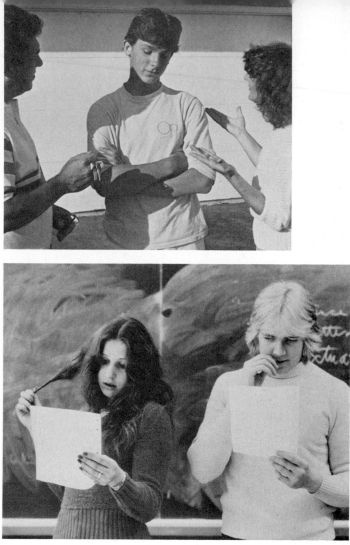

A. Think about the effective and ineffective uses of bodily action.

1. Which speakers use strong, smooth, or purposeful gestures and movements to enhance and clarify their communications? Which speakers are using distracting, awkward, or unpurposeful movements?

2. Which speakers use revealing facial expressions and good eye contact? Which speakers show blank or nervous facial expressions and little or no eye contact? How is this lack of eye contact likely to hinder their communication?

3. Which speakers illustrate relaxed, confident posture? How does this kind of posture help their communication? Which speakers illustrate poor, slouchy posture? How does this kind of posture detract from their communication?

4. Which speakers seem to be using bodily language that is suited to speaker, subject, and occasion? Which speakers seem to be using unsuitable bodily action?

5. In which speaking situations do you think the listener or audience is likely to be responding positively to the speaker's bodily movement? In which situations are the speakers likely to be getting feedback from the listener's or audience's bodily movements? In which speaking situations are the speakers likely to be unaware of or ignoring the feedback from the listener or audience?

B. With two or more other students, discuss the meaning being conveyed in each picture. Base your decisions on bodily actions and the setting. You will note that meanings of bodily movements are not as precise as those of words. Then think of alternate ways of communicating the same meaning.

C. Work with a small group of students. Extend what you decide is the subject, purpose, and attitude revealed by one of the pictures into a short, wordless skit. Pantomime your meaning with gestures, posture, facial expressions, etc., but use no words. The other students in the class should try to determine upon which picture you are basing your skit.

Guidelines

Use the following guidelines to make your body language more effective.

1. **Posture.** Your posture should be upright but not stiff. When standing, keep your head up and your shoulders back. Don't lean on the podium or table as you speak. When sitting, avoid slumping. It makes you appear to be uninterested and hurts your ability to produce effective sounds.
2. **Movement.** Move enough to show those with whom you are speaking that you are energetic but avoid purposeless pacing or fidgeting.
3. **Gestures.** Make your gestures purposeful, appropriate, smooth, and economical. Keep them related to what you are saying. Avoid stilted, artificial movements of hands and arms. Practice your speeches in front of a mirror.
4. **Expression.** Facial expressions, like gestures, can clarify meaning and provide emphasis. Dealing with a serious subject with a smile on your face or trying to suggest enthusiasm while your expression is blank sends a confusing message. Practicing before a mirror can help you analyze how well you match your expressions to your thoughts.
5. **Eye Contact.** As you speak with people, concentrate on how they are reacting to what you are saying. By looking for feedback from those with whom you are speaking, you will be able not only to judge their reactions but also to convince them of your interest.

Preparing and Presenting

Work with four to six other students. To begin with, engage in these exercises to make each of you more aware of the communicative power of movement. Take turns completing each of the following. No one should say any words as these activities are performed.

1. Pretend that you are looking for fleas on a frisky young kitten.
2. Play an imaginary game of ping pong with three others in your group. Have the other members of your group act as if they are watching the game.
3. Take turns within your group (a) feeling the texture of a piece of cloth, (b) picking up a frightened young bird, (c) feeling the falling rain, (d) experiencing the warmth of a camp fire during a chilly evening.

4. Walk as though you are (a) struggling to get through heavy snow, (b) moving through thick brush, (c) on a sidewalk covered with ice, (d) barefoot on a rocky beach.
5. Using only your face and general posture, but no gestures, take turns demonstrating that you feel (a) happy, (b) angry, (c) frightened, (d) ill, (e) amazed, (f) seasick.

When your group has completed these exercises, prepare the following for presentation to your class. Select music on record or tape that you will interpret through movement, gestures, and facial expressions. For example, you might select a passage from the *William Tell Overture* and act out a ride on a roller coaster, or use a 1950s rock number as background for an enactment of a group learning to ski. Your group's presentation should not last longer than four minutes.

After you have listened to the record or tape several times, plan the actions each of you will perform. Write a brief description of your plan. List the main ideas you will be trying to communicate. Under each main idea, list the major actions each of you will perform.

Practice the performance several times. Use your practice session to strengthen your interpretation. If a videotape recorder is available, make a tape of your performance in order to see it as the class will.

Evaluation Checklist

When each group has completed its presentation, the other members of the class should evaluate the group's performance on the basis of the following criteria. Rate the performance on a scale from 1 (Poor) to 5 (Excellent). Be prepared to give reasons for each rating you give. The questions in parentheses will help you do so.

Category	Rating
1. The major idea or set of ideas was clearly communicated by the group. (How do the responses of the class compare to your written description?)	
2. There were no movements distracting from the intended interpretation. (What might have been done instead of the distracting actions?)	
3. The group contributed to the intended meaning through the specific use of posture, facial expression, and arm and hand movement.	

Chapter 1 Review

Summary

The first important element of learning to be a good communicator is to understand yourself. Becoming aware of your interests and your attitudes toward yourself and others will help you evaluate your communication skills.

The second element is your mind. You can improve your thinking skills by strengthening your imagination; by sharpening your senses of sight, hearing, touch, smell, and taste; and by understanding how your experiences influence the knowledge you acquire.

The third element is language. You need to use language that is appropriate to the situation and the idea you are trying to express. Transition words can make clear the relation of one idea to the one that came before and the one that follows. Figures of speech make your ideas vivid to your listeners.

The fourth element is your voice. Strive to articulate clearly and pronounce words correctly. Also vary the rate, pitch, and loudness of your speech to make your voice more interesting and attractive.

The fifth element is your body. Appropriate posture, facial expression, and bodily movement enhance and emphasize your speaking.

Reviewing Vocabulary

Number your paper from 1 to 18. Next to each number, write the letter of the group of words that correctly defines the words.

1. denotation
2. personification
3. transitions
4. rate
5. feedback
6. gesture
7. diaphragm
8. trachea
9. eye contact
10. analogy
11. cliché
12. loudness
13. expression
14. simile
15. connotation
16. interference
17. larynx
18. message

a. a powerful curved muscle separating the chest and the abdominal cavity
b. the use of hands, face, body, and voice to enhance one's speech
c. anything that interrupts or alters the message between a speaker and a listener
d. the volume of a sound
e. facial expression used to clarify meaning and provide emphasis
f. an extended comparison between two things ordinarily considered unlike
g. a trite phrase
h. the speed of speech
i. response from listeners
j. words or phrases that connect ideas
k. a comparison of two things using *like* or *as*
l. the voice box
m. what a speaker conveys to a listener
n. the dictionary definition of a word
o. a type of metaphor in which an object is given human qualities
p. direct visual contact with listeners
q. the windpipe
r. what a word suggests because of its associations

Reviewing Facts and Ideas

1. How does a self-evaluation of your speaking skills help you become a better communicator?

2. What is feedback? Why is it important for a speaker to look for it?
3. How can strengthening imagination improve thinking skills?
4. How can sharpening senses aid thinking skills?
5. When you communicate with others, why is it important to consider their background? In what ways do past experiences contribute to our present perceptions?
6. What is articulation? How can you improve your articulation?
7. What is pronunciation? What are ways you can improve your pronunciation?
8. Give two reasons why you should vary the rate, pitch, and loudness of your speech.
9. How do posture, movement, and gestures enhance your speech?
10. How do facial expressions and eye contact enhance your speech?

Discussing Facts and Ideas

1. Discuss the way in which the various speech elements—attitudes and thought, language, voice, bodily action—interact in communication. For example, talk about ways in which gestures can contradict the meaning of words as well as support them. Consider how a tone of voice can affect the interpretation of the message.
2. Think about speaking experiences you have had. Remember that speaking and listening are not limited to addressing an audience but include many informal situations, such as conversations. Which speech elements do you feel you use most confidently? Which pose the most problems for you?
3. English is not the native language of many people in the United States. At the library, look up the extent of differences in language throughout different parts of the country. Discuss what barriers or challenges these language differences create for speakers and listeners. Some people have proposed that these barriers should be overcome by legislating English as the official language of the nation. Discuss the advantages and disadvantages of such a proposal.

Applying Your Knowledge

1. Watch a live or taped version of a television talk show. As an alternative, make a videotape that includes several televised interviews of athletes. After you have viewed approximately 15 minutes of the program, analyze the speaking and listening you observed. Discuss how well each of the speakers used each of the speech elements—thought and attitude, language, voice, bodily action. Which elements seemed to cause the most problems? Which were used most effectively?
2. Work with another student in your class. Introduce him or her to the class. As you plan your introduction, ask the other student to complete the following phrases as a way of helping you become acquainted.

> I always . . . .
> I like . . . .
> I am happiest when . . . .
> I would never . . . .
> People turn me off when they . . . .
> If I only had a year to live, I would . . . .

Your classmates may want to add to the list of phrases or delete some. Use your partner's answers in your introduction. After a series of students have been introduced, check on listening skills by recalling what you can about the students who have been introduced so far.

Analyzing Your Career Interests

Whether you enter the job market now or later, you need to decide what career would best suit your abilities and interests and which careers offer the best future. Answering the following questions can help you plan your career.

School

- Which subjects do I enjoy most? Which ones do I like least? Which ones inspire me to do work on my own?
- In which subjects do I get the best grades? Which require the most work? Which do I find easiest? Which are hardest?

Experience

- If I have had jobs, what did I like most and least about them?

Preferences

- What work activities interest me most?
- Do I prefer being indoors or outdoors?
- Do I prefer working with people, things, or ideas?
- Do I prefer working independently or as part of a group?
- Do I prefer working in a highly structured environment or under changeable conditions?
- Would I prefer to live in the city, in a town, or in the country?
- What kinds of activities or situations do I dislike most?
- How well do I respond to authority? Would I want to have authority over others, or want others to have authority over me?

Goals

- In what financial or social position will I be most happy?
- How much financial security do I need? Would I be willing to take risks in order to achieve my financial goals?

Activity

1. Answer each of the preceding questions. After thinking about your answers, write a brief summary of your talents, interests, and goals. Write down at least one possible career that would suit you.

Reporting an Incident

One of the most important skills in giving an accurate report of an incident to the police, insurance investigators, or other authorities is the ability to understand and communicate cause-and-effect relationships. To begin with, the person giving the report must be able to distinguish causes from effects. Moreover, this person must also be aware that:

- causes precede effects.
- not all the events that preceded an incident helped cause it.
- more than one cause can contribute to an effect.
- if there are several causes, they may not contribute equally to an effect.

The best way to arrive at correct cause-and-effect explanations is to intelligently and persistently question yourself and others who witnessed the incident.

Activities

1. A person involved in a traffic accident often is called upon to explain why the accident occurred. As a citizen you may be concerned with other kinds of incidents, such as vandalism or arson, in which the authorities must search for a cause or explanation. Make a list of the types of incidents in which citizens may be asked to provide cause-and-effect explanations. Search newspapers and magazines to find one example of each of the kinds of incidents on your list. Bring your examples to class and discuss the possible cause-and-effect explanation of each incident. If the newspaper or magazine article reveals the cause of the incident, discuss the consequences for the people involved if this cause is reported inaccurately to the authorities or insurance investigators.
2. Talk with a police officer about traffic accidents. For each accident you discuss, ask the officer to distinguish causes (speeding, negligence, drunk driving) from effects (injured drivers, damaged vehicles).
3. Search the newspapers for examples of faulty reasoning from cause to effect. (For example: "Coach Pinson wore the same shirt for ten days while the Mariners were on their winning streak.") Bring in three examples to discuss with the class.

Communicating with Others

After working through this chapter, you should be proficient at the following skills:

Lesson	Skills
Lesson 1	• recognizing the causes of conflict • communicating in order to resolve conflict
Lesson 2	• preparing for interviews
Lesson 3	• preparing interview questions
Lesson 4	• conducting interviews
Communicating on the Job	• making an oral inquiry about a job
Communicating as a Citizen	• interviewing candidates and public officials

Communicating to Resolve a Conflict

Not every conversation is a pleasant or friendly experience. A conversation may end in an argument or conflict among the people involved. Or a conflict may grow over a period of days or weeks before it finally breaks out into an open disagreement. Most conflicts result from imperfect communication. They can often be resolved through communication as well.

The following six causes are probably the most common sources of conflict among friends and acquaintances:

1. **Prejudice.** A prejudiced person assumes that everyone having a particular age, background, appearance, or accent will think and act in the same way. Once prejudiced people make up their minds, they may not bother to find out the truth.

2. **Lack of information.** A conflict may develop because a person knows only part of the truth but assumes that he or she knows everything. People who listen to rumors, for example, often act on inadequate information. They may misinterpret the actions of others because they did not check the facts.

3. **Verbal confusion.** Although it seems trivial, many people quarrel because they attach different meanings to the same word. For example, Gloria may tell Ron that his manners are extremely "gracious." Gloria means this as a compliment, but Ron, to whom "gracious" implies "phony," is offended.

4. **Different values.** Even when people share the same ideas of right and wrong, they may not perceive a problem in the same way. To one person, for example, conserving energy may be a serious principle of her life; to her friend, it may be a very minor concern. People who do not understand one another's values may find themselves in conflict when they did not expect it.

5. **Misplaced emotions.** Some people may quarrel, not with those who have made them unhappy, but with those who are most convenient. For example, a person with a headache may snap at a friend who asks him how he feels. Such an emotional reaction is unfair to the victim and does not affect the barking dog, which caused the headache in the first place.

6. **Desire to dominate.** Often, a conflict will continue because neither of the people involved will admit that he or she was wrong. Some people insist on having the last word in an argument. Others always insist on giving orders and will never take them. Many people feel that compromising means losing their dignity.

As you can see, most of the conflicts described could have been prevented if people were more willing to communicate their ideas, emotions, and interests to one another. Sometimes shyness keeps people from communicating, and at other times pride. The most important person in resolving a conflict is often a **mediator**—someone who knows both or all the people involved, and who can see both sides of the dispute. A mediator can encourage people to discuss their true feelings and can separate the important issues from the trivial ones. However, even a skillful and sensitive mediator can do little unless the people involved are willing to resolve their conflict.

Working with the Model

The following scene shows a kind of conflict that you have probably encountered at school or in your neighborhood. As you read the scene, put yourself in the place of each of the characters and try to understand the way he feels.

(Scene: the school yard at lunchtime. Hugh is just finishing a sandwich as Ken and Ervin walk by.)

Ken: Hi, Hugh!

Hugh: *(Mumbling)* H'lo, Ken. *(He walks away rapidly.)*

Ervin: I know that guy, don't I?

Ken: Sure, that's Hugh Lonsdale, a good buddy of mine. You must have seen him at basketball practice.

Ervin: Yeah, well, he didn't look too glad to see me.

Ken: Oh, I think he's not feeling too good; he hurt his knee in a game last semester—

Ervin: I've seen that look around this school before. That's the old "You-transfer-guys-from-East-High-can-drop-dead" look.

Ken: Oh, no, Erv, I'm sure Hugh doesn't feel that way. I'll bet you two would really get along. You have a lot in common, you're going to be on the team—

Ervin: Forget it.

Ken: *(Seeing Hugh)* There's Hugh . . . I'm going to get him over here. *(Shouting)* Hey, Hugh!

Ervin: So long.

Ken: No, wait . . . *(Shouting)* Hey, Hugh! *(To Ervin)* Please wait, Erv, I just want to introduce you—

Ervin: No way, man. I know where I'm not wanted. *(He goes.)*

Hugh: *(Coming up)* Well, your friend didn't last long, did he?

Ken: Listen, Hugh, I just wish you could get to know him—

Hugh: Him? You're nuts! I wouldn't even shake hands with that guy. I'd be afraid he'd steal my watch.

Ken: What do you mean?

Hugh: Those guys from East High are all thieves. They steal anything that isn't nailed down.

Ken: You don't know what you're talking about.

Hugh: Don't I? What about those thefts from the lockers last week? What about all the money that was taken?

Ken: Thefts? I only heard of one: Susan Spielman lost a book.

Hugh: I heard they took her purse with twenty dollars in it. I heard there were four or five other cases, but someone's hushing them up so we won't come down hard on those East High bums.

Ken: But Erv's no thief, he's a really nice guy—and he's never harmed you. Come on, Hugh, what's really eating you? Is your knee still giving you trouble?

Hugh: Yeah, it hurts whenever I play. Instead of being on the team, I'll be shooting baskets in the back yard.

Ken: I'm awfully sorry to hear that, Hugh. But that's no reason to be mad at Erv—just because he'll be on the team and you won't.

Hugh: It makes no difference. I just don't want to associate with people like that.

Ken: People like *what*, Hugh? If you could just get to know some of the students from East High . . . . Listen, Coach Wolf has been giving out passes to the Marauders game tomorrow night. Why don't you come? We could go have a pizza afterwards.

Hugh: Is that friend of yours going to be there?

Ken: Erv? Yes, but you don't have to sit next to him. Just be civil—

Hugh: Listen, if this Ervin and his bunch want to be accepted, they should make the first move. Let *them* come to *us*. It's our school, after all.

Ken: Hugh, we're talking about *people*—people who have their pride, too. How do you think they feel, being cold-shouldered like this?

Hugh: *(Going)* Let 'em come to us. That's all I say.

Ken: Will you go to the game?

Hugh: I don't know . . . maybe. I'll think about it and give you a call.

Ken: You won't regret it. . . . See you later, Hugh.

A. Think about the different sources of conflict in this scene.
   1. Find two examples of prejudice on the part of different people.
   2. Find an example of a conflict caused by lack of information.
   3. Find an example of misplaced emotions.
   4. Find at least one example of a person who wants to dominate others or have the last word.
B. Think about the people involved in this scene.
   1. Which person does the most to cause the conflict? Which person does the least? Explain your answer.
   2. What steps does Ken take to try to resolve the conflict? How well do his actions seem to be based on his understanding of Ervin and Hugh? What actions, if any, seem to be miscalculated?
   3. In what way is this conflict caused by a failure in communication? How do you think the conflict could have been prevented in the first place?
   4. Do you think Ken's efforts to bring Ervin and Hugh together will be successful? Explain your answer.
   5. How do you think this conflict could be resolved?

Guidelines

The following steps are the most important ones in resolving a conflict.

1. **Establish communication.** Nothing can happen if people are not speaking to one another. They must be willing to talk about their differences without fighting. A mediator can persuade people to get together and talk in a pleasant, neutral setting.

2. **Exchange information.** Often, a conflict will exist because people have been misled by rumors or half-truths. A basic step toward resolution is to talk about the facts of the case. Sometimes a problem will disappear once the truth becomes known.

3. **Try to understand others.** People who want to resolve a conflict must understand one another's emotions and point of view. They must be willing to listen to another person's story. They should make an effort to be sympathetic.

4. **Define your terms.** When a conflict results from verbal confusion, it is important for people to explain exactly what they meant. In such cases, understanding why the words were misinterpreted will usually eliminate the problem.

5. **Define your values.** People cannot be reconciled unless each of them understands the other's principles, beliefs, and priorities. Explaining these may not always convert one person to the other's opinion. However, people who disagree on questions of values can still respect one another's integrity.

6. **Get to the root of the problem.** A conflict may arise because of a person's prejudice, an emotional problem, or a deep-seated resentment. Unless these causes come into the open, the conflict may continue unresolved.

7. **Find common ground.** When the people in a conflict have discussed their feelings, values, and points of view, they should be able to agree on important issues. If they belong to the same family, attend the same school, or work for the same company, they should

have many goals, values, and problems in common. Agreement on these qualities can become the basis for resolving the conflict.

8. **Be willing to compromise.** If they truly want to resolve a conflict, both or all the parties must be willing to give up something they want. This does not necessarily mean compromising their principles. It does mean conceding that they may have been mistaken or misinformed, or that other points of view may also be worthwhile.

Preparing and Presenting

Work with two other students. Think about the conflict that was presented in the Model section of this lesson. Think about ways in which that conflict could be resolved through better communication. With the other students, write a script in which Ken, Ervin, and Hugh solve their differences. In your script, try to use as many of the rules for resolving conflicts as you can.

When the script is complete, rehearse it in a group, with each of you taking one of the three roles. As you rehearse the script, you may wish to rewrite it in order to make the characters and the conflict more convincing. When the script is finished, act it out before the class.

Evaluation Checklist

Ask the other students in your class to evaluate your script for resolving the conflict on the basis of the following criteria. Rate each script on a scale from 1 (Poor) to 5 (Excellent). Be prepared to give reasons for each answer you give.

Category	Rating
1. The script illustrates several methods of resolving a conflict.	
2. The characters and the conflict are realistic and convincing.	
3. The resolution of the conflict, in light of the personalities involved, is likely.	

If other groups of students have written scripts for resolving the conflict, listen to them and compare them with your own.

Preparing for Interviews

Good interviews do not happen by accident. They are the result of careful planning by interviewers who have researched their subjects and have foreseen the possible difficulties. First, think about the purpose of your interview. Are you trying to gather information for some writing or speaking you will do later? Are you seeking a job from the person or an endorsement for something you want to do? You should make firm arrangements for the time, place, and setting of the interview. These should be convenient for you and the interviewee. Confirm arrangements the day before the interview.

Make sure you are informed on the topic of the interview. For example, learn any specialized vocabulary needed to talk about the subject. Seek current information and be aware of controversies that may surround the topic.

Examine your own attitude toward the interviewee and the topic you will be talking about. Before you interview a person, learn as much about him or her as possible. Such background information will save time during the interview and enable you to ask questions that will lead to more interesting answers. There are many sources of information. If the person you are interviewing is well known, check the *Readers' Guide to Periodical Literature* for magazine articles about him or her. If the person is an author, you may be able to find an autobiography in *Contemporary Authors*. Scientists are listed in *American Men and Women of Science*. There are specific reference books for men and women in sports, business, politics, religion and other professions. Your librarian should be able to help you.

If the person you are interviewing is known only in your community, there may be information available through checking in the index to your local newspaper or by questioning people familiar with life in your city or region. You may wish to write or phone the interviewee in advance and ask for a brief biographical sketch to help you in preparing questions.

You should plan your opening remarks in advance. These should include a statement of the purpose of the interview and your first question or questions.

Finally, make the necessary arrangements for recording the conversation. This includes agreeing with the interviewee as to how information will be recorded. Two possible ways you can record a person's responses during an interview are (1) written notes and (2) tape recording. Each method has advantages and disadvantages.

Written notes are easy to refer to after the interview is over. You can rewrite and reorganize them before you turn the interview into a paper

or article. A convenient way to take written notes is to write your interview questions in advance on separate index cards or separate pages of a notebook. As you ask each question, record the response underneath it. The disadvantage of written notes is that you must write down each response before you can ask the next question. This slows down the interview, and you may lose some information unless you write rapidly. If you take written notes, be sure to reread and clarify them while the interview is fresh in your mind. Once your notes are "cold," you may not be able to decipher them.

Tape recording is usually more convenient for the interviewer and the interviewee and lets you record a person's exact words. Some people, however, are made nervous by tape recorders. Be sure to have the interviewee's permission before using one. Make sure that any special equipment to be used is in working order. Remember also to bring enough tape and spare batteries. The disadvantage of tape-recorded responses is that they must be transcribed, and it is difficult to find a specific question and response without advancing and rewinding the tape many times.

Working with the Model

Kris is going to interview a columnist from a local newspaper. To prepare for the interview, she has completed the items on a pre-interview checklist.

PREINTERVIEW CHECKLIST

Person to be interviewed: Ed Rosenberg
Purpose of interview: To learn about his series of exposés of waste and inefficiency in city government

____ 1. **Confirm arrangements with interviewee.**
   In response to my letter, Ed Rosenberg has agreed to be interviewed in his office at the *Times* on Saturday, July 5, from 11:00 A.M. until noon. If necessary, he says, we can continue over lunch. The day before the interview, I'll confirm.

____ 2. **Arrange interview setting.**
   We can speak in Ed's office.

____ 3. **Become informed on interview topic.**
   Vocabulary: I've researched the city agencies Ed writes about: Public Works Board, Harbor Commission, Foothill Water District Board, and others. I've read his articles carefully for three months. I have also discussed Ed's series with my Civics teacher, who gave me useful information.
   Current information: Ed's continuing exposé of the Water District is being covered in several newspapers, and I've read other articles as well as his columns.
   Controversies: Editorials in the *Mirror* have called Ed irresponsible—get his reaction on this.

____ 4. **Examine own attitudes toward topic and person.**
   Ed Rosenberg is one of my heroes, so I'll have to make an effort to ask him tough questions about his use of evidence.

____ 5. **Prepare opening remarks for interview.**
   After reminding Ed of the purpose of my interview, I'll ask him, "How did you first become aware of the problem of waste in the city government?"

____ 6. **Plan how to record interview.**
   Ed has given me permission to tape-record the interview. This will enable me to ask follow-up questions if Ed makes an interesting remark on a subject I had not covered in my prepared questions. Also, I will have a record of Ed's exact words—important when writing about such a complicated subject. (Memo: Buy new batteries, three 60-minute cassettes.)

A. Think about Kris' preinterview checklist.
   1. What is the purpose of the interview?
   2. How will each item that Kris has checked off help her to achieve that purpose?
   3. Name at least two other purposes for which Kris might have wanted to interview Ed Rosenberg.
   4. Suppose that Kris had wanted to interview Ed Rosenberg about journalism careers for young people. Which parts of her checklist would she have had to change? Which parts would remain the same?
B. Read an interview in a newspaper or magazine or listen to an interview on radio or television.
   1. What was the purpose of the interview? If the purpose was not clear, do you think this was the interviewer's fault?
   2. How well prepared was the interviewer? Find at least five things about the interview that show how much (or how little) preparation the interviewer had done.

Guidelines

Making a preinterview checklist should enable you to arrive for an interview well prepared. It should allow you to speak in comfortable surroundings, without interruption, for as long as is necessary. You should be able to ask intelligent questions and record the interviewee's responses easily and accurately.

A preinterview checklist should include the following items. It may not always be possible to do everything listed under each step. However, you should go through every step in order, to be sure you have not forgotten anything important.

PREINTERVIEW CHECKLIST

Person to be interviewed: _____

Purpose of interview: _____

Think about the different purposes you might have. You might want to obtain information about the person and topic in order to prepare an article or paper. You might want information that will help you make a major decision—for example, what courses to take in order to prepare for a career. Also consider the interviewee's purpose in speaking to you. The person may want to share important information about new developments in science, business, or government. Or the person may want to publicize a project, film, or book. Both of you should agree on what the purpose of the interview will be.

____ **1. Confirm arrangements.**
Prepare a letter introducing yourself and giving the purpose of the interview. Specify the best time and place for you but accept any arrangement the interviewee prefers.

____ **2. Arrange interview setting.**
Decide what would be the ideal setting. Be sure that you will be free from interruptions and distractions. If the interviewee's home or office would not be suitable, be prepared to suggest an alternative setting.

____ **3. Become informed.**
Decide what books and magazines you would read and what people you would talk to in order to learn about the topic and the interviewee. List special vocabulary words you should understand and look up these words. Also list one or two sources of current information on the topic, and at least one controversy connected with it.

____ **4. Examine attitudes.**
List both your positive and negative attitudes toward the person and the topic. List the difficulties these attitudes might create. Describe ways you could overcome these difficulties.

____ **5. Prepare opening remarks.**
Write out opening remarks, including the first question or questions you will ask. Be sure to remind the person of the purpose of the interview.

____ **6. Plan how to record interview.**
Decide whether you will write down or tape-record responses (see pages 55–56). List materials you will need. Describe how you will get the interviewee's permission if you use a tape recorder.

Preparing and Presenting

Working with another student, select a celebrity, politician, scientist, author, or other well-known person you would both like to interview. Then, working independently, prepare preinterview checklists. Follow the checklist form given in the Guidelines section of this lesson. Complete every step on the checklist that you can do without actually contacting the interviewee. Be sure to do research on the person and topic of your planned interview. As you complete each step, check off that item on your list. Type your checklist or write it neatly. Exchange checklists with the other student.

Evaluation Checklist

As you read each other's checklists, evaluate them on the basis of the following criteria. Rate them on a scale from 1 (Poor) to 5 (Excellent). Be prepared to give reasons for each rating you give. The questions in parentheses will help you do so.

Category	Rating
The interviewer . . . 1. Made the purpose of the interview specific and clear (How could it be made more clear?)	
2. Listed steps that were closely related to the purpose of the interview (In what ways could each step do more to achieve the purpose of the interview?)	
3. Listed steps that were *practical*, i.e., that he or she would have the time, influence, or sources of information to complete	
4. Listed steps that were *appropriate* for the interview	
5. Set up conditions under which the person would likely be willing to be interviewed	

Preparing Interview Questions

Writing effective questions is the most important part of preparing for an interview. Good questions will help you obtain interesting, informative responses. Weak questions will lead to dull, confusing, uninformative responses. Try to avoid asking questions that can be simply answered *yes* or *no*. Ask for specific information in your questions. One way to get this information is by preparing questions that begin with *who, what, where, when, how,* or *why.*

You should be prepared to ask **follow-up questions**. One kind of follow-up question can be asked when the interviewee gives you an unexpected piece of information. You should follow up the person's response by asking for further information on the subject, even though it is not covered in your prepared questions.

A second kind of follow-up question should be asked when the interviewee has used a term or name with which you are not familiar. Ask for a brief explanation before you continue with your prepared questions.

When you have finished asking a series of related questions, summarize the interviewee's responses before you go on to the next group. Such a summary will enable the person to correct any misunderstanding you may have about his or her responses.

Working with the Model

Professional interviewer Larry Wilde conducted the following interview with Woody Allen in the late 1960s (this was before Allen's career as a movie director). As you read the interview, think about the interviewer's purpose and the way his questions help achieve that purpose.

Wilde: Woody, what made you stop writing for other comedians and become one yourself?

Allen: Writing for other comedians as a lifetime pursuit is a blind alley. I never had any intention of continuing writing for other comedians before I started performing. At that time, I was just writing for them to earn a living. And I was interested in writing for the theatre, which I'm still interested in doing. But then I got interested in performing. It occurred to me it might be a good avenue of expression. So I decided to try it. But there is no future in being a TV writer. You can hack around from show to show and you're always worried—is the comedian you're writing for going to be dropped because of bad ratings? And if he is dropped you may find yourself moving three thousand miles to the other coast to write for a new comedian. It's a rough business.

Wilde: When you began creating material for your act, did you first decide what your image was and then begin to write?

Allen: No. There was never any sense of image. I still don't have any sense of that at all. I just wrote what I thought was funny and wanted to perform it. I found after a year or two of performing some sort of image formed itself. The critics and the people would come away and agree on certain images they had of me . . . certain aspects. . . . I think the worst thing I could do would be to believe the images of me I read in the newspapers.

Wilde: Then you're simply doing what you feel is the right thing for you?

Allen: Yeah, whatever I feel is funny, I do, no matter what it is, without any regard to the subject matter, and if an image emerges, fine!

Wilde: Is it easier to write jokes for yourself than it was for the other comedians?

Allen: It has different problems. Other comedians are much less selective. I would write jokes for ten other comedians and they would use eight out of ten, finally, in putting together their acts . . . and it would work. I find I'm much more cowardly. I use like one out of ten jokes. I'm much more selective with my own material. I pamper myself more.

Wilde: You write ten jokes and only choose one. After a while what percentage of the jokes work for you?

Allen: What finally remains in my act is really a very, very small percentage of what I come up with. When I write a piece of material . . . something occurs to me at some point, an idea, a notion that I think would be funny or something that actually happened to me and I try and develop a long story on it with as many laughs coming as close together as possible. I find after I'm finished I have a lot of jokes, a lot of remarks to make—comments—and as I look at them I find ninety percent of them don't meet the standards I would like to present publicly to an audience. Then I condense what was a twenty-minute thing to six minutes and I go out and do it, and I find my judgment was wrong on part of it. The audience is not laughing at some parts where I thought they would laugh. They're laughing at things I couldn't imagine they would laugh at, so I adjust it further and it comes down to four minutes, and gradually it's honed down. So in order to get a half hour act it takes me a long time, and I have to write a lot of material.

Wilde: How do you go about writing a piece of material for yourself?

Allen: There are two ways I have of working. One is spontaneously, where during my daily activities funny things occur to me. Ideas for jokes, premises. I write them down.

Wilde: Excuse me, what do you mean by a "premise"?

Allen: A premise would be like: If I was caught in an elevator during the blackout, trying to move a piano by myself. Now, that's not good for one joke. I found that that would lead me to a whole funny story of how I decided to move from one apartment to another in the same building . . . why I decided to move, what was wrong with the first apartment, how I looked for the second apartment, why I didn't have moving men do it because I wanted to do it myself, and finally the hard work of doing it. Trying to lift the piano and getting into a little elevator with it . . . trying to hold it up for the minute it takes to go up to the twentieth floor, and then the blackout comes and I'm stuck for six hours trying to hold the piano up. I find each step of the way should be told with as strong a joke as possible.

Wilde: Then by "premise" you mean a story that has a beginning, a middle, and an end?

Allen: Exactly. That idea which gives you a plot line to talk about for an extended length of time.

Wilde: And allows you to hang jokes or laughs on.

Allen: Right. As opposed to a single joke that would occur to me.

Wilde: I didn't mean to interrupt you. Then what do you do?

Allen: That's all right. So these premises or single jokes occur to me. I could be walking down the street or shaving, and I write them down on anything handy, like matchbooks or napkins, and I throw them in a drawer at home. Then when the time comes that I've got to get new material for appearances, I take them and lay them out in the room and I see which jokes are worth going for. I then combine those with the ones I write by mechanical process. That is, sitting down, without notes—just knowing that in three nights I'm going to appear . . . and I've got to prefabricate a piece of material.

Wilde: Since it takes a certain amount of time to break in jokes or lines, or a premise, would you take a chance on a major TV program with material you had just written two or three days before?

Allen: I wouldn't want to and try to avoid it as much as possible. Sometimes it's unavoidable, and sometimes I have gone on television with things I have never edited or done anyplace before. I find it's not as good as things I've done before but that's because . . . say a routine I want to do consists of twenty laughs, and if I do it in a club, I find there's really only sixteen laughs and finally four laughs are knocked out because they consistently don't work. The bit becomes tight and has a lot of punch . . . but if I do that routine on television first and I discover there are four weak spots, it's been seen by everybody. It's too late, and those four weak spots considerably weaken the whole thing.

Wilde: Do you try out new jokes on friends or anybody who will listen, as some comedians do?

Allen: Not really, because I find it doesn't mean anything. It can only be discouraging.

Wilde: You wait until you get in front of an audience?

Allen: Yeah, that's really where it counts. And not these late second-show spots where a lot of performers feel they should try out a new piece of material because if it doesn't go over they won't get hurt very much. The best thing to do is to come right out and lead with your best. Your Saturday night full-house show is the perfect opportunity, because the conditions are right and the new material stands a better chance. You're asking for trouble by breaking in material under any conditions that are not the best. If you tell it to friends, it's very depressing. They'll say, ''Yes, this joke is very funny, but that one doesn't thrill me too much.'' There's no point in hearing that from one or two people. It's better to do the joke before two hundred people. If someone says that joke isn't so great, I get very shaky and I might not try it on the floor.

Wilde: How do you go about creating a joke? The actual process?

Allen: That's very hard to answer. It depends on circumstances. When you do it, say when you're hired to write for Sid Caesar, there's a lot of different ways of doing it than you'd do it for yourself.

Wilde: How about just for yourself?

Allen: It's very, very intangible, really. Suppose I'm going to write the story about trying to move the piano. I try to take it right from the top. As far back as I can go. For instance, the first thought that occurs to you is getting stuck with the piano, and then I start retracing this backwards. Why am I moving myself? Because I don't want to spend the money on moving men. Why do I want to move? Because I don't like my apartment and I always have trouble with apartments. Why do I always have trouble with them? What other apartments have I lived in? What was my apartment in Brooklyn like? Why was it poor? Because my parents couldn't afford very much rent. What did my parents do for a living? I find this can go back and back forever. So I might start with the business about the piano by saying my mother married my father because he was a cabdriver and finally through a lot of stories of how she met him and how they moved to Brooklyn and how they got their apartment and by a lot of circuitous talk, a lot of jokes hopefully, I finally get up to the part of the piano.

Wilde: Someone taking a course in journalism or creative writing or how to write a novel can learn certain basic methods and techniques. Are there also rules for creating jokes?

Allen: I don't think you can learn to write jokes. Not good ones. You can learn certain mechanical things—to create variations of other jokes written, even good variations, but it's nothing you can learn. It's purely inborn.

Wilde: Are there different kinds of jokes?

Allen: I don't know what you mean by that.

Wilde: Well, some jokes are two or three sentences, others last for five or six sentences. They have names.

Allen: There are names that drift around, like a "one-liner" or an "ad-lib," but that's no advantage or help to you when you're writing material. . . . You can't learn how to write funny things . . . how to write individual jokes.

Wilde: Then it depends on the individual mind seeing a specific incident and seeing it humorously and expressing the humor he sees in words?

Allen: Yes. That's what is so tricky about it. Given an absolutely straight sentence, with no punch line to it whatsoever, you can have twenty people read the sentence, and Jonathan Winters reads it or W. C. Fields—it's just going to be funny without changing a word, for some intangible, built-in thing that's beyond reason. You see, it's not the jokes. . . . It isn't the jokes that do it, and the comedian has nothing to do with the jokes. It's the individual himself.

A. Think about the purpose of the interview you have just read.
 1. How would you state the purpose of the interview?
 2. Which questions show the purpose of the interview most clearly?
 3. Write three other questions that could have been asked to help achieve the purpose of the interview.
 4. Suppose Wilde had never interviewed a comedian before. What might the purpose of his interview have been? Which questions do you think he would have asked? What additional questions do you think he would have asked?
 5. Suppose this interview had been conducted in 1981, after Allen had directed several successful movies. What do you think might have been the purpose of the interview then? Write at least three questions that would help achieve that purpose.

B. Think about the interviewer's questions.
 1. Of the twenty questions the interviewer asked, how many appear to have been prepared in advance? How many are follow-up questions?
 2. Identify two follow-up questions based on information that the interviewer had not expected to hear. Why do you think he asked each of these questions?
 3. Identify two follow-up questions in which the interviewer is asking for clarification. At what other places in the interview do you think he might have asked for clarification?
 4. Find the two places in the interview where Wilde says, "Excuse me" or apologizes. Why would it be a good idea to say such things while asking follow-up questions?
 5. Write at least two further follow-up questions that might have been asked in this interview.

Guidelines

Good interview questions encourage good responses from the person you are speaking with. The following table shows seven differences between good questions and poor questions.

A good question . . .	A poor question . . .
• encourages an extended answer • is stated concisely	• can be answered "Yes" or "No" • takes so long that the interviewee loses track of the question
• is based on a sound knowledge of the topic • encourages a specific, informative answer • makes the interviewee think before answering • shows an original or unusual perspective on the topic	• reveals the interviewer's lack of preparation • encourages a vague, rambling answer • permits a glib, unthinking answer • is obvious and has probably been asked dozens of times by other interviewers
• builds on preceding responses	• is asked because it was next on the list, even if it is inappropriate

Activity

1. The following interview contains four poor questions. Read the interview and then decide which characteristic of good questions in the above table each question fails to meet.

Sportscaster: Great game! Has the team ever played better?

Coach Jones: Nope.

Sportscaster: I don't suppose you've had a season like this since you won the pennant in 1976. Do you feel as great this year as you did then?

Coach Jones: Well, actually . . . we lost the pennant in '76.

Sportscaster: I think that must really be something, I mean, having players you can be so proud of. . . . I wonder if Chuck Woodbridge will make it off the bench this season. . . . And didn't Ed Murphy play well despite injuries? Aren't you proud, you know, a 14-2 season . . . ?

Coach Jones: I didn't get all of your questions. . . . Did you say Ed? Yeah, he played well, but who did you say I was keeping on the bench? Rick?

Sportscaster: Chuck . . . oh, never mind, I have a few more questions here . . . um, do you think the team can go all the way to the pennant?

Coach Jones: Sure, why not?

Preparing and Presenting

Working with another student, decide on a person you would both like to interview. The person may be famous, such as a politician, entertainer, or sports figure. Or the person may be well known only within a given field, such as science or business. In either case, the person's achievements should be interesting enough to justify an interview. Research the person to gather material for an interview. You should each decide on the purpose of your interview and write down the purpose. Then write ten good interview questions that would lead to informative responses. Think about the information you have learned about the interviewee. Think of a subject area in which the person might give you unexpected information in his or her responses. Write at least two follow-up questions you could ask in response to this information. Think of a subject area in which the person might say something you would not understand. Write two follow-up questions you could ask so that the interviewee would clarify these remarks.

Evaluation Checklist

Exchange your list of questions with the other student. As you read each other's lists, evaluate them on the basis of the following criteria. Rate the questions on a scale from 1 (Poor) to 5 (Excellent). Be prepared to give reasons for each rating you give. The questions in parentheses will help you do so.

Category	Rating
The interviewer . . . 1. Had a clear purpose of the interview (In what ways, if any, could the purpose be made clearer or more appropriate?)	
2. Used prepared questions that achieved the purpose of the interview (What other questions, if any, could also achieve this purpose?)	
3. Showed understanding of the topic (Which questions, if any, show a lack of preparation? What sources could the interviewer consult in order to write better questions?)	
4. Used questions that were well organized into introduction, body, and conclusion	
5. Used questions that follow the rules given in the Guideline section (How could these questions be improved to abide by the Guidelines?)	
6. Used appropriate follow-up questions where needed (Are they based on information the person is likely to give in his or her response? What other follow-up questions should the interviewer be prepared to ask?)	

Conducting Interviews

After you have prepared for an interview and have written questions that will produce informative answers, the next step is to organize the interview so that it will go smoothly.

Organize your interview questions into three parts: introduction, body, and conclusion. In the *introduction*, remind the person being interviewed of the purpose of the interview. Ask the opening question you have prepared. Because your opening question should help put the interviewee at ease, it should not require too long or complex an answer.

In the *body* of the interview, ask your other prepared questions. You should be ready to change the order of your questions if it will help the conversation flow smoothly. For instance, if the interviewee brings up a topic at the beginning of the interview that you had planned to discuss later, you should ask your prepared questions at that point rather than waiting. You should also be ready to ask follow-up questions about unexpected topics or topics that need clarification.

In the *conclusion* of the interview, ask your final questions. These should be more general questions about the person's life, work, or future plans. Then summarize the responses you have received throughout the interview and ask the interviewee to clarify any points you have not understood. Obtain permission to use the interview material and agree on the person's right of approval. (For example, if you are going to publish the interview, agree on whether the interviewee has the right to approve or revise the manuscript.) Thank the interviewee and send him or her a letter of thanks the next day.

Working with the Model

Ross is interviewing Cathy Imamura, a young novelist, for a local newspaper. As you read the interview, notice the way the questions are organized.

Ross: Cathy, at the age of twenty, you've just published your first novel—a science-fiction novel. I'm going to be asking you about your writing and your new career. But first, I think our readers would like to know about your background. Can you tell us something about your family, and how you got such an early start as a writer?

Cathy: Well, Ross, there's really very little extraordinary about my family. My parents run a small garage, and my mother also works as a bookkeeper. My older brother is a graduate student in physics, and my sister's in high school. None of them is a writer, but I've been writing ever since I was a kid.

Ross: How long would that be?

Cathy: Oh, I started at a very early age—eight or ten, perhaps. I know I was writing stories by the time I was twelve—I still have some of them. Of course, they're pretty bad.

Ross: How many other people read your stories?

Cathy: No one—I was too shy! It wasn't until I was in high school that I felt confident enough to let someone read my work. Fortunately, I received real encouragement.

Ross: Who encouraged you?

Cathy: Miss Vollmer, my English teacher—I hope she's reading this, she's really a wonderful person! She read my stories—I had *reams* of them!—and urged me to polish the ones that showed promise.

Ross: "Reams" of stories?

Cathy: At least twenty. Poor Miss Vollmer—she read them all! She helped me decide on four that I should try to publish.

Ross: How successful were you in getting them published?

Cathy: Well, I had beginner's luck. The first story I submitted was "Old Ironsides"—a very short, humorous story about a robot. An editor liked it, bought it, and published it. I was absolutely amazed. I was paid fifty dollars, and I felt as though it were a million.

Ross: What luck did you have with the other stories?

Cathy: Very little, at first. I had two rejections in a row, and I was very discouraged. It was a hard time, because I was just entering college, and I didn't know if I'd have enough time to write. But Miss Vollmer gave me pep talks, and my parents were very supportive. They told me they had a lot of faith in me, and they trusted me to make the right choices. As it turned out, I was able to write *and* go to school—if I disciplined myself. And then I had my second sale.

Ross: "The Ravens of the Moon"? I read that when it came out last year, and I thought it was a wonderful story.

Cathy: Thank you, I really appreciate that, because it was so difficult to write. The story takes place in the distant future. It's about two children who discover they have telepathic powers and who have to escape from the authorities in order to avoid being killed. Most of the story describes the gradual discovery of these powers—and that is such a hard thing to write about! I went through four drafts, and I had to do more work on the story after it was accepted. I'm still not entirely happy with it.

Ross: And yet the story had a very favorable reception. How did that make you feel?

Cathy: Good, of course . . . I was very pleased that others liked it. But, you know, a writer really has to please herself first. I'm my own severest critic.

Ross: When did you begin work on your novel?

Cathy: Oh, I began *Footsteps on a Distant Star* when I was seventeen. But at first it was just an adventure story, and I lost interest in it after thirty or forty pages. Then, in my freshman year, I took it out of my desk and started work on it again. I realized that it could become a novel with ideas as well as adventures.

Ross: How easy was it to complete *Footsteps*?

Cathy: Oh, terribly hard. As you know, the book is about a group of people who are exiled from earth because of their political ideas. They believe in democracy, freedom of speech, and so forth at a time when it's not safe to do so. They're supposed to go to a prison planet in the Centaurus system, but there's an accident with the space-warp drive—very convenient for the author!—and they wind up on an uninhabited world. And there they have to put their political ideas into effect, and they find it isn't so easy.

Ross: Critics have praised your descriptions of these colonists trying to put democracy in action while struggling against a hostile environment. How difficult were those scenes to write?

Cathy: Not as difficult as you might think—that was what excited me about the novel, and I had plenty of ideas. Actually, the star-drive stuff gave me the most trouble. But my brother, who is in physics and is a real whiz, read those parts over and gave me some very good pointers. He said it was less important to make the physics accurate, since hyperspace is all fantasy, any-how, than to make it *convincing*. And I think I succeeded.

Ross: That was just before you submitted the novel for publication?

Cathy: No, that was when I spent all summer rewriting it for the third time! Then I asked one of my magazine editors to recommend a book publisher with a science-fiction list. He recommended three, and the first one took *Footsteps* as a paperback original, after I'd made some changes.

Ross: What were those changes?

Cathy: Mostly shortening the book by some 10,000 words. That was very painful, but I realize now that the novel is better for it.

Ross: In general, how "painful" is writing for you?

Cathy: Quite painful, I'm afraid. "Old Ironsides" was a snap to write, but that was a fluke. The other stories and the novel involved a lot of drudgery, as well as the excitement of creating charac-ters and new worlds.

Ross: What science-fiction writers have influenced you?

Cathy: Well, Ursula Le Guin, of course. All the critics see her influ-ence. There are other writers I admire greatly, but I don't think I could ever write like them. Philip K. Dick, for example: he writes such funny dialogue, and he has wonderful characters. That's really his private preserve, though, and I don't think I could ever poach on it.

Ross: What are you working on now?

Cathy: I have a second novel. I'm almost halfway through the first draft, and I may finish it by the end of the year. But you have to remember that I'm a full-time student, and until I get my B.A., writing is only a sideline.

Ross: How much time are you able to give to writing?

Cathy: One to two hours a day. That seems like very little time, but if you really *write* during that hour or two, you'd be amazed how much you can accomplish.

Ross: How rapidly *do* you write—if you don't mind answering?

Cathy: Three pages a day, about twenty pages a week. That means that the first draft of a novel would take me six to ten months. Of course, professionals work much faster, but right now I'm more concerned with quality than quantity.

Ross: Cathy, in this interview you've spoken a great deal about your luck and about the help you've received from others. I think most readers, though, would see you as a hard-working writer who has really earned her success. Drawing on your own experience, what advice would you give to other writers who are just starting out?

Cathy: In three words: Stick with it. Write, write, revise, and write some more. Finish what you begin, submit your best work, and don't become discouraged. It's possible you may never be successful, but unless you try—and I mean *really* try—you'll never know what you could have done.

A. Think about the introduction of the interview.
   1. What is the purpose of Ross' opening remarks?
   2. What is the subject of the first question? Why is this a good question with which to begin the interview?
B. Think about the body of the interview.
   1. In what order are the questions arranged?
   2. How many of these are follow-up questions?
   3. Write two other follow-up questions that Ross might have asked.
   4. One of Ross' remarks is a statement rather than a question. How could he have turned this into a question?
C. Think about the conclusion of the interview.
   1. How does Ross summarize the interview? In what other way could he have summarized it?
   2. What is the subject of the concluding question? Why is this an appropriate question to ask at the end of the interview?
   3. Write at least two other concluding questions that Ross could have asked Cathy Imamura.
D. Listen to an interview on radio or television. As you listen, take notes on the number and kinds of questions the interviewer asked in each part of the interview. As you look over your notes, see if you can identify the introduction, body, and conclusion of the interview. Think about how clear, interesting, or informative the interview was and decide whether it was well organized or whether it could have been better organized.

Guidelines

The following guidelines can help make an interview pleasant and informative.

1. **Maintain a friendly, interested attitude.** Make it clear that you are eager to learn about the person and the topic. Always be polite, even if the interviewee is irritable. If the conversation wanders from the subject, bring it back tactfully. Say, "I'd like to get back to this subject," rather than "You didn't answer my question." Don't badger a person who obviously does not want to answer a question. Polite, patient persistence will produce the best results.

2. **Be alert for nonverbal cues.** Observe the interviewee's facial expressions, posture, and gestures. If the person appears restless, he or she may feel that you don't understand the topic. If the person appears puzzled, you may have asked a confusing question that you should clarify. If the interviewee seems pleased by a particular line of questioning, you should ask follow-up questions on that topic.

3. **Make continual checks for understanding.** Ask follow-up questions whenever the interviewee talks about a person, book, or issue you do not understand. Summarize an especially long or complicated answer and ask the interviewee if you have understood it correctly. At the end of the interview, briefly sum up the person's responses and ask if he or she has anything to add.

Activity

1. Listen to an interview on radio or television. Note any places in the interview where the interviewee seems irritated, bored, or offended by the questions. Observe how the interviewer handles—or fails to handle—such reactions. Evaluate the interviewer's behavior. Decide in what ways the interviewer handled the interviewee's reactions well, and in what ways the interviewer should have acted differently.

Preparing and Presenting

Working with another student, decide on a person to interview. It can be one of the people you chose in the previous lessons, or it can be another person. One of you will role-play the interviewer, and the other the interviewee. Each of you should research the person independently. The interviewer will gather material on questions to ask. The interviewer should also do all the steps in the preinterview checklist that will help prepare good questions. The interviewee will gather material that he or she can use in answering possible questions. Although you should not rehearse the interview as you would a play, you should discuss the topic and possible questions to be sure that you are both prepared.

Role-play your interview before the class. Your prepared questions should take about ten minutes. Your follow-up questions may add three to five minutes to the length of the interview.

Evaluation Checklist

Ask your classmates to use the following checklist in evaluating your interview. Each item may be rated on a scale from 1 (Poor) to 5 (Excellent). Be prepared to give reasons for each rating you give.

Category	Rating
The interviewer . . . 1. Showed thorough knowledge of interview topic	
2. Understood vocabulary of interview topic	
3. Was aware of current information and controversies on topic	
4. Had good opening remarks which restated purpose of interview	
5. Asked clear questions that led to informative answers	
6. Organized interview into introduction, body, and conclusion	
7. Was sensitive to interviewee's responses and nonverbal clues	
8. Asked follow-up questions where appropriate	
9. Used summaries where appropriate	
10. Maintained polite, friendly, interested attitude	

Chapter 2 Review

Summary

Communicating effectively with others can help you resolve conflicts and obtain information. Most conflicts result from imperfect communication. They can often be resolved through a better communication of ideas, emotions, and interests. To resolve a conflict, try to:

1. establish communication
2. exchange information
3. understand others
4. define your terms and values
5. get to the root of the problem
6. find common ground
7. be willing to compromise

A good interview requires detailed preplanning and organization. The careful interviewer should:

1. plan the purpose of the interview
2. arrange for the setting, time, etc.
3. become informed on the topic of the interview
4. examine his or her own attitudes toward the topic and person
5. prepare opening remarks and how to record the interview

The most important part of preparation is writing effective questions. They should ask for specific information, not simple *yes* or *no* answers. Also think of appropriate follow-up questions. Organize your prepared questions into the introduction, body, and conclusion so that the conversation will flow smoothly.

Reviewing Vocabulary

To demonstrate your understanding of the word or phrase below, use each of them in a sentence.

mediator   follow-up question

Reviewing Facts and Ideas

1. Name the six causes of conflict among people. Which do you think is the most common barrier to good communication? Why? What can one do to avoid this barrier or to overcome it once it exists?
2. What is a mediator? In what ways can a skillful, impartial mediator help resolve conflicts? What kinds of qualities should a good mediator have?
3. Name the eight steps in resolving a conflict. Which ones do you find yourself using the most? Why? Which step(s) do you tend to pay too little attention to?
4. What is the purpose of completing a preinterview checklist? What are the main steps in completing this checklist? What problems might occur due to a failure to complete one?
5. Why is it important to become informed about the topic and the interviewee? What problems might result due to being uninformed?
6. What is the main characteristic of a good interview question? Why are questions that can be answered *yes* or *no* weak?
7. Which method of recording an interview—written notes or tape recording—do you think is best? Why?
8. What is the purpose of follow-up questions? What are the two main kinds of follow-up questions?
9. In which section of the interview does the interviewer ask the bulk of the prepared questions?
10. What is the purpose of an interview introduction? How can you help put your interviewee at ease in the introduction? What does a good interviewer do in the conclusion of the interview?

Discussing Facts and Ideas

1. Reflect on conflicts you have had with others in recent months. Was the conflict created by one or more of the six causes enumerated on page 49? Discuss your experiences with the class. Note which causes seem to be most common.
2. With three or four other students, think about a conflict that occurred recently in your classroom. Discuss whether or not miscommunication was the root of the problem and whether or not communication played a major role in the solution. Talk about which, if any, of the steps in resolving conflict listed in lesson one of this chapter were used effectively. Discuss which approaches could have resolved the conflict more quickly or easily had the participants used them.
3. Think of a famous person you would like to interview. Discuss with your teacher and other members of the class what information you would like to obtain from your interview. Talk about the possible ways you could find out background information before beginning the interview. Then discuss what prepared questions you would ask this person in order to ensure a well-organized, interesting interview.
4. To resolve conflict and contribute effectively in an interview session, you need to respect your listeners. You can show respect for listeners by being aware of their backgrounds, looking at controversial topics from their viewpoints, seeking topics about which you share viewpoints, and being sensitive when you discuss embarrassing or painful subjects. Discuss situations in which speakers demonstrate that they respected the listener. Discuss situations in which speakers failed to show such respect and examine what the consequences of this lack of respect were.

Applying Your Knowledge

1. With a small group of your classmates, view a popular television program, such as a situation comedy. Determine whether or not the central conflict is caused by one of the six sources of conflict discussed in this chapter. Then assign various characters for each of your group to assume and role play a solution to the conflict, taking an approach other than the one used in the program. One student should take notes and share the results with the class.
2. Divide your class into interview teams. Each team should interview one adult and one student. Obtain information during the interview about recent experiences the interviewees have had with interpersonal conflict. Try to discover how the conflict came about and what was done to solve it. Each team should share the results of its interviews with the class.
3. The ability to conduct a conversation with someone you do not know very well is a very important speech communication skill. At a party, school meeting, or other gathering, pick a person with whom you are only slightly acquainted and carry on a conversation with him or her. Try to converse for at least five minutes *and let the other person do half of the talking*. Keep the following in mind:

   a. Look for people who are interested in talking.
   b. Ease into a conversation.
   c. Introduce yourself. Let the person know something about you, not just your name.
   d. Make the conversation a learning opportunity.
   e. Be polite.

Without using names of the persons with whom you spoke, share the results of your conversation with your classmates.

COMMUNICATING ON THE JOB

Inquiring about a Job

Many of the job inquiries you make will be oral rather than written. You may phone about a job you have seen advertised, or you may speak in person to a personnel manager or job recruiter. Whether you make such inquiries by phone or in person, you should remember several points:

- Know the name and title of the person to whom you must speak.
- Have ready a list of questions about the job, including questions about qualifications, responsibilities, hours, pay, and benefits.
- Have pen and paper ready in order to take notes on your conversation.
- Identify yourself clearly at the beginning of the conversation. If necessary, add helpful information, such as "We talked at my high school's Career Day last week."
- Explain the reason for your inquiry. For example, are you interested in an interview, or do you just want information?
- Listen carefully to the other person and be prepared to answer questions about your work experience and interests.
- Follow up your conversation with a letter or phone call confirming the arrangements made during the conversation, or simply thanking the person in case you have decided not to inquire further about the job.

Activities

1. Read the help-wanted ads in your local newspaper. Select three ads for jobs in which you might be interested. Working with another student, take turns role-playing a telephone inquiry about each job. You can be asking for an interview or simply requesting more information about the job.
2. Invite a personnel director or recruiter from a local company to speak to your class. Ask him or her about the problems young people have when inquiring about job openings. Ask why some job applicants are successful and others are not.

Interviewing Candidates and Public Officials

As a citizen, you should learn to question public officials effectively about their duties and responsibilities. As a voter, you should be able to question candidates about their platforms and qualifications. When interviewing a candidate or public official, remember these points:

- Have your questions written out beforehand.
- Write good interview questions that require clear, detailed responses. Avoid questions that can be easily evaded or answered "yes" or "no."
- Treat candidates and officials politely and respectfully but don't be overawed by their titles.
- If a candidate or official answers in "officialese"—jargon that is difficult to understand—rephrase your question to obtain a clearer and more specific answer.

Activities

1. Interview three candidates for student government (or members of student government) about their experience and qualifications, and the offices they are seeking (or currently occupy). Compare their responses on the following topics:

   - the importance of student government
   - the most significant problem confronting your school
   - their solutions for such a problem
   - their plans for the school's future
   - how student government can help you or your class
   - how you or your class can help student government

2. Interview a person in city or community government about his or her duties, responsibilities, and plans. You might question a supervisor, a member of the school board, an official in the assessor's office, a member of the police commission, or a candidate for one of these positions. Ask questions on the following topics:

   - how the official is made accountable to the public
   - what laws or regulations require the official to share information with the public
   - the major problems in the official's job
   - the future scope and responsibility of the position the official holds

Group Discussion

After working through this chapter, you should be proficient at the following skills:

Lesson	Skills
Lesson 1	• making a prediscussion outline
Lesson 2	• understanding the different roles of group members
Lesson 3	• working effectively in small groups
Communicating on the Job	• interviewing for a job
Communicating as a Citizen	• solving a community problem

Making a Prediscussion Outline

Conducting a **group discussion** can be a particularly effective means of exploring a specific problem and arriving at a solution to it. Working together, group members share their ideas and build on one another's contributions to solve the problem.

Members of a successful problem-solving discussion group must understand and use the four steps in the **problem-solving process**. These are the steps:

1. Begin by describing and understanding the problem. This step may involve defining the symptoms, scope, and causes of the problem.
2. Next, identify specific **criteria**, or standards, by which all the possible solutions to the problem can be judged. Notice that these criteria are established before the possible solutions are explored.
3. Then, identify and define all the possible solutions to the problem. It is especially important to keep an open mind during this step in the problem-solving process, so that all possible solutions may be considered by the group.
4. Finally, evaluate each possible solution according to the criteria you have established. On the basis of these evaluations, select the best solution to the problem.

The members of a problem-solving discussion group should keep these four steps in mind while preparing for the discussion. The first step in preparing for the discussion is to do research. Each group member should gather facts, statistics, and opinions about the problem, the possible solutions to the problem, and the criteria by which those solutions might be judged. To do so, each member should read books and magazines, listen to relevant programs on television and radio, and conduct interviews. One good source for locating articles is the *Readers' Guide to Periodical Literature*. Your reference librarian should be able to guide you to sources for the area of special knowledge you are investigating. When you are gathering information, make sure that it is authoritative, up-to-date, and unbiased.

While doing research, each discussion group member should take notes on his or her findings and should then organize those notes into a prediscussion outline. In preparing and using their outlines, the group members must understand that each person's outline is a summary of the information he or she has gathered during research. It is not a specific outline showing how the discussion will be conducted. During the actual group discussion, each group member will refer to his or her own outline. However, each group member should also be prepared to consider new facts and ideas contributed by the other group members.

Working with the Model

Edrill and the other members of her group chose to consider this problem: What special provisions should be made for the education of physically disabled children? Edrill did research on the problem. Then she prepared the following prediscussion outline. Study Edrill's outline, thinking about how she collected facts and opinions and how she organized those facts and opinions in her outline.

Discussion problem: What special provisions should be made for the education of physically disabled children?

I. What is the problem?
   A. Public Law 94-142 (Education for All Handicapped Children Act) requires "free and appropriate public education" for all school-aged disabled children (*Newsweek*, Sept. 4, 1978).
   B. How to determine what an "appropriate" education is and how to provide it is the responsibility of individual school districts.
   C. Scope of the problem: There are more than eight million disabled children in the U.S. (Donahue, *America*, April 14, 1979); "roughly one-tenth of all children are handicapped" (Gliedman and Roth, *The Unexpected Minority*).

II. What criteria should be used to evaluate possible solutions?
   A. Solution should have positive psychological and educational effect on disabled children.
   B. Solution should have at least no negative psychological or educational effect on nondisabled students whom it involves.
   C. Solution should not cost any more than any other, equally effective solution.
   D. Solution should meet the requirements of federal law.

III. What are the possible solutions?
   A. No special provisions should be made. Disabled children who are able to take advantage of regular classroom facilities should do so; others should be the responsibilities of their own parents (Interview, local taxpayer).
   B. Disabled children should be assisted in participating in regular classes as much as possible. Additional educational and support services should be offered according to each child's needs (Donahue). Further, nondisabled children should be educated to understand physical disabilities (Leishman, *McCall's*, April 1978). This approach is usually called "mainstreaming."
   C. Disabled children should be grouped together and taught in special classrooms. The unusual needs caused by their physical disabilities should be directly met by specially trained teachers (Interview, parent of 8-year-old girl with cerebral palsy).

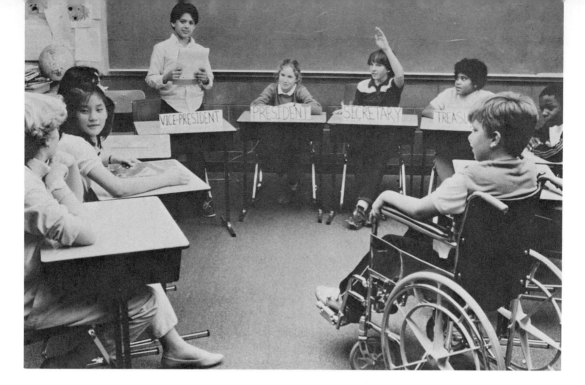

IV. How well does each solution meet the established criteria?
    A. No special provisions should be made.
        1. This would have positive psychological and education effect
           only for slightly disabled children, who can adjust readily to a
           regular classroom; its effect for most disabled children
           would be negative, since they would feel excluded from
           "normal" activity and would not receive public education
           (Interview, elementary school principal).
        2. Since it would not significantly change the make-up of regu-
           lar classrooms, it would not have much effect on nondisa-
           bled students.
        3. This approach would actually lower current spending for
           education (Interview, elementary school principal).
        4. This approach does not meet legal requirements for free
           public education for all disabled children.
    B. Disabled children should be "mainstreamed" into regular
       classrooms.
        1. Positive psychological and educational effects include in-
           creased pride, enthusiasm, self-confidence, ability to deal
           with other people, and motivation to learn (Bernstein, *To-
           day's Education*, Feb./Mar. 1980). Negative effects, how-
           ever, may include too much competition with standards
           physically disabled children are not prepared to meet and
           decreased opportunity "of mixing with other children who
           have similar disabilities (which can be helpful in assisting the
           child to assess the effects of his or her disability upon his or
           her achievement)" (Bowe, *Handicapping America*).

2. The effect on nondisabled children who are taught to understand disabilities and to learn and work with physically disabled children is usually positive (Daley, *Better Homes and Gardens*, Sept. 1979). However, some people express concern that the educational needs of nondisabled children may be neglected by teachers who give too much attention to the physically disabled students in the classroom (*Newsweek*, Sept. 4, 1978).

3. Congress has allotted funds to assist school districts, but providing full educational facilities and support systems for disabled children will necessitate additional spending by most school districts. It may even require some cutbacks in their regular educational programs (*Newsweek*, Sept. 4, 1978).

4. This approach meets legal requirements by providing "free and appropriate public education" for disabled children.

C. Disabled children should be grouped together and taught in special classrooms.

1. Smaller class size and specially trained teachers may provide educational benefits; however, negative effects include decreased opportunity for mixing with nondisabled children and increased probability of "labeling and stigma" (Bowe, *Handicapping America*).

2. Nondisabled children face no risk of disruption or decreased attention in the classroom. However, the lack of consistent, positive experiences with disabled children may be considered a negative effect.

3. Because of the small class size and special facilities required, special education classes are more expensive than regular classes. Establishing such special classes, however, is usually less expensive than is providing special assistance to students throughout the school district, as required in mainstreaming (Interview, elementary school principal).

4. This approach meets legal requirements by providing "free and appropriate public education" for disabled children.

A. Think about the prediscussion outline Edrill prepared.

1. What specific sources did she consult in doing her research? What notes about her sources did she include in her prediscussion outline? How might she use those notes about her sources when she participates in the group discussion?

2. How did Edrill organize the information in her outline? How will the organization of her outline help her participate in the group discussion?

3. When Edrill participates in the group discussion, she should be ready to help the group members agree on the definitions of several key terms. One of those terms is *physically disabled chil-*

dren. What other terms used in her prediscussion outline should Edrill be prepared to help define?

4. How did Edrill evaluate each of the possible solutions she included in her outline? How did she use each of the criteria she established?

5. Edrill might have included a final note in section IV of her outline. That note would have indicated which solution she considers best. Based on the information in her outline, which solution do you think Edrill would have chosen? Why do you think she would have chosen that solution?

Guidelines

Think about the following guidelines as you prepare to participate in a problem-solving group discussion.

1. There are four steps in the problem-solving process.

    a. **Describe and understand the problem.**
    b. **Identify specific criteria for evaluating possible solutions to the problem.**
    c. **Identify and define possible solutions to the problem.**
    d. **Evaluate each possible solution according to the established criteria.**

2. Each member of the group should research the problem, gathering relevant facts and opinions. Ask yourself the following questions about each source.

    *   Is it up-to-date? Check the date of publication of a periodical, the copyright date of a book, and the dates of books or events mentioned in the text to be sure that your information is current.
    *   Is it thorough? Consider whether the source treats a subject in depth or merely provides pictures and vague generalizations.
    *   Is it unbiased? Read carefully to detect any political, social, or economic bias in the source.
    *   Is it authoritative? Most reliable sources have footnotes or bibliographies that refer you to other, more detailed treatments of the subject. Periodical and encyclopedia articles by qualified authors are usually signed.
    *   Is it consistent with what you know? Compare the facts in each source with the facts in other books, articles, and encyclopedias.
    *   Do other experts consider it a reliable source? Teachers, authors, and librarians can tell you which sources, in their areas of special knowledge, are most accurate and complete.

3. Each member of the group should prepare a prediscussion outline. In that outline, each member organizes and records the information he or she gathered in research. The information should be organized in the order of the four steps of the problem-solving process.

Preparing and Presenting

Join four to seven other students in forming a discussion group. With the other members of your group, select an issue to consider in a problem-solving discussion. If you wish, you may choose one of the following problems.

- What should the federal government do to improve care for the aged?
- What should citizens do to decrease violence in their neighborhoods?
- What programs (if any) should be provided to prepare high school students for parenthood?
- What part should competitive sports play in the high school curriculum?
- What specific requirements for high school graduation should be imposed on all students?

Once you have selected a problem, work independently to gather information and opinions on it. Use a variety of sources in your research. Read at least one book chapter, two magazine articles, and one reference book article. Also, watch one radio or television program on the problem. If possible, interview at least two people who have knowledge or experience that relates to the problem. Take particular care in recording your sources, so you can quickly refer to them if other group members have questions about your information.

After you have completed your research, write an outline that will help you participate in a discussion of the problem. Your outline should have four main sections, corresponding to the four steps in the problem-solving process. Prepare your outline using only the left half of each page. You will be able to use the right half for taking notes during the discussion.

Evaluation Checklist

Evaluate the other students' outlines on the basis of the following criteria. Rate the outlines on a scale from 1 (Poor) to 5 (Excellent). Be prepared to give reasons for each rating you give.

Category	Rating
The outline . . . 1. Defined technical or unusual terms	
2. Clearly and specifically defined the problem	
3. Included adequate criteria for evaluating solutions	
4. Included adequate solutions in the third section of the outline	
5. Indicated, if applicable, that one solution is definitely the best	
6. Included comprehensive evaluations in the final section	
7. Identified all the sources of information	
8. Shows that the student did enough research to prepare for the discussion	

Understanding the Roles of Group Members

During a problem-solving discussion, group members may relate to other group members in many different ways. One person, the group leader, is committed to a formal role. The other members assume informal roles, either positive or negative.

Each problem-solving discussion group should have one leader. The leader accepts specific responsibilities toward the other group members. First, he or she must make any necessary arrangements for the group's meeting. Then, during the discussion, the group leader is responsible for keeping the discussion directed toward its goal, the exploration and solution of a specific problem. Usually, this involves encouraging group members to participate, keeping group members from discussing unrelated issues, and tactfully resolving any conflicts that may arise between group members. The discussion group leader should concentrate on guiding the other group members and must be especially careful to avoid giving too much attention to his or her own ideas.

The informal roles that discussion group members most often assume are listed in the chart below. During a discussion, each group member usually plays at least several of these informal roles. Group members who know and understand the informal roles that may be played during a group discussion can evaluate and improve their own participation. They can also respond constructively to the participation of other group members.

INFORMAL ROLES PLAYED BY GROUP DISCUSSION MEMBERS

Positive Roles

Information Seeker	One who asks questions to elicit information
Information Giver	One who gives the group facts and data
Opinion Seeker	One who asks the opinion of others
Opinion Giver	One who gives the group his or her opinions
Summarizer	One who recalls and briefly restates contributions made by various group members
Builder	One who listens thoughtfully and adds to the contributions of others
Procedural Technician	One who reminds other members of the routines and processes necessary to successful group functioning
Vision Builder	One who sees possibilities ahead
Reality Tester	One who seeks to verify the accuracy of information contributed by others
Boundary Tester	One who tries to stretch the group's thinking
Mediator	One who helps resolve conflicts and helps maintain harmony
Expediter	One who keeps the group moving toward the accomplishment of its purpose

Negative Roles

Dominator	One who tries to talk all the time and fails to listen to others
Interrupter	One who does not give others a chance to fully express their ideas
Thoughtless Agreer	One who enthusiastically supports any—and every—point of view
Forecaster of Doom	One who sees only the negative aspects of every issue
One-Track Thinker	One who repeatedly returns to the same issue
Supercritic	One who finds fault but fails to make constructive criticisms
Put-Down Artist	One who finds fault with other group members
Silent Observer	One who never expresses his or her ideas and opinions
Wanderer	One who digresses from the main point of the discussion

Working with the Model

Seven group members had researched and prepared prediscussion outlines on the problem, "What special provisions should be made for the education of physically disabled children?" Then they met as a group to discuss the problem. The leader of the group was Lucy. The other members of the group were Edrill, Jeremy, Carmine, Susan, Alvin, and Felipe. Read the following transcript of part of their discussion. As you read, think about the different roles played by each group member.

Lucy: We have agreed on four basic criteria for evaluating possible solutions. I think, then, that we're ready to discuss exactly what the possible solutions are.

Edrill: I spoke with one taxpayer who suggested that we should make no special provisions at all for educating disabled kids. I think I should mention, by the way, that this person doesn't have any children. I've been noticing that the people who really oppose spending money on education don't have children of their own. You'd think that they would understand that public education affects everyone—not just parents and kids.

Jeremy: I know what you mean. Some of the people in our apartment building think they shouldn't have to pay taxes for the schools—just because their kids have all finished school already. No wonder our school district is short of funds!

Lucy: You're right, that is a problem. But right now we should get back to Edrill's main point. One possible solution that has been suggested is that public schools should not have to make any special provision for educating physically disabled children.

Carmine: Yes, I read a letter in last month's *Tribune* that expressed the same idea. If disabled kids can't take advantage of whatever the regular classroom provides, then it's up to their parents to educate them.

Susan: But that's just not fair! Kids who have physical disabilities need an education just as much as kids without physical disabilities—maybe more. And think about how *different* it would make you feel if you weren't even allowed to go to school.

Lucy: You're making a good point, Susan, but let's wait with the evaluation until we have mentioned all the possible solutions. Alvin, do you have any ideas about other possible solutions we should be considering?

Alvin: *(shakes his head)*

Felipe: I read several magazine articles about a general program called mainstreaming. This usually involves including physically disabled kids in—

Edrill: Oh, yeah, mainstreaming really seems to be the answer. It helps disabled kids and nondisabled kids. Of course, some people aren't enthusiastic about mainstreaming, but there are always some people who are afraid of anything different.

Lucy: It's good that you're enthusiastic about one of the solutions, Edrill, but let's give Felipe a chance to finish explaining it. Remember, we want to consider each solution before we begin our evaluations.

Felipe: Well, with mainstreaming, physically disabled kids are included in regular classrooms as much as possible. But that doesn't mean that they're just left to work things out on their own. They're given any special help they need in addition to the regular classroom instruction.

A. Think about how Lucy acted as the leader of the group discussion.
1. How did she summarize what the group had already accomplished?
2. How did she guide the group members in continuing the discussion?
3. How did she try to keep the discussion focused on the problem?
4. How did she attempt to involve everybody in the discussion?
B. Think about the informal roles played by the other members of the group.
1. What role did Edrill assume when she first spoke?
2. How did Jeremy respond to Edrill's irrelevant comments?
3. Which students assumed these roles at least once in the recorded section of the discussion: Information Giver, Interrupter, Silent Observer?
C. Evaluate each member's contribution in the recorded section of the group discussion.
1. How did each member help advance the discussion?
2. What specific suggestions would you make to help each member improve his or her contribution to the discussion?

Guidelines

Whenever you participate in a group discussion, you should consider the variety of roles that each group member might play.

1. The leader of the group discussion has a formal role to fill. He or she is responsible for making arrangements for the group meeting. During the course of the group discussion, the leader is responsible for stimulating participation, resolving conflicts, and keeping the discussion focused on the problem to be considered.
2. The members of a discussion group may assume various informal roles during the course of a problem-solving discussion. These roles may be positive; they may help to advance the discussion. These roles may also be negative; they may detract from the purpose of the discussion. Understanding these different informal roles will help you contribute positively to the group discussion and respond constructively to other group members.

Preparing and Presenting

With the other members of your group, role-play the different discussion-group roles. Before you begin, each member should select a specific role to play and should announce his or her role to the rest of the group members. One member should choose the role of group leader. Half of the remaining members should choose positive informal roles. The other half should choose negative informal roles.

Work together to act out one section of a problem-solving group discussion. You may base the content of your discussion on the content used in the transcript in the Working with the Model section of this lesson. Or, if one of your group members has completed his or her prediscussion outline, you may base the content of your discussion on one specific section of that student's outline.

Remember that, in this activity, you should concentrate on playing specific roles. Later you will have an opportunity to actually conduct your group discussion and to work with the information you have gathered.

As you and the other group members act out the discussion, think about how it feels to play each kind of role. Also think about how you spontaneously respond to the roles played by other group members and about how you could respond in a constructive manner.

After the members of your group have acted out their roles for several minutes, change roles. A different member should assume the leader's role. Members who had assumed positive informal roles should

adopt negative informal roles. Members who had assumed negative informal roles should adopt positive informal roles. Again, announce the specific roles you intend to play and act out one of the four sections of a problem-solving group discussion.

You may wish to continue changing roles until every member has had an opportunity to act out the role of group leader. If your group does this, be sure that you act out a different role each time.

Evaluation Checklist

Evaluate the group discussion on the basis of the following criteria. Rate each other on a scale from 1 (Poor) to 5 (Excellent). Be prepared to give reasons for each rating you give.

Category	Rating
1. Each group leader stimulated participation, resolved conflicts, and kept the discussion focused on the problem at hand.	
2. The other members of the group assumed their informal roles with a clear understanding of each role.	
3. The members who played positive informal roles helped advance the discussion.	
4. The members who played negative informal roles showed understanding of the effects of negative actions.	

Working Effectively in a Small Group

If a discussion group is to be successful in exploring and solving a problem, all the group members must work together toward that goal. Working together requires that members listen thoughtfully to one another and build on what has already been said. It requires that they wait for one person to finish expressing his or her thoughts before they begin to speak. It also requires that they approach each contribution with interest and with open minds.

In order to work together successfully, discussion group members must be considerate of one another's feelings. They must respect one another's intentions, ideas, and emotions, and they must understand that differences of opinion can be resolved constructively.

Working with the Model

The following transcript records another section of the group discussion on the problem, "What special provisions should be made for the education of physically disabled children?" The members of the group are Lucy (who is the group leader), Edrill, Jeremy, Carmine, Susan, Alvin, and Felipe. Read the transcript and think about how each group member listens and responds to the contributions of the other members.

Lucy: We seem to have covered the evaluation of our first possible solution. Let's go on to see how our second possible solution, mainstreaming, measures up against our criteria.

Jeremy: In terms of psychological and educational benefits to disabled children, I read some pretty exciting things about mainstreaming. Provided a disabled child is given enough support, being in a so-called regular classroom with other kids the same age can be really positive. The kid's self-image and even the kid's ability to learn are improved.

Carmine: I read the same kinds of articles. Some very exciting things *can* happen. But that's not the way it always works out. When we consider mainstreaming, we have to think about the disabled kids who end up overwhelmed and frustrated, too.

Edrill: Oh, don't be so negative, Carmine. Try to look on the bright side of this issue.

Felipe: Carmine's just trying to help us be realistic. Physically disabled kids do have to deal with special problems. If those problems prevent the kids from keeping up with the rest of the class, they're just going to feel defeated. And defeat is never positive—psychologically or educationally!

Susan: You're right, Felipe. On the other hand, to make a fair evaluation, we have to assume that mainstreaming will be carried out thoughtfully and carefully. At its best, mainstreaming involves a thorough evaluation of each child's total situation, followed by a placement that will best meet all the child's needs. Disabled kids who cannot benefit from regular classroom work—for *whatever* reason—shouldn't be forced out of a better situation. That's the point that Public Law 94-142 makes about "the least restrictive environment."

Lucy: It looks like, in terms of our first criterion, mainstreaming gets a mixed rating. It can have both positive and negative effects on disabled children. What about in terms of our second criterion—its effect on the nondisabled kids who are involved?

Felipe: I think mainstreaming gets the same kind of rating here—mixed.

Carmine: I know what you mean. When it's well done, mainstreaming seems to have a terrific effect on everybody. All the kids— disabled and nondisabled—learn more because they're learning together. And they're learning from each other.

Susan: That's right. But when it isn't done carefully—

Edrill: Oh no! Here comes another put-down.

Susan: I'm just trying to be fair. If mainstreaming isn't done right, everybody's education can suffer. And nondisabled kids— instead of developing healthy and accepting attitudes—can build up new kinds of resentments against people who appear to be different.

• • • •

Lucy: Now that we have evaluated each of the three possible solutions, we need to work on choosing the one solution we consider best.

Carmine: I think that a program of mainstreaming seems most effective. It benefits both disabled and nondisabled kids, and it clearly complies with the law.

Felipe: That's true, but there is another criterion to consider. Mainstreaming is clearly the most expensive of the three possible solutions.

Susan: According to our phrasing of that criterion, expense is really only a consideration if all the other effects are equal.

Lucy: That's right, Susan. So now we need to be sure that everyone agrees on the superiority of mainstreaming in terms of our other three criteria. Jeremy, what do you think?

A. Think about how each member contributed to the group discussion.
   1. Which group members showed that they were listening thoughtfully to the contributions of others? How did they respond to those contributions?
   2. Which group members showed that they were not listening carefully and that they were not concentrating on the group's purpose?
   3. Which group members showed consideration of the feelings of others? How did their consideration help advance the discussion?
   4. Which group member did not show consideration of the feelings of others? How did that lack of consideration disrupt the discussion?

B. Think about how the group members began trying to agree on the best solution to the problem.
   1. What standards did they try to use in judging the possible solutions?
   2. What do you think happened in the rest of the discussion? Which solution do you think the group members chose as best? Why do you think they chose that solution?
C. Think about what changes might enhance the group discussion.
   1. How might each group member's contribution be changed to show involvement in the group's task, consideration for the feelings of others, and respect for the ideas posed by others?
   2. What might the other group members do to decrease the disruptive effect of Edrill's comments?
   3. What might the other group members do to encourage Alvin's involvement in the discussion?

Guidelines

The following guidelines will help you participate constructively in a group discussion.

1. Work with the other group members toward the accomplishment of the group's purpose. Listen thoughtfully to the facts and opinions contributed by others. Be ready to add your own facts and opinions, but also be ready to change your mind in response to new ideas.
2. Be considerate of the feelings of others and respect the ideas they suggest. Any strain in the relationships among group members may detract from the accomplishment of the group's purpose.

Preparing and Presenting

With the other members of your group, conduct a group discussion about the problem you selected and researched.

Before you begin, choose one member of the group to act as the discussion leader. That person should review the responsibilities of a group leader (see the previous lesson). The other group members should review the positive informal roles that can be played by discussion group members (see the previous lesson).

As the group discussion develops, you should consider, in order, the four steps in the problem-solving process. Each group member should refer to his or her outline for specific facts, quotes, and sources. Each of you should remember, however, that your outline is not intended as an outline for the group discussion. Rather, you should use your outline as a reference for the specific information and ideas you gathered in preparing for the discussion.

After the members of the group have evaluated each of the possible solutions raised during the discussion, you should try to agree on the best solution. If there is disagreement about which solution is best, try to combine different solutions to come up with one that everyone accepts, or try to find some additional information about one of the original solutions that will make that solution acceptable to everyone in the group.

Evaluation Checklist

Evaluate your problem-solving discussion on the basis of the following criteria. Rate each discussion on a scale from 1 (Poor) to 5 (Excellent). Be prepared to give reasons for each rating you give.

Category	Rating
1. Each group member helped advance the discussion.	
2. Each group member had researched and considered the problem before the discussion.	
3. The group leader guided the discussion well and kept it moving.	
4. Group members built on comments or questions that had just been made.	
5. The group leader solved the specific problems that arose.	
6. The group members dealt well with disagreements that arose.	
7. The discussion dealt with each step in the problem-solving process thoroughly.	

Chapter 3 Review

Summary

Conducting a group discussion can be an effective means of exploring a specific problem and arriving at a solution. Members of a problem-solving discussion group must understand and use these four steps.

1. describe and understand the problem
2. identify specific criteria for evaluating possible solutions to the problem
3. identify and define possible solutions to the problem
4. evaluate each possible solution according to the established criteria

To prepare for the group discussion, each member should research the problem and prepare a prediscussion outline organizing and recording the information he or she gathered in research.

In the discussion itself, a group leader fills the formal role of stimulating participation, resolving conflicts, and keeping the discussion focused on the problem. The other members may assume various informal roles, some of which are positive (advancing the discussion) and some of which are negative (detracting from the purpose of the discussion). All group members must work together toward exploring and solving the problem. A successful discussion requires that members listen thoughtfully to each other, be considerate of the feelings of others, and respect the ideas they suggest.

Reviewing Vocabulary

In your own words, define each of the words or group of words below.

group discussion
criteria
problem-solving process

Reviewing Facts and Ideas

1. What are the four steps in the problem-solving process?
2. Why is a group discussion an effective means of exploring a problem?
3. Why is it necessary for you to take notes and prepare an outline of the information you gather?
4. What are the main responsibilities of the group discussion leader?
5. How do the members who fill positive roles promote a constructive discussion?
6. How do the members who fill negative roles hinder a constructive discussion?
7. Why is it especially important in a group discussion to listen to one another?
8. Why is it important in a group discussion to keep an open mind?
9. Why is consideration of the feelings of others in a group discussion important?
10. In a group discussion, respect for the ideas others suggest helps the group accomplish its purpose. Why is this respect particularly important for discussing a fairly complex problem?

Discussing Facts and Ideas

1. Many groups, such as families, clubs, and civic organizations, deal with problems that can be approached as a group. Discuss the benefits of such groups solving their problems according to the problem-solving process described in this chapter. Talk about the problems that could be avoided by using this process.
2. Group discussion leaders must be careful not to become too involved in the give and take of the discussion. Discuss what the problems might be for a group if the leader begins to take positions on the issues being considered.
3. The preceding lessons focused on using group discussion for problem solving. What are some other possible purposes of group discussion? Discuss what the advantages and disadvantages of using group discussion for these other purposes might be.
4. A common joke maintains that a camel is a horse put together by a committee. Discuss how a poorly performed group discussion might indicate that there is a grain of truth in this joke.

Applying Your Knowledge

1. Invite your school librarian to talk with your class concerning the best general reference sources of information about particular areas of knowledge (for example, science, business, history, or current events). Ask the librarian to describe different standard reference works and how they can be used to discover vital information. Then familiarize yourself with the reference room of your school library.
2. *Brainstorming* is a special type of group discussion that is useful in generating ideas. When a group brainstorms, everyone is encouraged to put ideas before the group without anyone evaluating those ideas. The leader's task becomes one of encouraging participation and of helping participants keep track of the ideas being suggested. These ideas can be evaluated later in terms of standards agreed to by the group. To get an idea of how brainstorming works, select one of the following topics and brainstorm possible answers. Remember that no judgments should be made about answers as they are suggested.

   a. How can we improve school spirit?
   b. What is the best way to take notes in a class?
   c. How can young adults best be assured of getting enough physical exercise?
   d. What are the qualities that are most important to a successful popular music group?
   e. How can we help improve our school's appearance?
   f. What are the best ways to discipline a pet?
   g. What are some unique gifts that can be made for under five dollars?

3. With three or four other students, select a problem that you could explore as a group. It can be a problem as simple as how to reduce talking in movie theatres or as complex as how to dispose of nuclear waste. Then focus on the second step of the problem-solving process—identifying the specific criteria for evaluating possible solutions to the problem. Brainstorm as a group, jotting down every idea put forth. Then condense the criteria you come up with to the four most important ones that you would likely use if you were actually to research the problem, define possible solutions, and evaluate them. Be sure to take into consideration such basic factors as cost, safety, time, ease of implementation, benefit to the majority, and harmful side effects.

Being Interviewed for a Job

When you are interviewed for a job, you must present yourself as competent, confident, and likeable. Here are important guidelines to follow.

- Arrive a few minutes early for the interview.
- Dress neatly, even if good clothes are not required for the job.
- Bring an extra copy of your résumé, a list of references, your social security card, and a pen.
- Be prepared to answer questions about your education, experience, qualifications, and interests.
- Be confident and polite, but communicate your enthusiasm about the job.
- Don't slouch, smoke, mumble, or chew gum.
- Ask intelligent questions about the job and the company.
- Be alert to cues that the interview is over.
- Next day, write a letter thanking the interviewer for his or her time and interest.

Activities

1. Invite a person who conducts interviews with prospective employees to speak to your class. Ask the interviewer to describe the qualities he or she looks for in an interviewee and to list the things that a person being interviewed can do to improve his or her chances of being hired.
2. Research three or more jobs, making a list of qualifications, duties, hours, pay, and chances for promotion for each job. Working with another student, role-play an interview for one of these job positions. Let the class decide by ballot whether the person being interviewed should get the job and ask them to discuss the reasons for their decision.

Solving a Community Problem

To solve a problem that faces your community, follow these general rules.

1. **Define the problem.** What exactly is wrong? How many people does the problem affect? Is it limited to a few families on one block, or does it involve an entire neighborhood? Can the problem be solved? Is it the responsibility of a single person or agency, or will I have to do research to find someone who will help solve it?

2. **Contact people who can help you.** Enlist friends, neighbors, and other members of your community on your side. Explain the seriousness of the problem, and why you should all be concerned about it.

3. **Define possible solutions.** Follow the problem-solving sequence (see page 81). Select only the most workable solutions and be sure that they will eliminate the causes of the problem.

4. **Decide whether you need official help.** Many community problems can be solved if the people involved cooperate with one another. Other problems, however, may require the help of the city council, the public works department, or other government agencies. In most cases, you will get the fastest help if you go directly to the person with the most power: the mayor, the council member for your district, or the highest-placed person on a board or agency.

5. **Keep track of the problem and its solutions.** Don't simply drop the problem on an official's desk. Watch to see how well it is solved.

Activity

1. Working with three other students, define a problem that affects your community. It can involve conflicts between neighbors, or it can be a public problem such as vandalism. Discuss the different people you could enlist to help you solve the problem and the different suggestions they might have. Then role-play a problem-solving session before the class. During the session, try to find at least three possible solutions and identify three people or agencies that might help you. Ask the class to suggest further solutions.

Interactive Listening

After working through this chapter, you should be proficient at the following skills:

Lesson	Skills
Lesson 1	• using the techniques of active listening • providing feedback to people you are talking with • taking part in an interesting, friendly conversation
Communicating on the Job	• knowing what careers in communication are available
Communicating as a Citizen	• knowing what communication methods are used by the hearing impaired

Listening to Communicate

To really communicate with others, you must listen to them carefully and actively. In a conversation, speaker and listener share equally in the responsibility for achieving clear, harmonious communication. An inattentive or passive listener can do as much to cause a breakdown in communication as a speaker who isn't sure what he or she wants to say.

Think of some of the enjoyable conversations you've had, and of some of the difficult ones. How did the people in the enjoyable conversations let the speaker know that they understood (or didn't understand) what was being said? How did they show their interest in one another and in the topics being discussed? In the difficult conversations, what kinds of behavior seemed to lead to communication problems? Becoming aware of the kinds of behavior that lead to enjoyable or difficult conversations is the first step in learning to listen to communicate.

Working with the Model

A group of high school seniors were talking after school one day, and their thoughts turned to what they were going to do after high school. As you read the following transcript of their conversation, look carefully at the listening skills each student displays.

Sara: My parents are really after me to make up my mind about next year. I'm just not sure.

Ingrid: Me too. I really get it from home about my schedule and grades. Guess I'll have to do better.

Maurice: I think Sara had something else in mind. Sara, didn't you mean you are being told to decide what college you're going to attend?

Sara: Right. I'm being pushed to go to Smith. Actually, I'd rather take the extra money that it would require and buy myself a new car. What are the rest of you going to do?

Tova: Sara, I'm not sure I understood you correctly. Do you mean you don't care if you go to college?

Sara: Sure. Just because my parents want me to, doesn't mean I have to go to college. Do you do everything your parents want you to do?

Jerry: None of us does. But how can you get a decent-paying job without a college diploma? My counselor . . .

Sara: Oh, counselors don't know so much. My friend Wayman from Redmond didn't even finish high school, and he's already earned enough to buy a new sports car and a lot of fancy ski equipment.

Maurice: What does your counselor say, Jerry?

Jerry: That if you finish college, you will earn 20 to 30 percent more than if you stop with high school.

Sara: Everyone can make up statistics to make a point.

Maurice: Have any of you visited any of the state colleges?

Ingrid: *(looking up from the school paper she has been reading)* What happened in French today?

Jerry: What's that got to do with what we're going to be doing next year?

Ingrid: Huh?

A. Different students should take the parts of Sara, Ingrid, Maurice, Tova, and Jerry and read this conversation aloud. This will help you get the feeling of the conversation so that you can complete the questions and activities that follow.

   1. What comments in the conversation reveal that a person was actively listening to what was being said? What comments show that a listener was not paying attention?

   2. As you watched the students read through the conversation in the model, what nonverbal cues showed that some members of the group were not giving their full attention to the conversation?

   3. Extend the conversation by having the students role-play what they think will happen as the group keeps talking. For example, how will Jerry deal with Ingrid's response? As the role playing

continues, take notes on the various kinds of listening behavior the participants demonstrate.

4. List several examples from the model and from your notes on the roleplaying of occasions when a member of the group didn't understand something that was said. What, if anything, did the listener do in each case to clarify the speaker's remarks? In each case, what else might the confused listener have done to understand the speaker's remarks?

5. Not all efforts to let a speaker know that you, the listener, don't understand a comment need come in the form of spoken remarks. What (if any) nonverbal cues were used by the students role-playing the extended conversation to indicate their reactions to what was being said? What other nonverbal cues might have been used?

B. Drawing from your observations of the role playing and from your own listening experiences in conversations, make a list of suggestions of how people could improve their listening behavior. Then restate your suggestions as a list of guidelines for effective listening.

Guidelines

Follow these guidelines for being a good listener.

1. **Give active attention to what is being said.** When you are not speaking yourself, you should be alert and responsive to the remarks of others. Try to understand what is being said from the speaker's point of view. Be open-minded and alert for new ideas and viewpoints.

2. **Provide feedback and let the speaker know whether he or she has been understood.** You can provide feedback by asking the speaker to repeat what was said or to expand on his or her comments by giving examples. Another way to provide feedback is to repeat what you heard and ask the speaker whether or not you have understood him or her.

3. **Work to clarify comments you don't understand.** Sometimes simply asking a question or paraphrasing a comment can clear up any confusion. Sometimes you may have to ask several questions before a speaker's remark is clear. In any case, never pass up an opportunity to clarify a speaker's remark because you're afraid that asking questions will make you look foolish.

4. **Be courteous.** When you disagree with the remarks of others, do so in a way that conveys your respect for them as persons. Focus your responses on the ideas expressed, not on the personality or shortcomings of the speaker.

Preparing and Presenting

The class should divide into groups of three or four. Each group should begin by listing five current events from your school, your community, and the nation. As you discuss these events, decide which of them is most interesting to all of you and which event is likely to have the greatest impact on your lives in the next five years. For example, you might talk about the championship football game being played this weekend, a fight at city hall over whether there is to be a curfew for those under 18, or the problems this country is having with oil prices. You may decide that the curfew issue is the most interesting, but that the cost of oil is likely to have the greatest impact on your lives. After your group has reached agreement, select one member of your group to join representatives of other groups in the next round of activities.

The representatives of five to eight groups should form a small circle for discussion. Then chairs should be arranged for others in the class so that they can easily see and hear these representatives. While the rest of the students listen, the representatives should attempt to decide among themselves which of the events discussed in the original groups is most interesting and which will have the greatest long-term impact. The students listening to the representatives should take notes on the listening skills each representative displays. After five minutes, the representatives should stop their discussion. Each representative's listening skills should be rated aloud by three members of the audience, according to the guidelines presented in the Evaluation Checklist.

Evaluation Checklist

Three students from the audience should evaluate the listening skills of each representative according to the following criteria. Rate each representative on a scale from 1 (Poor) to 5 (Excellent). Be prepared to give reasons for each rating you give.

Category	Rating
The listener . . . 1. Gave active attention	
2. Provided feedback	
3. Sought to clarify	
4. Was courteous	

Chapter 4 Review

Summary

One of the keys to good communication is careful listening. In a conversation the listener is just as responsible as the speaker for achieving clear communication. Listeners can improve their listening skills by following the guidelines below.

A good listener should:

1. give active attention to what is being said
2. provide feedback to let the speaker know whether he or she has been understood
3. cooperate to clarify comments he or she does not understand
4. be courteous

Reviewing the Facts and Ideas

1. What is meant by the phrase *active listening*? How does it differ from *passive listening*?
2. What is feedback? Why is providing feedback to a speaker important to a good conversation? What are two ways to give feedback?
3. How can a speaker know he or she's being carefully listened to? What are some nonverbal clues that the listener is not giving his or her full attention?
4. What can a listener do if he or she doesn't understand a comment?
5. When you disagree with someone's remarks, why is it important to focus on the ideas, not the speaker personally?

Discussing Facts and Ideas

1. Discuss the differences between active listening and hearing what is said.

2. Some actions intended to provide feedback for a speaker might actually cause confusion. Think about times when you thought you knew how you were being interpreted only to discover later that you had misread your listener. Compare your experiences with those of others.
3. Make a list of the three most embarrassing moments you have had because you failed to listen well. Compare your list with those of your classmates. What were the most common types of listening errors that contributed to the embarrassing situations?

Applying Your Knowledge

1. People who are lonely or isolated particularly value good listeners. Seek out someone who is in a hospital or a convalescent center, someone who is new in your school, or a relative you haven't talked with in a long time. Visit him or her in person if possible, or if not in person, by telephone. Concentrate on practicing your "active" listening skills as you talk with this person.
2. Active listening often helps you understand others better. Make a list of people whom you think you don't like or whom you find uninteresting. Engage in a conversation with two of them, concentrating on using your active listening skills. Prepare a written report of new information you learn from them. Without using the names of the people with whom you talked, discuss with your classmates whether actively listening to these people helped you gain a better appreciation of them.

Exploring Careers in Communications

Careers in communications are not limited to public speaking and broadcasting. The following careers all require highly developed skills in speech communication.

Actor
Air traffic controller
Commercial artist
Counselor
Director of plays, films, or
    television
Editor of newspapers,
    magazines, or books
Executive
Executive secretary
Fund-raiser
Guide
Interpreter
Manager (any business)
Mediator
Newspaper reporter or
    freelance writer

Personnel director
Politician
Producer of films, plays, or
    television
Psychologist or psychiatrist
Public relations worker
Radio announcer
Receptionist
Salesperson
Teacher
Telecommunications worker
Television announcer or
    newscaster
Union organizer or
    representative

As you explore career possibilities, you should ask yourself how the ability to speak well and communicate effectively with other people can help you in your future jobs.

Activities

1. Invite one or more people with occupations on the preceding list to speak to your class. Ask each speaker to describe the ways in which effective speech skills have helped him or her do the job and receive promotions.
2. Working with another student, research the ways in which speaking skills are used in one of the preceding occupations. Then select a situation that shows these skills in use. You might select a film director explaining a role to an actor, an editor telling a reporter how to write a story, or a guide showing your town to a group of tourists. Role-play this situation before the class.

Being Aware of Communication Methods Used by the Hearing-Impaired

About 14 million Americans have some hearing impairment, and about 2 million of these are deaf—that is, unable to hear or understand speech. Those with severe hearing impairments must rely on sight for communication.

Lip reading is used by many hearing-impaired people to understand what others are saying. Much information is lost, however, if speakers move their lips very little or turn their heads so that their mouths are not visible. Hearing-impaired people also use two kinds of **manual communication**. One kind, the **manual alphabet**, uses the fingers to represent each letter of the alphabet. The other kind, **sign language** or **signing**, uses gestures of the hands and arms to represent words and ideas. Often, all three methods are used together. A person who is interpreting for hearing-impaired people will use signing to convey basic ideas. At the same time, the person will move his or her lips to reinforce the words and spell out unusual words or names using the manual alphabet.

Interpreters using sign language often appear on television programs, especially news or public affairs shows. Recorded programs may be **captioned**. Some captions are printed subtitles that are seen by all viewers. Other programs are **closed-captioned** and must be decoded by special machines. Some hearing-impaired people also communicate by a machine called a *TTY*, which uses a telephone to type out and send messages.

Activity

1. Observe an interpreter "signing" a speech or news program on television. See how often you are able to understand the interpreter's gestures. Also compare the interpreter's speed with that of the speaker. If possible, invite an interpreter to speak to your class and explain the language and symbols he or she uses.

Unit Introduction: Your Audience and You

Speaking to an Audience

A Case Study

Several years ago, a fire on a Bay Area Rapid Transit train underneath San Francisco Bay claimed the life of a fireman and caused the tunnel to be shut down for safety reasons. BART officials learned that many passengers were confused by the wordy instructions they were given by the train operators. BART hired Dr. Elizabeth Loftus, a psychologist, to write a brief, clear evacuation message. Here is Dr. Loftus' 131-word announcement.

"May I have your attention, please? A fire has been reported on this train. BART Central would like you to leave the train for your own safety. Please leave the train now and walk slowly to the opposite tunnel. Follow these instructions for going to the opposite tunnel. The instructions to the opposite tunnel will be repeated while you are leaving the train.

"Open your own doors now. To get to the opposite tunnel, take the sidewalk to the nearest tunnel door. Then go through two tunnel doors, and you will be in the opposite tunnel. Once you are in the opposite tunnel, continue to walk along the sidewalk and tracks so that other people can come through the doors. As you leave the train, please help any people who need help."

Think and Discuss

Dr. Loftus believes that an emergency message must be simple, clear, and reassuring. How clear do you think her message is? What key phrase is repeated many times? Why do you think this phrase is repeated so often?

Do you think you would be reassured by this message? What ideas or sentences in the message are designed to prevent panic? What expressions might help reassure people that someone competent is in charge?

In Unit Two, "Speaking to an Audience," you will learn the most effective ways you can communicate information to other people. You will learn how to persuade people to agree with you and how to take notes on a lecture or speech.

Unit Introduction: Your Audience and You

This unit will concentrate on developing your skills in giving expository and persuasive speeches to an audience. An **expository speech** is a speech whose main purpose is to explain something or to convey information. A **persuasive speech** is a speech whose main purpose is to convince the audience that they should think or act in a certain way.

Whenever you communicate with other people, you have an **audience**. Often your audience is very small, as in the conversations, interviews, and discussions considered in the previous unit. Sometimes, however, you may have a large audience of dozens or even hundreds of people. Whatever the size of your audience, you need to understand how and why they are reacting to your speech. You will need to adjust all of the elements of speech—your thought processes, attitudes, voice, language, and body movement—as you deal with different audiences and as you recognize the varied responses of different members of a single audience.

When speaking to an audience, you must think about what you are saying, why you are saying it, and to whom you are saying it. For example, you may be telling an anecdote, giving a campaign speech, or explaining a scientific theory. Your purpose may be to entertain, to

persuade, or to inform. For each of these purposes, you need to know different things about your audience. Suppose you were telling a humorous story. You would want to make sure that your audience would find the story funny. They should share your ideas of what is humorous and what is not. You also should be sure that your audience will not be offended by what you intend to say. You would want your listeners to be able to understand all the references you make to people and places without your having to explain them.

If you are going to understand an audience, you must develop skill in both observing people and understanding how your own feelings interact with your observations to form opinions about these people. A person's age, background, clothes, and way of speaking may cause us to assume certain things about him or her. Some of our observations about people may give us valuable information about them. Others may be based on prejudice or fear. Use the following checklist to learn more about the way you observe people.

OBSERVATION CHECKLIST

1. Age	Am I assuming that this person is too young to understand me or too old to be interested in what I have to say? How can I learn what people are really like, so that age difference will matter less?
2. Background	If this person comes from a different racial, ethnic, or religious background than I do, am I assuming that he or she is hostile to me? Am I allowing the prejudices of others to keep me from communicating with this person?
3. Appearance	Do I feel intimidated because this person is taller, more muscular, or better dressed than I am? Or am I assuming that because my appearance is better, it is all right for me to behave impolitely?
4. Language	If a person's English is better than mine, am I embarrassed to speak? If someone's English is worse, do I assume that he or she is too ignorant to understand me? How can I choose my language so that I communicate well with a specific person or group of people?

As you prepare to speak to an audience, you need to move beyond observations of individuals to analysis of the specific audience you will be addressing. The following checklist can assist you with your analysis.

AUDIENCE ANALYSIS CHECKLIST

1. Knowledge	What do people in the audience know about you and the subject of your speech?
2. Attitudes	What feelings do the people in the audience have toward you and the subject of your speech?
3. Interests	What are the main interests of the people in your audience? What relationships exist between these interests and your topic?
4. Events	What recent events have strongly influenced the people in your audience?
5. Purpose	Why will the people in the audience be present?
6. Competition	Will other activities occurring at the same time as your speech or in the immediate future compete with your efforts to get the audience's attention?

Once you have analyzed your audience, you need to make use of your findings. First, you must recognize that you use information about your audience to help you communicate what you wish to communicate. Some speakers mistakenly conclude that they are supposed to understand an audience in order to tell the audience members what they want to hear. Such an approach compromises one's integrity and, in the long run, will lead to the loss of credibility for a speaker.

In order to communicate effectively with others, you must show that you respect their intelligence, feelings, and opinions. Make a habit of looking at controversial subjects from the points of view of others. This will help you demonstrate to your audience that you respect their viewpoints, even though you may disagree with them.

Don't talk down to an audience. If you fail to give them credit for knowing as much as they do, people are likely to be offended. If it becomes necessary for you to discuss sensitive subjects, choose your language very carefully. As you speak on such matters, watch alertly for audience reaction that suggests members of your audience are not responding as you had expected them to.

In this unit you will prepare and present expository and persuasive speeches. In all instances, learn as much as you can about your audience and then plan and deliver your presentation with that knowledge of your audience uppermost in your mind.

Activities

1. Think of a person you know well. List things that a stranger might observe about this person. Include details of age, appearance, clothing, and speech. Decide whether a stranger would want to know or communicate with this person as a result of such observations. Then write down how you feel about and communicate with the person. Talk with two or three other students. Use your notes as a basis for the conversation. Seek agreement in your discussion on the kinds of personal characteristics that seem to have the most effect on whether you believe you can communicate with a person.

2. Think of an incident in which a person was able to communicate successfully with other people whose opinions he or she did not share. Think of another incident in which a speaker showed no respect for the opinions of his or her listeners. Describe these incidents briefly to other students in your class. Ask other students to compare their experiences with yours.

3. Find a detailed article on how to grow a vegetable garden (or on some other reasonably complicated process) and distribute a copy of the article to everyone in your class. After others have read your article, explain how you would adapt the material in the article for speeches to three different audiences. If you are talking about growing a vegetable garden, you might have the following audiences.

   a. a ten year old who is interested in planting a first garden
   b. a group of people your age who are not particularly interested in gardening
   c. a gardening club of adults

After your explanation, discuss your ideas with others in the class. Find out how they would adapt a speech to the knowledge, attitudes, interests, events, purpose, and competing activities that might be expected to be present for each audience.

Speaking to Explain

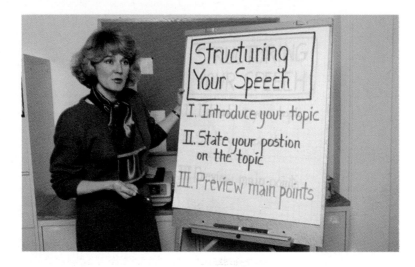

After working through this chapter, you should be proficient at the following skills:

Lesson	Skills
Lesson 1	• explaining a familiar process
Lesson 2	• organizing the information in an expository speech
Lesson 3	• preparing and using speaking notes
Lesson 4	• using visual aids
Lesson 5	• adapting a speech to your audience
Lesson 6	• developing confidence and polish
Lesson 7	• responding to questions from listeners
Lesson 8	• giving an analytical expository speech
Communicating on the Job	• explaining a work process
Communicating as a Citizen	• giving testimony

Explaining a Familiar Process

You have undoubtedly explained a process—how to do something or how something works—many times in your life. You may not have realized it, but each time you explained something, you were giving a short expository speech. Many expository speeches are given to explain how to do something. The process the speaker explains to the audience may be some simple task, such as how to build a greenhouse, or it may be a more complex process, such as how a scientist reasons.

There are three steps to preparing a speech that explains a process. First, fix the specific purpose of the speech firmly in mind. In this case, the purpose is to inform the audience about a particular process. Usually, it is best to write your specific purpose—for example, "This speech will explain to my speech class how to make woodblock prints." Next, think through all the steps in the process and the order in which they occur. These steps will be the main ideas in your speech. Finally, arrange the speech in a pattern that will help your listeners grasp the explanation of the process.

The introduction of a speech should clearly present its purpose as well as arouse the reader's interest. There are several techniques you can use to effectively introduce your speech, whether it is a process speech or any other kind. In the model below, Thomas Huxley uses a literary allusion (to a play by Molière) as well as a reference to the experience of the audience itself. Other techniques are using quotations, anecdotes, personal references, definitions, historical background, or even audiovisual aids.

Similarly, you can make your conclusions more interesting and effective by using a quotation (as well as any of the other techniques), particularly if it refers back to the introduction or body, thus tying together the speech.

Working with the Model

Like baking a cake, reasoning scientifically is a process. Nearly a hundred years ago, British scientist and philosopher Thomas Huxley faced the task of explaining how a scientist reasons to an audience of the general public. A portion of that explanation follows. Study it carefully, and then answer the questions that follow it.

The method of scientific investigation is nothing but the expression of the necessary mode of working of the human mind. You will understand this better, perhaps, if I give you some familiar example. You have all heard it repeated, I dare say, that men of science work by means of induction and deduction. It is imagined by many that the operations of the common mind cannot be compared with these processes, and that they have to be acquired by a sort of special apprenticeship to the craft.

There is a well-known incident in one of Molière's plays, where the author makes the hero express unbounded delight on being told that he had been talking prose during the whole of his life. In the same way, I trust, you will be delighted with yourselves, on the discovery that you have been acting on the principles of inductive and deductive philosophy during the same period. Probably there is no one here who has not in the course of the day had occasion to set in motion a complex train of reasoning of the very same kind as that which a scientific man goes through in tracing the causes of natural phenomena.

A very trivial circumstance will serve to exemplify this. Suppose you go into a fruiterer's shop, wanting an apple. You take up one, and, on biting it, you find it is sour. You look at it, and see that it is hard and green. You take up another one, and that too is hard, green, and sour. The shopman offers you a third. But before biting it you examine it, and find that it is hard and green, and you immediately say that you will not have it, as it must be sour, like those that you have already tried.

Nothing can be more simple than that, you think. But if you will take the trouble to analyze and trace out into its logical elements what has been done by the mind, you will be greatly surprised. In the first place,

you have performed the operation of *induction*. You found that, in two experiences, hardness and greenness in apples went together with sourness. It was so in the first case, and it was confirmed by the second. True, it is a very small basis, but still it is enough to make an induction from. You generalize the facts, and you expect to find sourness in apples where you get hardness and greenness. You found upon that a general law, that *all hard and green apples are sour*; and that, so far as it goes, is a perfect induction.

Well, having got your natural law in this way, when you are offered another apple which you find is hard and green, you say, "All hard and green apples are sour; this apple is hard and green, therefore this apple is sour." That train of reasoning is what logicians call a *syllogism*. And, by the help of further reasoning, you arrive at your final determination: "I will not have that apple." So that, you see, you have, in the first place, established a law by *induction*, and upon that you have founded a *deduction*, and reasoned out the special conclusion of the particular case.

Well now, suppose, having got your law, that at some time afterwards you are discussing the qualities of apples with a friend. You will say to him, "It is a very curious thing, but I find that all hard and green apples are sour!" Your friend says to you, "But how do you know that?" You at once reply, "Oh, because I have tried them over and over again, and have always found them to be so."

Well, if we were talking science instead of common sense, we should call that an *experimental verification*. And, if still opposed, you go further, and say, "I have heard from the people in Somersetshire and Devonshire, where a large number of apples are grown, that they have observed the same thing. It is also found to be the case in Normandy, and in North America. In short, I find it to be the universal experience of mankind wherever attention has been directed to the subject." Whereupon, your friend, unless he is a very unreasonable man, agrees with you, and is convinced that you are quite right in the conclusion you have drawn. He believes, although perhaps he does not know he believes it, that the more frequently experiments have been made, and results of the same kind arrived at, the more certain is the ultimate conclusion, and he disputes the question no further. He sees that the experiment has been tried under all sorts of conditions, as to time, place, and people, with the same result. He says with you, therefore, that the law you have laid down must be a good one, and he must believe it.

In science we do the same thing. The philosopher exercises precisely the same faculties, though in a much more delicate manner. In scientific inquiry, it becomes a matter of duty to expose a supposed law to every possible kind of verification. We take care, moreover, that this is done intentionally, and not left to a mere accident, as in the case of the apples. And in science, as in common life, our confidence in a law is in exact proportion to the absence of variation in the result of our experiments.

A. Look carefully for any unusual words or terms and for the main ideas in Huxley's explanation.
   1. Make a list of any words or terms Huxley used that you do not understand. Some of the terms in the model, such as *fruiterer's shop* (fruit store), are probably not familiar to you. Discuss with other students the words on your lists, until you are all certain you understand every sentence in the model. Consult a dictionary if necessary.
   2. What main ideas was Huxley trying to explain as he described the processes of induction and deduction?

B. Consider the fact that Huxley's lecture was given in the nineteenth century.
   1. How much of Huxley's explanations of induction and deduction made sense to you? Explain why you were confused by whatever didn't make sense to you.
   2. Rewrite in your own words Huxley's explanations of these methods of thinking. First, write a definition of inductive thinking and a definition of deductive thinking. Then think of an example to illustrate each kind of thinking. Finally, tell your complete explanation to a friend. You can tell how effective your explanation is by asking your friend whether he or she understood it.

Guidelines

In the model, only a portion of Huxley's speech was reprinted. A complete expository speech must be arranged in an introduction, body, and conclusion. The following outline is one example of how such a speech can be arranged.

OUTLINE FOR AN EXPOSITORY SPEECH

Format	Suggestions
I. Introduction A. Get the attention and interest of the audience.	Use any of the common techniques discussed on page 119.
B. State your topic and purpose.	State them specifically and clearly.
C. Preview your speech. (optional)	Briefly mention each of your main ideas.

II. Body
A. State main idea #1.
  1. Present supporting material.
  2. Present supporting material.
B. State main idea #2.
  1. Present supporting material.
  2. Present supporting material.
C. State main idea #3.
  1. Present supporting material.
  2. Present supporting material.
	Develop each main point using appropriate examples, illustrations, and details. Provide enough transitions so that the audience can clearly follow your speech from one idea to the next.

III. Conclusion A. Restate your main ideas.	Briefly summarize them. Don't state them in full again.
B. Clinch your central idea in a memorable way.	Emphasize any fact or example that you feel strongly illustrates your purpose.

Sometimes this organization is described by the rule "tell your listeners what you are going to tell them, tell them, and then tell your listeners what you have told them."

Preparing and Presenting

Prepare a three-minute expository speech on how to do something. Choose your own topic or use one of these:

- how to make potato salad
- how to eat a pomegranate
- how to warm up before jogging
- how to keep your Boston fern (or other plant) alive
- how to hook up your new speakers to your old receiver
- how to replace the plug on an electrical appliance
- how to throw a curve ball
- how to get a part-time job
- how to operate a video cassette recorder
- how to give a large dog a bath

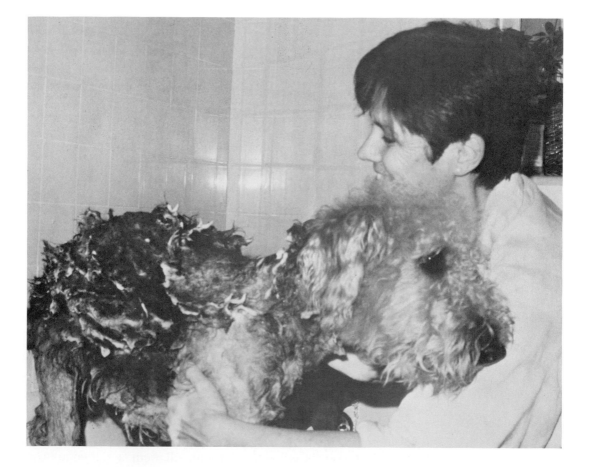

Work through the following steps to prepare your speech:

1. Write your specific purpose. Your purpose is to inform or explain; your specific purpose is to explain the process you have chosen to the class.
2. Make sure you know the major steps (main ideas) involved in the process and the order in which they are performed.
3. Prepare an outline of your speech, including an introduction, body, and conclusion. Use the format on page 123.
4. Practice your speech by giving it to a partner. Have your partner write down anything that is unclear. After your practice session, adjust your speech so that the main ideas are clear.

Give your speech to the class.

Evaluation Checklist

Evaluate each classmate's speech on the basis of the following criteria. Rate each speech on a scale from 1 (Poor) to 5 (Excellent). Be prepared to give reasons for each rating you give. The questions in parentheses will help you do so.

Category	Rating
The speaker . . . 1. Presented a clear, specific purpose	
2. Presented a clear statement of the process to be explained	
3. Had main steps (main ideas) that were organized in a logical order	
4. Included the main ideas in the summary	
5. Gave a speech that was close to the assigned length (If the speech was too long, how could the speaker get it closer to the assigned length?)	
6. Clearly described the process he or she set out to explain (If anything is unclear, how could the speaker make this part of the speech more clear?)	

Preparing an Expository Speech

Arranging your information in patterns helps your listeners understand what you have to say. A **chronological pattern** presents the parts of a speaker's information in the order in which they occurred. For example, you would tell your audience how to prepare a car for a new paint job by describing each of the steps in chronological order. **Spatial patterns** present the information in terms of physical spaces that are familiar to the audience. If you give a speech about the cheeses of France by explaining which cheeses come from each region of France, you are using spatial organization.

A **topical pattern** presents subdivisions of the subject of the speech, discussing the significant people, ideas, and events associated with each subdivision. If you organized your talk about French cheeses in terms of the three major categories of cheese—soft, semisoft, and hard—you would be using a topical pattern.

There are two other patterns, but speakers use them less often than these first three. Speakers sometimes organize their information in terms of causes and their effects, and sometimes in terms of problems and their solutions.

Begin planning your expository speech by choosing a topic and narrowing it to workable proportions. Suppose you choose genetic engineering as your topic. You could narrow this topic to the research applications of genetic engineering or to the industrial applications of genetic engineering. If you decide to talk about the industrial applica-

tions of genetic engineering, you could narrow your topic even further and talk about the development of a bacterium that ingests oil spills.

At this stage, you should write your specific purpose. In any expository speech, your general purpose is to transmit information. In this expository speech, your specific purpose is to tell the class about the development of a bacterium that ingests oil spills.

The next step is to decide which pattern will do the most to make your information easy to understand. You are then ready to begin outlining your speech.

In outlining a speech, it is acceptable to write supporting items as phrases. You will condense your outline even further when you prepare your speaking notes.

Working with the Model

In 1964, President Lyndon Johnson gave a speech to the graduating class of the University of Michigan. In this section of his speech, the President tells his audience how Americans can build the Great Society.

I have come today from the turmoil of your capital to the tranquility of your campus to speak about the future of our country. The purpose of protecting the life of our nation and preserving the liberty of our citizens is to pursue the happiness of our people. Our success in that pursuit is the test of our success as a nation. For a century we labored to settle and to subdue a continent. For half a century, we called upon unbounded invention and untiring industry to create an order of plenty for all our people. The challenge of the next half century is whether we have the wisdom to use that wealth to enrich and elevate our national life, and to advance the quality of our American civilization.

Your imagination, your initiative, and your indignation will determine whether we build a society where progress is the servant of our needs, or a society where old values and new visions are buried under unbridled growth. For in your time we have the opportunity to move not only toward the rich society and the powerful society, but upward to the Great Society. The Great Society rests on abundance and liberty for all. It demands an end to poverty and racial injustice, to which we are totally committed in our time. But that is just the beginning. The Great Society is a place where every child can find knowledge to enrich his mind and to enlarge his talents. It is a place where leisure is a welcome chance to build and reflect, not a feared cause of boredom and restlessness. It is a place where the city of man serves not only the needs of the body and the demands of commerce, but the desire for beauty and the hunger for community.

It is a place where man can renew contact with nature. It is a place which honors creation for its own sake and for what it adds to the understanding of the race. It is a place where men are more concerned with the quality of their goals than the quantity of their goods. But most of all, the Great Society is not a safe harbor, a resting place, a final objective, a finished work. It is a challenge constantly renewed, beckoning us toward a destiny where the meaning of our lives matches the marvelous products of our labor.

So I want to talk to you today about three places where we begin to build the Great Society—in our cities, in our countryside, and in our classrooms. Many of you will live to see the day, perhaps 50 years from now, when there will be 400 million Americans; four-fifths of them in urban areas. In the remainder of this century urban population will double, city land will double, and we will have to build homes, highways and facilities equal to all those built since this country was first settled. So in the next 40 years we must rebuild the entire urban United States.

Aristotle said, "Men come together in cities in order to live, but they remain together in order to live the good life."

It is harder and harder to live the good life in American cities today. The catalogue of ills is long: There is the decay of the centers and the despoiling of the suburbs. There is not enough housing for our people or transportation for our traffic. Open land is vanishing and old landmarks are violated. Worst of all, expansion is eroding the precious and time-honored values of community with neighbors and communion with nature. The loss of these values breeds loneliness and boredom and indifference. Our society will never be great until our cities are great. Today the frontier of imagination and innovation is inside those cities, and not beyond their borders. New experiments are already going on. It will be the task of your generation to make the American city a place where future generations will come, not only to live but to live the good life. . . .

A second place where we begin to build the Great Society is in our countryside. We have always prided ourselves on being not only America the strong and America the free, but America the beautiful. Today that beauty is in danger. The water we drink, the food we eat, the very air that we breathe, are threatened with pollution. Our parks are overcrowded. Our seashores overburdened. Green fields and dense forests are disappearing.

A few years ago we were greatly concerned about the Ugly American. Today we must act to prevent an Ugly America.

For once the battle is lost, once our natural splendor is destroyed, it can never be recaptured. And once man can no longer walk with beauty or wonder at nature, his spirit will wither and his sustenance be wasted.

A third place to build the Great Society is in the classrooms of America. There your children's lives will be shaped. Our society will not be great until every young mind is set free to scan the farthest reaches of thought and imagination. We are still far from that goal. Today, eight million adult Americans, more than the entire population of Michigan, have not finished five years of school. Nearly 20 million have not finished 8 years of school. Nearly 54 million, more than one-quarter of all America, have not even finished high school.

Each year more than 100,000 high school graduates, with proved ability, do not enter college because they cannot afford it. And if we cannot educate today's youth, what will we do in 1970 when elementary school enrollment will be 5 million greater than 1960? And high school enrollment will rise by 5 million. College enrollment will increase by more than three million. In many places, classrooms are overcrowded and curricula are outdated. Most of our qualified teachers are underpaid, and many of our paid teachers are unqualified. So we must give every child a place to sit and a teacher to learn from. Poverty must not be a bar to learning, and learning must offer an escape from poverty.

But more classrooms and more teachers are not enough. We must seek an educational system which grows in excellence as it grows in size. This means better training for our teachers. It means preparing youth to enjoy their hours of leisure as well as their hours of labor. It means exploring new techniques of teaching, to find new ways to stimulate the love of learning and the capacity for creation.

These are three of the central issues of the Great Society. While our government has many programs directed at those issues, I do not pretend that we have the full answer to those problems. But I do promise this: We are going to assemble the best thought and the broadest knowledge from all over the world to find those answers for America. . . .

A. Think about how President Johnson structured his speech.
   1. The purpose of this speech is to inform the listeners. How does President Johnson state the specific purpose of his speech? In what part of his speech does he tell the audience his specific purpose?
   2. What are the three "central issues of the Great Society"? How does knowing that the speech is organized around three issues help you identify what pattern of organization is being used? What pattern has President Johnson used to organize his information?
   3. If President Johnson had traced the evolution of the major problems in America from 1960 up until the time of the speech in 1964, what kind of pattern would he have been using? What kind of pattern would involve discussing the problems of the West, then the Midwest, the South, and the East?
B. Think about the speaker, the listeners, and the occasion.
   1. Why is it particularly appropriate to speak to a group of graduating seniors about "the future of our country," "the challenge of the next half century," and "the opportunity to move . . . upward to the Great Society"? What challenge is the President presenting when he says, "Your imagination, your initiative, and your indignation will determine whether we build a society where progress is the servant of our needs, or a society where old values and new visions are buried under unbridled growth"?
   2. Why do you think President Johnson chose the pattern of organization he did? What makes his pattern more appropriate than a chronological pattern for presenting the problems of the nation?
   3. Suppose the President had been addressing the mayors of the nation's ten largest cities on ways to reduce the problem of violent crime. What pattern of organization might he have used?

Guidelines

Once you have chosen and narrowed a topic, written a specific purpose, and arranged the main ideas necessary to accomplish that purpose in a definite pattern, your next task is to develop your main ideas. Main ideas may be developed in six different ways.

1. Use *definitions* to explain the meaning of an idea. In the third paragraph of his speech, President Johnson spends several sentences defining his concept of the Great Society.

2. Use *examples* to demonstrate an idea. When President Johnson says, "We must seek an educational system which grows in excellence as it grows in size," he gives "better training for our teachers" as one example of how this can be done.

3. *Comparison* or *contrast* may be used to develop main ideas. President Johnson contrasts the traditional concept of "America the beautiful" with the reality of pollution, to develop his idea that the countryside must be reclaimed.

4. *Narratives*, brief anecdotes, can be used to develop main ideas. For example, President Johnson could have developed his idea of the gravity of the pollution problem by telling the story of a family who returns to their favorite lakeside campsite, a place of unspoiled beauty, only to find the lake polluted and the fish dead.

5. *Testimony* or *quotations from experts* can be used to develop main ideas. In his speech, President Johnson quotes Aristotle to reinforce his idea that cities should be places where people can live well, not just survive.

6. *Statistics* are a useful means of developing main ideas. President Johnson states that in 1964 nearly 54 million adult Americans, nearly one-quarter of the population at that time, had not even finished high school. This statistic develops the main idea that America is still far from its goal of adequately educating its youth.

Activity

1. List the main ideas in President Johnson's speech and the method or methods he used to develop each one. Why are statistics a better method than quotation of an expert to develop his idea about the need to improve education in America? Why did President Johnson use a quotation instead of statistics to develop his idea about the quality of life in the cities? Discuss these questions with other students in your class.

Preparing and Presenting

Prepare an outline, using the format on page 123, for a five-minute expository speech on one of the following topics, or on a topic of your choice:

- fitness
- the natural resources of your state
- the location of the major oil fields in America

Use these steps to prepare your outline:

1. Select your topic.
2. Do enough research to become familiar with your topic.
3. Narrow your topic.
4. Write the specific purpose of your speech.
5. Complete your research, using several sources.
6. Decide what pattern to use to organize your information—topical, spatial, or chronological—or whether to organize it in terms of causes and their effects, or problems and their solutions.
7. Write an outline of the main points of your speech. State your main points as sentences.
8. Add supporting ideas and examples for each main point. State supporting items as sentences or phrases.

Share your completed outline with another student. Explain why you chose the kind of pattern you did to organize your information. Modify any part of your outline that the other student finds unclear.

Evaluation Checklist

Evaluate another student's outline based on the following criteria. Rate the outline on a scale from 1 (Poor) to 5 (Excellent). Be prepared to give reasons for each rating you give.

Category	Rating
The student . . . 1. Narrowed the topic enough to be presented adequately in five minutes	
2. Stated the specific purpose clearly in the introduction	
3. Used a pattern of organization that clearly and logically fit the speech topic	
4. Developed each main idea with enough detail to make it clear to the audience	
5. Included an introduction, body, and conclusion in the outline	

Preparing and Using Speaking Notes

Once you have completed your outline, you can begin thinking about delivering your speech. You can make your speech livelier and more spontaneous by maintaining good eye contact with your listeners, so that they feel you are really talking to them. To maintain contact with your listeners and observe how they are responding to your speech, you must keep from looking down at your speaking notes too often.

Properly prepared notecards free you from the necessity of reading your speech word-for-word. Once you have completed your outline, list the main ideas of your speech on 3″ × 5″ notecards. Under each main idea, write a word or phrase that will remind you of its supporting ideas and examples. Suppose that one of your main ideas is that many writers have used their experiences in other jobs as material for their books. Your supporting idea might be that several physicians have used their medical knowledge in novels and stories, and your examples might be the doctor-writers Michael Crichton, A. J. Cronin, and J. G. Ballard. Your notecard for this main idea would look like this:

> II. Many writers use experiences in other jobs as material
> A. Doctor-writers
>   1. Crichton
>   2. Cronin
>   3. Ballard

Such notecards remove any fear of forgetting your speech and let you give your listeners the attention they deserve.

Oral reports are one expository speaking situation in which carefully prepared notecards are especially helpful. Sometimes your teacher will already have chosen and named a topic for you, and sometimes you will choose the topic yourself. In both cases, the key to giving a good oral report is understanding the assignment. Be sure that the written purpose of your speech fulfills the assignment.

Using notecards is sufficient for most speeches, but you may need to write out the entire speech if it is unusually long or complex. Type or print the manuscript on one side of the paper. Number the pages clearly. This will help you establish eye contact with your audience instead of burying your head in the paper.

To gain confidence in manuscript speaking, use these guidelines. Stand and read your entire speech aloud as if you had an audience, or get a friend to listen as you read. Concentrate on making the meaning clear. Rework sections that you or your listener were not satisfied with. Finally, read the entire speech again in a relaxed manner. Concentrate on expressing the ideas with precision, power, and excitement. For further help on manuscript speaking, see page 374.

Working with the Model

After their biology class had completed a study module on how plants repond to their environment, Lauren Smith and Jason Martinson were asked to prepare short oral reports. Here is the assignment they were given.

Using at least three sources, prepare an oral report to give to the class during the first week of October. Your report should be from ten to fifteen minutes long. It should explore in detail one of the relationships that we have studied between plants and their environment. Be sure to include at least two examples for each main idea in your report. If you use a chart or other visual aid, be sure that the lettering is large enough to be read from the back of the room. End your report by giving two sources where your listeners can read more about your topic.

Lauren and Jason both decided to do reports on the relationship between water supply in the environment and plant life. Read the notecards each of them prepared:

Jason's Notecards

(1)

<u>purpose:</u> to explain relationship between water
supply and plant life to my biology class
<u>intro:</u> we all know too little water will cause plants to die,
but the relationship between water supply and
plant life is more complex than that: plants adapt
not only to amount of water, but to frequency of
water supply

(2)

<u>main ideas:</u>
  <u>plants adapt to <u>amount</u> of water</u>
  A. cactus
    1. leaves modified into spines to prevent water
        loss
    2. barrel cactus—storage tissue
        (SHOW DRAWING OF CROSS-SECTION OF
        BARREL CACTUS)
  B. mesquite: extra long roots

  <u>plants adapt to <u>frequency</u> of water</u>
  A. In areas w/dry seasons, trees are seasonal too—
      that is, deciduous (lose their leaves)
  B. In Sahara, some herbs complete entire life cycle in
      2-wk. wet season

conc.:   (3)
1. plants adapt to both <u>amount</u> & <u>frequency</u> of water
   supply
2. water supply is probably the most impt.
   environmental factor in determining a plant's
   characteristics
3. for more info: Rost et al., <u>Botany</u>; Raven & Curtis,
   <u>Biology of Plants</u>

Lauren's Notecards

Water is important in the life of plants
   You can see one kind of adaptation to water supply
   when you look at cactus
Plants also adapt to the frequency of water supply

Deciduous trees have a life cycle adapted to a seasonal
water supply
   see Rost, <u>Botany</u>
The next time you water your houseplants, remember
that water supply is probably the most important thing in
a plant's environment!

A. Imagine that you were given the same assignment as Jason and
   Lauren.
   1. When are you expected to give your report?
   2. What directions have you been given about structuring your
      report?
   3. For how long are you to speak?
   4. What guidelines has the teacher provided about the use of visual
      aids?
   5. How many sources are you to use in preparing your report?
   6. What specific information are you to give your listeners?
   7. Why has the teacher given this assignment—to review material
      you covered previously, to introduce a new topic, or to study in
      depth something the class already has some knowledge about?

B. Read carefully the notecards prepared by Lauren and Jason.
1. Which report will fulfill the assignment most accurately? Reread the assignment and discuss how each student's notecards fulfill or fail to fulfill it.
2. Which set of notes will help the audience grasp the purpose of the speech? Why?
3. Review the outline for an expository speech given on page 123. Which set of notes most resembles the outline? How do you think writing notes in this format will help the speaker? How will it help the audience?
4. Which set of notes will best help the audience grasp the speaker's main points? What does that set of notes remind the speaker to do to help the audience remember the main points?
5. Which set of notes contains a reference to a visual aid? What may happen to a speaker who plans to use a visual aid but includes no reference to it in his or her notecards?
6. What definition has been included in the notecards? How might this help the listeners during the speech?
7. Jason has numbered his notecards. How might numbering the notecards help a speaker?

Guidelines

Follow these suggestions in preparing your speaking notes.

1. Your speaking notes should be small enough so that they do not distract your listeners. Three-by-five-inch notecards are an ideal size and are stiff enough to be held easily.
2. Print the information on your cards large enough so it can be read at a glance from arm's length.
3. Arrange your notes so that the main ideas can be picked up at a glance. Underline major thoughts, capitalize items so you can spot them easily, and use color coding for any point you want to emphasize.
4. Write information on only one side of each card.
5. Number your cards. Don't experience the panic of dropping your cards just before the speech and being unable to get them back in order.
6. Limit the total number of cards to as few as possible while still retaining a comfortable number of reminders of your main points.
7. In deciding what to include on your cards, you may want to select specific quotations that you want to state accurately, facts or figures that are complicated or difficult to remember, phonetic spellings of hard-to-pronounce words, and precise definitions of confusing terms.

Preparing and Presenting

Read carefully the outline you prepared in the previous lesson. Imagine yourself giving your speech and think about what words or phrases most vividly bring your main ideas to mind. Then turn your outline into notecards. Your main ideas, stated in complete sentences in your outline, may become abbreviated sentences or phrases in your notecards. Your supporting ideas and examples may become single words.

When you have finished, look carefully through your outline again. Does your speech contain any information—statistics or quotations—that you must cite exactly? If so, write this information into your cards in full, exactly as you will deliver it. Do you use any terms which may need to be defined for your audience? Add such definitions now, along with any notes on when to use visual aids. Check that your cards are easy to read and number them.

Now give your speech for a classmate. As you deliver your speech, look at your notes as little as possible. The purpose of this practice session is to see how well your notecards work. Although it is important to keep your speaking notes as brief as possible, they must effectively remind you of everything you want to say and contain any numbers or passages you want to quote verbatim.

Evaluation Checklist

Evaluate your classmate's speech on the basis of the following criteria. Rate each speech on a scale from 1 (Poor) to 5 (Excellent). Be prepared to give reasons for each rating you give. The questions in parentheses will help you do so.

Category	Rating
The speaker . . . 1. Gave a clearly organized speech (What additional information or change in organization would make the speech clearer?)	
2. Handled the notecards in a way that was not distracting (What movements, if any, took your attention away from the speech?)	
3. Delivered the speech smoothly and naturally (What parts, if any, were awkward?)	

Preparing and Using Visual Aids

Since people receive information through their eyes as well as their ears, a visual aid will often increase your ability to communicate information in a speech. To decide whether you could improve your speech by using a visual aid, read carefully through your outline, looking for kinds of information that are best communicated visually as well as verbally. Here are some kinds of information to look for.

- the main ideas and examples in your speech, to help your listeners follow them more easily (see the chart on the left below)
- technical or unusual terms (see the chart on the right below)

Traditional Energy Sources	**Natural Gas Industry: Important Terms**

I. Oil
  A. Location of Established Fields
  B. New Fields
    1. Alaska
    2. North Sea
    3. Alberta, Canada
  C. Role of OPEC
 	
II. Natural Gas
  A. Present Resources
  B. Exploring for Natural Gas
  C. Storing Natural Gas
	• Acetylene
	• Butane
	• Propane
	• Ethane
	• Ethylene
	• Methane
	• Hydrocarbon
	• Petrochemicals

- information that you want your audience to compare with previous information in your speech (Visual aids help communication whenever you ask your audience to consider two things at once, since words restrict you to presenting pieces of information one at a time.)
- information that is difficult to visualize, such as the structure of an intricate piece of machinery
- information about something unlike anything your audience has ever seen (such as the exotic fish found in very deep water)
- information that is usually accompanied by a visual reference (For example, newspaper stories about archeological discoveries almost always contain maps.)

There are several types of visual aids you can use to illustrate your information. Three-dimensional *models* (in materials such as cardboard, wood, cloth, plaster, or plastic) can be used to explain structure:

the structure of an ancient Roman villa, the human skeleton, the earliest ice skates, or DNA. *Maps* are useful in speeches on history, politics, exploration, or ecology. *Charts* can be used to show the organizational structure of a company or a government agency. Pie charts, bar charts, and graphs are particularly useful when you want your audience to compare two or more pieces of information. (Notice the effect of presenting the same information—the number of flu cases between December and April—in the two graphs below. The line graph emphasizes the progress of the flu epidemic. The bar chart emphasizes the difference in the number of cases each month.)

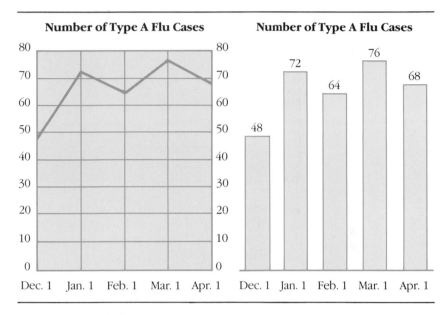

Diagrams help your audience understand the relative size and position of the parts of something, such as the parts of an engine or of the heart. *Photographs* or *color slides* let your audience see something totally unfamiliar to them, such as a snow leopard. After you have decided which ideas in your speech to supplement with visual aids, think carefully about what kind of visual aid will most help your audience understand each idea.

When you prepare a chart or diagram, be sure that it is orderly and attractive and that any lettering is large enough to be read from the back of the room. If you will be using special equipment such as a slide projector, be sure that it is in working order and that you understand its operation. Indicate in your notecards where in your speech you will use each aid and practice using the aids when you practice your speech. When you give your speech, remember not to block your listeners' view of each aid and not to look at it continuously as you talk.

Working with the Model

Here is the visual aid Jason Martinson used during his speech on water supply and plants:

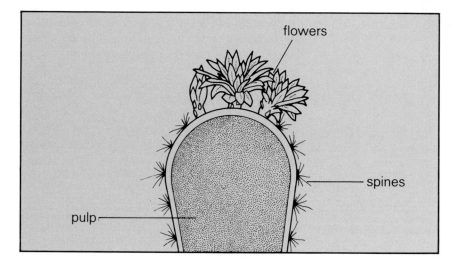

A. Reread Jason's notecards on pages 134–135.
   1. What piece of information has Jason decided to supplement with a visual aid? Why did he choose to use a visual aid with this particular item?
   2. Where else in his speech might Jason have used a visual aid? What terms in the speech might be new to the audience, or what information might be difficult to remember?
B. Think about the type of visual aid Jason decided to use.
   1. What type of visual aid did Jason choose?
   2. Why do you think Jason used this visual aid instead of color slides of a barrel cactus?
   3. Jason's father offered to buy him a cross-section of a real barrel cactus. What would be the advantages and disadvantages of Jason's using a real barrel cactus, instead of the visual aid he prepared?
   4. When Jason explained that the leaves of cactus have become spines to prevent water loss through evaporation, he passed several different kinds of cactus spines around the room for the class to see. What are the advantages and disadvantages of using a visual aid in this way? How else might Jason have shown the class what the spines of several different types of cactus look like?

C. Borrow from your audiovisual department and bring to class an example or a picture of each of the following visual aids: slides and 35-millimeter projector; transparency and overhead projector; film and 8- or 16-millimeter projector; videotape cassette; video tape recorder and monitor; flipchart and stand; poster; chalkboard; working model (as in the photo below); map; handout. Discuss with your teacher and other students the advantages and disadvantages of each of these visual aids, in terms of cost, ease and scope of use, preparation time, and effectiveness with different audiences. What other visual aids can you identify?

Guidelines

A few simple rules will help you use visual aids effectively.

1. Be sure the aid is large enough so that the smallest detail you want your audience to see is visible from every point in the room.
2. Stand so that you are not blocking your audience's view of the aid.
3. If the aid requires the use of special equipment, such as a slide projector or a video tape recorder, make sure you can operate the equipment. Just before your speech, check to make sure that the equipment is working properly.
4. Make the aid neat and attractive.
5. Do not look at the aid continuously as you talk. Point out each major feature in the aid briefly, but keep your eyes on the audience to see whether they are understanding your speech.
6. Be cautious about distributing materials to be looked at by listeners. Such activity will probably distract them from your speech instead of aiding communication. (You may, however, wish to distribute such materials immediately after your speech.)

Preparing and Presenting

Read carefully through the outline you prepared in Lesson 2 of this chapter, looking for ideas or examples that could be communicated more effectively with the help of a visual aid. Make a list of these ideas and examples.

Next, think carefully about what kind of visual aid will best help your listeners understand each idea or example on your list. For example, if one of your main ideas is the location of oil fields in America, you

will want to use a map like the one shown here, rather than color slides. Write the visual aid for each idea opposite it on your list. On the note-cards you prepared for the previous lesson, indicate at what point in your speech you will use each visual aid.

Now prepare your visual aids. Be sure that all parts of each aid, including all lettering, will be visible to everyone in the class. (Notice the size of the lettering on the pie chart and picture graph below.) When you practice your speech, include the use of your visual aids as part of your practice.

Give your speech to the class. Look at your listeners as you use each visual aid—remember that you are communicating with them, not it.

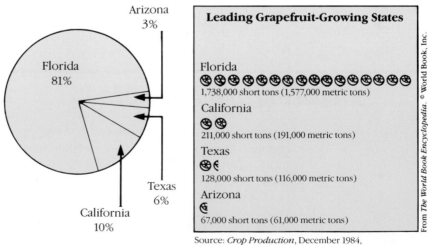

Source: *Crop Production*, December 1984,
U.S. Department of Agriculture. Figures are for 1984.

Evaluation Checklist

Evaluate your classmate's speech on the basis of the following criteria. Rate each speech on a scale from 1 (Poor) to 5 (Excellent). Be prepared to give reasons for each rating you give. The questions in parentheses will help you do so.

Category	Rating
The speaker . . . 1. Used visual aids that made his or her ideas or examples easier to understand	
2. Used visual aids that were appropriate to the ideas communicated (What other kind of visual aid, if any, would have been more effective in communicating one of the speaker's ideas? Why?)	
3. Used notes and aids without distracting the audience's attention away from the content (How can the speaker overcome this problem?)	
4. Used visual aids that were clearly visible to everyone in the audience	

LESSON 5

Adapting a Speech to Your Audience

Imagine that you are an experienced mechanic and that you've been invited to give a short talk to your uncle's senior citizen group. You have decided to talk about your hobby: restoring vintage cars. You feel you have prepared a good speech—your information on how to restore a Duesenberg engine is clearly organized in a chronological pattern, and you even have photos of each step in the process.

As you deliver your speech, you notice that people don't seem to be paying much attention. Your audience is easily distracted and not overly sympathetic. Later your uncle explains their reaction: most of your listeners didn't know enough about cars to understand your explanation. Moreover, most of them expected a talk on how to save money by doing minor repairs themselves. Naturally, they were disappointed and bored by your speech.

A successful speaker takes the audience's knowledge, needs, and interests into account.

Working with the Model

The following speech was given by Thomas J. Watson, Jr., the son of the founder of IBM, to the graduating class of Brown University in 1964. As you read it, be particularly aware of the speaker, the listeners, and the occasion. Try to find all the ways in which Watson, a successful executive with one of the nation's largest corporations, has adapted his speech to this group of inexperienced college seniors.

Twenty-seven years ago I sat where you now sit in the graduating class of 1937 at Brown University. I'm sure I seem several generations away from you in age, but these twenty-seven years have gone so quickly that it's not at all hard for me to remember that vivid day of my own graduation. Strangely enough, the one thing about that day that I cannot remember is what the commencement speaker had to say. My thoughts, like yours, were targeted upon my family and my friends and my plans for the summer. But of one thing I'm sure: If the speaker made a short speech, I know I blessed him.

Therefore, I surmise, there is only one sure way to earn a place in your memory and that is to be brief. I will.

My subject today is in the general area of self-protection. I want to spend a few moments contrasting the drive for physical protection in

144

and out of college with the great difficulty all of us have through life in protecting the non-physical parts of our being.

In college sports, one is constantly protecting one's body with all kinds of devices, from shoulder pads to shin guards. Even in later life, we continue this drive for physical safety with such things as padded dashboards and shatter-proof windshields. All these things help to keep one's body safe and unmarked, and they are good things.

However, all of you graduating today possess something much more important to you than your body. I am speaking to you of your mind, your spirit, your ability to think and speak independently, and your ability at this point as college seniors to stand up and be counted with a clear and firm position on nearly any of the issues which affect your life or the life of the nation.

The fundamental convictions and principles which help you to form your firm, clear position are your most precious possession. Paradoxically, all the wonderful equipment available for shielding the body is worthless for protecting the spirit and the mind.

What then can you do to protect these priceless personal assets? You can't hide them; you can't smother them; you can't rely on some kind of padding. On the contrary, you can protect them only by exposing them to danger, only by defending your personal beliefs regardless of opposition and, like tempered steel, toughening your convictions by the hot shock of conflict.

If you succeed in preserving your principles in the years ahead, without becoming so radical that nobody will listen or follow your example, you will become a part of that elite group in the world which Crawford Greenwalt, Chairman of the DuPont Company, calls the "uncommon man." . . .

It may seem fantastic to you that you could lose this outspoken ability you have been developing throughout your scholastic career. Yet it's a fact that the mass world in which we live tends to etch away the tough hard bumps of conviction and belief. I venture to predict that not one of you will be at work very many years before you will have to look into your heart and answer some very difficult questions. Your answers will, in a very real sense, begin to determine whether your parents, this institution, and the world in which you have lived have produced a common or uncommon human being.

You will have to choose between the safe, conservative silent position and the choice of speaking your mind, of stating your true position and thereby earning yourself some enemies.

Will you develop the reputation of being outspoken, sometimes uncooperative but always honest in supporting what your beliefs indicate is right?

Or will you be a steadfast, reliable . . . [person] who can always be counted on to cooperate? . . .

All the great . . . [people] of history have had to answer the same critical questions. Each had to choose between the safe protection of the crowd and the risk of standing up and being counted. And you can find no truly great . . . [individuals] who took the easy way.

For their courage some suffered abuse, imprisonment, and even death. Others lived to win the acclaim of their . . . [contemporaries]. But all achieved greatness.

Through history, examples are abundant:

- Columbus
- Charles Darwin
- Galileo, who confirmed the theory that the earth traveled about the sun, and who for his affirmation became a prisoner of the Inquisition.

- Socrates, who told his judges at his trial: "Men of Athens, I honor and love you; but I shall obey God rather than you, and while I have life and strength, I shall never cease from the practice and teaching of philosophy."

If we turn to our own times, we can all of us recall other . . . [people] of other lands who refused to take the easy way out, who stood up against the current for what they believed right and just. Nehru in India, de Gaulle in France, Churchill in England.

And in our own country, it wasn't easy in 1956 when the British, French and Israeli forces invaded Egypt—in the midst of an American presidential election—for the President of the United States, Dwight D. Eisenhower, to condemn the use of force and to call upon the aggressors to get out. But he did it—and the electorate overwhelmingly upheld his courage.

And it wasn't easy for another American President of a different political party—John F. Kennedy—to take an unequivocal stand on civil rights, when that stand might have cost him votes of the South, which in the 1960 election gave him his tiny margin of victory. But he did it and thereby added a post-publication chapter to *Profiles in Courage*. . . .

All these . . . [people], despite their great variety, had something in common. Every single one of them put principle first, safety second; individuality first, adjustment second; courage first, cost second. . . .

We need more such . . . [people], more than ever before, living at this hour. The issues are the biggest in history—the need for courageous dialogue greater than ever. . . .

Now suppose you try, in your own manner, to follow this course. What will happen to you?

Well, Nicholas Murray Butler, the great President of Columbia University at the beginning of this century, said that the world is made up of three groups of people.

A small elite group who make things happen.

A somewhat larger group who watch things happen.

And the great multitude who don't know what happens.

This means that the leaders, the makers of opinion in the world, are a very limited group of people.

So as you stand and are counted you will first run into the group who equate newness with wrongness. If it's a new idea, it's uncomfortable and they won't like it. These are the conventionalists.

Second, you're sure to meet cynics, people who believe anyone who sticks his neck out is a fool. I am sure all of you have heard of measures which passed the Congress in a breeze on a voice vote, and later go down to crashing defeat where some Congressman insists that every vote be recorded in the *Congressional Record*.

Third, you'll run into the group of people who believe that there are certain taboo questions that should not be debated. These suppressors of dissent think that once a stand has been taken it is forever settled.

Disarmament, the admission of Red China to the U.N., a change in policy toward Castro or Vietnam—all such touchy subjects, these people warn, should be left alone.

If you stand up and are counted, from time to time you may get yourself knocked down. But remember this: . . . [Someone] flattened by an opponent can get up again. . . . [Someone] flattened by conformity stays down for good. . . .

Follow the path of the unsafe, independent thinker. Expose your ideas to the dangers of controversy. Speak your mind and fear less the label of "crackpot" than the stigma of conformity. And on issues that seem important to you, stand up and be counted at any cost.

A. Think about how Watson has taken the audience's knowledge, needs, and interests into account.
   1. What is the purpose of Watson's speech? Why is this purpose well adapted to his audience?
   2. How does Watson capture the audience's interest by letting them know that he knows how they feel? Where in his speech does he do this?
   3. What experiences familiar to his audience does Watson use to illustrate his main ideas?
   4. What authorities familiar to his audience does Watson quote to support his main ideas? How does he give his audience information about authorities with whom they may be unfamiliar?

B. Think about the speaker, the listeners, and the occasion.
   1. This speech was given on a college campus by an important executive of a major American corporation. Discuss how Watson would have had to change his speech to present it to a philanthropic organization like the Elks, many of whose members are themselves in business. How might Watson have modified the purpose of his speech? What examples (both experiences and authorities) might he change?

2. Imagine that Watson was asked to speak to the PTA. How might he modify the purpose of his speech? Which experiences and examples in his speech might he have to change?

Guidelines

You should let your audience know that you are aware of their knowledge and interests from the very beginning of your speech. A good introduction has the following characteristics.

1. It directs the attention of the audience to the topic of the speech.
2. It makes the purpose of the speech clear.
3. It ties the speech to the knowledge and interests of the audience.
4. It uses humor or other attention-getting techniques to further the purpose of the speech rather than merely to entertain.
5. It includes a linkage or bridge to the body of the speech. Often this bridge is a preview of the main ideas of the speech.

Preparing and Presenting

Prepare an outline of a five- to ten-minute speech in which you define a concept for your audience. You may choose a concept from the biological or physical sciences, from sports, from the arts, or from politics and the social sciences. Your speech will answer the question "What is . . . ?" (for example, "What is genetic engineering?"). It should contain a definition of the concept, plus a brief explanation of how the concept works.

Your definition should tell the class what sport, science, art, or social science your concept belongs to, what class within that area your concept belongs to, and what characteristics set it apart from other similar concepts. For example, the term *general anesthesia* belongs to medicine, specifically to the class of anesthesia, denoting the loss of sensation. Unlike the similar concept *local anesthesia*, general anesthesia involves the entire body and results in loss of consciousness as well as loss of sensation. Be sure not to use any technical words your audience may not know in your definition.

In the rest of your speech, explain how the concept works. First, use a metaphor or simile to help explain how your concept works (review how Watson used the metaphor of padding to explain the concept of self-protection of the mind and spirit). Then, give one or more examples of how your concept works. Use one of the following concepts or a concept of your own (with your teacher's approval):

The Arts
montage
collage
opera
a cappella singing
Expressionism

Science
solar energy
photosynthesis
immunization
gravitation
"greenhouse effect"

Social Science/Politics
buffer state
laissez-faire
superego
behaviorism
colonialism

Sports
blocking
power play
birdie
dressage
dunk shot

To begin your preparation, analyze your audience by completing the Audience Analysis Checklist on page 116. Share your analysis with two other students. Discuss the differences and similarities in your analysis of the class. In particular, see whether you agree on the class's probable knowledge of and interest in each of the concepts the three of you have chosen.

As you complete work on your speech, be sure that your introduction reflects the knowledge about your audience you gained in completing the Audience Analysis Checklist. Share your introduction with the other two students.

Evaluation Checklist

Evaluate each other's outline and audience analysis on the basis of the following criteria. Rate them on a scale from 1 (Poor) to 5 (Excellent). Be prepared to give reasons for each rating you give.

Category	Rating
The outline and analysis . . . 1. Showed a good knowledge of the audience	
2. Showed a clear understanding of the audience's interest in his or her topic	
3. Gave details about the audience's opinions and beliefs that would ensure the effectiveness of his or her speech	
4. Included an introduction that would be interesting and effective to the specific audience addressed	

Developing Confidence and Polishing Your Speech

In a recent survey, adults rated speaking before a group as their number one fear. They were more afraid of giving a speech than of accidents, of heights, or of death. Columnist Erma Bombeck jokingly suggested that, in order to deal with this fear, you should "demand a podium capable of supporting a dead body (yours) up to 187 pounds. Throw yourself over it, being sure to hook your arm over the microphone so you won't slip away." Maybe you have seen speakers who seemed to be taking this advice. You probably weren't very impressed with their skill. In this lesson you will learn to develop confidence and to polish your speech for its eventual delivery to an audience.

Many famous performers and people who work with such performers have offered advice concerning what is commonly called "stage fright." Author and television personality George Plimpton observed that "very few speakers escape the so-called 'butterflies.'" He suggested that the best way of dealing with them is to recognize that they are beneficial rather than harmful.

It may not be easy to remember this advice when you are getting ready to speak and are struck by the familiar symptoms of cold hands, sudden loss of memory, trembling legs and arms, dry mouth, rapid pulse, and a lump in your throat. A certain amount of tension, however, is essential for a good performance, even among the most successful professional performers. Sports psychologist Dr. David Coppel's clients have included Olympic athletes who need help in developing enough confidence to perform under great stress. He emphasizes the importance of concentrating on the performance as a key to success. Actors have long recognized that eliminating distracting thoughts is an essential ingredient to successful stage performing. Concentrating on breathing deeply before you speak and learning to relax your entire body before you speak can also help.

However, really confident speaking depends most on thorough preparation and practice. You may have heard stories of how Abraham Lincoln would jot down ideas on the back of an envelope as he sat listening to another speaker and then give a polished performance when it was his turn to speak. There is some evidence that Lincoln did jot down ideas on the backs of envelopes. There is much more evidence that Lincoln was a successful speaker because of long hours of practice, during which he sought the critical assistance of others to help him perfect the content and delivery of his speeches.

Holding a practice session gives you a listener's reaction to your speech before you have to face your audience. This listener's ability to give you valid criticism is an important advantage of the practice session; if you've been doing something wrong, practicing by yourself will just strengthen this mistake you've been making.

Before you schedule a practice session, review your speech to be sure that you have already completed these steps.

- Link the topic of your speech to subjects that are familiar to your listeners.
- Organize your information in a pattern: chronological, spatial, topical, by cause and effect, or by problem and solution.
- Use metaphors and other figures of speech to make your explanations more vivid.
- Use audio and visual aids to increase your listeners' interest and comprehension.

Working with the Model

To complete the Preparing and Presenting section of the previous lesson, Missy decided to define and explain the concept of mutualism. Before they gave their speeches, the students in Missy's class were required to hand in a speech outline and a practice record of at least one practice session. Read Missy's outline carefully to find its strengths and weaknesses. Then read the practice record George completed when he, Jane, and Sherry listened to Missy practice her speech.

Missy's Outline

Specific Purpose: To explain the biological concept of mutualism to my speech class

I. Introduction
   A. *To gain audience's attention:* Most of us think of friendship as a relationship that is mutually beneficial. Friends depend on each other, and each one benefits from the relationship. But did you know that this sort of relationship also exists in nature? When two species depend on each other and each one benefits from the relationship, biologists call this relationship *mutualism*.
   B. Today I'm going to answer the question "What is mutualism?"

II. Body
   A. Mutualism is a relationship between two species, from which both benefit.
      1. The concept is from biology.
      2. Mutualism is a kind of symbiosis (symbiosis: interdependence of two species).

   a. mutualism differs from *commensalism*, a kind of symbiosis in which one member benefits and the other is unaffected
   b. mutualism differs from *parasitism*, in which one member benefits at the cost of the other

  B. Mutualism is like the friendship between two neighboring families with tight budgets.
   1. If Mrs. Smith teaches the Gomez children to ice skate and Mr. Gomez teaches the Smith children to draw, both families have benefited from the relationship.
   2. Both families live better because of the relationship, because without it the families would have to pay for ice skating and art lessons.

  C. There are many examples of mutualism in nature.
   1. *Rhizobium* bacteria live on the root nodules of legumes like peas and peanuts. The plants benefit because the bacteria change the nitrogen in the soil into a form the plants can use.
   2. Certain small birds obtain food by eating the insect parasites from the backs of African Cape elk. The elk benefit from removal of the parasites.
   3. Certain protozoa find a protected home in the intestinal tract of termites. The termites benefit because the protozoa digest the cellulose in the wood the termites eat.

III. Conclusion
  A. Mutualism is a relationship between two species that benefits both of them.
  B. You can think of mutualism as nature's "good neighbor policy."

George's Practice Record

PRACTICE RECORD

Person(s) Listening *Jane* *George* *Sherry*

When *12/8/88* Where *Jane's house* Length of speech *10 minutes*

Specific Purpose (as heard by listener) *To explain the concept of mutualism.*

Main Ideas (as heard by listener) *1) Mutualism is a biological partnership from which both parties benefit; 2) Mutualism is like friendship; 3) Mutualism occurs only at the microscopic level.*

Audience Adaptation	poor			good		Comments
To their knowledge	①	2	3	4	5	*What exactly is a species? You don't define "symbiosis."*
To their interests and feelings	1	2	3	④	5	*I'm not interested in biology, but I can understand the benefits of friendship.*
Language and Examples						
Concrete	1	②	3	4	5	*You should have given examples of commensalism and parasitism.*
Vivid	1	2	③	4	5	
Appropriate	1	2	3	4	⑤	*Your explanation in terms of neighbor families was good!*
Voice						
Loudness	1	2	3	④	5	*It's easy to hear you.*
Variety	1	②	3	4	5	*You tend to speak in a monotone.*
Pronunciation	1	2	3	4	⑤	*You're able to pronounce all the scientific terms.*
Articulation	1	2	3	4	⑤	
Bodily Action						
Movement	1	2	3	④	5	*Your movements look relaxed and natural.*
Eye Contact	1	②	3	4	5	*Not enough! It seems you don't know we're there.*

Suggestions

1. Define "symbiosis".

2. A visual aid listing each type of symbiosis would help, especially if you used arrows to indicate the dependent relationships. Using a visual aid might help you develop better eye contact, too.

A. Reread the Preparing and Presenting assignment in the previous lesson and think about how Missy's outline fulfills that assignment.
   1. What is the specific purpose of Missy's speech?
   2. How does Missy's speech fulfill the assignment given her class?
   3. How does Missy link her topic to something familiar to her audience? Where in her speech does she do this? Why do you think she does it in this portion of her speech?
   4. How does Missy define mutualism for her audience? Where in the speech does she do this?
   5. What metaphor or simile does Missy use to help her audience understand the concept of mutualism? Where in the speech does she do this?
   6. What examples of mutualism does Missy give her audience? How effective do you think these examples are? Explain why you find them (or don't find them) effective.
   7. Which of the patterns for organizing information that you studied on page 126 does Missy's outline most resemble? Why (or why not) is the pattern she used effective?

B. Read George's practice record carefully.
   1. George's practice record shows that he thinks mutualism occurs only at the microscopic level, even though this is not the case. Why has George received this false impression? How can Missy change her speech to avoid giving her listeners this false impression?
   2. What two reasons does George give for suggesting that Missy use visual aids?
   3. What visual aids do you think would most help you understand Missy's main ideas?
   4. What problems does George have with the language in Missy's speech? How can she solve these problems?

C. Suppose that you are Missy and that you have just reviewed the practice record completed by George.
   1. George thinks that you didn't define *symbiosis*, but you know from your outline that you intended to, and you're almost certain that you did. How can you use the practice records completed by Jane and Sherry to see whether you really did define symbiosis in your speech?
   2. What aspects of your speech and your delivery would you feel were successful?
   3. What aspects of your speech and delivery need more work? How would you go about improving each of them?

D. After reading the practice record completed by George, what information will you particularly look for in the practice records completed by Jane and Sherry?

Guidelines

Keep the following points in mind as you practice your speaking.

- During practice sessions seek to understand your fears and put them in their place. Remember that most audiences are like the person you have chosen to help you in the practice session. They want you to succeed. To them, you will not seem as nervous as you feel.
- During practice sessions try the following relaxation routine. Just before you move to the place where you will be speaking, take a deep breath and then swallow. Yawn several times. Press your fingertips together. Walk at a normal pace to the location of your speech. Pause and arrange your notes and thoughts. Make sure your weight is evenly distributed on both feet and press the balls of your feet against the floor. Then look up at your audience and begin speaking.
- Work with someone in whom you have confidence, someone with whom you are comfortable.
- Agree beforehand with your listeners which items should be stressed during the practice session. Use the practice record form in this lesson. Make sure that you all agree on the meaning of the terms in the practice record before the practice session takes place. You may want your listeners to concentrate on evaluating one or two aspects of your speech, such as its organization or your use of gestures.
- Practice your speech as if you were actually giving it. Don't sit in a chair and mutter your speech. Stand up and deliver it as if you were in front of your final audience.
- Work to avoid being overly sensitive to constructive criticism. Listen carefully and give fair consideration to each of your listeners' suggestions.
- When helping others, seek to be constructive in your remarks. Make sure to remark on things the speaker is doing well as well as to note things that should be corrected.
- Take advantage of practice sessions to try out new ideas. If they don't work, drop them and try others—that is what practice is for.

Preparing and Presenting

Arrange a session to practice the speech you prepared in the previous lesson. Ask three of your classmates to help you during this session. Before your practice session, check your outline against Missy's outline in this assignment to make sure you have satisfied all of the requirements of the assignment. Prepare your speaking notes and any audio or visual aids needed to help make your speech more vivid. You may find that giving your speech to a tape recorder and then listening to it played back will help you develop the confidence you need for your presentation to an audience.

Meet your classmates at the time and place agreed to for the practice. At the beginning of the session, give your "audience" blank practice sheets like the one in this lesson. Mention any aspects of your speech or delivery you would like them to pay special attention to. Then repeat the relaxation sequence described under the preceding guidelines, being particularly careful to pause before you start speaking.

Give your speech to your classmates just as if they were the final audience for whom your speech is intended. Obtain their comments on the practice sheets and discuss them.

Evaluation Checklist

Carefully read the practice records completed by your three classmates and then complete each of the following steps.

1. Ask your three classmates to explain anything in their practice records that you don't understand.
2. Ask your classmates to describe in detail the things they felt you did especially well in your speech.
3. Ask your classmates to discuss their suggestions for how you can improve your speech. Pay particular attention to how well they feel you accomplished your specific purpose—this is the best measure of the effectiveness of your speech.
4. At the end of your outline, write a brief summary of the strengths and weaknesses of your speech, as reflected in the three practice records. Then write a list of the steps you will take to improve your speech. Turn your outline and the three practice records in to your teacher.
5. Revise your speech, based on the suggestions you received during the practice session.

Giving an Expository Speech and Responding to Questions

Expository speeches are often followed by a question period. How well you answer your listeners' questions will strongly influence their opinion of your speech as a whole.

The best way to prepare for answering questions is to become thoroughly familiar with your topic. Once you know your topic in depth, you will be able to use several other techniques for answering questions effectively. For example, you can ask a questioner to clarify his or her question—that is, to make it more clear. You can repeat a question to be sure that everyone in the room knows what question you are about to answer. If a listener asks several questions at once, you can answer them one at a time, repeating each question before you answer it.

Working with the Model

When Missy finished her speech on the concept of mutualism, the students in her biology class asked her some questions. Read this transcript of the question period:

Missy: *(concluding her speech)* . . . and so you can see that mutualism is a relationship between two species that benefits them both. You can think of mutualism as nature's good neighbor policy! Do any of you have questions?

Brenda: Isn't the lichen an example of mutualism? But how can one plant be an example of a relationship that involves two different species?

Missy: Let me answer those questions one at a time. Yes, you're right; the lichen is an example of mutualism. Now, what was your other question?

Brenda: How can a single plant be an example of mutualism, if mutualism always involves two different species?

Missy: That's a tricky one. You see, what we call a lichen really is two plants: an alga living in a mutualistic relationship with a fungus.

Tom: Can you explain how that works?

Missy: I'm afraid I don't remember the exact nature of the relation-ship between the plants.

Larry: I remember. Lichens grow in cool, dry environments. The alga, which has chlorophyll, manufactures food for itself and for the fungus, which can't manufacture its own food be-cause it has no chlorophyll. The fungus captures and stores water for both plants.

Missy: Thanks, Larry. Are there any other questions?

Maurice: Are there other examples of mutualism on the nonmicro-scopic level?

Missy: Oh yes—there are lots of them.

Tom: Lots of what?

Missy: I'm sorry, Tom. I should have repeated the question. Maurice asked whether there were other examples of mu-tualism on the nonmicroscopic level, and I said that there were lots of them. The first one that comes to mind is the mutualistic relationship that exists between certain fish that live in the waters around coral reefs and the shrimp that inhabit those waters. A shrimp stands on the coral and waves its antennae to attract the fish. The shrimp then eat the parasites clinging to the fish. You can see that this rela-tionship benefits both the shrimp and the fish. Any more questions?

Janine: My biology teacher last semester said that lichens were an example of symbiosis.

Missy: I'm not sure I understand your question.

Janine: Well, my teacher said that lichens were an example of symbiosis, but you say that they're an example of mutualism.

Missy: Oh, I understand you now. In a way, your teacher and I are both right. You see, although some people use the term *symbiosis* to describe what I've been calling *mutualism*, others use *symbiosis* to describe any kind of interdependence between species, beneficial or not. Since *symbiosis* is used in these two different ways, many people prefer to use *mutualism* to make it clear that they are describing a mutually beneficial relationship between species.

A. Think about the techniques Missy used in answering the questions from her audience.
   1. Brenda asks Missy two questions at the same time. How does Missy answer Brenda? What does Missy do to make sure that the audience remembers the second question before she answers it?
   2. What might have happened if Missy had pretended to know the answer to Tom's question and bluffed a response? How might Larry and the others who did know the answer have reacted? What effect might Missy's discovered bluff have had on her listeners' attitude toward the rest of her speech?
   3. What technique did Missy use to make sure that everyone in the class knew what question Maurice had asked?
   4. Janine did not really ask a question at first. How did Missy get Janine to put her statement into question form before she attempted to answer it? What techniques did Missy use to clarify the question in a tactful manner? How did this help to reduce any tension that might have been caused by Janine's seeming to challenge the information in Missy's speech?
   5. Tom seems very interested in Missy's speech. What might have happened to Missy's hold on her audience's attention if Tom had kept on asking questions without giving the others a chance to participate? What techniques do you think a speaker can use to keep an individual from monopolizing the question period?
B. Build your skill in answering questions by working with three other students in a question-answering group. Each member of the group will pick a topic and spend five minutes answering questions about it. Pick your topic and then answer questions from the other three students. Answer each question as completely and accurately as you can. Don't try to answer questions beyond your knowledge; just admit that you do not know the answer. Ask the others to clarify

questions when necessary and repeat any particularly long or complicated question before answering it, so that everyone in the group will know what question you are answering. (When you are answering questions before a group of ten or more people, it's a good idea to repeat every question before answering it.) After you have answered questions for five minutes, ask the other group members which of your answers were unclear or incomplete. Rephrase these answers to make them as clear and specific as possible.

Guidelines

Follow these guidelines when you answer questions from your listeners.

1. Be sure you understand a question before you attempt to answer it. If you aren't sure what a question means, ask your questioner to clarify it.
2. Be sure your audience knows what question you are answering. Unless you are speaking to a very small group, repeat each question before answering it.
3. If you are asked several questions at once, answer them one at a time. If your first answer is very long, ask your listener to repeat his or her other questions.
4. Make your answers direct and understandable. Limit your answer to the question you have been asked. Use specific examples in your answer. Use concrete language and adapt your language to your audience.
5. Watch your listeners to be sure they understand your answers. If they look confused, you may not have understood the question in the first place, or they may not have understood your answer. If this happens, ask that the question be repeated and repeat your answer as well.
6. If you don't know the answer to a question, don't bluff.
7. Treat the people who ask you questions with respect, even if they don't all treat you that way.

Preparing and Presenting

Prepare to present the speech you outlined and practiced in the previous lessons.

First, review your notecards and your Audience Analysis Checklist. Then make a list of the questions you think your audience is likely to ask at the end of your speech. Do any additional research necessary to make yourself feel thoroughly prepared to answer their questions.

Next, review the question-answering techniques Missy used in the Working with the Model section of this lesson. Give your list of questions to a friend and have him or her ask them in a way that lets you practice your question-answering techniques. For example, have your friend ask you several questions at once, a question that must be clarified, and a question that seems to challenge the information presented in your report.

Finally, give your speech defining a concept to the class.

Evaluation Checklist

Evaluate each classmate's speech on the basis of the following criteria. Rate each speech on a scale from 1 (Poor) to 5 (Excellent). Be prepared to give reasons for each rating you give. The questions in parentheses will help you do so.

Category	Rating
The speaker . . . 1. Had a clear, specific purpose	
2. Achieved his or her specific purpose	
3. Used an introduction that captured the audience's attention and properly introduced the topic (How could the introduction be improved?)	
4. Used an effective and logical pattern of organization (What other pattern, if any, would have been more effective?)	
5. Used adequate details to make the speech understandable (What additional information or details, if any, would have made the speech more understandable?)	
6. Used question-answer techniques effectively (What other techniques, if any, would have helped him or her do a better job of answering questions?)	

Giving a Speech that Analyzes a Work of Literature or Art

Now that you have given several expository speeches, you are ready to work on a speech that requires more preparation. Often you will be asked to give an oral report analyzing a topic from an area you have been studying. This kind of speech is called an **analytical expository speech**. In it you may analyze a speech, a poem, a novel, a piece of music, or a short story for your audience.

As you analyze something for your audience, you will answer one or more of the following questions:

- **What does it mean?** What are the literal meanings in your selection? What implicit or suggested meanings does it contain?
- **How does it convey meaning?** How does the sequence of ideas in your selection help convey its meaning? What other devices (such as rhyme or alliteration in a poem) help to convey its meaning? How are these elements organized?
- **Why was it created?** If you are analyzing a work of literature, you will deepen your audience's understanding of it by explaining why it was created, especially if its author created it in response to a particular event.
- **What is its value?** Is your selection good or poor, compared with the best-known examples of its kind? In what ways is it different from other poems, plays, or stories?

There are several steps to preparing an analytical expository speech. First, **analyze your audience**. Will they be familiar with the novel, play, poem, or story you are analyzing? If not, give them enough background information so that they will be familiar with the examples you use in your analysis. This may mean summarizing the plot of a novel before you present your analysis of one of its chapters, or it may mean explaining the circumstances that led a poet to write the poem you are analyzing.

Second, **read expert analyses of your selection**. Even if your own analysis differs considerably from those you read, the opinions of experts can add to your audience's understanding of your selection. If you decide to quote a literary critic or other authority in your speech, be prepared to rephrase or expand his or her remarks to help your listeners understand them. Also be prepared to define any unusual or technical terms in the expert's remarks.

Be careful to keep your analysis distinct from that of the experts, and to separate fact from opinion. One way to do this is to clearly *identify all expert sources* you use in your speech. Give the audience enough information about the authorities you cite to make it clear that they are knowledgeable sources.

The third step is to **prepare your speech** so it will be easily understood by your audience. Use your Audience Analysis Checklist to find some link between your audience's interests or opinions and the topic of your speech. Then use this link in your introduction to capture your audience's attention and direct it to your topic. Present your analysis in a pattern that makes it easy for your audience to understand. Remember that you are asking them to understand in a few minutes an analysis that may have taken you several weeks to prepare. Use language appropriate to your audience and explain any technical terms in your speech.

Working with the Model

The students in Jewel's class were asked to analyze a poem, play, speech, or short story for the class. Jewel decided to analyze a poem by Stevie Smith, a modern English poet. Before beginning her analysis, Jewel passed out copies of the poem and asked her classmates to read it. Read the poem carefully and then read Jewel's analysis.

Not Waving but Drowning

Nobody heard him, the dead man,
But still he lay moaning:
I was much further out than you thought
And not waving but drowning.

Poor chap, he always loved larking
And now he's dead
It must have been too cold for him his heart gave way
They said.

Oh no no no, it was too cold always
(Still the dead one lay moaning)
I was much too far out all my life
And not waving but drowning.

—Stevie Smith

Jewel's Analysis

Have you ever tried to communicate your feelings to someone, but found that you just weren't getting through to that person? I think most of us have that experience at one time or another. Stevie Smith's poem "Not Waving but Drowning" is about that kind of failure in communication. It sounds like a very simple poem at first, but—as I am going to show you—there's a great deal of meaning in it.

Stevie Smith, who died in 1971, was really named Florence Margaret Smith. She didn't make her living as a poet, but as a secretary. For many years, people did not take her poems very seriously. They sounded almost like nursery rhymes, and Stevie Smith illustrated them with cartoonlike drawings. In fact, this poem is effective just *because* it is so short and easy to read. It has only twelve lines, and not one word is wasted.

First, let's look at the poem's *literal* meaning, the basic meaning of the words. There are two voices speaking in the poem. One speaker is a man who has just drowned. The other voice belongs to his friends on the beach. They saw him waving his arms, trying to get help. However, they thought he was "larking"—that is, clowning around, having a good time. Now that the man is dead, they blame his death on the coldness of the water. The dead man, however, knows differently. He says, "It was too cold always / . . . I was much too far out all my life, / And not waving but drowning."

Now, when we read the last stanza, we realize that the poem is about much more than a man who has drowned in the ocean. Dead men, after all, cannot speak. Yet it is very important in this poem that we should know what the dead man is saying, what he knows that the others do not. The clue is in the line "I was much too far out all my life." If you think about it, you understand that he has been "drowning" for years. Even while he was alive, he was asking people for help. But throughout his life, nobody understood him.

In this poem, then, the ocean is not just a literal, real ocean. It is a *symbol*—that is, it stands for something else. I think you can see that the ocean stands for human life. In fact, we often speak of life as an ocean. We talk about "embarking on a new career," of being "overwhelmed by difficulties."

Now let's see how this symbol helps us understand the poem. In the first stanza we find out that a man has "drowned." This may mean that the man is actually dead, but it might also mean that he's been overwhelmed by problems. Why didn't people help him? Unfortunately, they couldn't tell he was in danger. He says, "I was much further out than you thought"—but, of course, no one hears him when he says this.

In the second stanza, we hear from the other people. They're mildly sorry for him, but not very sympathetic. They say, "Poor chap"—that doesn't show very great emotion. Listen to the seventh line of the poem: "It must have been too cold for him his heart gave way." I think that line is meant to be read very rapidly, without any expression. This line is a *cliché*. It shows how little people understood about the drowned man.

In the last stanza, we hear from the dead man again. "It was too cold always," he says. What he means, I think, is that he was always treated coldly, without any affection or interest. In the same way, he was "too far out"—that is, too far away from people. In a sense, the people on the shore are right when they say, "His heart gave way." The man's heart broke because he did not have the love or friendship of other people.

The line "And not waving but drowning" appears twice in the poem. It is also used in the title. Maybe you can understand this line better if you think about some person you know who is always doing things to attract attention. Perhaps the person wears strange clothes, or talks too much, or behaves wildly. We usually say, "Oh, he's just having a good time"—in other words, "he always loved larking." We think a person like that is always "waving"—that is, trying to show us how much he's enjoying himself. But suppose the person is actually "drowning," suffering from loneliness and the feeling that people are cold toward him. Perhaps the things he does to attract our attention are really a plea for our love and understanding. After reading this poem, maybe you'll think about that person again. Ask yourself whether he or she is "not waving but drowning."

You can see, then, that this little poem is about one of the most important problems in people's lives: understanding when other people need our help. Yet because the poem is so simple, its meaning strikes us almost immediately. Only a very fine poet could speak to us so well in so few words. Stevie Smith, too, must have felt such a lack of communication in her own life. As the English poet Philip Larkin wrote, "For all the freaks and sports of her fancy, . . . Miss Smith's poems speak with the authority of sadness."

A. Think about the four questions you should answer in an analytical expository speech and how they apply to the poem.
   1. Find the part of her speech where Jewel answers the question "What does it mean?" How does Jewel organize the answer to this question?
   2. Find the part of her speech where Jewel answers the question "How does it convey meaning?" What aspects of the poem does Jewel point to in answering this question?
   3. How does Jewel deal with the question "Why was it created?" Find the part of her speech where she suggests an answer.
   4. How does Jewel answer the question "What is its value?"
B. Think about the way Jewel's speech illustrates her knowledge of her audience.
   1. How does Jewel connect the knowledge and interests of her audience to the topic of her speech? At what places in her speech does she do this?
   2. What background information does Jewel give her audience to help them understand the poem?
C. Think about the way Jewel organized her speech.
   1. What does Jewel do to attract her audience's interest?
   2. What aspect of the poem does she discuss first?
   3. What aspect of the poem does she discuss next?
   4. What point does Jewel make in her conclusion?
   5. Do you think Jewel's conclusion would have been more effective if she had summarized her main points? Explain why or why not.

Guidelines

When you are preparing an analytical expository speech, be careful not to confuse your opinions about the object of your analysis with facts about that object. For example, critics' *opinions* about the merit of Dickens' novels have varied greatly since the time they were written. However, it is a *fact* that almost all of them were great popular successes when they first appeared.

As you present your opinions, make it clear that they are your own. When you present the analytical opinions of others, be sure to give your source, and enough background about the source to make it clear that he or she is an acknowledged expert.

An analysis usually presents one perspective, or viewpoint, on a subject on which several points of view are possible. When you are preparing an analytical expository speech, concentrate on *explaining* your point of view rather than on convincing others that it is the right one. Do not be sarcastic toward your subject. Even if you dislike a poem or story, it is not necessary to belittle the work or its author in order to present an intelligent, informative analysis.

Preparing and Presenting

Prepare an analytical expository speech that will take about ten minutes to present. Choose the topic of your speech from one of these four groups. Ask your teacher to approve your topic before you begin work.

Television production:	Select a dramatic special or series.
Film:	Select a recent or older movie.
Literary work:	Select a short story, speech, novel, poem, or play.
Live concert:	Select a concert you attended recently or will attend before the date of your speech.

Once you have selected a topic from one of these groups, follow these steps in preparing your speech:

1. Familiarize yourself thoroughly with the topic of your speech.
2. If they are available, read informed analyses of your topic by acknowledged experts.
3. Analyze your audience's knowledge of and opinions about the topic of your speech.
4. Narrow your topic.
5. Write the specific purpose of your speech.
6. Prepare an outline of your speech.
7. Prepare an introduction that will get your listeners' attention by linking your topic with their interests and opinions.
8. Prepare your speaking notes.
9. Practice your speech.

Present your speech to the class. After you have finished your speech, answer questions from your listeners.

Evaluation Checklist

Evaluate each other's analytical speeches on the basis of the following criteria. Rate the speeches on a scale from 1 (Poor) to 5 (Excellent). Be prepared to give reasons for each rating you give. The questions in parentheses will help you do so.

Category	Rating
The speaker . . . 1. Showed a good understanding of and familiarity with the topic	
2. Made his or her specific purpose clear	
3. Established a link between the topic and the audience by appealing to their interests and opinions	
4. Accurately and effectively previewed the main points (If the speaker did not preview the main points, how could he or she have done this?)	
5. Used adequate examples to support the main points	
6. Gave background information about the topic, if necessary	
7. Gave adequate information about the experts cited	
8. Gave definitions for unusual or technical terms (What terms should have been defined but were not?)	
9. Organized the information in the speech in a clear, logical pattern	
10. Analyzed the subject answering one or more of the following questions: What does it mean? How does it convey meaning? Why was it created? What is its value?	

Chapter 5 Review

Summary

Expository speaking, or speaking to explain, involves careful organization and planning whether your purpose is to explain a process or to explain your understanding of a selection. You should choose and narrow your topic, write a specific purpose, and arrange your main ideas in an outline form. Use plenty of details, examples, testimony, or statistics, etc., to fully develop each of your main ideas.

Notecards and visual aids can make your expository speeches more effective. Glancing at notecards to keep your main ideas in mind or reading specific quotations, facts, figures, or definitions can make your speech more smooth and more interesting. Visual aids help make your ideas or examples easier to understand. Make sure they are attractive and clearly visible. Both notes and visual aids should always be used in a way that enhances your speech, never distracts from it.

Adapt your speech to your audience, taking into account the audience's knowledge, needs, and interests. Preparing your speech with such things in mind will enable you to better capture and hold their attention. Also speak with confidence and polish by concentrating, relaxing, and, most importantly, thoroughly preparing and practicing your speech.

If you have to answer questions from your audience, repeat each question before answering it. If the question is not clear, ask the questioner to clarify it. Answer one question at a time directly and clearly and look for feedback to see if your audience understood what you said.

Reviewing Vocabulary

Write the sentences below and insert the correct group of words from those in the box.

> spatial pattern
> topical pattern
> chronological pattern
> analytical expository speech

1. An explanation of how time-lapse photography works would most likely be organized according to a _____.
2. Brynn gave her _____ on an old Norwegian folk story.
3. A _____ is best for discussing the differences among three kinds of bicycles.
4. Jeremy plans to arrange his speech on popular ski resorts in the East, North, and West according to a _____.

Reviewing Facts and Ideas

1. What is the main purpose of an expository speech? In what part of a speech is its specific purpose usually stated?
2. What kind of organizational pattern do most process speeches follow?
3. In what part of your speech are the main ideas developed? What are the six chief ways to develop main ideas?
4. One purpose of using notecards is to remind you of your main points. What are two other common reasons to refer to notecards?
5. What is the main purpose of using a visual aid? How can you ensure that the aid does not take up too much attention?

6. Why is it important for a speaker to take the audience into consideration? What are some likely results of a speaker's lack of audience awareness?
7. What are two ways you can improve your confidence and polish when speaking to others?
8. Name three question-answering techniques. Why is it important to clearly and tactfully answer your listeners' questions?
9. What is the main purpose of an analytical speech? Is it appropriate, then, to try to convince your audience that your interpretation is the only right one?
10. Why is it important to analyze your audience when preparing for an analytical speech? In what part of the speech would you likely include a link between your audience's interests and the topic of your speech? Why?

Discussing Facts and Ideas

1. Often when people say they are explaining something, they are really trying to get other people to agree with them—to persuade them. Often when people say they don't understand, they mean that they do not agree. Discuss what the real differences are between explaining and persuading. Why is it important for you to know which of the two is the real purpose when you are speaking or listening?
2. You have been encouraged to outline an expository speech carefully but not to write out each word of the speech. Discuss some of the advantages and disadvantages of writing out an entire speech.
3. Think of the person you know who is able to explain things to you more clearly than anyone else. Make a list of the reasons you believe he or she is so successful. Discuss the items on your list with others in the class. Which items appear most frequently? Why?

Applying Your Knowledge

1. As a citizen and future voter, you should understand the documents that express the ideas on which this country was founded. Prepare an explanation of the following paragraph from the Declaration of Independence:

   We hold these truths to be self-evident, that all men are created equal, that they are endowed by their Creator with certain unalienable Rights, that among these are Life, Liberty and the pursuit of Happiness.

   Share your explanation with another student in the class. Talk about any differences of interpretation you have. If you still have questions, seek clarification from your teacher or from one of the social studies teachers in the school.
2. Select one of the amendments to the U.S. Constitution that make up the "Bill of Rights." Explain it to your class.
3. As a student you are in the midst of an experience that is of great interest to many members of your community. Work with your teacher to organize a program in which you explain to local community clubs what is happening at your school. Many of these organizations are looking for programs and will be pleased to provide you with an opportunity to speak. Organize your program so that different students explain what is happening in different parts of your school. For example, one might talk about the current emphasis in math classes, another might describe the activities of the athletic program, and a third might talk about programs being put on by the music department. Be sure to find out how much time the organizations have allotted for your program and tailor your presentations to their time requirements. If possible, arrange the programs so that each speaker has an opportunity to answer audience questions.

Explaining a Work Process

Both at school and at work, you will often have to explain a process to another person. The process may be as simple as the routine for punching a time card, or it may be as complicated as the rules for using a computer terminal.

Whatever the process is, your explanation should have three parts. In the **introduction**, explain to the other person why the process is important and what steps you will be describing. In the **body**, explain the steps one at a time, demonstrating or illustrating each of them. As you speak, observe your listener, to be sure he or she understands what you are saying. After each step, ask whether the person understands what you have said. In the **conclusion**, briefly go over the steps again and remind your listener of any important rules or warnings.

Activities

1. Pretend that a member of your class is a new student at your school. Explain to this student a process that takes place at your school; for example:

   - how to prepare a class schedule
   - how to register for a class
   - how to have a teacher sponsor your organization
   - how to find and check out a library book

2. Pretend that a member of your class is a co-worker in a business or office. Explain a work process to this student; for example:

   - how to use a cash register
   - how to prepare a fast-food lunch
   - how to take a customer order on the phone
   - how to find an item in the stock room

Giving Testimony

At some point in your life you may be required to testify under oath in the course of a trial or before an investigating committee or commission. The purpose of testimony is to present facts and evidence from which other people (a judge, a jury, or committee members) will draw conclusions. A witness should follow these rules.

1. Listen carefully to the entire question. Do not interrupt the questioner or anticipate what he or she is going to say.
2. Answer only what was asked in the question.
3. If you do not understand a question, ask for clarification.
4. State your answer in terms of facts—things you have seen, heard, and done.
5. Do not give your opinion unless you are asked. If asked for your opinion (for example, "Which person was the aggressor?"), be prepared to cite facts in order to explain it.
6. Take your time answering questions. Do not allow yourself to be rushed.
7. Remain calm. Do not lose your temper, even if you feel you are being baited, made fun of, or attacked.
8. Do not evade the question or conceal any facts that should be part of the answer. Remember, your oath included a promise to tell "the whole truth."

Activity

1. Observe a committee investigation on television or in person. Learn the purpose of the investigation and the reasons why particular witnesses were called. As you listen to the questioning of witnesses, observe whether or not the questioning is relevant to the purpose of the investigation. Observe also whether the witnesses' testimony seems likely to help the purpose of the investigation, or whether committee members are using the testimony to gain publicity for themselves. Report on your findings to the class.

Speaking to Persuade

After working through this chapter, you should be proficient at the following skills:

Lesson	Skills
Lesson 1	• thinking critically as a persuasive speaker
Lesson 2	• using appeals to logic
Lesson 3	• using appeals to emotion
Lesson 4	• using identification
Lesson 5	• combining appeals to logic, emotion, and identification
Communicating on the Job	• making a sales presentation
Communicating as a Citizen	• evaluating your credibility as a speaker

Critical Thinking and Persuasive Speaking

Your thinking skills are like any other skill. They can be improved by analyzing, determining what improvements are needed, acquiring new strategies, and practicing. In order to be an effective speaker, you should develop the following kinds of thinking skills.

1. **Perceiving:** your ability to observe, compare and contrast that which you observe, and to understand the point of view from which perceptions are being made
2. **Arranging:** your ability to group, classify, place in order of sequence, discover patterns, and to place in order of importance
3. **Inquiring:** your ability to question and to analyze, including determining what is relevant and whether something is fact or opinion
4. **Inferring:** your ability to recognize underlying assumptions and to make generalizations as well as your understanding of cause-and-effect relationships and skill in making predictions
5. **Reasoning:** your ability to make decisions, exercise judgments, arrive at conclusions from specific examples, and recognize specific examples or draw specific conclusions once you are aware of general rules

Although you will not have mastered all of these skills by the time you have finished with this chapter, the more proficiency you develop in each, the better speaker you will be.

Working with the Model

In 1872 Susan B. Anthony was arrested in New York for voting in the Presidential election. She was fined $100.00, but she refused to pay the fine and appealed the sentence. The following speech was delivered in 1873. It represents a milestone in the movement for women's suffrage.

On Woman's Right to Suffrage

I stand before you tonight under indictment for the alleged crime of having voted at the last Presidential election, without having a lawful right to vote. It shall be my work this evening to prove to you that in thus voting, I not only committed no crime, but, instead, simply exercised my citizen's rights, guaranteed to me and all United States citizens by the national constitution, beyond the power of any state to deny.

The preamble of the federal constitution says:

"We, the people of the United States, in order to form a more perfect union, establish justice, insure domestic tranquillity, provide for the common defense, promote the general welfare, and secure the blessings of liberty to ourselves and our posterity, do ordain and establish this Constitution for the United States of America."

It was we, the people; not we, the white male citizens; nor yet we, the male citizens; but we, the whole people, who formed the Union. And we formed it, not to give the blessings of liberty, but to secure them; not to the half of ourselves and the half of our posterity, but to the whole people—women as well as men. And it is a downright mockery to talk to women of their enjoyment of the blessings of liberty while they are denied the use of the only means of securing them provided by this democratic-republican government—the ballot.

For any state to make sex a qualification that must ever result in the disfranchisement of one entire half of the people is to pass a bill of attainder, or an *ex post facto* law, and is therefore a violation of the supreme law of the land. By it the blessings of liberty are forever withheld from women and their female posterity. To them this government has no just powers derived from the consent of the governed. To them this government is not a democracy. It is not a republic. It is an odious aristocracy; a hateful oligarchy of sex; the most hateful aristocracy ever established on the face of the globe. This oligarchy of sex, which makes father, brothers, husband, sons, the oligarchs over the mother and sisters, the wife and daughters of every household—which ordains all men sovereigns, all women subjects, carries dissension, discord, and rebellion into every home of the nation.

Webster, Worcester, and Bouvier all define a citizen to be a person in the United States, entitled to vote and hold office.

The only question left to be settled now is: Are women persons? And I hardly believe any of our opponents will have the hardihood to say they are not. Being persons, then, women are citizens; and no state has a right to make any law, or to enforce any old law, that shall abridge their privileges or immunities. Hence, every discrimination against women in the constitutions and laws of the several states is today null and void.

A. Perceiving
   1. From what point of view does the speaker make her speech? In what ways do you think this speech might have been different if it had been made by a man who favored women's suffrage?
   2. How does the speaker use comparisons/contrasts to make her point?

B. Arranging
   1. Where does the speaker present her statement of the proposition? Is it clearly stated?
   2. Why does the speaker immediately quote a passage from the United States Constitution? How is it related to her main argument?

C. Inquiring
   1. Much of the speaker's argument hinges upon definitions. Think about the connotations of the following phrases. State the emotional appeal each suggests.

      "the blessings of liberty to ourselves"   "odious aristocracy"
      "the people"   "hateful oligarchy of sex"
      "bill of attainder"   "women are citizens"

   2. Does the speaker rely more heavily upon fact or opinion? Find and give examples of facts and opinions from the speech.

D. Inferring
   1. The speaker uses cause/effect relationships to support her position. What are some of the effects she names of denying women the right to vote?
   2. What is the effect of the question "Are women persons?" that begins the last paragraph?
   3. In what sense is the speaker's strong position in the last sentence a statement of prediction? Do you think that her appeal would have been as effective if she had not made such a bold prediction? Why?

E. Reasoning
   1. What definition does the speaker give for *citizen*? What conclusion does she wish her listeners to draw from this definition?
   2. What is the specific conclusion the speaker draws from the following premises?
      • All citizens have the right to vote in order to secure the blessings of liberty.
      • Women are citizens.

Guidelines

The following suggestions will help you be a more effective critical thinker.

1. Strive to gain an accurate perception of the world around you. Observe carefully, using all of your senses. Because your senses can be fooled—things may not be what they appear to be—you need to interpret what they tell you with care.
2. Remember that the words you use to name what you see affect your interpretation of it. Specialized vocabularies both help and hurt efforts to observe. Think how specialists in computer science and sports use terms to help them and how these same terms interfere with others' ability to understand what the specialists are thinking.
3. When you are trying to make sense of what you have observed, look for similarities and differences. Employ figurative language that reveals you have made effective comparisons. Learn to use analogies, personification, similes, and metaphors.
4. Try to determine which things are important and which are not. Look for common characteristics, which enable you to group ideas, things, and concepts.
5. Questions are most effective when they are based on careful observation. Be curious. Question answers that seem too simple but review what you already know in your mind before you ask your questions.
6. Facts are verifiable. You and others will agree on facts even when you hold different opinions. The best opinions are ones that can be clearly supported by facts.

Avoid the following logical fallacies in your thinking and speaking and try to recognize them in the speech of others.

A. **Oversimplifying the issue** results in statements that may sound persuasive but that distort the truth; for example:

> On this issue, we have a clear choice between a policy that will lead to national disgrace and disaster, and a policy that will lead to strength, peace, and prosperity.

Unless you can offer facts to support such a statement, listeners will not be persuaded.

B. **Begging the question** means stating a position that needs to be proved as though it had already been proved; for example:

> The issue of this campaign is whether Mayor Grey, who has had a disgraceful four years in office, deserves another chance.

The real "issue," however, is whether Grey's record can be shown to be disgraceful. The speaker who avoids having to prove this by *assuming* it is begging the question.

C. **Misleading statistics** sound factual, but they may not prove what the speaker wants them to. For example, magazines often conduct surveys to learn whether Americans are content with their jobs, incomes, and personal lives. Not surprisingly, most of the responses come from people with enough leisure and money to read magazines and answer questionnaires. Such people are often contented with their lives, but their answers do not provide useful information about the population as a whole. If a speaker uses such a survey as evidence, you should point out how unreliable it is.

D. ***Post hoc ergo propter hoc***, or **confusing "after" with "because,"** is a common error; for example:

> During the governor's term of office, the cost of living has doubled. Are you going to reelect a man who made you poorer?

The fact that something happened *after* a person became governor does not mean that it happened *because* he became governor. The speaker has to demonstrate the cause-and-effect relationship.

E. **Reasoning backward** assumes that because members of a particular group have a characteristic in common, anyone with that characteristic must belong to the group; for example:

> Communists are always talking about peace. Senator Flower talks about peace. Therefore Senator Flower must be a communist.

Obviously, it is possible to talk about peace without being a communist. Unsound though it is, backward reasoning leads to many dangerous accusations.

179

F. **False analogy** means using a figure of speech to make a comparison and then reasoning from the comparison as though it were a fact:

> Politics is like a football game. In football, if a player doesn't follow the signals, the coach pulls him off the field. Obviously any politician who doesn't obey the head of the party should be kicked out of the party.

Although there may be a superficial resemblance, the real world of politics is infinitely more complicated than a game of football.

Preparing and Presenting

Read the excerpts from Emrich's eulogy of Lincoln found on pages 405–406. Discuss the use of comparisons in this speech with another. Work with that student to find examples of written or spoken materials that reveal good and poor use of comparisons. Columns on the editorial pages in your local newspaper and commentary on radio and television will provide you with examples.

Bring to class the examples of materials that best demonstrate effective critical thinking and those that you believe reveal poor thinking on the part of the speaker or writer. Prepare a poster for the bulletin board that includes good and bad examples of each kind of thinking skill.

Evaluation Checklist

Evaluate each others' posters on critical thinking on the basis of the following criteria. Rate the posters on a scale from 1 (Poor) to 5 (Excellent). Be prepared to give reasons for each rating you give. The question in parentheses will help you do so.

Category	Rating
1. The poster contains good examples of critical thinking skills. (Does it contain examples of each kind of thinking skill: perceiving, arranging, inquiring, inferring, and reasoning?)	
2. The poster correctly identifies examples of poor critical thinking skills.	

Using Appeals to Logic

When you make any persuasive speech, your general purpose is to convince your listeners that they should think or act in a certain way. When you plan a persuasive speech, you should begin by clarifying the specific purpose of that speech: Precisely what do you want your listeners to think or do? That specific purpose is called the **position** of your speech.

One effective way to develop a persuasive speech is to support your position with **logical arguments**. Your logical arguments must be objective reasons that directly support your position. These arguments should not involve personal preferences or opinions. In turn, each logical argument in your speech must be supported by **evidence**—factual illustration, statistics, expert testimony, or other specific details about the argument.

In order to plan an effective persuasive speech developed with logical arguments, research your topic thoroughly, consulting a variety of sources. You must also think about your audience. Consider which arguments and which kinds of evidence will be understandable and convincing to your listeners. In addition, you must organize your persuasive speech clearly and carefully. The most effective kind of organization for a persuasive speech developed with logical arguments is shown in the following chart.

Introduction	Draw your listeners' attention to the topic of your speech. State your position on the topic.
Body	Clearly state each logical argument. After the statement of each argument, present evidence to support that argument. (In most cases, you should present your most effective argument last, to leave a strong impression with your listeners.)
Conclusion	Restate your position and summarize your arguments in support of that position.

Working with the Model

Until 1858, Jewish citizens were excluded from holding office in the British Parliament. For many years before the law was changed, the members of Parliament debated the issue of whether Jews should be allowed to be elected to the legislature.

In 1830, a member of Parliament from Oxford (referred to in the following speech as "my honorable friend the Member for the University of Oxford") made a speech asserting that it was logical to exclude Jews from office. Three years later, Thomas Babington Macaulay replied to that member's speech. The specific purpose of Macaulay's speech was to persuade his listeners that, contrary to his opponent's main point, it was illogical to exclude Jews from office. In spite of the fact that Macaulay's speech was delivered in the middle of the nineteenth century, it still presents a strong and relevant argument against bigotry in all its many forms.

Read the following excerpt from the introduction and part of the body of Macaulay's speech. Look for Macaulay's position, the three logical arguments he presents, and the evidence he uses to support those arguments.

I recollect, and my honorable friend the Member for the University of Oxford will recollect, that when this subject was discussed three years ago, it was remarked that the strength of the case of the Jews was a serious inconvenience to their advocate, for that it was hardly possible to make a speech for them without wearying the audience by repeating truths which were universally admitted.

My honorable friend the Member for the University of Oxford began his speech by declaring that he had no intention of calling in question the principles of religious liberty. He utterly disclaims persecution, that is to say, persecution as defined by himself. It would, in his opinion, be persecution to hang a Jew, . . . or to imprison him, or to fine him; for every man who conducts himself peacefully has a right to his life and his limbs, to his personal liberty, and to his property.

But it is not persecution, says my honorable friend, to exclude any individual or any class from office. . . . He who obtains an office obtains it not as a matter of right, but as a matter of favor. He who does not obtain an office is not wronged; he is only in that situation in which the vast majority of every community must necessarily be. There are in the United Kingdom five and twenty million Christians without places [in Parliament]; and, if they do not complain, why should five and twenty thousand Jews complain of being in the same case? In this way my honorable friend has convinced himself that, as it would be most absurd in him and me to say that we are wronged because we are not sec-

retaries of state, so it is most absurd in the Jews to say that they are wronged because they are, as a people, excluded from public employment.

Now surely, my honorable friend cannot have considered to what conclusions his reasoning leads.

Does he really mean that it would not be wrong in the legislature to enact that no man should be a judge unless he weighed twelve stone [168 pounds], or that no man should sit in Parliament unless he were six feet high? We are about to bring in a bill for the government of India. Suppose that we were to insert in that bill a clause providing that no graduate of the University of Oxford should be governor general or governor of any presidency, would not my honorable friend cry out against such a clause as most unjust to the learned body which he represents? And would he think himself sufficiently answered by being told, in his own words, that the appointment to office is a mere matter of favor, and that to exclude an individual or a class from office is no injury? Surely, on consideration, he must admit that official appointments ought not to be subject to regulations purely arbitrary, to regulations for which no reason can be given but mere caprice, and that those who would exclude any class from public employment are bound to show some special reason for the exclusion.

My honorable friend has appealed to us as Christians. Let me then ask him how he understands that great commandment which comprises the law and the prophets. Can we be said to do unto others as we would that they should do unto us, if we wantonly inflict on them even the smallest pain? That by excluding others from public trust we inflict pain on them my honorable friend will not dispute. As a Christian, therefore, he is bound to relieve them from that pain, unless he can show, what I am sure he has not yet shown, that it is necessary to the general good that they should continue to suffer.

But where, he says, are you to stop if once you admit into the House of Commons people who deny the authority of the Gospels? . . . I will answer my honorable friend's question by another. Where does he mean to stop? Is he ready to roast unbelievers at slow fires? If not, let him tell us why; and I will engage to prove that his reason is just as decisive against the intolerance which he thinks a duty as against the intolerance which he thinks a crime. Once admit that we are bound to inflict pain on a man because he is not of our religion, and where do you stop? Why stop at the point fixed by my honorable friend rather than at the point fixed by the Member for Oldham, who would make the Jews incapable of holding land? And why stop at the point fixed by the honorable Member for Oldham rather than at the point which would have been fixed by a Spanish inquisitor of the sixteenth century? When once you enter on a course of persecution, I defy you to find any reason for making a halt till you have reached the extreme point.

A. Think about the introduction of Macaulay's speech, contained in the first three paragraphs.
 1. How does Macaulay direct his listeners' attention to the topic of his speech?
 2. What is Macaulay's position on that topic? In which sentence does Macaulay state his position?
B. Think about the three arguments Macaulay presents in the final three paragraphs of the excerpt. Notice that each paragraph presents one logical argument (objective reason) in support of Macaulay's position. Each argument, however, is stated at or near the end of the paragraph.
 1. What is the first argument in support of Macaulay's position?
 2. What evidence supports that first argument?
 3. What is the second argument in support of Macaulay's position?
 4. In supporting that second argument, Macaulay uses the phrase "that great commandment which comprises the law and the prophets" to refer to what we call "the golden rule." What is that rule?
 5. What evidence supports Macaulay's second argument?
 6. What is the third argument in support of Macaulay's position?
 7. What evidence supports that third argument?
C. Think about an appropriate conclusion for this portion of Macaulay's speech.
 1. If you were preparing the conclusion, how would you restate Macaulay's position?
 2. How would you summarize Macaulay's arguments in support of that position?

Guidelines

When you plan a persuasive speech developed with logical arguments, you should keep in mind the following guidelines:

1. Decide on and clearly state the specific purpose of your speech. The sentence that states your specific purpose is called the *statement of your position*.
2. Research the topic of your speech. Knowing as much as possible about the topic will allow you to select the best arguments and evidence in support of your position.
3. Think about your audience. Select arguments and evidence that your listeners will understand and accept.
4. Follow this list of sixteen steps when you prepare a persuasive speech. Not every step may be appropriate to every speech you make, but you should follow them in this order to avoid omitting any important elements.

a. Select a topic narrow enough to be covered in the time allotted you.
b. Find out what positions people hold on this topic.
c. Research the arguments supporting and opposing each position.
d. Decide on your position on the topic.
e. Analyze your audience—its background, interests, and prejudices.
f. With your position and audience in mind, complete your research, using a variety of reliable sources.
g. Decide which arguments will be most effective with your audience.
h. Outline the main arguments of your speech and the evidence you will use to support each argument.
i. Outline the arguments and evidence you will use to refute the opposing position.
j. Decide what visual aids, if any, will help make your speech more effective.
k. Prepare the introduction and conclusion of your speech.
l. Prepare notes for your speech and practice it alone, preferably before a mirror.
m. Practice your speech before at least one other person and ask the person for his or her response.
n. Revise your speech in accordance with the person's response and practice it again.
o. Deliver your speech before an audience.
p. Analyze your speech and the audience's response and apply what you learn to future speeches.

Preparing and Presenting

Select a topic for a persuasive speech. If you wish, you may choose one of the following topics.

- equal rights for women
- the rights of minors
- the use of nuclear power
- government surveillance of private citizens
- citizens' rights to own handguns

Think about your chosen topic and decide what you would like to convince listeners to think or do in respect to that topic. Then write a one-sentence statement of your position.

Plan a persuasive speech that uses appeals to logic in support of your position. Begin by researching your topic. Consult at least four different sources.

After you have gathered information, think about the audience (your fellow students) for whom your speech is intended. Evaluate your possible arguments and evidence in terms of the interests and experiences of your listeners. Select at least three major arguments in support of your position. Select at least two items of evidence in support of each argument.

Write an outline for your persuasive speech. Organize your speech according to the plan shown on page 181. (Your outline should have three main parts: I. Introduction; II. Body; III. Conclusion.)

Evaluation Checklist

Exchange outlines with another student and evaluate each other's speech outline on the basis of the following criteria. Rate the outlines on a scale from 1 (Poor) to 5 (Excellent). Be prepared to give reasons for each rating you give. The questions in parentheses will help you do so.

Category	Rating
1. The topic of the speech is introduced effectively. (How might this introduction be made more effective or more interesting?)	
2. The statement of the position is clearly presented. (What changes, if any, are needed to clarify the position?)	
3. The logical arguments given support the position. (Which arguments, if any, are personal preferences or opinions rather than objective reasons? Which, if any, might not be understandable or convincing to an audience of your fellow students?)	
4. The evidence clearly and logically supports each argument. (Which arguments, if any, are not directly supported by factual illustrations, statistics, expert testimony, or other specific details? Which items of evidence, if any, might not be understandable or convincing to an audience of your fellow students?)	
5. The conclusion of the speech is effective. (How might the conclusion be made more clear or more effective?)	

Using Appeals to Emotion

Rather than appealing to the listeners' minds, as logical arguments do, some persuasive speeches appeal to the listeners' emotions. Emotional appeals are based upon the three kinds of basic needs all people have: physical needs, psychological needs, and social needs. **Physical needs** involve the life and health of an individual's body; examples of physical needs include the need for food and the need to avoid physical pain. **Psychological needs** involve an individual's inner life; examples of psychological needs include the need for love and the need for self-respect. **Social needs** involve an individual's relationship to a group; examples of social needs include the need for freedom and the need for acceptance by others. Appeals to emotion are intended to convince listeners that accepting the speaker's position will satisfy one or more of these basic needs.

When you plan to use appeals to emotion in a persuasive speech, you must constantly consider your position, the specific purpose of your speech. You should be sure that each appeal you choose will lead your listeners to accept that position.

Being able to make such judgments, of course, involves knowing your audience thoroughly. You must be familiar with your listeners' most important needs, with their interests, and with their fears. If you misjudge your audience, your appeals to their emotions will not be successfully persuasive.

In organizing a persuasive speech with appeals to emotions, you may want to develop your position before you state it. For example, you might begin by interesting listeners in the topic of your speech. Then you might present statements, examples, or short **anecdotes** (brief stories) that appeal to specific emotions and that will sway your listeners in favor of your position. By the time you reach the conclusion of your speech, you should have already succeeded in persuading your listeners to accept your position. This may be the most effective time to state that position directly to the audience.

When you present a persuasive speech developed through appeals to emotion, you should use particularly vivid language. You may also want to employ voice tones and gestures that depict greater intensity than you might show in other kinds of speeches. Be careful, however, that you do not confuse forceful speaking with shouting.

Also be careful, as you plan and present a persuasive speech with emotional appeals, that you avoid unfair and dishonest persuasive techniques. Such techniques as telling lies or half-truths, calling names, using obscenities, and making irrelevant personal attacks are unethical and, in many cases, harmful.

Working with the Model

In 1976, Representative Barbara Jordan of Texas was the keynote speaker at the Democratic National Convention. Read the following excerpt from the speech she made on that occasion. As you read, think about the specific purpose of Jordan's speech and about the appeals she uses to achieve that purpose.

From the Keynote Speech

There is something special about tonight. What is different? What is special? I, Barbara Jordan, am a keynote speaker.

A lot of years passed since 1832, and during that time it would have been most unusual for any national political party to ask that a Barbara Jordan deliver a keynote address . . . but tonight here I am. And I feel that, notwithstanding the past, my presence here is one additional bit of evidence that the American Dream need not forever be deferred.

Now that I have this grand distinction, what in the world am I supposed to say? . . .

I could list the many problems which Americans have. I could list the problems which cause people to feel cynical, angry, frustrated;

problems which include lack of integrity in government; the feeling that the individual no longer counts; the reality of material and spiritual poverty; the feeling that the grand American experiment is failing or has failed. I could recite these problems, and then I could sit down and offer no solutions. But I don't choose to do that. . . .

The citizens of America expect more. They deserve and they want more than a recital of the problems.

We are a people in a quandary about the present. We are a people in search of our future. We are a people in search of a national community.

We are a people trying not only to solve the problems of the present: unemployment, inflation . . . but we are attempting on a larger scale to fulfill the promise of America. We are attempting to fulfill our national purpose; to create and sustain a society in which all of us are equal. . . .

Let's all understand that these guiding principles cannot be discarded for short-term political gains. They represent what this country is all about. They are indigenous to the American idea. And these are the principles which are not negotiable. . . .

And now we must look to the future. Let us heed the voice of the people and recognize their common sense. If we do not, we not only blaspheme our political heritage, we ignore the common ties that bind all Americans.

Many fear the future. Many are distrustful of their leaders, and believe that their voices are never heard. Many seek only to satisfy their private work wants, to satisfy private interests.

But this is the great danger America faces: that we will cease to be one nation and become instead a collection of interest groups—city against suburb, region against region, individual against individual, each seeking to satisfy private wants.

If that happens, who then will speak for America?

Who then will speak for the common good? . . .

Are we to be one people bound together by common spirit sharing in a common endeavor, or will we become a divided nation?

For all of its uncertainty, we cannot flee the future. We must not become the new puritans and reject our society. We must address and master the future together. It can be done if we restore the belief that we share a sense of national community, that we share a common national endeavor. It can be done.

There is no executive order, there is no law that can require the American people to form a national community. This we must do as individuals, and if we do it as individuals, there is no President of the United States who can veto that decision.

As a first step, we must restore our belief in ourselves. We are a generous people, so why can't we be generous with each other? We need to take to heart the words spoken by Thomas Jefferson:

"Let us restore to social intercourse that harmony and that affection without which liberty and even life are but dreary things."

A nation is formed by the willingness of each of us to share in the responsibility for upholding the common good.

A government is invigorated when each of us is willing to participate in shaping the future of this nation.

In this election year we must define the common good and begin again to shape a common future. Let each person do his or her part. If one citizen is unwilling to participate, all of us are going to suffer. For the American idea, though it is shared by all of us, is realized in each one of us.

And now, what are those of us who are elected officials supposed to do? We call ourselves public servants, but I'll tell you this: we as public servants must set an example for the rest of the nation. It is hypocritical for a public official to admonish and exhort the people to uphold the common good if we are derelict in upholding the common good. More is required of public officials than slogans and handshakes and press releases. More is required. We must hold ourselves strictly accountable. We must provide the people with a vision of the future.

If we promise as public officials, we must deliver. If we as public officials propose, we must produce. If we say to the American people, "It is time for you to be sacrificial; sacrifice"—if the public official says that, we (public officials) must be the first to give. We must be. And again, if we make mistakes, we must be willing to admit them. We have to do that. What we have to do is strike a balance between the idea that government should do everything and the idea, the belief, that government ought to do nothing. Strike a balance.

Let there be no illusions about the difficulty of forming this kind of a national community. It's tough, difficult, not easy. But a spirit of harmony will survive in America only if each of us remembers that we share a common destiny; if each of us remembers, when self-interest and bitterness seem to prevail, that we share a common destiny.

I have confidence that we can form this kind of national community. . . .

We cannot improve on the system of government handed down to us by the founders of the Republic; there is no way to improve upon that. But what we can do is to find new ways to implement that system and realize our destiny.

Now, I began this speech by commenting to you on the uniqueness of a Barbara Jordan making the keynote address. Well, I am going to close my speech by quoting a Republican president, and I ask you that as you listen to these words of Abraham Lincoln, relate them to the concept of a national community in which every last one of us participates: "As I would not be a slave, so I would not be a master. This expresses my idea of democracy. Whatever differs from this, to the extent of the differences is no democracy."

A. The specific purpose of Jordan's speech is to persuade her listeners that they must work together in forming a national community based on the principles of democracy. Think about how the speech is organized around that purpose.
   1. Which single sentence in Jordan's speech do you consider the direct statement of her position?
   2. How does the introduction of Jordan's speech capture the listeners' interest in her position?
   3. How does the main portion of her speech develop that purpose?
   4. How does the conclusion emphasize that position?
B. Think about the appeals to emotion which Jordan uses to develop her persuasive speech.
   1. Read the following appeals to emotion from Jordan's speech. On which kind of basic need—physical, psychological, or social—is each appeal based?

   "to create and sustain a society in which all of us are equal"
   "the reality of material . . . poverty"
   "problems which cause people to feel cynical, angry, frustrated"
   "only if each of us remembers that we share a common destiny"

   2. Find four other examples of appeals to emotion in Jordan's speech. On what kind of basic need is each appeal based?
C. Think about the audience to whom Jordan's speech is addressed.
   1. Who are the people in the audience?
   2. How do the appeals Jordan uses show her understanding of those people?

Guidelines

These guidelines will help you plan and present an effective persuasive speech developed with appeals to emotion.

1. Appeals to emotion are based on the three kinds of basic needs common to all people: physical needs, psychological needs, and social needs. When you select the specific appeals to use in your speech, you must think carefully about the needs, interests, and fears of the people in your audience.
2. Use vivid language, a forceful voice, and clear gestures when you present your speech.
3. Carefully avoid unfair persuasive techniques, such as lying, calling names, using obscenities, and making irrelevant personal attacks.

Preparing and Presenting

Choose a product, real or imaginary, to use as the topic of a persuasive speech. Select a specific audience, such as preschool children or wealthy middle-aged adults, for your speech. Think about the emotional appeals that will most effectively convince the members of that audience of their need for your product. Plan a brief persuasive speech, developed with at least two specific appeals to emotion, that will persuade the people in your audience to use the product.

After you have planned and rehearsed your speech, select a partner. Have your partner listen as you give your persuasive speech. Then listen as your partner gives his or her persuasive speech.

Evaluation Checklist

Evaluate each other's persuasive speeches on the basis of the following criteria. Rate the speeches on a scale from 1 (Poor) to 5 (Excellent). Be prepared to give reasons for each rating you give. The questions in parentheses will help you do so.

Category	Rating
1. The position of the speech was directly stated in an appropriate part of the speech. (In what other part of the speech might the position have been more effectively presented?)	
2. The speaker used appropriate emotional appeals to develop the speech. (On what kind of basic need was each appeal based?)	
3. The appeals to emotion were well suited to the members of the audience. (What other appeals to emotion might have been better suited to that audience?)	
4. The word choices, tone of voice, and gestures were effective. (What changes in these factors might have made the presentation of the speech more effective?)	
5. The speaker avoided using unfair persuasive techniques. (If the speaker used any, how might those unfair techniques have been avoided?)	

Using Identification

The effectiveness of a persuasive speech can be greatly enhanced if the listeners think of the speaker as a person very much like themselves (or very much like their best images of themselves). As such, the speaker becomes a person whom the listeners can trust and believe.

Whenever you present a persuasive speech, you should encourage the members of your audience to identify with you. To do so, you must establish your own credibility, or believability, in the minds of the audience. You must also evoke the goodwill of the audience. Specific techniques for achieving these goals are listed in the chart below.

You can also use your method of delivery to encourage identification. If you project self-confidence and a genuine enthusiasm when you speak, your listeners will want to believe you.

HOW TO ENCOURAGE IDENTIFICATION	
To Establish Credibility	**To Gain Goodwill**
• Speaker has an established reputation. • Speaker has demonstrated knowledge of the topic. • Speaker is sincere. • Speaker appears trustworthy to audience members.	• Speaker stresses interests in common with audience. • Speaker identifies self with person or cause audience admires. • Speaker compliments audience on its positive qualities.

Working with the Model

In 1933, in the middle of the Great Depression, Franklin Delano Roosevelt was inaugurated into his first term as President. Read the following excerpt from the beginning of his inaugural address. As you read, notice how directly Roosevelt encourages the members of his audience to identify with him.

From the First Inaugural Address

I am certain that my fellow Americans expect that on my induction into the Presidency I will address them with a candor and a decision which the present situation of our Nation impels. This is preeminently the time to speak the truth, the whole truth, frankly and boldly. Nor need we shrink from honestly facing conditions in our country today. This great Nation will endure, will revive, and will prosper. So, first of all, let me assert my firm belief that the only thing we have to fear is fear itself—nameless, unreasoning, unjustified terror which paralyzes needed efforts to convert retreat into advance. In every dark hour of our national life a leadership of frankness and vigor has met with that understanding and support of the people themselves which is essential to victory. I am convinced that you will again give that support to leadership in these critical days.

In such a spirit on my part and on yours, we face our common difficulties. They concern, thank God, only material things. Values have shrunken to fantastic levels; taxes have risen; our ability to pay has fallen; government of all kinds is faced by serious curtailment of income; the means of exchange are frozen in the current of trade; the withered leaves of industrial enterprise lie on every side; farmers find no market for their produce; the savings of many years in thousands of families are gone.

More important, a host of unemployed citizens face the grim problems of existence, and an equally great number toil with little return. Only a foolish optimist can deny the dark realities of the moment.

Yet our distress comes from no failure of substance. We are stricken by no plague of locusts. Compared with the perils which our forefathers conquered because they believed and were not afraid, we still have much to be thankful for.

A. Think about the audience to whom this speech is directed.
   1. Who are the listeners in Roosevelt's audience?
   2. How does Roosevelt show that he knows his audience well?

B. Think about the techniques Roosevelt uses to establish his own credibility.
   1. What is Roosevelt's established reputation at the time of this speech? How does he refer to that reputation in the first sentence of his speech?
   2. What is Roosevelt's demonstrated knowledge of his topic? How does he refer to that knowledge?
   3. How does the following sentence indicate Roosevelt's sincerity? "Only a foolish optimist can deny the dark realities of the moment." In what other ways does Roosevelt show his sincerity?

C. Think about the techniques Roosevelt uses to evoke the goodwill of his audience.
   1. How do the following sentences stress the interests and efforts Roosevelt has in common with his listeners?

   "Nor need we shrink from honestly facing conditions in our country today."
   "In such a spirit on my part and on yours we face our common difficulties."

   Find at least two other sentences in which Roosevelt emphasizes his unity with his listeners.

2. Reread the last two sentences in the first paragraph of the speech. With whom is Roosevelt identifying himself? Why could he expect the members of his audience to admire those leaders?
3. What positive quality in his listeners does Roosevelt compliment in the final sentence of the first paragraph?

Guidelines

When you give a persuasive speech, you should encourage your listeners to identify with you, to regard you as a person like themselves who can be trusted and believed. These guidelines will help you.

1. Establish your own credibility.
2. Evoke the goodwill of your listeners.
3. Speak with self-confidence and genuine enthusiasm.

Preparing and Presenting

With a partner, select a persuasive speech to analyze. For example, you may select a campaign speech, a sales presentation, or a persuasive speech made before a legislative body. You may choose a speech that you attended or one that you heard broadcast on television or on the radio. If you wish, the speech may be one presented by a fictional character in a television drama or a film.

Listen carefully to the speech that you and your partner select. As you listen, think about how the speaker encourages identification on the part of his or her listeners.

After the speech, write a four-paragraph analysis of the speaker's success in encouraging audience identification. In the first paragraph, examine the speaker's efforts to establish his or her own credibility. Consider each of the techniques listed in the chart on page 194 and cite specific examples from the speech.

In the second paragraph, examine the speaker's efforts to evoke the goodwill of the audience. Consider each of the techniques listed in the chart on page 194 and cite specific examples from the speech.

In the third paragraph, examine the speaker's method of delivery. Consider the self-confidence and the enthusiasm he or she displayed while speaking and, once again, cite specific examples.

In the final paragraph of your analysis, summarize the effectiveness of the speaker's attempts to encourage audience identification. Also suggest specific changes in the content or delivery of the speech that might have improved the audience's identification with the speaker.

Evaluation Checklist

Evaluate each other's analysis on the basis of the following criteria. Rate the analysis on a scale from 1 (Poor) to 5 (Excellent). Be prepared to give reasons for each rating you give. The questions in parentheses will help you do so.

Category	Rating
The analysis . . . 1. Appropriately evaluated the speaker's effectiveness in establishing his or her credibility (Which examples most clearly typify the techniques he or she used? Which techniques did he or she fail to use?)	
2. Appropriately evaluated the speaker's effectiveness in evoking the goodwill of the audience (Which examples most clearly typify the techniques he or she used, or failed to use?)	
3. Appropriately evaluated the effectiveness of the speaker's delivery (How did the members of the audience seem to react to the speaker's self-confidence and enthusiasm, or to the lack of self-confidence and enthusiasm?)	
4. Made specific suggestions for improving audience identification (Which of your partner's suggestions seem most appropriate? Which of yours?)	
5. Noted how the speaker's success (or failure) in encouraging audience identification enhanced (or detracted from) the effectiveness of his or her persuasive speech	

Using Identification with Appeals to Logic and Appeals to Emotion

As you listen to and evaluate persuasive speeches, you will probably find that the most convincing speeches do not rely only on logical arguments or only on appeals to emotion. In many cases, a combination of these two methods of development results in the most effective persuasive speech.

When you plan a persuasive speech, consider including both logical arguments and appeals to emotion. Select a logical argument for each main point that is based on common sense or fact. Select an appeal to emotion for each main point that involves a basic physical, psychological, or social need. As you choose your main points, remember to consider both your position and your audience. Be certain that each main point will be clearly understandable and convincing to your listeners.

When you plan your speech, also think about the techniques you can use to encourage your listeners to identify with you. Consider how you can best appear credible and self-confident to the members of your audience, and consider how you can evoke their goodwill. If your listeners regard you as familiar and trustworthy, they will be more readily persuaded by your speech.

Working with the Model

In 1894 Captain Alfred Dreyfus, a French army officer, was accused of selling military secrets to Germany. Although much of the evidence against him had been forged, Dreyfus was convicted by a secret court martial and condemned to life imprisonment on Devil's Island. Proof of Dreyfus' innocence was found in 1897, but the army refused to reopen the case. This controversy divided France into two factions: those who believed Dreyfus had been convicted largely because he was a Jew and those who believed the army should be supported at any cost.

In 1898 the novelist Émile Zola published an article entitled "I Accuse!" He accused politicians and officers, by name, of framing Dreyfus, concealing evidence, and deliberately encouraging public anti-Semitism. Zola knew he would be charged with libel, and he wanted to use his trial to reopen the Dreyfus case. Zola was convicted and fled to

England to avoid imprisonment. Shortly afterwards Dreyfus was pardoned, and eventually he was entirely cleared.

As you read the following excerpts from Zola's speech to the jury, observe the way he uses appeals to logic, appeals to emotion, and identification to argue his case.

If I am standing here before you, it is by my own wish. I alone decided that this dark, monstrous scandal should be brought under your jurisdiction. I alone, of my own free will, chose you—the highest source of French justice—in order that France might at last know everything, and reach a verdict. My acts have had no other purpose, and my person is nothing. I have sacrificed my person so that I could place in your hands, not only the honor of the army, but the imperiled honor of the nation. . . .

You know the legend that has grown up: Dreyfus was condemned justly and legally by seven infallible officers, whom we cannot even suspect of error without insulting the entire army. He pays with deserved tortures for his abominable crime. And since he is a Jew, a Jewish syndicate has been established, an international syndicate of people without national allegiances, in order to save the traitor at the price of shameless bribery. Next, this syndicate piles crime on crime, buying consciences, throwing France into disastrous confusion, determined to sell her to the enemy, to plunge France into a general war, rather than to renounce its terrible plan.

There it is. It's very simple—even childish and imbecile, as you see. But with this poisoned bread the dirty press has been nourishing our people for months. And we must not be astonished if we are witnessing a dangerous crisis, for when you sow folly and lies, you reap madness.

Certainly, gentlemen, I do not insult you by thinking that you have been taken in by such nursery tales. I know you, I know who you are. You are the heart and mind of Paris, of my great Paris, where I was born, which I love with an infinite tenderness, which I have studied and written about for forty years. And I know what is now going on inside your brains; for before coming to sit here as the defendant, I was seated there, in the jury box where you are. There you represent the average point of view, you illustrate wisdom and justice in the mass. Soon I will be with you, in thought, in the room where you deliberate. I am convinced that your effort will be to safeguard your interests as citizens, which are, naturally, the interests of the entire nation. You may make mistakes, but you will make mistakes with the idea that in serving your own welfare, you serve the welfare of all.

I see you with your families in the evening, under the lamplight. I listen to you chatting with your friends. I accompany you into your factories and shops. You are all working people, some in trade, some in industry, some in the professions. And your anxiety over the deplorable state into which business has fallen is legitimate. Everywhere the present crisis threatens to become a disaster. Receipts fall off, business deals become more difficult. So the thought which you have brought here, the thought I read on your faces, is that there has been enough of this scandal, and you must put an end to it.

You have not reached the point of saying, like many: "What does it matter to us whether an innocent man is on Devil's Island?" But you tell yourselves, just the same, that the agitation by us, who hunger and thirst for truth, is not worth all the evil we are accused of causing. And if you condemn me, gentlemen, only one thought will underlie your verdict: the desire to calm your own seas, to revive business, the belief that in striking at me you will be putting an end to a campaign that is harmful to the interests of France.

I do not defend myself. But what a blunder you would make, if you believed that in striking at me you would reestablish order in our unhappy country! Don't you understand now that the country is dying of the darkness in which they so obstinately keep her? The mistakes of government officials pile up on top of mistakes; one lie necessitates another, and the mass becomes overwhelming. A judicial blunder has been committed; and in order to hide it, it has been necessary to commit a new offense every day against common sense and justice. . . .

Today they ask you to condemn me, in my turn, because, seeing my country on such a terrifying course, I have cried out in my anguish. Condemn me, then! But it will be another mistake, a mistake whose burden you will bear throughout history. And my condemnation, instead of restoring the peace which you desire, which we all desire, will only sow new passion and disorder. The cup, I tell you, is full to the rim. Do not make it overflow! . . .

The Dreyfus case—ah, gentlemen, the Dreyfus case has become very small at this moment. It is very far away, compared to the terrifying question which it has raised. It is no longer a question of the Dreyfus case. It is a question of whether France is still the France of the Declaration of the Rights of Man, the France which gave liberty to the world, and which ought to give the world justice. Are we still the most noble, the most fraternal, the most generous nation? Are we going to protect our reputation in Europe for justice and humanity? Are not all our victories now called into question? Open your eyes, and realize that the French soul, to be in such confusion, must have been shaken to its depths by these terrible dangers. A nation is not turned upside down in this way unless its moral existence is in peril. This is an hour of extraordinary gravity; the safety of the nation is at stake.

And when you have grasped this, gentlemen, you will feel that only one remedy is possible: to speak the truth, to render justice. Everything that holds back the light, everything that piles darkness on darkness, will only prolong and aggravate the crisis. The role of good citizens, of those who feel the overriding necessity to put an end to this business, is to demand broad daylight. There are many of us who believe this.

Men of letters, philosophers, scientists are rising on every side in the name of intelligence and reason. And I am not speaking of foreigners, of the shudder that has shaken all Europe. Yet the foreigner is not necessarily the enemy. Let us not consider the nations who might be our enemies tomorrow. But great Russia, our ally, or generous little Holland, or all the sympathetic northern peoples, or the French-speaking lands of Switzerland and Belgium—why are their hearts so full, so over-flowing with brotherly suffering? Do you imagine that France is isolated from the world? When you cross the frontier, do you want them to forget your traditional reputation for justice and humanity?

Perhaps, gentlemen, like so many others, you are waiting for a clap of thunder—the proof of Dreyfus' innocence, falling from the sky like a bolt of lightning. Truth does not behave in that way. She requires some searching, some intelligence. The proof! You know very well where it is, where we could find it! . . . And if it is impossible for the present to seek it out where it is, the government—which is ignorant of nothing, which is as convinced as we are of the innocence of Dreyfus—when it sees fit, and when there are no risks, will find the witnesses who will at last give us light.

Dreyfus is innocent, I swear it! I stake my life on it, I stake my honor! In this solemn hour, before this tribunal which represents human justice, before you, gentlemen of the jury, who are the very incarnation of my country, before all France, before the whole world, I swear that Dreyfus is innocent! By my forty years of labor, by any authority that labor may have conferred upon me, I swear that Dreyfus is innocent! By all that I have achieved, by the name that I have made for myself, by the works I have added to French literature, I swear that Dreyfus is innocent! Let all that melt away, let my works perish, if Dreyfus is not innocent! He is innocent!

Everything seems to be against me: the two legislative Chambers, the civil power, the military power, the newspapers with the widest circulation, the public opinion which they have poisoned. And I have on my side only the ideal—an ideal of truth and justice. But I am content, for I will win!

I did not want my country to be the victim of lies and injustice. You may condemn me here. One day France will thank me for having helped to save her honor.

A. Think about the appeals to logic that Zola makes in his speech.
   1. In what part of the speech does he appeal to the jurors' ability to tell truth from falsehood?
   2. In what passage does he explain how the present crisis came about?
   3. In what passage does he try to account for the lack of proof on his side of the case?
   4. Why do you think Zola makes as few appeals to logic as he does?
B. Think about the appeals to emotion in this speech.
   1. In what passages does Zola appeal to the jurors' sense of fairness?
   2. In what passages does he appeal to their patriotism and national pride?
   3. What other emotions does Zola appeal to?
C. Think about Zola's use of identification in this speech.
   1. How does he present himself to the jurors?
   2. How does he explain his ability to understand the jurors' thoughts and feelings?
   3. In what passages does Zola ask to be judged on the basis of his talent and reputation?
D. At the time he made this speech, Zola was fairly certain he would be convicted. If he believed this, why do you think he made this speech? Why do you think he made the specific appeals that he did? In what ways do you think the speech might have been different if Zola had thought he would be acquitted?

Guidelines

Very often, logical arguments and appeals to emotion can be combined to develop a particularly effective persuasive speech. When you combine these methods of development, remember to keep the following guidelines in mind.

1. Use logical arguments in presenting main points that are based on common sense or fact. Be sure each logical argument directly supports your position and will be understandable and convincing to your audience.
2. Use appeals to emotion in presenting main points that are based on basic physical, psychological, or social needs. Be sure each appeal to emotion directly supports your position and will be understandable and convincing to your audience.
3. Plan to use specific techniques that will encourage your audience to identify with you. If you establish their identification with you early, your listeners will be particularly willing to be persuaded by your speech.

Preparing and Presenting

With three or four other students, select a topic on which you can all prepare persuasive speeches. You and the other members of your group may wish to choose one of the following topics.

- violence on television
- the budget for national defense
- cigarette smoking in public buildings
- career-directed education for high school students
- a national draft for two years of public service

Working independently, plan a persuasive speech on the topic that you and the other group members have chosen. Decide on your position on that topic. Also select an audience for the persuasive speech in which you will present that position. You may choose your fellow students as an audience, or you may choose another kind of group.

If necessary, do research on the topic of your speech. Then select three or more main points that will persuade your listeners to accept your position. Your main points should include both logical arguments and appeals to emotion.

Write a complete outline for your speech. In your outline, include notes on the methods you will use to encourage the members of your audience to identify with you.

With the rest of your group, discuss the speech outline prepared by each group member. Talk about the statement of position, the logical arguments, the appeals to emotion, and the methods for encouraging audience identification presented in each student's outline. Help each group member improve his or her outline as necessary.

After you have revised and improved your own speech outline, practice presenting your speech. Ask the other members of your group to listen as you speak and to suggest specific ways in which you might improve your tone of voice, rate of speaking, use of gestures, and projection of self-confidence and enthusiasm.

Finally, present your speech to the other students in your class. If you have selected an audience other than your fellow students, identify your intended audience before you begin your speech.

Evaluation Checklist

Evaluate each persuasive speech on the basis of the following criteria. Rate the speech on a scale from 1 (Poor) to 5 (Excellent). Be prepared to give reasons for each rating you give. The questions in parentheses will help you do so.

Category	Rating
1. The statement of position was convincingly presented. (How might it have been more effectively phrased or placed in the speech?)	
2. The logical arguments presented to support the position were sound. (Which ones, if any, were not appropriate to the topic or to the audience? What other logical arguments, if any, should have been presented?)	
3. The appeals to emotion presented to support the position were effective. (Which ones, if any, were not appropriate to the topic or to the audience? What other appeals to emotion, if any, should have been presented?)	
4. The techniques used to encourage the audience to identify with the speaker were successful. (What other techniques, if any, should have been used?)	
5. The delivery of the speech was persuasive. (What changes in voice or gestures would have made the speech more convincing?)	
6. Considering the overall impression, the speech was persuasive. (What one change would have been most important in improving the effectiveness of the speech?)	

Chapter 6 Review

Summary

Effective persuasive speaking depends heavily on your ability to develop your thinking skills. The skills below will help you become a better critical thinker.

1. Perceiving
2. Arranging
3. Inquiring
4. Inferring
5. Reasoning

In preparing for a persuasive speech, clearly draft your specific purpose and the statement of your position, carefully research your topic, and adapt the arguments you plan to use to your specific audience. The material you choose to support the statement of your position will depend upon the kind of persuasive speech you are giving. The first kind is based mainly upon an appeal to logic and reasoning supported by evidence; the second kind is based mainly upon an appeal to emotion (appealing to the audience's physical, psychological, or social needs); the third kind is based upon the use of identification plus a combination of the first two.

Using identification, establishing yourself as a credible speaker deserving the audience's trust and goodwill, is also an important persuasive skill. Encouraging your audience to identify with you early in a speech will better ensure they will be persuaded by your speech.

Reviewing Vocabulary

Number your paper from 1 to 14. Next to each number write the letter of the group of words that correctly defines the word(s).

1. oversimplify
2. anecdotes
3. evidence
4. *post hoc*
5. position
6. false analogy
7. inferring
8. physical needs
9. social needs
10. psychological needs
11. misleading statistics
12. reasoning backward
13. begging the question
14. logical argument

a. needs involving an individual's relationship to a group
b. confusing *after* with *because*
c. ability to make generalizations
d. brief stories
e. to simplify an issue to such an extent that distortion results
f. needs involving an individual's life and physical health
g. a misleading figure of speech (comparison) from which one reasons
h. stating a position that needs to be proved as if it were true
i. facts, statistics, etc., used to support an argument
j. statistics that sound factual but that are unreliable
k. needs involving an individual's inner life
l. objective reason that supports a position
m. assuming that people belong to a group because they have a characteristic in common with that group
n. specific purpose of a persuasive speech

Reviewing Facts and Ideas

1. Of the five thinking skills discussed on page 175, which ones do you think you need to spend the most time developing? Why?

2. Confusing "after" with "because" is a very common logical fallacy. What are some popular superstitions that exemplify this error in thinking?
3. What is the statement of your position? Where does it usually come in a persuasive speech? Why? When is it most effective to present a formal statement late in the speech?
4. What are the main points of support in a persuasive speech appealing to logic called? What are the characteristics of these?
5. What are the most common kinds of evidence used to support logical arguments?
6. What are the three kinds of needs upon which emotional appeals are based? Why does appealing to these basic human needs sometimes help to convince audience members to accept your position?
7. Why are vivid language, a forceful voice, and clear gestures particularly effective in a persuasive speech developed with appeals to emotion?
8. What is identification? How does encouraging it enhance a persuasive speech?
9. What can a speaker do to establish credibility with an audience?
10. What can a speaker do to gain the audience's goodwill?

Discussing Facts and Ideas

1. Which are the most common fallacies in reasoning that can be found in radio and television advertising? Why do people continue to be influenced by these appeals if they are false?
2. A frequently raised question about persuasive speaking is whether the ends justify the means. That is, does the fact that your position is good or right justify using any kind of argument (even false statements) in order to get others to accept the "good" position? Discuss this question. See if you can find some examples of speakers who seem to agree that the end justifies the means.

Applying Your Knowledge

1. An effective persuasive speaker, and a person who is effectively listening to persuasive speakers, must be knowledgeable about a wide variety of subjects. Select a major weekly news magazine. Use the four most recent issues to prepare a list of speaking topics. With your classmates write thirty to fifty topics, each on a separate slip of paper. Place the topics in a box. At the beginning or toward the end of your class period, a student, chosen by your teacher, will draw two of the slips from the box and read them silently. The student will return one slip and use the other as the topic for a three-minute, impromptu persuasive speech. Organize the speech using the simple pattern of a statement of a specific purpose followed by no more than three major points, each with some support, and a summary for a conclusion.
2. The various kinds of persuasive appeals can be made easier to master if you use some imagination. Give a brief speech to your class on one of the following topics. (You and your teacher may want to add similar subjects to the list.)

   a. Roses are better than daffodils.
   b. Grapes are better than bananas.
   c. Standing is better than sitting.
   d. Talking is better than singing.
   e. Running is better than walking.
   f. Crying is better than laughing.
   g. The opposite of any of the above.

   Obviously you could argue the opposite of each statement, i.e., that daffodils are better than roses. When you make your presentation, be sure to include one logical argument, one emotional appeal, and one appeal to get the audience to identify with you.

Making a Sales Presentation

Very few products or services can sell themselves. First-rate sales-people can inspire customers with a desire to buy and the feeling that they are making the right decision. Effective sales presentations are based on extensive practice, experience, and knowledge of human psychology. Several principles, however, are always true.

- A good sales presentation has the qualities of a good persuasive speech. It uses facts, figures, and other evidence to promote a product. It meets and answers the listeners' objections to the product, and it is delivered with conviction and enthusiasm.
- An effective salesperson uses questions and observations to learn about his or her customers. How much money do they have to spend? Are they seriously interested in buying, or only comparison shopping? What are they looking for in a product—for example, do they value glamour or efficiency more highly?
- If there is more than one customer, a good salesperson finds out what features each person is most interested in and then emphasizes those features when speaking to that customer.
- A good salesperson never argues with customers—even if they are wrong. The salesperson should continually observe the customers' reactions and change the presentation accordingly.
- A good salesperson knows when to stop talking and let the customers make up their minds. Whether or not the presentation results in a sale, the salesperson should give the customers a business card and urge them to stay in touch.

Activities

1. Working with three or more other students, select several products to shop for. (You should consider stereo equipment, bicycles, televisions, used cars, and other products students might reasonably be expected to buy.) Visit the stores individually and listen to the sales presentations. Then evaluate the presentations according to the guidelines above and report your findings to the class.
2. Work with another student. Each of you should prepare a different sales presentation for a product. Try to make the presentations equally appealing to customers. Then deliver your presentations before the class. Have the other students vote for the presentation more likely to make them buy the product.

Evaluating Your Credibility as a Speaker

To be an effective speaker, you must be *credible* to others. The following chart contains ten questions to evaluate a speaker's credibility. Each question may be answered by a score of 0 (Poorest) to 10 (Best).

Category	Rating
1. How well does the speaker know his or her subject?	
2. How accurately does the speaker report information?	
3. Does the speaker give due credit to sources of information and ideas?	
4. Does the speaker use sound logic?	
5. Does the speaker avoid deceptive techniques and loaded language?	
6. Are the speaker's facts and ideas consistent on different occasions?	
7. Does the speaker avoid gossip, rumor, and innuendo?	
8. Does the speaker show respect for others?	
9. Does the speaker avoid bragging?	
10. How would you rate the speaker's overall credibility, in speaking and in life?	

Activity

1. Use the preceding chart to evaluate five well-known speakers (for example, a politician, a city or state official, a newscaster, a business person, and a celebrity). Add up their scores in each category and see how they rank on a scale of 0 to 100. Compare your evaluation with those of other students in your class and discuss why you evaluated each speaker as you did.

Listening to Understand

After working through this chapter, you should be proficient at the following skills:

Lesson	Skills
Lesson 1	• recognizing a speaker's signposts • taking notes using outline format • recording the essential information in a speech or lecture
Communicating on the Job	• taking notes on a training lecture
Communicating as a Citizen	• appealing to a government agency

Listening and Taking Notes

You are probably used to taking notes when you do library research for a paper or a report. Taking notes on a speech or lecture, however, is different from taking notes on a book. You usually cannot ask a speaker to slow down so that you can take better notes. You cannot ask a speaker to repeat an earlier section of his or her speech. Furthermore, you will probably not have an outline of the entire speech in front of you as you write. When taking notes on a speech, you will record only the important points, and you will use a very simple outline form.

Effective note taking is based on effective listening. Listen for **signposts**—the words or phrases the speaker uses to tell you what part of the speech you are hearing; for example:

"To begin with . . ."   "On the other hand . . ."
"My first point . . ."   "In conclusion . . ."
"Secondly . . ."

Also listen for signposts that emphasize the ideas the speaker thinks are most important; for example:

"First and foremost . . ."   "Above all . . ."
"Let me remind you . . ."   "I repeat . . ."
"I cannot emphasize too strongly . . ."

The points that the speaker emphasizes should all go into your notes.

A speaker may outline a speech for the audience in advance. (For example, a teacher may write the main points of a lecture on the board.) Usually, however, you will be able to recognize only the speaker's main topics and the subtopics or supporting details. An **informal outline** format is best for recording a speech when you do not know in advance how it will be organized:

• First main topic
  —first subtopic
  —second subtopic
• Second main topic
  —first subtopic
  —second subtopic (and so forth)

When you take notes using the informal outline format, pay close attention to the relationships between the speaker's ideas. If you are not certain whether an idea is a main topic or a supporting detail, write it in whichever position is easier at the moment. When you review your notes afterward, you should be able to decide where the idea belongs.

Take your notes in the most concise form possible. Use phrases instead of sentences, and single words instead of phrases whenever you can. Use abbreviations, initials, and symbols rather than complete names. Later, reread your notes to be sure that all abbreviations and shortened expressions are understandable.

Working with the Model

Ronald Reagan delivered his inaugural address on January 20, 1981. Read the following passage from the beginning of the speech and then read the notes that Vincent took while watching the speech on television. As you read the notes, notice which ideas Vincent chose to record.

From the First Inaugural Address

These United States are confronted with an economic affliction of great proportions.

We suffer from the longest and one of the worst sustained inflations in our national history. It distorts our economic decisions, penalizes thrift, and crushes the struggling young and the fixed-income elderly alike. It threatens to shatter the lives of millions of our people.

Idle industries have cast workers into unemployment, human misery, and personal indignity.

Those who do work are denied a fair return for their labor by a tax system which penalizes successful achievement and keeps us from maintaining full productivity.

But great as our tax burden is, it has not kept pace with public spending. For decades we have piled deficit upon deficit, mortgaging our future and our children's future for the temporary convenience of the present.

To continue this long trend is to guarantee tremendous social, cultural, political, and economic upheavals.

You and I, as individuals, can, by borrowing, live beyond our means, but for only a limited period of time. Why, then, should we think that collectively, as a nation, we're not bound by that same limitation?

We must act today in order to preserve tomorrow. And let there be no misunderstanding—we are going to begin to act, beginning today.

The economic ills we suffer have come upon us over several decades.

They will not go away in days, weeks, or months, but they will go away. They will go away because we as Americans have the capacity now, as we have had in the past, to do whatever needs to be done to preserve this last and greatest bastion of freedom.

Vincent's Notes

- U.S. confronted by great "economic affliction"
  —inflation harms econ., citizens
  —idle indust.→unemployment
  —tax system penalizes achievemt, prod'ty.
  —high pub. spending "mortgaging future"
  ——→soc., econ. upheaval
  —nation living beyond means
- "Must act today in order to preserve tomorrow"
  —we (admin.) will
  —econ. ills came & will go slowly
  —Amer. have capacity to succeed

213

A. Think about the points made in Reagan's speech.
   1. What are the main topics of this passage?
   2. What are the subtopics and supporting details of this passage?
   3. What signpost words or phrases, if any, has Reagan used in this passage? Why do you think he has not used more signposts?

B. Think about Vincent's notes.
   1. What ideas or topics has Vincent included in his notes?
   2. What subtopics and details has Vincent omitted from his notes? Why do you think he omitted them?
   3. What abbreviations and symbols has Vincent used? Do you think they would be easy or difficult to understand? What other abbreviations do you think he might have used?
   4. What expressions has Vincent quoted directly from the speech? How has he indicated that these are exact quotes? Why do you think he did not record more direct quotations?

C. Some listeners prefer to take notes using a paragraph format. They write the main topic as the first sentence of a paragraph and underline it. Then they write the subtopics and details as sentences in the paragraph. Rewrite Vincent's notes using the paragraph format.

Guidelines

In order to take good notes, you need to have good listening habits. Try to practice the following habits while listening to a speech or lecture.

1. Have all your note-taking materials ready *before* the speech begins. Have a pen that writes well, a notebook with enough blank pages, and a firm surface on which to write.
2. When the speaker begins, concentrate entirely on what he or she is saying. Don't think about the people next to you, your other classes, or your plans for the weekend.
3. Identify the *purpose* of the speech as soon as you can and include it in your notes.
4. Listen for signpost words and phrases that identify the important points in the speech. Use underlining or symbols in your notes to make these points stand out.
5. Indent subtopics and supporting details to show their relation to the main topics. Include only the most important supporting details. Don't try to write down everything.
6. Use as many abbreviations, symbols, and initials as possible, but be sure that you will be able to understand them when you reread your notes.

7. As you listen, try to understand the speech rather than evaluate it. Listen carefully to the speaker's actual words instead of anticipating what he or she will say.
8. If you have failed to record a piece of information correctly in your notes, wait until the speech is over before you go back to insert it. Polishing your notes during the speech will cause you to miss more important information.
9. Pay special attention to unfamiliar vocabulary and new concepts. Be sure to record and define these correctly.
10. After the speaker has finished, ask questions (if possible) to clarify any information you are uncertain about.
11. Review your notes while the speech is fresh in your memory. Make sure they are both legible and understandable. Rewrite any passages that you think might be difficult to understand a few weeks or months from now. Note any topics on which you need additional information.

Activity

1. Listen to a recording of a speech by a politician or other public figure. As you listen, take notes on a section of the speech lasting two to three minutes. Several days later, reread your notes and try to write out that section of the speech as it was originally delivered. Then listen again to the recording. See how many of the important points you wrote down in your notes and how many you missed. Think about ways in which you could have listened more carefully and taken better notes.

2. Collect notes taken by students who are in a social studies class together but who are not in your class. Make copies of those notes, leaving off the name of the teacher and of the student. Preferably with the teacher's help, determine which notes are most accurate. Discuss which notes would be most helpful in studying for a test. How might the kind of test the teacher gives affect which set of notes would be most helpful?

Preparing and Presenting

Work with a partner. Choose a lecture, speech, or program on which you can both take notes. Listen carefully to the speech, paying particular attention to signpost words and phrases. Take notes in the informal outline format, making the main points and subtopics clear.

Reread your notes and rewrite any information that you think might be difficult to understand. If necessary, recopy your notes. Exchange the notes with your partner. Compare the information contained in your notes with the information in your partner's notes.

Evaluation Checklist

Evaluate your partner's notes on the basis of the following criteria. Rate the notes on a scale from 1 (Poor) to 5 (Excellent). Be prepared to give reasons for each rating you give.

Category	Rating
My partner . . . 1. Recorded all or most of the main topics	
2. Recorded all or most of the subtopics and supporting details	
3. Correctly identified the main topics as main topics and the subtopics as subtopics	
4. Used abbreviations and symbols that were easy to understand	
5. Took notes that accurately reflected the content and meaning of the speech	

Chapter 7 Review

Summary

Taking good notes of a speech requires good listening habits. The following guidelines will help you take concise, clear notes.

1. Identify and write down the purpose of the speech as soon as you can.
2. Record only the important points, usually in an informal outline format.
3. Listen for signposts to help you understand the important points and transitions.
4. Indent subtopics and supporting details to show their relation to the main topics.
5. Use phrases and single words whenever possible. Don't try to write everything down in full.
6. Utilize as many abbreviations, symbols, and initials as possible.
7. When the speech is over, ask questions (if possible) to clarify any uncertainties.
8. Review and rewrite your notes while the speech is fresh in your memory.

Reviewing Facts and Ideas

1. What are signposts? What two kinds of signposts are frequently used? Give an example of each.
2. What are the chief characteristics of an informal outline? Why is this outline format best for note taking?
3. Why is it helpful to indent subtopics and supporting details?
4. For the purposes of taking good notes, why is it better to try to understand a speech rather than to evaluate it?
5. Why should you skip over a passage you missed or recorded incorrectly rather than to try to add to or polish it during the speech?

Discussing Facts and Ideas

1. Discuss the ways different teachers have of letting you know what information should be included in your notes. Which ways seem to be most effective?
2. Some students think that using a tape recorder is a good way to take notes in class. Discuss the advantages and disadvantages of this approach.
3. Chapter 7 includes examples of "signposts" that help alert the listener to changes in thought. Discuss other words that can be used as "signposts." What are other key words or phrases that may not be "signposts" but could be important in helping you prepare notes? (For example, "This is not in the book.")

Applying Your Knowledge

1. Take notes of 10 minutes of a newscast on television using the format below. Use the right side of the paper for supporting information.

Main Topics	Notes on Each Topic
President's speech	President criticizes Congress
	President appeals for citizen support
	President praises Sec'y of State
Hurricane	Storm damage in Florida is great
	Storm misses L.A.

Taking Notes on a Training Lecture

When you start a new job or learn a new skill, you will need to take accurate, useful notes on the oral instructions you are given. Follow these guidelines for taking notes on a training lecture.

- Listen carefully for the major steps in the procedure being taught and be sure to record the steps in the right sequence.
- Be precise in recording figures and other technical information (measurements, times, sizes, numbers, colors, and so forth). Your notes should be clear and accurate enough that anyone could use them as a guide.
- Don't hesitate to ask the instructor to repeat or clarify information.
- Check the accuracy of your notes by going over them with the instructor (if possible) and by doing the procedure yourself.

Activities

1. Ask another student to explain a task or procedure to you while you take notes on it. Then, using your notes as a guide, explain the procedure to the student who lectured to you. Compare the accuracy of your notes and find ways in which they might be improved.
2. With other members of your class, arrange to visit a business (such as a garage, a printing plant, or a fast-food restaurant) or one of the shops in your school. Ask a supervisor to explain a procedure to your group while you take notes. Then compare your notes with the other students'. Decide whose notes would be the best guide to carrying out the procedure and explain why.

Appealing to a Governmental Agency

At some time you will probably need to appeal to a governmental official or agency to take action on a problem. Whether you and your community receive the help you want will depend on your understanding of the agency's powers and the persuasiveness of your presentation. Keep the following guidelines in mind.

- Be sure that you understand your problem and that all your facts and figures are accurate.
- Learn which agency or official can help you. Don't waste time appealing to people who are powerless.
- Learn about the personality, powers, and biases of the official you will be speaking to.
- Have a specific action that you want the official to take.
- Make an appointment to see the official and arrive on time.
- Present your case in a well-organized manner, using your strongest facts and arguments. Be concise and end your presentation with a summary of your case and request for action.
- Speak effectively and sincerely, but avoid emotional displays. Be respectful, but not awestruck.
- When you have finished your presentation, ask for a specific date or time when you can learn whether action has been taken.
- Follow up your appeal by speaking to or phoning the official to see what action has been taken.

Activities

1. Arrange to meet with a city or county supervisor, a school board member, or another public official who has the power to take action on local problems. Ask about the ways citizens persuade this official to help solve problems and which methods are most effective.
2. Working with several other students, identify a local problem that you believe needs action by a public agency. You might ask for action on poor streets, defective traffic signals, or other problems. Prepare a concise, well-organized presentation on the problem. If your teacher decides that you should make the presentation, make an appointment to speak to the appropriate official. You may present your case with a single spokesperson. However, if the problem is complex, you may divide the presentation among several people. Report on your presentation to the class.

Unit Introduction: Communicating in a Democracy

Parliamentary Procedure and Debate

A Case Study

In 1980 two speech professors, using computers and market research techniques, developed a "perfect" campaign speech on foreign policy, designed to appeal to everybody and offend nobody. The ideas of the speech were vague and not specific.

America requires a President who is experienced in diplomacy and capable of managing world stability. The international scene demands a chief executive who carries out a coherent and consistent foreign policy that can be understood and respected by allies and adversaries alike.

Today's international scene is one in which the major powers have reached military parity. What we must do is manage and stabilize our relationships with each other and maintain the balance of power.

The U.S. will continue to meet its responsibilities to its allies. However, to maintain world order, we will continue to seek and negotiate stable relationships with all nations.

The U.S. needs a President with a moral vision of promoting the welfare of mankind. America requires a leader who treats other nations with mutual respect; who promotes and encourages increased human rights and fundamental freedoms; who responds consistently in a calm, cool and reasoned manner.

Think and Discuss

Find five groups of words that you think were chosen for their reassuring effect. Tell why you think each phrase is reassuring.

Choose one sentence that states in a vague way something that this country should do. Then list at least two specific ways that thing could be done.

In Unit Three, "Parliamentary Procedure and Debate," you will think about some of the issues raised in this Case Study. You will learn ways of persuading people to agree with you wherever you are speaking.

Unit Introduction: Communicating in a Democracy

> Those who won our independence believed . . . that freedom to think as you will and to speak as you think are means indispensable to the discovery and spread of political truth.
>
> Justice Louis D. Brandeis

> To be free is not necessarily to be wise. But wisdom comes with counsel, with the frank and free conference of untrammeled men united in the common interest.
>
> President Woodrow Wilson

Effective Citizenry and the Communication Process

Effective speaking and listening skills are essential to a citizen in the United States or in any democracy. Because our form of government is so dependent on the free consideration of ideas, our courts have repeatedly emphasized that the right of freedom of speech is one of the most basic of our constitutional protections.

Before reading further, discuss the quotations above. First make sure you understand the meaning of each word in each of the statements. For example, what was Wilson talking about when he spoke of "free conference"? Of "untrammeled men"?

Next answer these questions in the course of your discussion.

1. Why is freedom to think and speak essential "to the discovery and spread of political truth"?
2. Why do you think Wilson believed "free conference" could produce wisdom?
3. What conditions might seem to justify restriction of free speech? For example, should people be permitted to yell that they are drowning when, in fact, they are not in any trouble? Should students be permitted to say whatever they want in a graduation speech?
4. What responsibilities do citizens in a democracy have when they exercise their freedom of speech?

Without good speaking and listening skills, a citizen cannot participate fully in community affairs and in democratic government. A citizen
needs to be able to listen carefully and critically to ideas and proposals
made by public figures and organizations in order to evaluate such
proposals. A citizen also needs to be able to present his or her ideas
clearly and persuasively in order to take an active role in the community
and in the political process.

Effective citizenry requires more than freedom for people to say
what they want to say. It demands people who are skillful in advocating
their positions and in analyzing the arguments made by others. Effective
citizenry also depends on fair rules for participation in meetings and
decisions, rules which protect the rights of all to speak out and to
advocate their ideas.

In addition there need to be speakers who are skillful enough to
oppose those who would trample others' rights. Otherwise, a speaker
with the abilities Hitler possessed can lead a nation to destruction.
Totalitarian governments often are led by individuals with great skills
as speakers.

Consider again the basic model of speech communication which
was introduced in Unit One.

The Communication Process

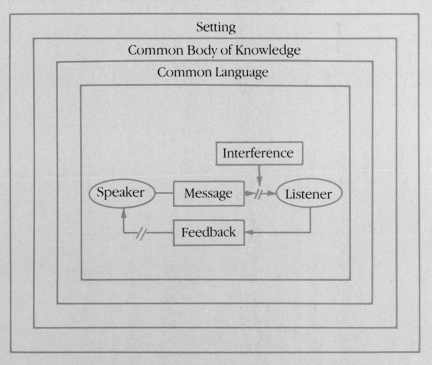

The protection given by the right of freedom of speech is part of the setting in which speakers and listeners interact as citizens in the United States. If citizens are to participate successfully in decision-making organizations, they must share a common body of knowledge, the rules and procedures to be followed in meetings. These rules depend very much on there being a common language. If speakers participating in deliberative bodies, such as a meeting of a city council, do not understand what a *motion* is or what *to call the previous question* means, it makes little difference how much freedom of speech the Constitution grants them.

When critical issues are being debated, there is often much interference, making it difficult for speakers and listeners to understand one another. Frequently, this interference is deliberately introduced into the situation by one or the other participant as a means of preventing others from achieving their objectives. Those who wish to interfere with free communication may rudely shout so loud that speakers cannot be heard. Or they may try something more sophisticated, such as introducing irrelevant arguments or making verbal attacks on the speaker. As you develop skills in parliamentary procedure and debating, keep in mind the model of the communication cycle. It will help you remember that the purpose of the rules of parliamentary procedure and debate is to facilitate effective and free communication.

Reread the report of the discussion at the beginning of the lesson.

1. What, if anything, would you add to your answers to the questions?
2. What, if anything, would you change?

Problem Solving and Decision Making

You will find the study of debate and parliamentary procedure becomes increasingly helpful as you become involved in community activities. Citizens who participate in local organizations—such as neighborhood action groups, precinct caucuses, or county committees—must be able to reach agreement on public issues and to take positions on those issues. Reaching agreement requires skillful discussion. All participants should have a chance to be heard on the issues they think are important. Speakers should focus discussion on the issues rather than on the personalities of the participants. Such focus requires the participants to be well informed on the issues and to consider the likely responses of others to their positions.

As a participant in a community or school group that has a problem to solve, it is useful to understand the four basic approaches to decision making.

Trial-and-error	Trying a likely solution to your problem and, if it doesn't work, trying alternative solutions until you find one that does work. This approach can waste time and money, but if little relevant information is available, it may be the only way.
Incremental	Taking a small step toward a decision, seeing if it is successful, taking the next small step, and so on until you reach a decision. This method, too, is time consuming, but when strong feelings are involved, this step-by-step approach may well be the best.
Rational	Analyzing all facts and problems logically, on the basis of certain ideas assumed to be true, and then drawing conclusions based on the analysis. This is the approach advocated by scientists. It is not always possible to have all of the information needed to make a purely rational decision.
Scanning	Identifying all possible solutions and developing standards for evaluating them. Standards may include whether there are the means to implement the solutions or whether the solutions are compatible with basic values or interests of the parties involved. Once you have examined all possible solutions and discarded some, continue to repeat the process until only one solution remains.

When you are working within a community or school group to solve a problem, you need to begin by defining the problem. Discover what is wrong. Start by asking questions such as the following. How

many people does the problem affect? Is it limited to a few families on one block, or does it involve an entire neighborhood? Is the problem the responsibility of a single person or agency? Will some research be necessary to find someone who can help solve the problem? Can the problem be solved?

Next, you need to contact people who can help you. Enlist friends, neighbors, and other members of your community. Explain the seriousness of the problem and why the community should be concerned about it. Then, using one of the decision-making strategies above, your group should seek the best possible solution to the problem.

Once you have decided on a solution, you may need to enlist official help. Some problems can be solved merely through active efforts by concerned individuals. Other problems will require assistance from responsible officials: city council members, school board members or administrators, or representatives of various local, regional, and state agencies. In most cases you will get the best help if you go to the individual with the most direct responsibility for dealing with the problem instead of the highest official available. For example, you may have much more success handling a zoning problem by dealing directly with the city planner than with the mayor. Don't drop your solution on someone's desk and forget it. After you have arrived at a solution, you need to develop a clear plan to bring your solution about. Then you must follow the plan until the problem is solved.

At each stage in the effort to solve a problem, you will find yourself called on to exercise a variety of speaking and listening skills. You will need to explain matters to others, conduct interviews, engage in group discussions, persuade others that your solutions are correct, and listen effectively to your coworkers and to those whose support you are seeking. You are apt to find yourself involved in a formal or informal debate with those who oppose you. You are also likely to participate in a number of meetings run by parliamentary procedure. As you study the material in Unit Three, keep in mind that the formalities of parliamentary procedure and of scholastic debate are not ends in themselves but vehicles that enable those who master them to be successful as citizens.

Activities

1. Define a problem that affects your community. It could involve conflicts between neighbors or a public problem, such as vandalism. Discuss the different people you could enlist to help you solve the problem and the different suggestions they might have. Then find at least three possible solutions and identify three people or agencies that might help you.
2. Invite a local political organizer or committee member to speak to your class. Ask the person to describe how local political organizations function and how they develop their positions on issues. Ask how debates and parliamentary procedure are used in the development of positions or issues.
3. Invite a person who is a leader in a business or in a government agency to speak to your class about the way decisions are made in his or her business or agency. Compare the process the speaker describes with the four approaches outlined in the preceding discussion. Ask if he or she uses debate and parliamentary procedure in the course of making decisions. If so, discuss the skills that the leader thinks are most important for their successful use. If not, discuss the processes that he or she uses instead and the communication skills these processes require.

Parliamentary Discussion

After working through this chapter, you should be proficient at the following skills:

Lesson	Skills
Lesson 1	• understanding the way a parliamentary body is organized • knowing the nine events of a meeting conducted according to parliamentary procedure
Lesson 2	• participating in a parliamentary meeting • introducing parliamentary motions
Communicating on the Job	• using an agenda
Communicating as a Citizen	• nominating a candidate for office

Planning a Meeting

Many clubs and other organizations adopt the rules of parliamentary procedure to conduct their meetings. The meetings of local civic groups and the meetings of your school's student council are probably conducted according to the rules of parliamentary procedure. The meetings of the United States Congress are conducted according to the same rules. Parliamentary procedure is used so widely and in so many diverse situations because it ensures that every group's meetings will proceed fairly and efficiently.

Parliamentary procedure cannot be used effectively in a meeting, however, unless all the participants make specific preparations for that meeting.

The person who will be in charge of conducting the meeting, called the **chairperson**, has the greatest responsibility in preparing for the meeting. The chairperson should write out an **agenda**, a list of things that will be done during the meeting. The nine events usually included in a meeting are shown, in order, in the chart on the following pages. The chairperson's agenda should list each of those nine events with specific notes on who will speak and what will be considered during that portion of the meeting. The written agenda should also include estimates of the time required for each portion of the meeting. These estimates will help the chairperson conduct the meeting efficiently and adjourn the meeting promptly.

Each member who plans to make a specific contribution during the meeting should discuss his or her plans with the chairperson. For example, a member who plans to present a committee report or introduce an item of new business should consult with the chairperson before the meeting. These premeeting discussions will help the chairperson plan the meeting accurately and allow time for each person's contribution. After confirming his or her plans with the chairperson, each member should prepare his or her contribution in detail by making notes for a report or by writing out a specific proposal. Contributions, such as committee reports or new items of business, particularly those filled with many important facts and figures upon which a group decision will be made, are sometimes typed in advance. Then copies can be distributed during the meeting so that the members can better follow the report or proposal.

All the other organization members should also prepare for the meeting. They should think about the issues that are likely to be considered during the meeting. If necessary, they should also review the rules of parliamentary procedure so that they can participate correctly in the meeting.

THE NINE EVENTS OF A MEETING CONDUCTED ACCORDING TO PARLIAMENTARY PROCEDURE

Call to Order The chairperson calls the meeting to order. Informal conversation ends and the rules of parliamentary procedure take effect.

Minutes of Previous Meeting The secretary reads the minutes and the chairperson asks for corrections. If someone has a correction, it is made, and the minutes stand approved as corrected. If there are no corrections, the minutes stand approved as read. If the minutes have been distributed in writing and everyone had copies prior to the meeting, the chair may simply ask for corrections. If there are none, the minutes stand approved as distributed.

Treasurer's Report The treasurer reports the balance of funds as of the previous meeting, the funds received since that meeting, the amount spent, and the new balance. This is *not* the part of the meeting to deal with issues related to the financial operations of the organization.

Correspondence The secretary reads letters sent to the organization (or distributes them if they have been duplicated). Issues raised by the letters are not acted on at this time. They are referred to appropriate committees by the chairperson or are scheduled for consideration later in the meeting under "new business."

Committee Reports Proper advance planning will ensure that only committees with something to report are called on. Committee recommendations may be acted on at this time.

Old Business Issues considered but not resolved at previous meetings are scheduled for further consideration at this point. Sometimes this part of the agenda is called "unfinished business."

New Business Issues being considered for the first time are introduced and discussed. When practical, members should be made aware before the meeting of issues scheduled as new business.

Announcements The chairperson and others may announce upcoming events and other matters of interest to members at this point in the meeting. Time will be saved if these announcements are prepared in writing and distributed to members.

Adjournment The meeting may be brought to an official close either when all business has been completed or when a majority of those in attendance vote for adjournment. Once the members of an organization have voted to adjourn, they can conduct no further business without convening a new meeting.

Working with the Model

Claire is the president of the Stevenson Service Club. To prepare for one of the club's meetings, Claire wrote the following agenda. Read the agenda carefully and think about the plan it presents.

AGENDA

Stevenson Service Club – April 13, 1987

1. Call to Order (3:15)
2. Minutes of Previous Meeting (5 minutes)
   a. Stan—read minutes
   b. Corrections and approval
3. Treasurer's Report—Tanya (5 minutes)
4. Correspondence—none
5. Committee Reports (10 minutes)
   a. Leah—community committee
   b. Miguel—fund-raising committee
   c. Malcolm—school grounds committee
   (No report from new students committee, sports committee, or social committee)
6. Old Business (10 minutes)
   a. New club representative for Student Council
   b. Orientation for foreign exchange students
   c. Banquet for outstanding community members
   d. Open to floor
7. New Business (20 minutes)
   a. Stevenson High fund-raising fair—Maxine
   b. Summer picnic for next year's freshmen—Lyle
   c. Entertainment program for senior citizens
   d. Open to floor
8. Announcements—Gary (5 minutes)
9. Adjournment (4:10)

A. Think about the agenda Claire prepared.
   1. How will the written agenda help Claire lead the club members in a productive and efficient meeting?
   2. How will the suggested times help Claire lead the meeting? Imagine that Tanya's report takes only three minutes instead of five. What do you think Claire will do? Imagine instead that the committee reports take fifteen minutes instead of only ten. What do you think Claire will do?
   3. Imagine Leah wants the club members to consider another item of old business. When will she have an opportunity to bring that item to the attention of the club?
   4. Imagine that, since the previous meeting, the Stevenson Service Club has received a letter from the Mayfield City Council, requesting assistance in a city clean-up campaign. When would the letter be read? When would a specific proposal regarding participation in the campaign be introduced?

B. Think about how other people should prepare for the meeting.
   1. What should each of these members do before the meeting: Stan, Tanya, Leah, Miguel, Malcolm, Maxine, Lyle, and Gary?
   2. What should the other club members do?

C. Think about your own experiences in attending meetings conducted according to parliamentary procedure.
   1. In what specific meetings did the chairperson follow a written agenda? How did the agenda help the chairperson conduct the meeting? What problems, if any, did the chairperson have in following the agenda?
   2. In what specific meetings did the chairperson seem not to have a written agenda? How could you tell that he or she did not have one? What problems arose because the chairperson had no written agenda?

Guidelines

Before the meeting of a club or organization, each member should make specific preparations.

1. The chairperson, who will conduct the meeting, should write an agenda, a list of what will happen during the meeting.
2. Members who plan to make specific contributions, such as presenting committee reports or introducing items of new business, should discuss their plans with the chairperson and should prepare their contributions in detail.

3. All the other members of the club or organization should think about issues likely to be raised during the meeting and should review the rules of parliamentary procedure as necessary.

Preparing and Presenting

Write a complete agenda for a meeting that will be conducted according to parliamentary procedure. You may write the agenda for a meeting of a real club or organization, or you may make up a club or organization. You may wish to use one of the following clubs.

Seaside High School Sailing Club
Central Chess Club
Main High School Debate Club
Ski and Surf Club
Latin Club
Jazz Club

Include in your agenda each of the nine events usually included in the order of business. Plan at least one item of correspondence, two committee reports, two specific items of old business, and two specific items of new business. Also include in your agenda a specific time for beginning the meeting, an estimated number of minutes to be spent on each event, and an estimated time for adjourning the meeting.

Evaluation Checklist

Exchange agendas with another student. Read each other's work carefully and then discuss both agendas. In the course of your discussion, evaluate each other's agendas on the basis of the following criteria. Rate each agenda on a scale from 1 (Poor) to 5 (Excellent). Be prepared to give reasons for each rating you give. The questions in parentheses will help you do so.

Category	Rating	
	Agenda A	Agenda B
The agenda . . . 1. Would be easy for a chairperson to use in conducting a meeting (How could the agenda be made easier to use?)		
2. Is complete (What should be added to make the agenda complete?)		
3. Includes only necessary information (What should be taken out of the agenda?)		
4. Presents a realistic estimate of the time involved in conducting the planned meeting (How should the estimates of time on the agenda be revised?)		

After you have discussed agendas with your partner, make any changes that are needed to improve your agenda.

Participating in a Meeting

In a meeting conducted according to parliamentary procedure, most business is accomplished by using motions. A **motion** is a proposal that specific action be taken. During appropriate portions of a meeting, any member may introduce a motion. Usually, the motion must be seconded and may then be discussed by all the members. Changes in the wording or the intent of a motion may be accomplished by **amendments**. Every motion brought before a meeting must be voted on, and the majority vote rules.

It is essential that every member understand the procedure used in introducing and acting upon a motion. Parliamentary motions are explained in detail in *Robert's Rules of Order (Revised)*, the most commonly accepted authority on parliamentary procedure.

During a meeting, the chairperson's main responsibility is to conduct the meeting. The chairperson gives each member who wants it permission to speak, but, with few exceptions, the chairperson may not introduce or second a motion and may not participate in the discussion or the voting, except to break a tie. The chairperson must always strive to be impartial in calling upon speakers. As he or she conducts the meeting, the chairperson must keep in mind one of the primary goals of parliamentary procedure: to ensure that the will of the majority is carried out and that the rights of the minority are protected.

Here is a description of five common parliamentary motions.

Main Motion

Intention: To obtain action on a proposal.

Member: "I move _____." The specific proposal should be stated simply and briefly. If the issue is complex, the motion should be written out and given to the chairperson.

Chairperson: "Is there a second?" Once the chairperson receives a seconding motion, he or she says, "It has been moved and seconded that _____. Is there any discussion? Since there is no further discussion, we will vote. All those in favor of the motion, which is _____, say aye (yes). All those opposed say no." Depending on the outcome of the vote, the chairperson then says, "The motion is carried" or "The motion is defeated."

Motion to Amend a Proposal

Intention: To change a proposal being considered by the group.

Member: "I move to amend the motion by (inserting, adding, substituting _____)." The amendment must be related to the proposal under consideration. It must not be just the opposite of the proposal under consideration.

Chairperson: After the motion to amend the proposal has been seconded, the chairperson says, "It has been moved and seconded to amend the motion by _____. Is there any discussion?" Discussion should be restricted to the amendment until it has been voted on. When the discussion has ended, or if there is no discussion, the chairperson says, "All in favor of amending the motion by _____, say aye. Opposed, say no." Depending on the outcome of the vote, the chairperson then says, "The amendment is carried. The question is now the motion as amended" or "The amendment is lost. The question is now the motion as originally stated, to _____."

Motion to Refer a Proposal to a Committee

Intention: To have a committee study a proposal.

Member: "I move that this matter be referred to the _____ committee." The motion can be worded to specify that a special committee be appointed by the chairperson or the organization to study the proposal. The motion can also include specific directions, such as "and that the committee report by (specified date or time)."

Chairperson: After the motion has been seconded, the chairperson says, "It has been moved and seconded that this matter be referred to the _____ committee. All those in favor of referring this matter, which is _____, to the _____ committee, say aye. Opposed, say no." Depending on the vote, the chairperson says, "The motion is carried. You have voted to _____" or "The motion is lost. The original motion is now before us."

Motion to Delay Action on a Proposal

Intention: To delay action on a proposal. Action may be postponed indefinitely or to a specified time. A proposal may also be "tabled," which stops action on it unless a later vote "takes it from the table."

Member: "I move that this matter be postponed" or "I move that this matter be postponed until (specified time)."

Chairperson: After the motion is seconded, the chairperson says, "It has been moved and seconded to postpone this matter to _____. Is there any discussion?" After discussion has ended, or if there is no discussion, the chairperson says, "All those in favor of postponing this matter to _____, say aye. Opposed, say no." Depending on the vote, the chairperson says, "The motion is carried. We will consider _____ at _____" or "The motion is lost. The original motion is now before us."

Motion to Move the Previous Question

Intention: To stop discussion on a motion and get the members to vote on it.

Member: "I move the previous question."

Chairperson: After the motion is seconded, the chairperson says, "The previous question has been moved." This motion is not debatable. "Shall we stop debate and order an immediate vote? All those in favor raise their hands (or stand). All opposed raise their hands." If two-thirds of those present and eligible to vote, vote in favor, then the motion passes. The chairperson then says, "The motion is carried. We will proceed at once to vote on the motion to _____. All those in favor say aye. Opposed say no." If the previous question is defeated, the chairperson says, "The motion is lost. We will return to the original motion. Is there any discussion on the motion to _____?"

Working with the Model

Read the following transcript from a portion of the Stevenson Service Club's meeting. Notice how motions are introduced and discussed according to parliamentary procedure.

Chair: The first item of new business is the Stevenson High fund-raising fair. Maxine.

Maxine: I move that we sponsor a booth at this year's fund-raising fair.

Malcolm: I second the motion.

Chair: It has been moved and seconded that we sponsor a booth at this year's fund-raising fair. Is there any discussion? Sergio.

Sergio: Maxine has a good idea, but her motion isn't quite clear. What kind of booth should we sponsor?

Phan: I move to amend the motion to read that we should sponsor a dart-throwing booth at this year's fund-raising fair.

Chair: Is there a second to the amendment?

Sergio: I second the amendment.

Chair: It has been moved and seconded that we amend the motion to read that we should sponsor a dart-throwing booth at this year's fund-raising fair. Is there any discussion? Maxine.

Maxine: The amendment helps make clear exactly what we should do. I think it's a good idea.

Chair: Isabel.

Isabel: I agree that the amendment does clarify the motion, but I'm getting tired of the dart-throwing booth. This will be the fourth year in a row that we've sponsored one. Shouldn't we try something different?

Chair: Setsuko.

Setsuko: The important thing to remember about the fair is that its purpose is to raise money. We have had the same kind of booth for several years, but it's always been very successful. I think the best way to contribute to the fair is to stick with something that works.

Chair: Julian

Julian: I think Setsuko's right. Besides, we already have most of what we need to set up a dart-throwing booth. If we switch to something new, we will have to commit more time and more money to the project.

Chair: Is there any further discussion? Hearing none, I will call for the question. All those in favor of amending the motion to read that we should sponsor a dart-throwing booth at this year's fund-raising fair, say "aye." Those opposed say "no." The amendment is carried. Is there any discussion on the motion as amended?

A. Think about what happened in the recorded portion of the meeting.
1. What main motion was introduced?
2. What had to happen before the club members could begin talking about whether or not they should sponsor a booth at the fund-raising fair?
3. What kind of motion did Phan make?
4. Imagine that Phan had said, "I move to amend the motion to read that we should not sponsor a booth at this year's fund-raising fair." What would have been wrong with his motion?
5. Imagine that, when Setsuko contributed to the discussion, she had said, "Don't be crazy, Isabel. Any fool knows that our dart-throwing booth is a big success. You only want to change it so that we can have a baseball-pitching contest. Then you'll be able to show off your good throwing arm!" What would have been wrong with Setsuko's contribution?

6. Imagine that, after the chair had asked for any further discussion on the motion as amended, Lyle had said, "I move that we plan a summer picnic for next year's freshman students." What would have been wrong with his motion?

B. Think about what might happen in the next portion of the meeting.

1. Imagine Janey wants to suggest that the proposal for sponsoring the dart-throwing booth be referred to the club's fund-raising committee. What should she say?

2. What would be necessary before Janey's suggestion could be discussed?

3. What might some of the club members say in discussing Janey's motion?

4. Imagine that, after several people have spoken, there seems to be no more discussion on Janey's motion. What should the chairperson say?

5. Imagine that most of the members vote against Janey's motion. What should the chairperson say?

6. Imagine that Nikki wants to end the discussion and to have the club members vote on the main motion as it has been amended. What should she say?

7. After Nikki's motion has been seconded, what should the chairperson say? If the majority of the members vote in favor of Nikki's motion, what should the chairperson say next? Then, if the majority of members vote for the main motion as amended, what should the chairperson say?

Guidelines

Remember these guidelines whenever you participate in a meeting conducted according to parliamentary procedure.

1. A proposal for specific action must be made as a motion. Usually, a motion must be seconded and may then be discussed by all members. Any motion introduced must be voted on. (See chart below for directions on using the basic parliamentary motions.)
2. Before he or she may speak during a meeting, a member must be called upon by the chairperson.
3. The chairperson's main responsibility is to conduct the meeting impartially. With few exceptions, the chairperson does not participate in discussion or voting.
4. The chairperson must not be partial in calling upon speakers. Everyone at the meeting should remember that one of the goals of following parliamentary procedure is to carry out the will of the majority while protecting the rights of the minority.

Using the Basic Parliamentary Motions

The business of a parliamentary meeting is carried on by means of motions—suggestions or proposals made by members who have been recognized by the chairperson. Specific purposes have specific motions. Some motions need seconds; others do not. Some may be debated; others may not. Some require majority approval; others require a two-thirds vote, or only approval by the chairperson. Effective organization members know how to use the following motions.

PURPOSE	MOTION	SECOND	DEBATE	VOTE
If you want to . . .	Then you should move to . . .	Will you need a second?	May the motion be debated?	Approval requires a vote which is . . .
1. Introduce business	Introduce a motion	Yes	Yes (A)	Majority
2. Consider motions which were tabled	Take from the table	Yes	No	Majority
3. Delay action	Lay on the table	Yes	No	Majority
4. Require an immediate vote	Call the previous question	Yes	No	Two-thirds
5. Modify a motion	Amend	Yes	Yes (A)	Majority
6. Correct or question a parliamentary error	Rise to a point of order (I)	Yes	No	Decision of chair
7. Clarify outcome of voice vote	Call for division of the house (I)	No	No	Majority, if vote is needed
8. Dismiss meeting for a specific (usually brief) time	Recess	Yes	No (A)	Majority
9. Dismiss a meeting	Adjourn	Yes	No (A)	Majority

(I) May interrupt speaker   (A) May be amended

Preparing and Presenting

With the other students in your class, participate in a meeting conducted according to parliamentary procedure. The class members should select as the agenda one of those written for the previous lesson. Then select one student to chair the meeting and other students to fill the specific roles called for in the agenda. (A secretary, a treasurer, at least two committee representatives, and at least two people to introduce specific items of new business will be needed.)

Those students who have specific roles called for in the agenda should plan what they will contribute to the meeting. The treasurer, for example, will need to prepare a report, and the students who are responsible for items of new business will need to plan their motions.

Students who do not have specific roles to play should prepare by reviewing the use of motions in parliamentary procedure, as explained in *Robert's Rules of Order (Revised)*.

When everyone is prepared, the chairperson should conduct the meeting, following the plan in the agenda.

Evaluation Checklist

After the meeting has been adjourned, form a group with two or three other students. With your group, evaluate the use of parliamentary procedure during the meeting on the basis of the following criteria. Rate the meeting on a scale from 1 (Poor) to 5 (Excellent). Be prepared to give reasons for each rating you give. The questions in parentheses will help you do so.

Category	Rating
1. Each participant had prepared for the meeting. (How did that preparation help make the meeting run smoothly?)	
2. Specific problems were prevented by the use of parliamentary procedure. (How were they prevented?)	
3. The use of parliamentary procedure helped the participants focus on only one issue at a time.	
4. The use of parliamentary procedure ensured that the will of the majority was carried out.	

Chapter 8 Review

Summary

Many clubs and other organizations adopt the rules of parliamentary procedure to ensure that their meetings proceed democratically, fairly, and efficiently. Before the meeting the chairperson, the person who conducts the meeting, writes an agenda, a list of what will happen during the meeting. Also members who plan to make specific contributions, such as presenting committee reports or introducing items of new business, should discuss their plans with the chairperson and prepare their contributions in detail. All the other members of the club or organization should think about the issues likely to be raised during the meeting and review the rules of parliamentary procedure if necessary.

In the meeting itself, most of the business is accomplished by means of motions, proposals for specific action. Most motions must be seconded and may then be discussed by all members. Every motion brought before a meeting must be voted on, and the majority rules.

Before members of a meeting may speak, they must be called upon by the chairperson. The chairperson must strive to be impartial because one of the goals of parliamentary procedure is to carry out the will of the majority while protecting the rights of the minority.

Reviewing Vocabulary

Decide which word or group of words from the box would correctly complete each sentence. Write the completed sentences.

---

chairperson
agenda
minutes of the previous meeting
treasurer's report
old business
adjourned
motion
motion to amend the proposal
motion to refer the proposal to the committee
motion to delay action on the proposal
motion to move the previous question

---

1. Because so many issues were left unresolved at the previous meeting, there will be a great deal of _____ at this meeting.
2. After all the new business had been concluded, the chairperson read several announcements and _____ the meeting.
3. Because Carl wanted a change in the proposal being considered, he made a _____.
4. The new _____ seemed nervous as he conducted the meeting.
5. Karen made a _____ until further information could be obtained about the need for the project.
6. When Lee read the _____, we were surprised at how much money had been received in dues since the previous meeting.
7. As the committee had more information than the rest of the members, Elizabeth made a _____.
8. "The next item on the _____ is the report of the Picnic Committee," said the chairperson.
9. Jan thought the discussion had gone on too long and made a _____.

10. There were no corrections when the secretary read the _____.
11. If you want to obtain action at a meeting, you make a _____.

Reviewing Facts and Ideas

1. What kinds of groups use parliamentary procedure?
2. What is the main purpose for using parliamentary procedure?
3. What are some of the main functions of a chairperson? What do you think the result would be if no chairperson conducted a meeting? Why?
4. What should a member who plans to present a committee report or introduce an item of new business do to prepare for a meeting?
5. What can members do to prepare for a meeting?
6. What are the nine events included in most agendas? Which one usually takes up the most time? Why?
7. What is a motion? How are motions introduced in a meeting?
8. Why do you think most motions must be seconded and then discussed by all of the members before a vote is taken?
9. Why do you think the chairperson cannot introduce or second a motion, or participate in the discussion or in the voting (except to break a tie)?
10. What book would one most likely consult to check on a detail of parliamentary procedure?

Discussing Facts and Ideas

1. Discuss how a chairperson should conduct a meeting to ensure that he or she remains impartial and that the majority's will prevails. How can he or she be sure, nevertheless, to protect the minority's rights? In your discussion consider what safeguards for democracy parliamentary procedure itself offers.
2. One way to delay action on a certain motion is to postpone it indefinitely or for a specified time. Discuss the possible reasons why a motion might be postponed. What are some advantages of postponing? What are some disadvantages?
3. Another way to delay an action is to *table* it. What are some of the possible reasons why a group might decide to table a motion? Discuss specific circumstances under which a group would want to table a motion.

Applying Your Knowledge

1. Visit a meeting of a local civic group, a school club or council, or another organization that uses parliamentary procedure to conduct its meetings. Observe the meeting and take notes on the proceedings. Be prepared to answer these questions. Did they follow the agenda given in Chapter 8? Was enough time given to discussion of motions? Did the chairperson conduct the meeting impartially? Did they complete one piece of business before going on to the next? Write down any effective contributions you observe as well as recommendations on how the meeting could have been conducted more smoothly. Write a brief summary of your evaluation and present it to your class.
2. Research the origins of parliamentary procedure and how it developed into its present form. Think about the contributions it makes to democratic organizations and write a summary of the history and contributions of parliamentary procedure to share with your class.
3. Sessions of Congress are televised. Arrange to view a session either at home or in class. Notice how parliamentary procedure is employed. Keep a list of requests to the chair by members and of motions made. If any of the requests or motions are unfamiliar to you, look them up in *Robert's Rules of Order*. Discuss with the rest of the class the reasons the members had for each request or motion.

COMMUNICATING ON THE JOB

Using an Agenda

Most meetings of organizations have to deal with several different types of business. For such a meeting to run efficiently, it should follow an *agenda*. An agenda is simply a list of things to be done during the meeting, the order in which they should be done, and (often) the names of the persons responsible for each piece of business.

The chairperson of the meeting draws up the agenda in advance. He or she may be assisted by several other members. This is the usual order of items on an agenda:

1. Call to Order
2. Reading of Minutes of Previous Meeting
3. Treasurer's Report
4. Correspondence
5. Committee Reports
6. Old Business (or Unfinished Business)
7. New Business
8. Announcements
9. Adjournment

For each of these categories, the chairperson should list the number and subject of expected reports, the names of the people reporting or giving background information, and the approximate time each piece of business will take. At any meeting, of course, some items on the agenda may be passed by quickly (for example, there may be no correspondence to read). Generally, new business will take the most time.

Activity

1. Draw up an agenda for a class organization or student government committee. Include the titles of specific items of business (for example, "School Orchestra Fund-raising Drive"), the names of the officers or members who will present each item, and an estimated time for each piece of business. Read the agenda to your class and ask for their suggestions of other items or details.

Nominating a Candidate for Office

The two purposes of a nominating speech are to explain why your candidate is qualified for a particular office and to make your audience feel enthusiastic about that person. The speech should create a sense of excitement that (you hope) will carry over into the voting. Follow these guidelines when preparing a nominating speech.

- List the requirements of the office and point out how well your candidate's experience and personality fulfill each requirement.
- Give examples of your candidate's intelligence, energy, warmth, judgment, patriotism, and loyalty. Relate these details to the office he or she is seeking rather than give the candidate's entire biography.
- Emphasize the superiority of your candidate without making personal attacks on the other candidates. Such attacks usually backfire and produce sympathy for the victims.
- Speak with conviction and enthusiasm. Use the candidate's name frequently, so that your listeners will associate it with the qualifications you are describing.
- Don't speak too long, or you will risk losing the audience's attention. Try to create a sense of rising excitement and end the speech with the name of your candidate.

Activities

1. Read or listen to a famous nominating speech for a presidential candidate made during a political convention. Decide what strategies the speaker used to make the candidate appear able, likeable, and electable. Listen for the use of anecdotes, the repetition of key words and phrases, and appeals to the audience's emotions. Report your findings to the class.
2. Write a nominating speech for a candidate for local, state, or national office. (The person can be an actual candidate, or someone you would like to see run for the office.) You and several other students should deliver speeches for different candidates to the class and let them vote for the candidate who was given the best nomination.

Debating

After working through this chapter, you should be proficient at the following skills:

Lesson	Skills
Lesson 1	• understanding the terms used in debate • preparing a debate brief • understanding how debate speeches are organized
Lesson 2	• giving a constructive speech and a rebuttal speech
Lesson 3	• participating in a Lincoln-Douglas style debate
Communicating on the Job	• avoiding common research mistakes
Communicating as a Citizen	• participating in a candidate debate

Preparing for a Debate

A **debate** is a competition between persuasive speakers. A formal debate usually involves two teams, each with two members, presenting in a specific sequence their arguments for and against a given resolution.

The following chart presents the most important terms used in a formal debate. Study the terms and their explanations.

Debate Terms

Proposition The formal statement of the issue to be debated. During the debate, the speakers take opposing sides on the proposition. The proposition for a debate should be a concisely worded statement that contains only one idea. It is a statement of policy, not of fact. It should propose a specific change in existing conditions or policies.

Affirmative The side of the debate that argues for the change advocated in the proposition. During the debate, the affirmative side presents arguments and evidence to support the proposition.

Negative The side of the debate that argues against the change advocated in the proposition. During the debate, the negative side presents arguments and evidence to oppose the proposition.

Argument The statement of an objective reason that directly supports the position of either the affirmative side or the negative side.

Evidence Facts, statistics, expert testimony, or other specific details that directly support an argument.

Brief A complete outline of all the necessary definitions, arguments, and evidence on both sides of a proposition.

Refutation An effort by speakers to answer or disprove arguments presented by the other side in a debate.

Constructive Speech The first speech given by each debater. Both affirmative and negative speakers use their constructive speeches to present the arguments in support of their positions. Except for the first speaker in the debate, they may also include some refutation in their constructive speeches.

Rebuttal Speech A speech in which refutation is the primary activity. Usually, each debater gives one constructive speech and, later, one rebuttal speech, half as long as the constructive speech. In his or her rebuttal speech, the debater may also try to bolster arguments refuted by the other side, clarify positions, and summarize arguments.

Successful participation in a debate requires thorough and careful preparation. Each debater must consider the proposition closely and must research both sides of the issue. In order to argue persuasively either for or against the proposition, and in order to convincingly refute opposing arguments, all the debaters must be completely familiar with both the affirmative and the negative positions.

Each debater should consult a wide variety of sources in researching the issue of the debate. When he or she has completed the research, the debater should organize all the information, arguments, and evidence into a complete outline, the debate brief.

The following outline shows the specific parts of a complete brief. A formal brief should be written as a sentence outline. Its purpose is to help the debater understand both sides of the debate issue; it also serves as a source of the specific information the debater will include in the outline for his or her debate speech.

Parts of a Brief

  I. Statement of the proposition

 II. Introduction
    A. Tell why the issue is important.
    B. Give a short history of the issue.
    C. Define controversial or vague terms. Include various possible definitions where necessary.
    D. State the main arguments.
       1. List the arguments for the affirmative side. Common arguments are that the proposed change is needed, that the change is practical, that the change is desirable, and that the advantages of making the change are greater than the disadvantages of making it.
       2. List the arguments for the negative side. Common arguments are that the proposed change is not needed, that the change is impractical, that the change is undesirable, that the disadvantages of making the change are greater than the advantages of making it, and that there are solutions better than those proposed by the affirmative side.

III. Body (This is the longest, most detailed portion of the brief.)
    A. State again each argument for the affirmative. After each argument, list the specific evidence that supports it. Cite the source for each item of evidence.

B. State again each argument for the negative. After each argument, list the specific evidence that supports it. Cite the source for each item of evidence.

IV. Conclusion
   A. Summarize the position and arguments of the affirmative side.
   B. Summarize the position and arguments of the negative side.

Working with the Model

Read the following outline. It shows the beginning of the brief Camilla prepared for a formal debate.

Debate Brief

I. Statement of the proposition: The teachers in Elementary School District 212 should be allowed to use corporal punishment to discipline their students.

II. Introduction
   A. Consideration of the use of corporal punishment to discipline students is important for two major reasons.
      1. Discipline problems in the elementary schools have increased steadily during the past five years.
      2. A group of teachers and parents has organized a campaign to change the current regulation against corporal punishment.
   B. Since Elementary School District 212 was established forty-three years ago, corporal punishment has never been permitted. On two occasions (approximately twenty years ago and eight years ago), unsuccessful efforts have been made to allow corporal punishment.
   C. The following definitions may be applied.
      1. "Teachers" should be considered the main classroom instructors for students in kindergarten through eighth grade. Some may want to include aides, classroom assistants, student teachers, or school administrators in this definition.
      2. Using "corporal punishment" may be defined as hitting students, in a controlled and supervised situation, either with the open hand or with a wooden paddle.
   D. The following are the major arguments for each side.
      1. The affirmative side can be expected to present these arguments.

         a. The use of corporal punishment will improve students' behavior.

b. A majority of the students' parents approve of the use of corporal punishment.
c. Corporal punishment does not violate the rights of students.
d. Abuses in the use of corporal punishment are easily prevented.

2. The negative side can be expected to present these arguments.

a. The use of corporal punishment will not significantly improve students' behavior.
b. Corporal punishment violates the rights of students.
c. The right to use corporal punishment is often abused.
d. Forms of discipline other than corporal punishment can more effectively improve students' behavior.

III. Body
  A. The affirmative arguments are supported by these items of evidence.
    1. The use of corporal punishment will improve students' behavior.

      a. After corporal punishment was ended in Los Angeles schools (1975), students' fighting and "general disregard for good behavior" increased markedly, according to Board of Education member Bobbi Fiedler (*U.S. News & World Report*, June 2, 1980).
      b. The superintendent of a school district in which corporal punishment is allowed notes that such punishment rarely has to be used more than once with the same child (Brenton, *Today's Education*, November/December 1978).

A. Think about what you have read in Camilla's debate brief.
   1. What is the issue of the debate?
   2. What is the proposition?
   3. What does the wording of the proposition indicate about the current use of corporal punishment in Elementary School District 212?
   4. What information on the importance and the history of the issue is included in the brief?
   5. Which terms are defined in the brief? What changes, if any, would you suggest for the definitions in the brief? What other terms, if any, do you think should be defined?
   6. What arguments for the affirmative are listed in the introduction? What arguments for the negative are listed in the introduction? What other arguments, if any, would you add?
   7. What indication, if any, about which side Camilla will support is included in the brief?

B. Think about what might be included in the rest of the brief.
   1. What arguments will be included in the body of the brief?
   2. What kinds of evidence might be included to support each argument?
   3. What information should be included after each item of evidence?
   4. What will be included in the conclusion of the brief?

C. Think about a debate you have heard, either in person or on television or radio.
   1. How well prepared did the debaters seem to be?
   2. What indication was there that the debaters were familiar with both sides of the issue?

Guidelines

When you prepare to participate in a formal debate, you should remember the following guidelines.

1. A well-stated proposition has the following characteristics.

   - It is a statement, not a question.
   - It contains only one idea.
   - It is worded so that the persons who argue for it (the affirmative) advocate a change from existing conditions.
   - It is precisely stated. Ambiguous terms are avoided, as are overly broad statements.
   - It must present a debatable issue, one that is not a question of fact and one that does not give either side a clear advantage.

2. Debaters on both the affirmative team and the negative team should research the issue of the debate thoroughly, consulting a variety of sources.
3. Each debater should organize the information he or she has gathered into a debate brief, a complete outline presenting the background of the issue and the arguments and evidence that support both sides of the issue.

Preparing and Presenting

Form a group with three other students. Together, select one of the following topics, or choose another topic that your teacher approves.

- government-supported day-care programs
- the closing times for polling places during national elections
- government control of oil companies
- national health insurance
- restrictions on the use of automobiles
- statewide requirements for graduation from high school

With the other members of your group, write a debate proposition on the issue you have chosen.

Then work independently to research that issue. Consult at least six different sources and take notes on the information, arguments, and evidence you find.

Use your notes to write a debate brief. Your brief should be a sentence outline and should include all the parts shown in the outline on pages 250–251.

Evaluation Checklist

With the other members of your group, decide who will be the two members of the affirmative team and who will be the two members of the negative team. Then compare your brief with the brief prepared by your teammate. Together discuss the two briefs and evaluate them on the basis of the following criteria. Rate each other's briefs on a scale from 1 (Poor) to 5 (Excellent). Be prepared to give reasons for each rating you give.

Category	Rating	
The brief . . . 1. Presents a complete explanation of the importance of the issue	Brief #1	Brief #2
2. Includes an accurate history of the issue		
3. Defines terms		
4. Includes main arguments for the affirmative side		
5. Includes no irrelevant arguments for the negative side		
6. Fully supports the arguments for the affirmative side with relevant evidence		
7. Fully supports the arguments for the negative side with relevant evidence		

With your teammate, combine the best information of the two briefs into one brief. Also take out any irrelevant information and do research to add any other needed information.

Participating in a Debate

Once the debaters have researched the issue and written their briefs, they must prepare the speeches they will make during the debate. The members of each team should divide the important arguments between themselves, so that all the arguments will be presented but none will be repeated. Each debater presents and supports his or her major arguments during the constructive speech and refutes the opposing team's arguments during the rebuttal.

The traditional pattern for speeches in a debate is as follows:

Constructive Speeches (6 minutes each)
  First Affirmative
  First Negative
  Second Affirmative
  Second Negative

Rebuttal Speeches (3 minutes each)
  First Negative
  First Affirmative
  Second Negative
  Second Affirmative

The debaters should carefully outline their constructive speeches, remembering all the methods and techniques of persuasive speaking. Except for the first affirmative speaker, each debater should allow some time in his or her plan for refutation of the previous speaker's arguments.

In the rebuttal, each debater attempts to refute the arguments presented by the other side and to rebuild the case of his or her own team. These rebuttal speeches, obviously, cannot be outlined in advance; they must show direct responses to the arguments and evidence presented by the other team. Debaters can, however, prepare for their rebuttal speeches by studying their briefs. Each debater's brief should clearly indicate what arguments and evidence the opposing team is likely to present. It should also include specific items of evidence that will be useful in refuting the opposing team's arguments.

Debaters should also prepare for their rebuttal speeches by listening carefully and critically during the debate. It is essential that each debater hear and understand the arguments of the other side in order to refute those arguments successfully.

The last two speakers in a debate (Second Negative and Second Affirmative) should also be prepared to summarize the cases developed by their teams. Both before and during the debate, these two debaters should make notes that will help them present clear and convincing summaries.

Working with the Model

Camilla, Vince, Fran, and Elena participated in a debate on the following proposition: The teachers in Elementary School District 212 should be allowed to use corporal punishment to discipline their students.

The following excerpt is from the beginning of Vince's speech of rebuttal during that debate. As you read the excerpt, think about the argument Vince is attempting to refute. Also think about the evidence he uses in that attempt.

Vince's Rebuttal

Camilla would have us believe that the use of corporal punishment in schools will develop positive behavior among the students. This is simply not the case. Recently, the National Education Association appointed a task force to study the effects of corporal punishment in the schools. That task force found that, instead of decreasing aggression on the part of students, corporal punishment actually increased the students' aggression. Members of the National Center for the Study of Corporal Punishment reached similar conclusions.

Hitting is, after all, an aggressive act. Elementary school students look on their teachers as role-models. When they see their teachers acting aggressively, they learn to act aggressively themselves. A university professor of psychology stated this problem most directly. "Violence breeds violence," he said. "There's a greater chance that children who are hit will hit other children, will retaliate directly against teachers, will take their hostility out on the school buildings."

A. Think about what the excerpt from Vince's speech tells about the debate.
   1. Is Camilla a debater on the affirmative team or the negative team?
   2. Is Vince a debater on the affirmative team or the negative team?
   3. What was one of the main arguments presented by the affirmative team members during their constructive speeches?
B. Think about how Vince tries to refute Camilla's argument.
   1. When and how does he restate Camilla's argument?
   2. When and how does he state his objection to the argument?
   3. What specific evidence does Vince use to refute Camilla's argument?
   4. Since Vince could not have outlined his rebuttal speech before the debate, where do you think he found the evidence that he used?

5. What other kinds of evidence might Vince have used?
6. How are the organization and presentation in this part of Vince's rebuttal speech like those for a persuasive speech developed with appeals to logic? (See pages 181 and 185–186).

C. Camilla will give her rebuttal speech after Vince has finished his.
1. How do you think she will try to rebuild the affirmative case?
2. What kinds of evidence might she use?

D. Think about a debate that you have heard, either in person or on television or radio.

1. How did the debaters organize and present the arguments and evidence in their speeches?
2. How did they attempt to refute the arguments of their opponents?
3. How did they try to rebuild their own cases?

Guidelines

The following guidelines will help you when you participate in a formal debate.

1. Before the debate, discuss your brief with your teammate and decide which major arguments each of you will present. Also decide which of you will be the first speaker and which the second speaker for your side. The responsibilities of the first speaker include introducing your side's case during his or her constructive speech. The responsibilities of the second speaker include summarizing your side's case during his or her rebuttal speech.
2. Outline your constructive speech, using the methods of planning and organization appropriate to a persuasive speech developed with logical arguments (see pages 181 and 185–186.)
3. To prepare for your rebuttal speech, study your brief carefully before the debate. During the debate listen carefully and critically to the debaters for the other side.
4. When you make your constructive and rebuttal speeches, present your arguments and evidence clearly and speak with confidence.

Preparing and Presenting

With your teammate, decide who will present and develop each major argument in your case. Also decide who will speak first and who will speak second.

Outline your own constructive speech and practice presenting it while your teammate listens. Together, discuss improvements that might be made in both your constructive speeches. Also discuss the arguments you expect the other side to present and the evidence you plan to use to refute those arguments.

Finally, with the other members of your group, conduct your debate before the rest of your class. Have one of the students serve as time keeper during the debate, signaling each speaker as the end of his or her allotted time approaches.

Evaluation Checklist

Have each student in your debate audience complete the form below. After the debate, study the other students' responses and discuss with the other members of your group how each debater might have improved his or her participation.

Debate Proposition: _____

_____

Before the Debate

I am

_____ strongly in favor of

_____ in favor of

_____ uncertain about

_____ against

_____ strongly against

the change advocated in the proposition.

After the Debate

I am

_____ strongly in favor of

_____ in favor of

_____ uncertain about

_____ against

_____ strongly against

the change advocated in the proposition.

I

_____ changed

_____ did not change

my opinion for the following reasons:

1. _____

2. _____

3. _____

4. _____

Participating in a Lincoln-Douglas Debate

In this chapter so far, you have learned about traditional forms of academic debate that center on policy questions, that is, on should something be done? The **Lincoln-Douglas debate** format involves propositions of value rather than policy. A suitable topic for a Lincoln-Douglas debate might be the following: "Resolved, that the least possible government is the best possible government." Arguments concerning such a question rely more on logical reasoning, philosophy, and theory and less on statistically based evidence.

Lincoln-Douglas debates are named for the famous confrontations between Abraham Lincoln and Stephen Douglas in 1860. Lincoln-Douglas debates feature one-on-one exchanges between two speakers. Although different specific patterns are used, the following is a typical pattern.

Affirmative Constructive Speech (7 minutes) The speaker for the affirmative presents her or his arguments.

Negative Cross-Examination (3 minutes) The speaker for the negative questions the affirmative speaker on the points she or he made in his or her constructive speech.

Negative Constructive Speech (8 minutes) The speaker for the negative presents his or her arguments.

Affirmative Cross-Examination (3 minutes) The speaker for the affirmative questions the negative speaker on the points she or he made in his or her constructive speech.

Affirmative Rebuttal (5 minutes) The affirmative speaker rebuts the points made by the negative speaker.

Negative Rebuttal (7 minutes) The negative speaker rebuts the points made by the affirmative speaker.

Affirmative Rebuttal (3 minutes) The affirmative speaker again rebuts.

One variation eliminates the cross-examinations. The affirmative constructive presentation is followed by a negative speech and a short closing affirmative speech. Variations can also involve audiences or special panels asking questions of the speakers.

You may be familiar with some of the formats used for candidate debates in recent elections. Some of these are examples of a Lincoln-Douglas debate in that they involve a direct clash between speakers. Others, which simply permit an audience to listen to speakers answering questions, are more properly viewed as forms of discussion than as examples of debate.

The supporting information for arguments for a Lincoln-Douglas debate may differ from that used for a traditional policy-option debate, but the way in which an argument is presented by the speaker remains basically the same. A speaker normally begins with a thesis statement and follows it with definitions, three or four supporting statements backed up by examples, and a conclusion. The affirmative speaker's main duty is to persuade listeners that the values he or she is arguing for best suit the public. On the other hand, the negative speaker must dismantle the other speaker's basic arguments and supply listeners with a reasonable alternative to the case presented by the affirmative speaker.

Working with the Model

The following speech was given by Charles Vice while he was a student at Biloxi High School in Mississippi. This is his opening affirmative speech in a debate about the welfare state.

A CHAMPIONSHIP LINCOLN-DOUGLAS AFFIRMATIVE SPEECH
The Welfare State Destroys Freedom

The resolution in today's debate is, "The welfare state destroys freedom." I, the affirmative, do not intend to debate the need for the welfare state, for the resolution does not lean in that direction. But, instead, I plan to debate whether or not the welfare state destroys freedom.

The welfare state is a social system based upon the assumption by a political state of primary responsibility for the individual and social welfare of its citizens, usually by the enactment of specific public policies (such as health and unemployment insurance, minimum wages and prices, and subsidies to agriculture, housing, and other segments of the economy) and their implementation directly by governmental agencies.

Destroy means to neutralize the effect of.

Freedom means liberation from some arbitrary power.

The very definition of a welfare state leads to the conclusion that it destroys freedom. As I stated earlier, the welfare state is a social system based upon the assumption by a political state, or government, of primary responsibility for the social welfare of its citizens. As a result, the government of countries with welfare economies has control over its citizens. This situation destroys the freedom of the citizens to care and look out for their own well-being. In a welfare state the government steps in and assumes the responsibility to "look out for" and "care for"

its citizens. And, in this process, the government greatly destroys the freedom of its citizens by not allowing the citizens to care for themselves.

The welfare state destroys the freedom of three main groups of people. The first group is the people who have to support the welfare state programs. The second is the people who receive the welfare state benefits. And the third is made up of the people who run the welfare state programs.

The freedom of the people who support the welfare state programs . . . is greatly destroyed. The people who support the programs are those who hold jobs. Before the employed person even gets his paycheck the employer must take out taxes and Social Security to help support the welfare state.

This practice destroys the employed person's freedom in two ways. It destroys his freedom of choice and his freedom to spend the money he makes as he pleases. The employee has absolutely no freedom to choose whether he wants to help support the welfare state. He is forced to support it. Before he even sees his check the money has already been taken. Thus, the welfare state destroys the freedom of choice that the employee should have.

The welfare state also destroys the freedom of the employee by taking his hard-earned money away with no real assurance that he will get it back. The money that comes out of the paychecks of today's employees is used on the people who need the help of the welfare programs right now. Suppose you were an employee paying welfare taxes. If the welfare tax payers in the future refused to support the welfare programs at that time, and you needed to fall back on the welfare system, there would be none to turn to. Thus, you would never be able to get back the money you paid when you were employed, if this situation occurred. And how do you have the freedom to spend your hard-earned money if a portion is taken out before you get your paycheck? You do not! In this sense, your freedom is completely destroyed by the welfare state.

The recipients of welfare programs have their freedom destroyed, also. There are millions of people across the world today who are dependent on the welfare state to survive. If the help from the welfare state were cut off, they would most surely die. Thus, the recipients' freedom of independence is destroyed. The welfare programs, because of the recipients' great dependence, start to control their lives—slowly at first, but gradually more and more. Thus, the recipients' freedom of self-control and independence are, again, completely destroyed.

Now let us look at how the freedom of the people who run the welfare state programs is destroyed. Their freedom of decency is destroyed. The lure of getting someone else's money is strong. Many, including the bureaucrats administering the programs, will try to get the money for themselves, rather than have it go to someone else. The temptation to engage in corruption, to cheat, is strong and will not always be resisted or frustrated. People who resist the temptation to cheat will use legitimate means to direct the money to themselves. They will lobby for legislation favorable to themselves, for rules from which they can benefit. This is an example of indirect indecency and corruption by people involved in the administration of the program. Thus the welfare state destroys the freedom of the people who run the welfare programs to be decent.

In conclusion, I have proven that the welfare state destroys the freedom of three main groups of people: (1) it destroys the freedom of the people who support the welfare state programs; (2) it destroys the freedom of welfare recipients; and (3) it destroys the freedom of the people who run the welfare state programs. This destruction of freedom is undisputable. Now I wait for a reply from the negative. Thank you.

A. Examine the overall format of the speech.
   1. Where does the introduction end and the body begin?
   2. Where does the body end and the conclusion begin?
   3. What are the main points of Charles Vice's argument?
B. Examine the definitions offered for terms in the debate proposition.
   1. Did Charles define all of the terms which you think should have been defined? What other terms should, in your opinion, have been defined? Why?
   2. Do you agree with his definitions? If not, what would you suggest as alternatives? Defend your alternative definitions.
C. Consider how you would respond.
   1. What major arguments would be most effective in responding to the ones contained in the speech? Work with another student to compile a list of such arguments.
   2. Assume you were debating on the opposite side from Charles' position. How would you state your case in your first negative speech?

Guidelines

The following guidelines will help you when you participate in a Lincoln-Douglas debate.

1. A suitable topic for a Lincoln-Douglas debate involves a question of value rather than a question of policy.
2. Before the debate decide what major arguments you will present.
3. Outline your constructive speech. You will normally begin with a thesis statement and follow it with definitions, three or four supporting statements backed up with examples, and a conclusion. If you are arguing on the negative side, you need to supply your listeners with a reasonable alternative to the case presented by the affirmative speaker.
4. To prepare for cross-examining the opposing speaker, prepare a list of possible questions before the debate. During the debate, listen carefully and critically to his or her affirmative speech.
5. To prepare for your rebuttal, study your brief carefully before the debate and listen to your opponent carefully and critically.
6. When you make your speeches, present your arguments and evidence clearly and speak with confidence.

Preparing and Presenting

Work with four to six other students preparing to take the affirmative or the negative side of a Lincoln-Douglas debate on one of the following topics or on another "value" question which meets with your teacher's approval.

- "The welfare state destroys freedom."
- "Protecting the environment is more important than economic progress."
- "Competition contributes more to personal growth than cooperation."

Prepare a constructive speech for the affirmative and negative side of each issue. Prepare a list of questions that you think might be useful in the cross-examination phase.

Practice your constructive speeches and cross-examination by working with a partner within your group.

Choose two members of your group to conduct a Lincoln-Douglas debate before your class using the format previously described but limiting the time to one half that listed for each speech. (For example, make the affirmative constructive speech 3½ minutes.) A member of your group should serve as time keeper.

Evaluation Checklist

As you listen to the students in your class present a Lincoln-Douglas debate on a values question, complete the form below. After the debate, share your ballot with the members of the class and with the speakers. Use the discussion of these ballots to help speakers improve and to give the other members of the class experience in analyzing issues involved in debating.

Evaluate the debate on the basis of the form below.

Debate Proposition _____

_____

_____

	Time	**Rating**				
		Excellent				**Poor**
Affirmative Constructive	___ minutes	5	4	3	2	1
Negative						
Cross-Examination	___ minutes	5	4	3	2	1
Negative Constructive	___ minutes	5	4	3	2	1
Affirmative						
Cross-Examination	___ minutes	5	4	3	2	1
Affirmative Rebuttal	___ minutes	5	4	3	2	1
Negative Rebuttal	___ minutes	5	4	3	2	1
Affirmative Rebuttal	___ minutes	5	4	3	2	1

Notes:

Affirmative _____

_____

_____

_____

Negative _____

_____

_____

_____

Rater _____   Date _____

Chapter 9 Review

Summary

A debate is a formal competition between persuasive speakers. Two teams (traditionally each with two members) present in a specific sequence their arguments for or against a given resolution. The affirmative side argues for the change advocated in the proposition. The negative side argues against the change advocated. After the debaters research the issue, they organize all the information, arguments, and evidence into a brief, a complete outline. The three main parts of a brief are:

1. Statement of the proposition—a statement of the issue to be debated
2. Introduction—in which the debaters explain why the issue is important, give a short history, define necessary terms, and state main arguments
3. Body—the longest and most detailed part in which the arguments and the evidence that supports them are presented
4. Conclusion—in which the debaters summarize the position and arguments

After this preparation, the team should decide which speaker is first and which is second. Then the speakers should outline their constructive speeches (traditionally six minutes long each) and their rebuttal speeches (traditionally three minutes long each). Each team member should listen carefully to the other speeches to help prepare for the rebuttal speeches. They should present their arguments and evidence as clearly and confidently as possible.

The Lincoln-Douglas debate format, named after the famous 1860 confrontation between Abraham Lincoln and Stephen Douglas, involves a proposition of value rather than policy. Instead of competition between two teams, it features a one-on-one exchange between two speakers. Whereas the traditional debate is composed of constructive speeches followed by rebuttal speeches, the Lincoln-Douglas debate is frequently composed of constructive speeches followed by direct questions to the opponent and replies (cross-examination).

Reviewing Vocabulary

Decide which word in the box correctly completes each sentence. Write the completed sentences.

```
debate
proposition
affirmative
negative
argument
evidence
brief
refutation
constructive speech
rebuttal speech
Lincoln-Douglas debate
negative cross-examination
```

1. A _____ is an appropriate format for arguing propositions of value.
2. Gerald's _____ was a convincing presentation of the arguments for his team's position.
3. The _____ to be debated was that the states should once again set all automobile speed limits.
4. A formal _____ should be written as a sentence outline.
5. Lillian's _____ to support her argument might have been more convinc-

ing if she had included more specific details and statistics.

6. To many in the audience, Felipe's _____ of the other side's arguments was completely convincing.
7. Claude's questions to the affirmative speaker during the _____ revealed the weaknesses of the affirmative position.
8. The two teams in yesterday's _____ were equally matched.
9. The _____ team presented very strong evidence in favor of the proposition.
10. Helen's last _____ gave a strong reason to support her side.
11. In his _____, Tim attempted to strengthen the arguments that the other side had refuted.
12. Which was the strongest argument against the proposition presented by the _____ side?

Reviewing Facts and Ideas

1. What is a debate?
2. What is a brief? What are the four main parts of a brief? Why do you think it is important to prepare one?
3. What kinds of evidence are commonly used to support an argument in a debate?
4. What is the difference between the constructive speeches and the rebuttal speeches? How long is each type of speech usually?
5. Each debate team traditionally has two members. What are the responsibilities of each member?
6. What is a Lincoln-Douglas debate? How did it get its name?
7. How many debaters participate in the Lincoln-Douglas debate format?
8. What kind of resolutions are debated in the Lincoln-Douglas debate format? How do the arguments differ from those of traditional debates?

9. What is the main duty of the affirmative speaker in a Lincoln-Douglas debate?
10. What is the main duty of the negative speaker in a Lincoln-Douglas debate?

Discussing Facts and Ideas

1. Discuss the differences between the topics used for scholastic forms of debate and those used in Lincoln-Douglas debate. Give at least three examples of suitable topics for each kind of debate.
2. Discuss the importance of preparing a brief on both sides of a question. If you were a lawyer, why would you want to prepare such a brief?
3. Most forms of scholastic debate place great value on logic as a means of persuasion. Discuss what you think the value of emotional appeals and identification would be if used in a scholastic debate.

Applying Your Knowledge

1. Invite adults who are former high school or college debaters to come to your classroom and debate a current subject. Give them the topic several weeks in advance. If necessary, change the time allotments of the Lincoln-Douglas format to fit within the time limit of your class.
2. Prepare to debate a subject of current interest and present your debate before a local civic organization. Ask the club members to complete a change of opinion ballot, giving you feedback on how well you argued the case. Be sure to find out in advance the specific length of time for the debate and the arrangement of the room in which you will be speaking.

Avoiding Common Research Mistakes

To take part effectively in group discussions, meetings, and other business situations, you need to have accurate facts and figures available. Inaccurate, out-of-date, or incomplete information can cause you embarrassment and damage your credibility. Study the following list of *don't*s to avoid common research errors.

- Don't begin your research without a specific goal in mind.
- Don't ignore what you already know about a topic. Use your knowledge to locate areas where more research is needed.
- Don't hesitate to ask for help from teachers, librarians, and experts.
- Don't consult obsolete or unreliable sources, even if they are more readily available.
- Don't consult sources that are too much alike—for example, only encyclopedias, or only news magazines.
- Don't record everything indiscriminately. Select only information that can help you.
- Don't record any fact without understanding it in its context.
- Don't record any important piece of information without verifying it with an independent source.
- Don't record information without also recording the author, title, date, and page number of the source.

Activity

1. Using at least three different *types* of sources, research one of the following topics. Obtain enough facts, statistics, and expert opinions for a ten-minute oral presentation on the subject.

    - deregulation of the airline and trucking industries
    - feasibility of solar power as an energy source for cities and factories
    - the all-volunteer army *versus* the draft

Participating in a Candidate Debate

A well-planned candidate debate can give the public valuable information on the issues and the candidates' positions. A debate should be planned according to these guidelines:

1. Determine the setting, questioners, question format, and number of participants well in advance. All the candidates should agree to the conditions.
2. Candidate debates have from three to five questioners, who may be journalists, officials, or local citizens. The questioners should discuss the questions they will ask, to be sure they are covering all the major issues. The chairperson introduces the candidates and questioners, times the candidates' responses, and selects audience questions.
3. In most candidate debates, the same question is asked of each candidate, who has a set time for his or her response. Questioners may ask follow-up questions. In two-candidate debates, each candidate is usually allowed a shorter time (one or two minutes) to respond to what the other candidate has said.
4. Hold the candidates to their allotted times, politely but firmly.
5. Encourage the candidates to answer the questions rather than deliver prepared speeches. When asking a follow-up question, you can politely remind the candidate that he or she has not answered the original question.
6. If members of the audience are to question the candidates, they should write their questions out and have them approved by the questioners. Most candidates will be unwilling to take unscreened questions.

Activity

1. Role-play a debate between candidates running for state or federal office. Students should take the parts of two candidates, three questioners, and a chairperson. Each of you should research the major issues and be prepared to ask or answer questions. Conduct the debate in front of the class and allow time for at least two questions. Ask the other students to evaluate the conduct of the debate and the quality of the questions and responses.

Critical Listening

After working through this chapter, you should be proficient at the following skills:

Lesson	Skills
Lesson 1	• evaluating persuasive appeals • giving a speech analyzing a persuasive appeal • identifying and analyzing techniques of propaganda
Communicating on the Job	• giving and accepting criticism
Communicating as a Citizen	• using critical listening to analyze a political speaker

Evaluating Persuasive Appeals

A speaker who wants your money, your vote, or your support may use every technique to sway you emotionally and intellectually. The speaker may use facts, statistics, emotional appeals, loaded language, generalizations, the names of famous people, and sometimes even outright lies in order to win you over. To evaluate persuasive appeals, you must be *alert* and *informed*. Be aware of the speaker's intentions and continually compare what the speaker is saying with what you know to be true. Be especially alert to the techniques of propaganda.

Propaganda is a one-sided argument that tries to win people over to a cause, such as a political movement. Its primary appeal is to the emotions, and when propagandists use facts they prefer to distort them. These are the principal techniques of propaganda.

1. **Loaded words and phrases.** Sometimes called "buzz words," these are expressions that produce an instant, unthinking reaction in an audience. Listeners will probably react positively to such words and phrases as *all-American, free enterprise, family man, justice, equality,* and *peace*. Most people will probably react negatively to *communism, oppression, bureaucracy, politician,* and *inflation*. Such words can be used in a meaningful way. But some audiences will react only to the good or bad associations of the words, not to the ideas behind them.

2. **Name calling.** Like the use of loaded language, name calling means attaching a label to a person. Labels such as *bureaucrat, subversive, big spender, warmonger,* and *extremist* can badly damage a politician's reputation. Yet the propagandist who uses such labels might not be able to find facts to justify them.

3. **Faulty generalizations.** There are two kinds of faulty generalizations.

   Hasty generalizations are based on too little evidence:
   > "After his first week in office, everyone agrees that Mayor Watson's policies are leading this city toward bankruptcy."

   Glittering generalizations are based almost entirely on prejudice. Some common generalizations are completely contradictory:
   > "This country is run by an establishment of millionaires and liberal professors."
   > "This country is run by an establishment of millionaires and conservative industrialists."

   Because faulty generalizations may contain a small grain of truth, people are often willing to accept them unquestioningly. This saves propagandists the trouble of using evidence to support their positions.

4. **The bandwagon.** Propagandists often urge people to jump on the bandwagon—to join in a movement or crusade simply because everyone else is doing it. People who want to feel part of a winning team are very vulnerable to this appeal. Often, those who do not join are made to feel insulted or threatened.

5. **Transference.** Many speakers, including propagandists, try to transfer the positive qualities associated with a place or party to their own cause:

> "Here in Philadelphia, in the shadow of Independence Hall. . . ."
> "We Republicans, the party of Abraham Lincoln. . . ."
> "We Democrats, the party of Franklin Delano Roosevelt. . . ."

Of course, such historic associations probably have little or nothing to do with what the speaker is advocating in the present. Propaganda uses such transference as a substitute for sound argument. Listeners are asked to use their emotions, not their minds.

6. **Testimonials.** A testimonial, or endorsement, by a movie star, sports hero, or other celebrity may draw everyone's attention to a candidate or campaign. Many voters feel that people who are glamorous, competent, and intelligent on the screen must be that way in real life. In fact, celebrities are no more or less competent to judge public issues outside their own fields than the rest of us are. Propagandists try to use the magic of celebrities' names to lure people to support dubious causes.

7. **The big lie.** The big lie is an outright, often outrageous, falsehood repeated loudly and often. Many people feel that if a politician or ruler sounds positive about a statement, it must be true. Propagandists who use the big lie exploit this feeling. A candidate may use the big lie technique to slander an opponent. A dictator may use it to blame his country's troubles on members of a single race, religion, or party. No matter how absurd it seems to those who know better, the big lie is extremely dangerous, especially when it can be spread by newspapers, radio, and television.

8. **Bias and Stereotyping.** A **bias** is a prejudice either for or against certain people, institutions, or ideas. A biased person has already made up his or her mind, often with very little information, and may be difficult to persuade. A bias toward a particular group of people—all members of a race, age group, nationality, religion, or profession—can lead to **stereotyping**. Stereotypes are all too common in speech and writing. Consider these:

> "All cheerleaders are silly airheads."
> "Football players are subhuman."
> "Women only go to college to get married."

Propagandists tend to cling to destructive prejudices even in the face of overwhelming evidence against them.

Working with the Model

Benito Mussolini, the head of the Fascist party, became dictator of Italy in 1922 after leading his Black Shirts in a march on Rome. Under Fascism, all other political parties were suppressed, and newspapers and radio became tools of government propaganda. King Victor Emmanuel III became a figurehead without real authority. Government, education, and industry were all dedicated to increasing Mussolini's power, enlarging the Italian army, and conquering weaker nations. In 1935 Mussolini invaded Ethiopia, whose ill-equipped people were soon defeated. In August, 1936, spectacular war games were conducted at Avellino, Italy. On August 30 Mussolini delivered the following speech to an audience of 20,000, and it was broadcast throughout the country. In the speech, Mussolini refers to the region as "Hirpinia"—the ancient Roman name for southern Italy. As you read the speech, observe Mussolini's persuasive appeals and his use of propaganda techniques.

The grand maneuvers of the fourteenth year of Fascism have ended. They have taken place, from the first to the last day, in an atmosphere vibrant with enthusiasm. The generous hospitality of the Hirpinian people has surrounded the participating soldiers. Comrades of

Hirpinia, your fervent patriotism and your dedication to the regime make you worthy of having the grand maneuvers of the first year of the Fascist Empire held in your magnificent territory!

Tomorrow, on the plains of Volturara, before His Majesty, Victor Emmanuel, King of Italy and Emperor of Ethiopia, will pass more than 60,000 men, 200 tanks, 400 pieces of heavy artillery, 400 mortars, 3,000 machine guns, and 2,800 armored cars. This concentration of men and arms is imposing, but it represents, at most, a modest and almost insignificant number compared with the total of men and arms on which Italy can surely count.

I invite Italians to take this declaration of mine absolutely to heart. Not despite the African war, but as a consequence of the African war, all the armed forces of Italy today are more efficient than ever. At any time, in the course of a few hours and after a simple order, we can mobilize eight million men. It is a formidable bloc that fourteen years of Fascist rule have prepared at white heat with great sacrifice. The Italian people should know that their internal peace will be protected, and with it the peace of the world.

With the most crushing of victories, in one of the most just wars, Italy, with war in Africa, has acquired an immense, rich, imperial territory, where for many decades she will be able to carry out the achievements of her labors and of her creative ability. For this reason, but only for this reason, we will reject the absurdity of eternal peace, which is foreign to our creed and to our temperament.

We desire to live a long time at peace with all. We are determined to offer our lasting, concrete contribution to the project of collaboration among peoples. But after the catastrophic failure of the disarmament conference, in the face of an armaments race already under way and irresistible from this time on, and in the face of political situations whose outcome is uncertain, the order of the day for Italians, for Fascist Italians, can be only this: We must be strong! We must be always stronger! We must be so strong that we can face any eventualities and look directly in the eye whatever may happen. To this supreme principle must be subordinated, and will be subordinated, all the life of the nation.

The conquest of the empire was not obtained by compromises on that table of diplomacy. It was obtained by fine, glorious, and victorious battle, fought with the spirit that has overcome enormous material difficulties and an almost world-wide coalition of nations. It is the spirit of the Black Shirt revolution, the spirit of this Italy, the spirit of this populous Italy, warlike and vigilant on sea, on land, and in the heavens! It is the spirit I have seen shining in the eyes of the soldiers who have maneuvered in these past days, the spirit we shall see shine when King and country call them.

Before concluding this meeting, I ask you: Were our old accounts settled? [*The crowd shouted*: "Yes!"]

And have we marched straight ahead until now? [*The crowd*: "Yes!"]

I tell you—I promise you—we shall do the same tomorrow and always!

A. Think about the purpose of Mussolini's speech.
1. Of what fact or feeling is Mussolini trying to persuade his audience?
2. Find at least two passages in the speech that show Mussolini is trying to appeal to a nationwide audience.
3. This speech was widely reprinted in Europe and America. What passages suggest that Mussolini was thinking of an international audience as well?

B. Think about the appeals to emotion in this speech.
1. Why do you think Mussolini would refer to the province by its ancient Roman name?
2. In the second paragraph, why does Mussolini list the numbers of men and weapons? What effect is he trying to create?
3. Find at least three passages in which Mussolini speaks of the Italian people in a way that is meant to encourage a feeling of unity.
4. Mussolini speaks of Italians overcoming "enormous difficulties" with "great sacrifice." What do you think such difficulties and sacrifices might have been? Do you think the sacrifices were voluntary? Why or why not?

5. If the King of Italy had no real power, why does Mussolini refer to him twice in this speech? Of what propaganda technique is this an example?
6. What is the purpose of Mussolini's questions to the audience at the end of the speech? Suppose you had been in the audience; would you have wanted to answer "No?" What would you have done?

C. Think about the propaganda techniques in this speech.
1. Find at least five examples of loaded words or phrases. What emotions are these words meant to produce?
2. Find at least three places where Mussolini uses faulty generalizations or exaggerations. What would have been the effect if he had paid more attention to the facts?
3. Find three uses of the bandwagon technique in the speech.
4. Find at least one use of the big lie in this speech.

Guidelines

When evaluating a persuasive appeal, you should ask yourself the following questions:

1. **Is the speaker making promises that he or she cannot fulfill?** A candidate may say, "If you vote for me, I'll turn this country around within a year." But listeners who understand complex national problems realize that no one person, no matter how competent, could solve them in such a short time. The better informed you are, the more easily you can tell serious promises from empty ones.

2. **Is the speaker suppressing or distorting facts in order to be more persuasive?** Speakers naturally want to emphasize their own achievements and belittle those of their opponents. They may misuse facts and figures in order to do this. For example, suppose a candidate announces, "When I was mayor of Metropolis, we virtually wiped out violent crime!" A check of newspapers might show a drop in the crime rate, but this is not the same as "wiping out" crime—nor does it prove that the mayor had anything to do with it. Such a use of facts is a **distortion** of the truth. Suppose another candidate announces, "Since Smith's party took over this city in 1964, the murder rate has doubled." That sounds like a frightening statistic, until you learn that during the same period the city's population tripled. By **suppressing**, or withholding, the additional fact about the population, the candidate has turned a fact into a falsehood.

3. **Does the speaker use innuendo to attack others?** Responsible speakers will attack their opponents directly, using facts in order to persuade their listeners. Irresponsible speakers may use **innuendo**—attacking a person by implication or association. For example, a candidate may say, "The mayor was seen having lunch with a man whose lawyer once represented organized-crime figures." The innuendo in this statement suggests a connection between the mayor and organized crime, but the connection is in fact very flimsy.

4. **Does the speaker offer positive alternatives?** It is easy to attack people and parties that are currently in office. It is difficult to suggest new programs that would work better. Be wary of speakers who are eager to criticize but who can offer only vague promises and suggestions for improvement.

5. **Is the speaker being consistent with previous speeches and writings?** A speaker who changes his or her positions in front of different audiences may only be interested in telling people what they want to hear. Compare the speaker's earlier speeches and writings with what he or she is saying today. Television reporters often do this, using videotape from their files. Remember, though, that consistency does not guarantee integrity. It is possible for a speaker to be consistently wrong or dishonest.

6. **Is the speaker using the techniques of propaganda?** These techniques, explained at the beginning of this lesson, include:

loaded words and phrases	the bandwagon	the big lie
name calling	transference	bias and stereotyping
faulty generalizations	testimonials	

The use of one or more propaganda techniques does not automatically prove that a speaker is irresponsible. Loaded language, faulty generalizations, and the transference of good qualities to people or programs that do not deserve them are all traditional in political speechmaking. You should, however, be suspicious of speakers who rely heavily on such techniques. Name calling and the big lie are techniques that have no place in responsible speech.

Preparing and Presenting

Find a persuasive speech on an issue that arouses strong emotions. You may look in books or in periodicals such as *Vital Speeches*. You may also listen to or watch recorded speeches. The speech should not run much over ten minutes. It should be on an issue that you either understand or can do research to learn about. Read or listen to the speech

several times and ask yourself the questions in the Guidelines section of this lesson. Make notes on the different persuasive appeals used by the speaker. Make an outline for a presentation in which you explain the persuasive appeals and give specific examples.

When you make your presentation to the class, begin by reading aloud or playing the speech you have studied. Ask the other students whether they found the speech persuasive and why. Then present your own observations.

Evaluation Checklist

After the presentation and discussion, evaluate each student's observations on the basis of the following criteria. Rate them on a scale from 1 (Poor) to 5 (Excellent). Be prepared to give reasons for each rating you give.

Category	Rating
The student . . . 1. Accurately explained the persuasive appeals in the speech	
2. Gave ample examples from the speech as evidence for his or her findings	

Chapter 10 Review

Summary

Critical listening skills are necessary to evaluate persuasive speeches. Many speakers, especially when their argument is weak, resort to using propaganda to win people over to a cause. Such a one-sided argument appeals primarily to the emotions and distorts the facts. Being alert and informed will help you detect propaganda tactics. The major propaganda techniques that you should be on the lookout for are:

1. loaded words and phrases
2. name calling
3. faulty generalizations
4. the bandwagon
5. transference
6. testimonial
7. the big lie
8. bias and stereotyping

Reviewing Vocabulary

Write the list of propaganda techniques in the Summary. Next to each write the letter of its definition.

a. the redirection of positive associations from one source to another
b. prejudice; holding an oversimplified or preconceived mental picture
c. terms charged with positive, negative, or hidden implications
d. an endorsement by a celebrity
e. attaching a label with negative connotations to a person
f. a movement or cause that propagandists urge audiences to support simply because everyone else is
g. an outright, often outrageous, falsehood repeated loudly and frequently
h. statements based either on too little evidence or on prejudice

Reviewing Facts and Ideas

1. What is propaganda? How can a listener guard against propaganda?
2. Why can loaded words and phrases be misleading?
3. How are name calling and innuendo alike?
4. What is the bandwagon technique? Cite an example of this technique from a popular advertisement or commercial.
5. Why is the use of testimonials often an irresponsible way to persuade?

Discussing Facts and Ideas

1. List the various propaganda techniques discussed in this chapter that were most familiar to you. Compare your list with those of others in your class. Speculate as to why some seem to be used so frequently, others less often.
2. Collect several issues of the local newspaper and examine the letters to the editor. Discuss the examples of various persuasive appeals that you find. Which are most frequently used? Which couldn't you find?

Applying Your Knowledge

1. Invite a current office holder or someone who has recently run for election to talk with your class about the use of propaganda and the need for critical listening during election campaigns.
2. Much attention has been given in recent years to Soviet programs of "disinformation." Investigate these programs by using the *Readers' Guide to Periodical Literature* to locate articles about them. Compare such Soviet efforts with our government's spreading of information. What are the similarities and differences?

Giving and Accepting Criticism

Both at school and at work, friends, teachers, co-workers, and supervisors will criticize your performance. Constructive criticism points out the weaknesses in a person's work and suggests ways in which he or she could improve. Remember these guidelines.

When giving constructive criticism:

1. Be sure that the words you use have the same meaning for your listener that they have for you.
2. Limit your criticism to a particular aspect of the job or assignment.
3. Your purpose should be to give the person information that will help him or her, not to tell everything you think about him or her. Focus on the behavior, not the personality. It's more helpful to say "Please proofread your typing" than "You're a poor secretary."
4. Tell the person what aspects of the job he or she does well.

When accepting constructive criticism:

1. Listen carefully. Find out what specific criticisms of your performance the other person is making.
2. Do not immediately defend your actions or performance. Think about whether the criticism is true.
3. Ask the other person for specific suggestions for improvement. Ask him or her to clarify any point you do not fully understand.
4. Try to correct your performance according to the other person's suggestions. Then ask in a pleasant way whether you are doing what he or she suggested. For example, ask, "Is this closer to what you had in mind?" rather than "Is this good enough for you?"

Activities

1. With a partner watch a person being interviewed on television. As you listen to the interview, take notes on how the interviewer could improve his or her interviewing. Then compare notes with your partner and decide what the two of you would say to this person if he or she came to you for constructive criticism.
2. Think of an instance in which you benefited from constructive criticism. Possible subjects might include clothing, table manners, study habits, mechanical skills, punctuality, or performance on a team. Prepare a brief speech in which you describe the criticism, your reaction to it, and the ways in which you changed your behavior in response to it. Deliver the speech to the class and ask the other students to discuss similar instances from their own experience.

Using Critical Listening

Candidates, politicians, and activists will frequently appeal to you for your support and vote. They may ask you to contribute to a campaign, write letters in support of a bill, sign a petition, or help elect someone to public office. Political speakers will use every skill and argument they have in order to persuade you. To tell the worthwhile appeals from the worthless ones, you must ask yourself these questions.

- Is the speaker using the techniques of propaganda? (See the previous lesson for a list of these techniques.)
- Is the speaker making promises that he or she cannot fulfill?
- Does the speaker use innuendo or distortions of fact to attack others?
- Does the speaker offer positive alternatives to the people or positions he or she attacks?
- Is the speaker being consistent with his or her previous speeches and writings, or is the speaker simply telling the audience what it wants to hear?

Activities

1. Listen to a recorded speech or editorial from radio or television. Decide what position the speaker is actually taking and what he or she wants the members of the audience to do. Analyze the speech by asking yourself the questions listed above. Then decide whether you agree with the speaker because of or in spite of what he or she said. Describe your findings to the class and compare your reactions to theirs.
2. Working with another student, prepare two brief speeches advocating the same position. One speech should use the techniques of good persuasive speaking, and the other should use deceptive and unsound arguments. Deliver your speeches before the class. Have them vote for the more persuasive speech and ask them to explain their reasons.

U N I T

Unit Introduction: Communicating as a Performer

Performing

A Case Study

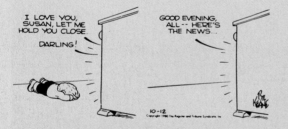

Think and Discuss

Study these six panels from the comic strip *Family Circus*. What do you think is happening on the television screen in each of the panels?

What is the little boy's reaction to each of the programs? Is he reacting in the way the broadcasters would like him to? Is he reacting to each situation in the way an adult would?

In the last panel, why do you think the boy has left the room? Do you know teenagers or adults who also prefer not to watch the news?

In Unit Four, "Performing," you will learn to entertain others by using your voice for story telling, oral interpretation, and radio drama and television drama. You will also think about an issue raised by this Case Study: how well or badly your television time is spent.

Unit Introduction: Communicating as a Performer

In this unit you will develop your skills in performing in a variety of situations. The same elements—attitudes, thought, language, voice, and bodily movement—are as important in speaking in performance as they are in the activities considered previously. The communication cycle described earlier remains an appropriate model for understanding the relation of performer and audience. However, those who speak as performers—the storytellers, oral interpreters, radio or television performers, and dramatic performers—share some things that distinguish their tasks from those of other speakers considered in the earlier units.

Before reading further, stop and discuss the following questions.

1. In what ways might the feedback performers receive differ from that other kinds of speakers receive?
2. What are some characteristics of the settings in which performers speak that might affect their speaking?
3. Many performers have to communicate other people's ideas. How might this change the communication process?
4. All speakers must use their memories. Why would memory be a particularly important tool for a performer?

The Performer and Feedback

When you are speaking with another individual, a small group, a debate opponent or attempting to explain to or convince an audience, you should adjust your presentation as you are making it. You do so based on the responses of the audience. Many times (although not always) a performer does not have the benefit of such direct feedback. Actors on a stage may hear the laughter and the applause of a theatre audience, but often the critical response they need to tell them whether they should change their interpretation does not come until after the entire performance.

Those on radio, in television, or in films have an even greater delay before they learn how their audience is responding. Sometimes radio and television performers stage their programs before a live audience to get more immediate responses to their efforts. More often they have to rely on the ratings obtained by radio and television broadcasters to determine how many people are listening to or watching the program. Similarly, the box office records tell film actors whether people are attending their films. However, such responses come long after the performance and generally have little effect on the performance as it happens. Moreover, ratings and attendance figures merely tell how many people saw or heard a performance, not how these people felt. Thus, they are not as helpful in improving future performances as immediate, direct feedback.

The Performer and the Medium

People have said that the medium is the message. That is, the medium, whether it be radio, television, or the stage, so shapes what is said that it becomes a part of what is said. For example, the time constraints of television newscasts tend to reduce major world events to what can be described with a few words or pictures in no more than three minutes. Thus, television newscasts create a far different message for viewers than newspapers with columns of print do. Similarly, radio, with its reliance on sound, produces different messages than do live performances or television performances in which a variety of visual images are added. The setting, or medium, not only affects the message but also dictates the means the performer uses to communicate with the audience. These tools include sound effects, special visual effects, music, lighting, costumes, and makeup.

The Performer and Another's Ideas

Frequently a performer interprets another's ideas to an audience. This introduces a whole series of new challenges to the performer. He or she must understand what the author of the material intended to communicate. Often the author's intentions are open to multiple interpretations, requiring considerable analysis of the material. This task is further complicated because the performer is expected to understand the author's intentions as interpreted by the director. Effectively communicating another's ideas requires more than understanding them. When you are trying to communicate your own ideas, you often have to experiment with language, voice, and movement in order to ensure that your audience clearly understands you. Similarly, a performer must experiment with language, voice, and movement in order to communicate the message clearly.

The Performer and Memory

As a speaker you use two kinds of memory.

1. Your ability to recall information so that you can make interesting and effective presentations
2. Your ability to remember specific words that you or others wrote as you make a memorized presentation

You usually use your ability to recall general information when engaging in the kinds of speaking activities discussed in the previous units. The performer often uses both kinds of memory.

In order to improve your skill in memorizing specific information, consider the following suggestions.

1. Focus your attention and interest on the material. Memorize in a place that is free of distractions.
2. Make sure you have a thorough understanding of what you are trying to memorize. Recalling information you understand thoroughly is much easier than recalling something you don't understand.
3. Rehearse the thought sequences—not the words. Break information down into small units but make sure each unit is a complete thought. Work to learn a group of closely related thoughts before moving on to another group.
4. Schedule your practice so that you work intensively when you are first learning the material and then repeat it at intervals after that. For example, you may want to repeat a poem you are memorizing a dozen or so times on the first day. Repeat it again the next day

several times and repeat it again several times within three days after that. Then repeat it again at least twice a week as long as you need to be able to recall it exactly.

5. Speak aloud. Many performers find that using a tape recorder or working with a partner helps the memorization process.
6. Find out when and where you function at your peak. As you practice, you may find that you concentrate best at certain times of the day or in certain locations. Some people find that reviewing memorized material just before going to sleep in the evening helps them.
7. Use association techniques. Remembering certain catch words, relating certain passages to personal experiences, or noticing specific patterns in the language may help you.

Activities

1. Invite a professional performer to talk with your class. You may want to ask a local actor or a radio or television personality. Ask him or her to discuss the four questions posed at the beginning of this lesson.
2. Work with another student and memorize the seven suggestions listed above for improving your ability to memorize. Once you are able to recite the entire list of suggestions word for word, practice several times on your own so you can recall the list after several weeks have passed.

CHAPTER 11

Story Telling and Oral Interpretation

After working through this chapter, you should be proficient at the following skills:

Lesson	Skills
Lesson 1	• identifying the important elements of a story • organizing a story, using specific details to make it clear • delivering a story in the most effective manner
Lesson 2	• understanding an author's ideas and emotions
Lesson 3	• preparing and giving an oral reading
Communicating on the Job	• using a telephone effectively
Communicating as a Citizen	• introducing a speaker

Telling a Story

You are probably used to telling stories and anecdotes, sometimes to entertain and sometimes to make a point. **Narrative speaking** is the art of telling a story well. A good narrative speaker plans his or her story carefully. He or she thinks about the incidents of the story, the order in which they occur, and the details that will make them vivid to the audience.

Whether you tell a story to illustrate a point or simply to entertain, you should plan and practice your story carefully. To plan a story, begin by identifying for yourself the essential elements: *who* is involved; *when* and *where* the story takes place; *what* happens. Next, decide what the most important or most exciting part of your story is. Then organize the events of your story in chronological order so that they lead up to that most important part. Finally, choose specific details that will make the story clear to your listeners. Avoid details—however interesting—that are not essential to the development of your story.

Once you have planned your story, you should practice telling it. As you practice, keep in mind the most important part of your story. Remember that everything in the story and everything in your telling of the story should lead up to that part. For example, you might try speaking slowly at first and then quickening your rate of speech as you move toward the most important part. Also try pausing just before you tell the most important part. Experiment with facial expressions and gestures that will emphasize the development of your story. As you practice, have a friend listen and comment on the effectiveness of your speaking techniques and actions.

Working with the Model

Moss Hart was a well-known American playwright. In his autobiography, *Act One*, Hart included the following story about an incident from his childhood. As you read the story, think about how Hart presented it.

It was the Christmas after my aunt had left the house, and since it was she who always supplied the tree and the presents for my brother and myself, this first Christmas without her was a bleak and empty one. I remember that I was more or less reconciled to it, because my father had worked only spasmodically throughout the year. Two of our rooms were vacant of boarders and my mother was doing her marketing farther and farther away from our neighborhood. This was always a sign that we were dangerously close to rock bottom, and each time it occurred I came to dread it more. It was one of the vicious landmarks of poverty that I had come to know well and the one I hated the most. As the bills at our regular grocer and butcher went unpaid, and my mother dared not even be seen at the stores lest they come to the doorways and yell after her publicly, she would trudge ten or twelve blocks to a whole new neighborhood, tell the new grocer or butcher that we had just moved in to some fictitious address around the corner, and establish credit for as long as she could. Thus we were able to exist until my father found work again, or all the rooms were rented, and she could pay our own grocer and butcher, and gradually the others. This time, however, they had all of them gone unpaid and my mother was walking twenty blocks or more for a bottle of milk.

Obviously Christmas was out of the question—we were barely staying alive. On Christmas Eve my father was very silent during the evening meal. Then he surprised and startled me by turning to me and saying, "Let's take a walk." He had never suggested such a thing before, and moreover, it was a very cold winter's night. I was even more surprised when he said as we left the house, "Let's go down to a Hundred and Forty-ninth Street and Westchester Avenue." My heart leapt within me. That was the section where all the big stores were, where at Christmastime open pushcarts full of toys stood packed end-to-end for blocks at a stretch. On other Christmas Eves I had often gone there with my aunt, and from our tour of the carts she had gathered what I wanted the most. My father had known of this, of course, and I joyously concluded that this walk could mean only one thing—he was going to buy me a Christmas present.

On the walk down I was beside myself with delight and inner relief. It had been a bad year for me, that year of my aunt's going, and I wanted a Christmas present terribly—not a present merely, but a symbol, a token of some sort. I needed some sign from my father or mother that they knew what I was going through and cared for me as much as my aunt and my grandfather did. I am sure they were giving me what mute signs they could, but I did not see them. The idea that my father had managed a Christmas present for me in spite of everything filled me with a sudden peace and lightness of heart I had not known in months.

We hurried on, our heads bent against the wind, to the cluster of lights ahead that was 149th Street and Westchester Avenue, and those lights seemed to me the brightest lights I had ever seen. Tugging at my father's coat, I started down the line of pushcarts. There were all kinds of things that I wanted, but since nothing had been said by my father about buying a present, I would merely pause before a pushcart to say, with as much control as I could muster, "Look at that chemistry set!"

or, "There's a stamp album!" or, "Look at the printing press!" Each time my father would pause and ask the pushcart man the price. Then without a word we would move on to the next pushcart. Once or twice he would pick up a toy of some kind and look at it and then at me, as if to suggest this might be something I might like, but I was ten years old and a good deal beyond just any toy: my heart was set on a chemistry set or a printing press. There they were on every pushcart we stopped at, but the price was always the same and soon I looked up and saw we were nearing the end of the line. Only two or three more pushcarts remained. My father looked up, too, and I heard him jingle some coins in his pocket. In a flash I knew it all. He'd gotten together about seventy-five cents to buy me a Christmas present, and he hadn't dared say so in case there was nothing to be had for so small a sum.

As I looked up at him I saw a look of despair and disappointment in his eyes that brought me closer to him than I had ever been in my life. I wanted to throw my arms around him and say, "It doesn't matter . . . I understand . . . this is better than a chemistry set or a printing press . . . I love you." But instead we stood shivering beside each other for a moment—then turned away from the last two pushcarts and started silently back home. I don't know why the words remained choked up within me. I didn't even take his hand on the way home, nor did he take mine. We were not on that basis. Nor did I ever tell him how close to him I felt that night—that for a little while the concrete wall between father and son had crumbled away and I knew that we were two lonely people struggling to reach each other.

A. Think about the organization of the story.
    1. Identify the *who, when, where,* and *what* of the story. When is each of these story elements presented?
    2. In what order are the story events organized?
    3. What is presented as the most important part of the story?
    4. How does the organization emphasize the most important part of the story? Imagine that Hart had continued his story by presenting several more events that took place on Christmas. How might those additions have altered the effect of the story?

B. Think about the development of the story.
    1. What specific details show how poor Hart's family was? How do those details help make the story clear to you?
    2. What specific details show that the gifts Hart wanted were too expensive? What effect do those details have on the development of the story?
    3. Imagine that the story included several specific details about Hart's tour of the pushcarts on previous Christmas Eves. What effect would those details have had on the story?

Guidelines

As you prepare to tell a story, remember the following guidelines.

1. Plan to include the essential story elements (*who* is involved, *when* and *where* the story takes place, and *what* happens) and to avoid any unnecessary information.
2. Plan your story to lead up to the most important or most exciting part. Arrange the events of the story leading up to that part in chronological order.
3. Include specific details that will help make the story clear to your listeners. Avoid details that do not directly develop the story.
4. Practice telling your story, being sure to emphasize the most important part.

Preparing and Presenting

Think of a story you would like to tell. If possible, choose a story from your own experiences—something that happened to you or something that you observed. You may choose a story because it is amusing or interesting or because it illustrates a point you want to make.

Carefully plan the organization and development of your story. Then practice telling your story to another student. Ask that listener to evaluate the organization and development of your story as well as your effectiveness in telling it. Encourage your listener to make specific suggestions that will help you improve your story and your delivery.

After you have practiced and improved your story, tell it to a group of other class members.

Evaluation Checklist

Evaluate each student's story on the basis of the following criteria. Rate each story on a scale from 1 (Poor) to 5 (Excellent). Be prepared to give reasons for each rating you give. The questions in parentheses will help you do so.

Category	Rating
The storyteller . . . 1. Introduced all essential story elements (Were any necessary elements left out? What unnecessary information, if any, was presented?)	
2. Organized the story events effectively (What changes in organization might make the events more effective?)	
3. Included effective specific details (In which parts of the story should more details have been used? In which parts were there too many details?)	
4. Had a purpose that was clearly evident in the reading of the story. (Was it intended to illustrate a specific point? If so, what was the main idea of the story?)	
5. Used good speaking techniques and movements to emphasize the most important part of the story	

Understanding a Selection's Ideas and Emotions

Oral interpretation is the art of reading aloud a story, poem, or speech. When you give an oral reading, your goal should be to convey the ideas and emotions in your selection as completely as possible. Your audience should gain as much from your reading as they would by reading the selection themselves. The first step in your preparation for giving a successful oral reading is to understand both the ideas and the emotions the selection contains.

Begin by looking for the major idea in your selection. Most selections contain one major idea supported by several minor ideas. If your selection is from a story or essay, each paragraph will usually contain a single idea that supports the major idea of the selection.

To understand the ideas in your selection, you must understand the words in which they are written. Use an unabridged dictionary to check the meaning of any words you don't understand fully. The meaning of a word is called its denotation. You must understand the denotation of each word the author has used if you are to fully grasp the ideas of the selection. In order to understand the feelings the author wishes to convey about these ideas, you must also be aware of what the words suggest. Such suggestions are called the connotations of a word. A word's connotation is the emotional message it carries. For example, *slender* and *thin* have almost identical denotations. *Slender*, however, suggests a pleasingly slim form. *Thin* can suggest a slimness that is not pleasing.

Reread your selection to find any figures of speech your author may have used. See Chapter 1, Lesson 3 for a detailed explanation of figures of speech. Figures of speech make ideas more vivid by presenting them through an unusual comparison. A figure of speech also contains an emotional message. This message helps to present the author's feelings about the ideas he or she is expressing.

Then look for other devices the author may use to create emotional emphasis and see what emotions are expressed through them. For example, has the author repeated sounds, words, or phrases to emphasize or build emotion? Has the author used a light, tripping rhythm to suggest humor, or a slow, heavy one to convey solemnity? Answering these questions will help you discover the emotions in your selection.

When you feel you understand the ideas and emotions in your selection, spend some time reading about its author. If possible, find out how your selection came to be written. This knowledge will deepen your understanding of the selection and improve your oral reading.

Working with the Model

Here are two selections for you to study at home and discuss in class. The first selection is from the inaugural address of President John F. Kennedy. In the second selection, a poet remembers his grandmother and the times he spent with her when he was a child. Read each selection at home, first silently and then aloud. Come to class prepared to answer and discuss the questions following the selections.

From the Inaugural Address

Mr. Chief Justice, President Eisenhower, Vice President Nixon, President Truman, reverend clergy, fellow citizens, we observe today not a victory of party, but a celebration of freedom—symbolizing an end, as well as a beginning—signifying renewal, as well as change. For I have sworn before you and Almighty God the same solemn oath our forebears prescribed nearly a century and three quarters ago.

The world is very different now. For man holds in his mortal hands the power to abolish all forms of human poverty and all forms of human life. And yet the same revolutionary beliefs for which our forebears fought are still at issue around the globe—the belief that the rights of man come not from the generosity of the state, but from the hand of God.

We dare not forget today that we are the heirs of that first revolution. Let the word go forth from this time and place, to friend and foe alike, that the torch has been passed to a new generation of Americans—born in this century, tempered by war, disciplined by a hard and bitter peace, proud of our ancient heritage—and unwilling to witness or permit the slow undoing of those human rights to which this Nation has always been committed, and to which we are committed today at home and around the world.

Let every nation know, whether it wishes us well or ill, that we shall pay any price, bear any burden, meet any hardship, support any friend, oppose any foe, in order to assure the survival and the success of liberty.

This much we pledge—and more.

To those old allies whose cultural and spiritual origins we share, we pledge the loyalty of faithful friends. United, there is little we cannot do in a host of cooperative ventures. Divided, there is little we can do—for we dare not meet a powerful challenge at odds and split asunder.

To those new States whom we welcome to the ranks of the free, we pledge our words that one form of colonial control shall not have passed away merely to be replaced by a far greater iron tyranny. We shall not always expect to find them supporting our view. But we shall always hope to find them strongly supporting their own freedom—and to remember that, in the past, those who foolishly sought power by riding the back of the tiger ended up inside.

To those peoples in the huts and villages across the globe struggling to break the bonds of mass misery, we pledge our best efforts to help them help themselves, for whatever period is required—not because the Communists may be doing it, not because we seek their votes, but because it is right. If a free society cannot help the many who are poor, it cannot save the few who are rich.

To our sister republics south of our border, we offer a special pledge—to convert our good words into good deeds, in a new alliance for progress, to assist free men and free governments in casting off the chains of poverty. But this peaceful revolution of hope cannot become the prey of hostile powers. Let all our neighbors know that we shall join with them to oppose aggression or subversion anywhere in the Americas. And let every other power know that this hemisphere intends to remain the master of its own house.

To that world assembly of sovereign states, the United Nations, our last best hope in an age where the instruments of war have far outpaced the instruments of peace, we renew our pledge of support—to prevent it from becoming merely a forum for invective—to strengthen its shield of the new and the weak—and to enlarge the area in which its writ may run.

Finally, to those nations who would make themselves our adversary, we offer not a pledge but a request: that both sides begin anew the quest for peace, before the dark powers of destruction unleashed by science engulf all humanity in planned or accidental self-destruction. . . .

My Grandmother Would Rock Quietly and Hum

in her house
she would rock quietly and hum
until her swelled hands
calmed

in summer
she wore thick stockings
sweaters
and gray braids

• • • •

mornings,
sunlight barely lit
the kitchen
and where
there were shadows
it was not cold

she quietly rolled
flour tortillas—
the papas
cracking in hot lard
would wake me

she had lost her teeth
and when we ate
she had bread
soaked in café

always her eyes
were clear
and she could see
as I cannot yet see—
through her eyes
she gave me herself

she would sit
and talk
of her girlhood—
of things strange to me:
   México
   epidemics
   relatives shot
   her father's hopes
  of this country—
how they sank
with cement dust
to his insides

now
when I go
to the old house
the worn spots
by the stove
echo of her shuffling
and
México
still hangs in her
fading
calendar pictures

        —Leonard Adamé

A. Think about the ideas in the two selections.
  1. What is the major idea of President Kennedy's speech? What
      ideas support this major idea?
  2. What do these words from President Kennedy's speech mean:
      signifying, forebears, asunder, ranks, sovereign, invective?
  3. President Kennedy refers to the beliefs of the people who
      fought the American Revolution when he says "the revolutionary
      beliefs for which our forebears fought are still at issue around
      the globe." What do these words mean? According to these "rev-
      olutionary beliefs," from where do human rights come? What

does the statement that such rights do not come from the "generosity of the state" mean? Compare what President Kennedy says about human rights with this paragraph from the Declaration of Independence.

> "We hold these truths to be self-evident, that all men are created equal, that they are endowed by their Creator with certain unalienable Rights, that among these are Life, Liberty and the pursuit of Happiness."

4. Explain the meaning of each figure of speech from President Kennedy's speech: "iron tyranny"; "those who foolishly sought power by riding the back of the tiger ended up inside"; "peaceful revolution."

5. Often in a poem, the major idea is not stated in any one group of words. Rather, the major idea may be the total impression created by all the ideas and descriptions in the poem. What is the major idea in the poem by Leonard Adamé? What supporting ideas contribute to the major idea?

6. *Papas* means potatoes. What do *tortillas* and *café* mean?

7. What does Adamé mean when he says his grandmother would rock and hum until her hands "calmed"? What does he mean by saying her father's hopes "sank/with cement dust/to his insides"? What do these lines tell you about how the grandmother's father earned his living in his new country?

B. Think about the emotions expressed in each of these selections.

1. The connotations of words convey emotional meanings. These phrases come from President Kennedy's speech: "the torch has been passed," "the ranks of the free," "master of its own house," "strengthen its shield of the new and the weak." What idea does each phrase convey? What emotion is suggested by the connotation of each phrase? How does the new president want Americans to view their country on his inaugural day?

2. President Kennedy begins his speech by saying he has just taken the presidential oath written by the founders of our country. After speaking of the past, he turns to the future. In speaking of the future, he uses the word *pledge* (another kind of oath) many times. What connotations does the word *pledge* suggest? Why do you think the president spoke of the oath he has just taken in the way he did? How might that statement make his audience feel about his pledges for the future?

3. President Kennedy uses repetition to create drama and emotional emphasis in his speech. Notice how he repeats the word *know* here: "Let all our neighbors *know* that we shall join with them to oppose aggression or subversion anywhere in the Americas. And let every other power *know* that this hemisphere intends to remain the master of its own house." Find three other

examples of repetition used for emotional emphasis in President Kennedy's speech. Discuss how repetition heightens emotional emphasis in each case.

4. Adamé says "always her eyes/were clear/and she could see/as I cannot yet see." What are the connotations of *see* in these lines?

5. In this poem Adamé presents his memories of his grandmother. Each memory has a slightly different emotional message. How can you tell by looking at the poem where one memory ends and another begins? What clue does this give you about how to find the emotional messages in a poem?

6. Adamé's poem tells about his memories of his grandmother and about her memories of Mexico. From one point of view, this poem is about how a people's cultural heritage is preserved through their memories. Explain how this idea is presented in the last stanza of the poem. What emotion or emotions do you find accompanying this idea in the last stanza?

C. Think about the background of each selection.

1. How does knowing that President Kennedy was inaugurated during one of the most prosperous periods in American history affect your evaluation of his speech? How might his speech have been different if his inauguration had occurred during the Depression, as did President Roosevelt's? (See the model on pages 194–195 for Roosevelt's first inaugural address.)

2. How does knowing that Adamé escaped from the poverty and disappointment suffered by his grandmother affect your evaluation of his poem?

Guidelines

When preparing for an oral reading, make sure you have a complete understanding of your selection.

1. Be sure to correctly identify the major idea of your selection.
2. Identify figurative language the author has used and evaluate what ideas and emotions this figurative language is meant to convey.
3. Make sure you understand what overall mood or emotion the author means to convey. Note specific words and phrases that suggest this mood to you.
4. Evaluate how the author uses phrasing, repetition, contrast, rhythm, or rhyme to convey ideas and emotions.
5. Add to your understanding of your selection by doing research on its author and the circumstances under which it was written.

Preparing and Presenting

Work with a partner. The two of you should choose one of the following selections to prepare for oral interpretation. (You may choose another selection instead, with your teacher's approval.)

Working separately, you and your partner should each study the selection to discover its ideas and emotions. Each of you should read the selection at home, first silently and then aloud. Discover the major idea of your selection, and as an example of this idea, write the lines or words in which it is presented. Then find each supporting idea and at least one group of words as an example of each supporting idea.

Then think about the emotions in your selection. Decide what the major mood or emotion is and find an example of a figure of speech, phrase, line, sentence, or group of words in which this emotion is expressed. Then find any supporting emotions and one example (one group of words) that expresses each.

Next, do some reading on your author and the circumstances under which your selection was written. Your reading may lead you to look at your selection in a new way, so that your interpretation of its ideas and emotions changes slightly.

Finally, arrange all your information in an outline. Your finished outline should look something like this:

I. Your Statement of Major Idea (example from selection)
    A. Supporting Idea (example)
    B. Supporting Idea (example)
    C. Supporting Idea (example)

II. Major Emotion
    A. Supporting Emotion (example)
    B. Supporting Emotion (example)
    C. Supporting Emotion (example)

III. Author Background That Relates to Selection
    A.
    B.
    C.

IV. Circumstances under Which Selection Was Written
    A.
    B.
    C.

Here is the group of selections. Each section is preceded by suggestions on its interpretation. However, remember that there are often several valid ways to interpret a selection, just as there are usually several valid ways to play a character in a stage drama.

HUMOR

The following selections are all humorous. Notice how the poets use a light, tripping rhythm to suggest humor. Notice too how Mark Twain keeps his audience wondering how his story will end, so that the humor of its final outcome is heightened by a release from suspense.

Father William

"You are old, Father William," the young man said,
   "And your hair has become very white,
And yet you incessantly stand on your head—
   Do you think, at your age, it is right?"

"In my youth," Father William replied to his son,
   "I feared it might injure the brain;
But now that I'm perfectly sure I have none,
   Why, I do it again and again."

"You are old," said the youth, "as I mentioned before,
   And have grown most uncommonly fat;
Yet you turned a back-somersault in at the door—
   Pray, what is the reason of that?"

"In my youth," said the sage, as he shook his gray locks,
   "I kept all my limbs very supple
By the use of this ointment—one shilling the box—
   Allow me to sell you a couple."

"You are old," said the youth, "and your jaws are too weak
   For anything tougher than suet;
Yet you finished the goose, with the bones and the beak;
   Pray, how did you manage to do it?"

"In my youth," said his father, "I took to the law,
   And argued each case with my wife;
And the muscular strength which it gave to my jaw
   Has lasted the rest of my life."

"You are old," said the youth, "one would hardly suppose
   That your eye was as steady as ever;
Yet you balanced an eel on the end of your nose—
   What made you so awfully clever?"

"I have answered three questions, and that is enough,"
   Said his father; "don't give yourself airs!
Do you think I can listen all day to such stuff?
   Be off, or I'll kick you downstairs!"

—Lewis Carroll

Don't Cry, Darling,
It's Blood All Right

Whenever poets want to give you the idea that something is particularly
        meek and mild,
They compare it to a child.
Thereby proving that though poets with poetry may be rife
They don't know the facts of life.
If of compassion you desire either a tittle or a jot,
Don't try to get it from a tot.
Hard-boiled, sophisticated adults like me and you
May enjoy ourselves thoroughly with *Little Women* and *Winnie-the-*
        Pooh
But innocent infants these titles from the reading course eliminate
As soon as they discover that it was honey and nuts and mashed potatoes
        instead of human flesh that Winnie-the-Pooh and Little Women ate.
Innocent infants have no use for fables about rabbits or donkeys or
        tortoises or porpoises.
What they want is something with plenty of well-mutilated corpoises.
Not on legends of how the rose came to be a rose instead of a petunia
        is their fancy fed.
But on the inside story of how somebody's bones got ground up to
        make somebody else's bread.
They'll go to sleep listening to the story of the little beggarmaid who
        got to be queen by being kind to the bees and the birds,
But they're all eyes and ears the minute they suspect a wolf or a giant is
        going to tear some poor woodcutter into quarters or thirds.
It really doesn't take much to fill their cup;
All they want is for somebody to be eaten up.
Therefore I say unto you, all you poets who are so crazy about meek
        and mild little children and their angelic air,
If you are sincere and really want to please them, why just go out and
        get yourselves devoured by a bear.

—Ogden Nash

From a Speech He Gave
on His Seventieth Birthday

I have had a great many birthdays in my time. I remember the first
one very well, and I always think of it with indignation; everything was
so crude, unaesthetic, primeval. Nothing like this at all. No proper ap-
preciative preparation made; nothing really ready. Now, for a person
born with high and delicate instincts—why, even the cradle wasn't
whitewashed—nothing ready at all. I hadn't any hair, I hadn't any teeth,
I hadn't any clothes, I had to go to my first banquet just like that.

Well, everybody came swarming in. It was the merest little bit of a village—hardly that, just a little hamlet, in the backwoods of Missouri, where nothing ever happened, and the people were all interested, and they all came; they looked me over to see if there was anything fresh in my line. Why, nothing ever happened in that village—I—why, I was the only thing that had really happened there for months and months and months; and although I say it myself that shouldn't, I came the nearest to being a real event that had happened in that village in more than two years.

Well, those people came, they came with that curiosity which is so provincial, with that frankness which also is so provincial, and they examined me all around and gave their opinion. Nobody asked them, and I shouldn't have minded if anybody had paid me a compliment, but nobody did. Their opinions were all just green with prejudice, and I feel those opinions to this day.

Well, I stood that as long as—you know I was courteous, and I stood it to the limit. I stood it an hour, and then the worm turned. I was the worm; it was my turn to turn, and I turned. I knew very well the strength of my position: I knew that I was the only spotlessly pure and innocent person in that whole town, and I came out and said so. And they could not say a word. It was so true. They blushed; they were embarrassed. Well, that was the first after-dinner speech I ever made.

—Mark Twain

SERIOUS LITERATURE

Like most well-written poems, the Yeats poem can be understood in several ways. It is a story about a magical event, but it is also a statement of how a man cannot settle for anything less than an ideal he has glimpsed for only a moment.

The Song of Wandering Aengus

I went out to the hazel wood,
Because a fire was in my head,
And cut and peeled a hazel wand,
And hooked a berry to a thread;
And when white moths were on the wing,
And moth-like stars were flickering out,
I dropped the berry in a stream
And caught a little silver trout.

When I had laid it on the floor
I went to blow the fire aflame,
But something rustled on the floor,
And some one called me by my name:
It had become a glimmering girl
With apple blossom in her hair
Who called me by my name and ran
And faded through the brightening air.

Though I am old with wandering
Through hollow lands and hilly lands,
I will find out where she has gone,
And kiss her lips and take her hands;
And walk among long dappled grass,
And pluck till time and times are done
The silver apples of the moon,
The golden apples of the sun.

—William Butler Yeats

MOOD AND ATMOSPHERE

Each of the following selections carefully creates an atmosphere or major emotion, using such emotions as fear, suspense, and mystery. In the first poem, notice that the speaker in the first two stanzas is the witch and that the speaker in the last stanza is her victim. The mood results partly from the witch's attempt to track her victim and partly from the results of her attempt. The short lines of the second poem make the mushrooms seem almost timid—until you read the last stanza. The second poem makes heavy use of repetition, assonance, and rhyme to convey ideas and emotions. If you choose this poem, decide what emotional effect is created by these devices.

The Witch

I have walked a great while over the snow,
And I am not tall nor strong.
My clothes are wet, and my teeth are set,
And the way was hard and 'ong.

I have wandered over the fruitful earth,
But I never came here before.
Oh, lift me over the threshold, and let me in at the door!

The cutting wind is a cruel foe;
I dare not stand in the blast.
My hands are stone, and my voice a groan,
And the worst of death is past.
I am but a little maiden still;
My little white feet are sore.
Oh, lift me over the threshold, and let me in at the door!

Her voice was the voice that women have,
Who plead for their heart's desire.
She came—she came—and the quivering flame
Sank and died in the fire.
It never was lit again on my hearth
Since I hurried across the floor,
To lift her over the threshold, and let her in at the door!

—Mary Elizabeth Coleridge

Mushrooms

Overnight, very
Whitely, discreetly,
Very quietly

Our toes, our noses
Take hold on the loam,
Acquire the air.

Nobody sees us,
Stops us, betrays us;
The small grains make room.

Soft fists insist on
Heaving the needles,
The leafy bedding,

Even the paving,
Our hammers, our rams,
Earless and eyeless,

Perfectly voiceless
Widen the crannies,
Shoulder through holes. We

Diet on water,
On crumbs of shadow,
Bland-mannered, asking

Little or nothing.
So many of us!
So many of us!

We are shelves, we are
Tables, we are meek,
We are edible,

Nudgers and shovers
In spite of ourselves.
Our kind multiplies:

We shall by morning
Inherit the earth.
Our foot's in the door.

—Sylvia Plath

307

RHYTHM, RHYME, AND FIGURATIVE LANGUAGE

These selections will give you a chance to study how poets use rhythm, rhyme, and figurative language to convey ideas and emotions vividly. The poem by Leigh Hunt presents a modern idea (or viewpoint) in a traditional poetic form for story telling: the ballad. Sandburg and Moore make expert use of language and rhythm to produce very vivid pictures of their subjects.

The Glove and the Lions

King Francis was a hearty king, and loved a royal sport,
And one day, as his lions fought, sat looking on the court.
The nobles fill'd the benches, with the ladies in their pride,
And 'mongst them sat the Count de Lorge, with one for whom he sigh'd:
And truly 'twas a gallant thing to see that crowning show,
Valor and love, and a king above, and the royal beasts below.

Ramp'd and roar'd the lions, with horrid laughing jaws;
They bit, they glared, gave blows like beams, a wind went with their paws;
With wallowing might and stifled roar they roll'd on one another,
Till all the pit with sand and mane was in a thunderous smother;
The bloody foam above the bars came whisking through the air;
Said Francis then, "Faith, gentlemen, we're better here than there."

De Lorge's love o'erheard the King, a beauteous, lively dame,
With smiling lips and sharp bright eyes, which always seem'd the same;
She thought, "The Count, my lover, is brave as brave can be;
He surely would do wondrous things to show his love of me;
King, ladies, lovers, all look on; the occasion is divine;
I'll drop my glove, to prove his love; great glory will be mine."

She dropp'd her glove, to prove his love, then look'd at him and smiled;
He bow'd, and in a moment leap'd among the lions wild;
The leap was quick, return was quick, he has regain'd his place,
Then threw the glove, but not with love, right in the lady's face.
"By heaven," said Francis, "rightly done!" and he rose from where he sat;
"No love," quoth he, "but vanity, sets love a task like that."

—Leigh Hunt

Four Preludes on Playthings of the Wind

1

The woman named Tomorrow
sits with a hairpin in her teeth
and takes her time
and does her hair the way she wants it
and fastens at last the last braid and coil
and puts the hairpin where it belongs
and turns and drawls: Well, what of it?
My grandmother, Yesterday, is gone.
What of it? Let the dead be dead.

2

The doors were cedar
and the panels strips of gold
and the girls were golden girls
and the panels read and the girls chanted:
    We are the greatest city,
    the greatest nation:
    nothing like us ever was.
The doors are twisted on broken hinges.
Sheets of rain swish through on the wind
    where the golden girls ran and the panels read:
    We are the greatest city,
    the greatest nation,
    nothing like us ever was.

3

It has happened before.
Strong men put up a city and got
    a nation together,
And paid singers to sing and women
to warble: We are the greatest city,
    the greatest nation,
    nothing like us ever was.
And while the singers sang
and the strong men listened
and paid the singers well
and felt good about it all,
    there were rats and lizards who listened
    . . . and the only listeners left now
    . . . are . . . the rats . . . and the lizards.
And there are black crows
crying, "Caw, caw,"
bringing mud and sticks
building a nest

over the words carved
on the doors where the panels were cedar
and the strips on the panels were gold
and the golden girls came singing:
> We are the greatest city,
> the greatest nation:
> nothing like us ever was.
The only singers now are crows crying, "Caw, caw,"
And the sheets of rain whine in the wind and doorways.
And the only listeners now are . . . the rats . . . and the lizards.

4

The feet of the rats
scribble on the doorsills;
the hieroglyphs of the rat footprints
chatter the pedigrees of the rats
and babble of the blood
and gabble of the breed
of the grandfathers and the great-grandfathers
of the rats.
And the wind shifts
and the dust on a doorsill shifts
and even the writing of the rat footprints
tell us nothing, nothing at all
about the great city, the greatest nation
where the strong men listened
and the women warbled:
> Nothing like us ever was.

—Carl Sandburg

Blessed is the man

who does not sit in the seat of the scoffer—
    the man who does not denigrate, depreciate, denunciate;
      who is not "characteristically intemperate,"
who does not "excuse, retreat, equivocate, and will be heard."

(Ah, Giorgione! there are those who mongrelize
    and those who heighten anything they touch; although it may
    well be
      that if Giorgione's self-portrait were not said to be
      he
it might take my fancy. Blessed the geniuses who know

that egomania is not a duty.)
    "Diversity, controversy; tolerance"—in that "citadel
      of learning" we have a fort that ought to armor us well.
Blessed is the man who "takes the risk of a decision"—asks

himself the question: "Would it solve the problem?
    Is it right as I see it? Is it in the best interests of
all?"
    Alas, Ulysses' companions are now political—
living self-indulgently until the moral sense is drowned,

having lost all power of comparison,
    thinking license emancipates one, "slaves whom they
themselves have bound,"
    Brazen authors, downright soiled and downright spoiled, as
      if sound
and exceptional, are the old quasi-modish counterfeit,

mitin-proofing conscience against character.
    Affronted by "private lies and public shame," blessed is the
    author
      Who favors what the supercilious do not favor—
who will not comply. Blessed, the unaccommodating man.

Blessed the man whose faith is different
    from possessiveness—of a kind not framed by things which
                      do appear"—
    who will not visualize defeat, too intent to cower;
whose illumined eye has seen the shaft that gilds the sultan's
tower.

                               —Marianne Moore

Beginning on page 403 there are other materials that can be used for practicing oral interpretation. The speeches found there also make effective use of rhythm and vivid language.

Evaluation Checklist

Exchange outlines with your partner. Read your partner's outline carefully and then answer the following questions. As you answer each question, remember that there is no single "correct" interpretation of a selection. If both you and your partner can support your evaluations of the major idea and emotion with examples from the selection, you may both have arrived at valid interpretations, even if your evaluations are different.

1. What did you identify as the main idea and supporting ideas of the selection? If your partner stated these ideas differently, modify your outline to reflect your partner's evaluation, if you feel that doing so will enrich your own interpretation.
2. What did your partner identify as the main emotion and supporting emotions of the selection? If your partner stated these emotions differently, modify your outline to reflect your partner's evaluation, if you feel that doing so will enrich your own interpretation.
3. What information (if any) did your partner discover about the author that you did not? If your partner's information adds to your understanding of the selection, modify your evaluation of its ideas and emotions accordingly.
4. What information (if any) did your partner discover about the circumstances under which your selection was written? If your partner found some information you did not and if this information adds to your understanding of the selection, modify your evaluation of its ideas and emotions accordingly.

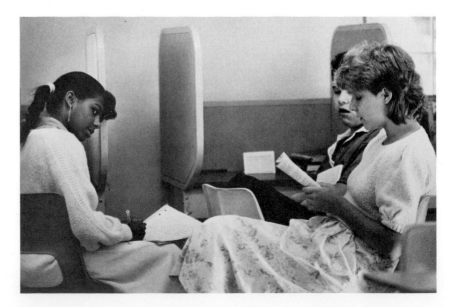

Preparing and Giving an Oral Reading

Now that you have analyzed the ideas and emotions in your selection, there is one more step to complete before you are ready to give your oral reading. You must prepare a **reading copy** of your selection, a copy marked to show exactly how you will read the selection to your audience. To do this, you must decide how you will use your voice to convey the ideas and emotions you've identified in the selection.

The first thing to remember is that your audience won't be able to see the punctuation in your selection. Therefore, you must read it so that they can hear every period, comma, or other punctuation mark. Begin by making a copy of your selection. Read through your selection and draw a vertical line after every punctuation mark.

Next, look at the examples of important ideas and emotions you listed in the outline for the previous lesson. Draw a vertical line after any idea or emotion that is important enough to require a pause. (Any major idea or emotion will probably require a pause.) Finally, read your selection aloud and draw a vertical line after any word at which it seems natural to pause.

Next, identify the emotional climax or most important statement in your selection. This passage may be a single sentence or several sentences long. It contains the single most important idea or emotion in your selection. When you practice giving your reading, you should build up to this passage.

Last, you should decide what reading rate and emotional tone are appropriate for your selection. For example, to heighten the irony in Sandburg's "Four Preludes on Playthings of the Wind," you would read the chant of the golden girls at a fast rate and in a lighthearted tone; you would read the description of an annihilated civilization at a slow rate and in a solemn tone. Remember that the emotional tone your voice suggests is created by the rate, pitch, and energy with which you read each part of your selection.

Now you are ready to prepare your reading copy. First, type or print your selection, ending a line every time you reach a vertical mark. (You do not need to transfer the vertical marks to your reading copy.) Be sure to leave ample margins and plenty of space between lines.

Next, mark any place where you want to pause for emphasis with a double line (‖). Then, underline any words or phrases you want to emphasize (many of these words or phrases will come from the examples in your outline). Draw brackets on each side of the climax of your selection, so you can see what passage you want to build up to.

Finally, make notes in the margin at each point where you want your voice to be softer or louder, where you want to vary the rate of your reading, or where you want to suggest a particular emotional tone.

Working with the Model

Douglas decided to prepare President Kennedy's inaugural speech as his oral reading. Study the following section of his reading copy.

So let us begin <u>anew</u> — || *moderate rate with great energy exhort audience*

remembering on both sides that civility is not a sign of

weakness,

and sincerity is always subject to proof.

Let us never <u>negotiate</u> out of <u>fear</u>.   *louder with*

But let us never <u>fear</u> to <u>negotiate</u>. || *emphasis*

<u>Let both sides explore</u> what problems unite us,

instead of laboring those problems which divide us.||

<u>Let both sides,</u>

for the first time,

formulate serious and precise proposals

for the inspection and control of arms—

and bring the <u>absolute power</u> to <u>destroy other nations</u>

under the <u>absolute control</u> of <u>all nations.</u> ||

<u>Let both sides seek</u>

to invoke the <u>wonders</u> of science

instead of its <u>terrors.</u>

<u>Together</u> let us explore the stars,

conquer the deserts,

eradicate disease,

tap the ocean depths,

and encourage the arts and commerce.||

<u>Let both sides unite</u>

to heed in all corners of the earth

the command of Isaiah—

to "undo the <u>heavy burdens</u>

and to <u>let the oppressed go free.</u>"||

And if a <u>beachhead</u> of <u>cooperation</u> *Confident tone*

may push back the <u>jungle</u> of <u>suspicion</u>,

<u>let both sides join</u> in creating a new endeavor,

<u>not</u> a <u>new balance of power</u>,

but a <u>new world of law</u>,

where the <u>strong are just</u>|| ⎫
                              ⎬ *emphasize*
and the <u>weak secure</u> || ⎬ *ending of*
                              ⎭ *each line*
and the <u>peace preserved</u>. ||

A. Think about how Douglas plans to use his voice to convey the ideas and emotions in his selection.

1. Douglas has divided his selection to help his listeners grasp which words belong together. He has typed one word group per line. Discuss how Douglas decided which words belong together. For example, how many of the lines in his reading copy end with a period, comma, or other punctuation mark? What lines end with an important word or phrase? What lines represent grammatical units, such as phrases or clauses? What line divisions represent places where it would be natural to pause?

2. What part of his selection did Douglas mark as the climax? Why do you think he chose this part? Do you think Douglas should have marked another passage as the climax? If so, identify the passage you think he should have marked and explain why you think it is the climax.

3. On a separate piece of paper, list the words and phrases Douglas has underlined. Looking only at your list, write the idea or emotion each item suggests. Then reread the selection and compare it with the list of emotions you have just made. How well do you think Douglas has identified the most important words presenting the ideas and emotions of his selection? What other words, if any, would you have underlined in the selection? Explain your choices.

4. At what points in his reading does Douglas plan to pause for emphasis? Explain how you think each of these pauses will help convey an important idea or emotion.

5. Read the notes Douglas has made on rate, loudness, and emotional tone. Explain how each of these notes will help him convey an important idea or emotion. What other notes on delivery (if any) should he have made? Why?

B. Think about what nonverbal communication would be appropriate for Douglas' selection.

1. Some speakers like to indicate on their reading copy places where they want to look up at their audience. At what places in his selection might Douglas have made such a notation?
2. Some speakers like to note places where they will make certain movements or gestures during their reading, while others prefer to let their interpretation be more spontaneous. What gestures would have been appropriate for Douglas' reading, and where in his selection would he have made them?
3. Discuss why Douglas decided not to include notes on nonverbal communication on his reading copy. For example, what problems can you think of that might arise if a speaker had too many marks on the reading copy?

Guidelines

Work from your reading copy when you practice your oral reading. Follow these guidelines when you practice.

1. When you begin a practice session, put your reading copy on a stand at arm's length. If you will not have a stand or podium to use when you give your reading, put your reading copy in a stiff, clear plastic cover so you can hold it easily.
2. Ask a classmate to listen to you as you practice. This classmate should note whether you are using enough eye contact with your audience. He or she should also point out any mannerisms that may distract the audience from your efforts to convey your author's ideas and emotions.
3. If possible, tape-record your practice session to find out whether you are emphasizing the sections you intended to and whether you are building effectively to the climax of your selection.
4. Be aware of the meaning of words and phrases as you speak them.
5. Vary the pitch, rate, and loudness of your voice to convey the author's ideas and emotions and to hold your listeners' interest.
6. Become familiar enough with your material so you can look up frequently to see your listeners' responses.

Preparing and Presenting

Prepare a reading copy of the selection you chose for oral interpretation in the previous lesson. Remember to mark off the groups of words that go together and then write or type one word group per line in your reading copy. Underline the words and phrases you want to emphasize and mark any places where you want to pause for emphasis. Decide what passage represents the climax of your selection and draw brackets on each side of this passage. Make notes in the margin to indicate where you want to vary rate, pitch, and emotional tone.

Practice your oral reading in front of a classmate, following the procedures set down in the Guidelines section of this lesson. Write your classmate's suggestions on your reading copy and then conduct a final practice session alone. Before you come to class, make enough copies of your reading copy for everyone in the class. When you give your oral reading, ask your classmates to take notes on your presentation.

Evaluation Checklist

Evaluate each student's presentation on the basis of the following criteria. You may use the notes you took during each oral reading as well as copies of each student's reading copy distributed after the oral reading. Rate each presentation on a scale from 1 (Poor) to 5 (Excellent). Be prepared to give reasons for each rating you give.

Category	Rating
The speaker . . . 1. Made the most important idea in the selection clear, emphasized words or phrases, paused for emphasis, or varied vocal rate or pitch to convey this idea	
2. Made the most important emotion in the selection clear and used his or her voice to convey this emotion	
3. Used nonverbal communication, such as gesture and eye contact, to convey the ideas and emotions in the selection	
4. Interpreted the major idea and emotion of the selection correctly	
5. Prepared the reading copy correctly	

Chapter 11 Review

Summary

Effective story telling, whether to inform or to entertain, requires careful planning and execution. First, be sure to include the essential story elements (the *who*, *when*, *where*, and *what* of the story). Second, arrange your events in chronological order leading up to the most important or most exciting part. Third, add details that will help make your story clear, vivid, and interesting to your listeners. Avoid any details that do not directly support your story. Fourth, practice telling your story, adjusting your rate and using facial expressions and gestures to emphasize the most important part or parts.

Oral interpretation is the art of reading aloud a story, poem, or speech. When you give an oral reading, your purpose is to convey the ideas and emotions of the selection as completely as possible. Analyzing the selection's language is the primary way of understanding the selection's central ideas and emotions. Notice both the denotations and connotations of important words, as well as the figures of speech, and other devices. Prepare a reading copy by typing or writing one word group per line, underlining words or phrases you want to emphasize, marking any pauses for emphasis, drawing brackets around the climax, and making marginal notes about how to deliver certain lines.

When you are presenting your oral interpretation, try to make the audience clearly understand the ideas and feel the emotions. Vary your pitch, rate, and loudness to emphasize the climax or the important sections and to hold the audience's attention.

Reviewing Vocabulary

Number your paper from 1 to 6. Next to each number, write the letter of the group of words that best defines the word(s) in dark type in the sentence.

---

a. the reading aloud of a story, poem, or speech
b. the dictionary definition of a word
c. a copy of a selection marked to show how it will be read
d. an expression that makes ideas more vivid by comparing them to things people have seen, touched, or felt
e. the art of telling a story
f. the emotional messages that words suggest

---

1. Janine forgot to add several crucial delivery notes to her **reading copy**.
2. The defense attorney's plea to the jury was filled with flattery and patriotic **connotations**.
3. Franz's **oral interpretation** of "The Raven" conveyed the eerie mood so vividly that we were on the edge of our seats.
4. The chef's **figure of speech** compared cooking a gourmet meal to conducting a symphony.
5. Mark Twain's short stories are perfect vehicles for practicing **narrative speaking**.
6. Technical writing demands that the **denotation** of every word be very clear and precise.

Reviewing Facts and Ideas

1. What are the essential elements of any story?
2. In what order are most story events organized? Why?
3. Why is it important to include specific details that support your story events?
4. What are ways to emphasize the most important part of your story?
5. What is oral interpretation? What is its purpose?
6. What is the difference between the denotation and connotation of a word? Which one carries more of the feelings that a selection conveys?
7. What are figures of speech? How do they make works of literature more vivid?
8. Besides figures of speech, what other devices can an author use to create emotional emphasis?
9. Why is it important to mark your reading copy?
10. What are the main steps of marking your reading copy of your selection?

Discussing Facts and Ideas

1. As young children, most people had a favorite story that was told by their parents or by someone else close to them. Discuss your favorite with others in the class. Why do you think some stories stick in your memory for so long while others have been long forgotten?
2. Discuss the characteristics of literature that make some works good and others poor for oral interpretation.
3. Read a contemporary poem or short story and then listen to a recording of the author reading that work. Discuss with the class the ideas and feelings in the material that become more evident when hearing it than when reading it.

Applying Your Knowledge

1. Locate a preschool or child care facility near your school. Arrange to tell the children stories. To help you know what kind of story the children of a given age will enjoy, ask the children's librarian at the public library. When you prepare your story, begin with an outline of the major events. Practice telling your story by repeating it to another student at least twice a day for a week before telling it to the children. When you tell your first story to the children, be sure to take with you another student who can help you review the presentation and help you to improve it.
2. The *Foxfire* books edited by Eliot Wiggenton contain many stories told to high school students by older people in the Georgia hills. You can use these works in several ways.
   a. Use them as a source of oral interpretative readings. The dialects as the students have reproduced them will challenge you, but the straightforward narratives are interesting.
   b. Use the interviews as models for your own interviews. As you read the materials these high school students have gathered and published, think of a number of people who can tell stories of your own community. Interview these people, using a tape recorder. Then retell the story yourself to the class. Let the class compare your version with the original taped version.

Using the Telephone Effectively

You should learn how to use the telephone to save yourself time and effort in making business contacts. You should also use it to make a good impression on the people you are dealing with. Remember these rules.

1. **Answer the phone politely.** Instead of simply saying "Yes?", "Hello?", or "What is it?", answer with useful information:
   "Glenn's Gaskets. Can I help you?"
   "Glenn's Gaskets, Jill Thomas speaking."

2. **Identify yourself to the person you are calling.** Instead of "Is Jim Fernandez there?" or "Let me speak to Jim Fernandez," give your name and a polite request:
   "Good afternoon, this is Jill Thomas from Glenn's Gaskets. May I speak to Jim Fernandez, please?"

3. **State your business clearly.** Don't waste the other person's time on irrelevant conversation. Tell him or her as briefly as possible why you are calling and exactly what you want. Give any information that will make it easier for the person to help you.

4. **Don't interrogate the person who answers the phone.** If you are told that a person is busy or in conference, don't try to find out what the person is really doing or with whom he or she is speaking.

5. **Leave clear messages.** Instead of saying, "I'll try later," leave your name and number and some information that will help the person who has to call you back:
   "Please tell Jim that Jill Thomas called about the schedule for delivering the gaskets. My number is 555-6200."

Activity

1. Working with another student, role-play one of the following telephone conversations, or another conversation your teacher approves, before the class.

   Student inquiring about a job opening
   Garage owner placing an order for mufflers
   Retailer checking when catalogues will be delivered

   Ask the other students to evaluate the conversation and to suggest ways in which both speakers could have made more effective use of the telephone.

Introducing a Speaker

Remembering these points will help you introduce a speaker with grace and poise.

1. Become familiar with the background and accomplishments of the person you will introduce.
2. Focus your introduction on the speaker's qualifications to speak on his or her subject to this particular audience.
3. Praise the speaker but don't embarrass him or her by making extravagant predictions that will be impossible to live up to.
4. Deliver your introduction in the form of a good expository speech.
5. Deliver your introduction with warmth and enthusiasm.
6. Be brief; don't steal attention from the speaker.

Activities

1. Prepare and deliver a speech of introduction for one of the following people or for another person of your choice. The person you introduce can be someone now living, a person from history, or a character from a novel or film.

   - Captain Ahab
   - your next-door neighbor
   - Queen Elizabeth I of England
   - one of your classmates

2. Do research on the background of a state or local politician and prepare a speech of introduction to present this person to your class. You might choose one of the following people.

   - a school board member
   - a member of the city council
   - a county commissioner
   - your mayor or city manager
   - a state legislator
   - a district attorney

CHAPTER 12

Radio and Television

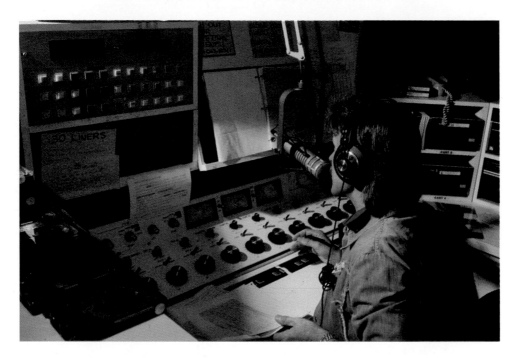

After working through this chapter, you should be proficient at the following skills:

Lesson	Skills
Lesson 1	• using voice and sound effects in radio dramas
Lesson 2	• rehearsing and presenting a radio drama
Lesson 3	• combining images and sound in a television script
Lesson 4	• communicating visual ideas in a shot sheet
Lesson 5	• producing a television script
Communicating on the Job	• working with others to solve a problem
Communicating as a Citizen	• presenting an award

Using Voice and Sound Effects in Radio Dramas

A **radio drama** is the oral interpretation of a story, poem, or play using voice, music, and sound effects prepared for dramatic presentation over the radio. In radio drama, the voice is especially important since it must be used to convey the action of the story as well as the emotions of the characters.

There are three characteristics of your voice that you can use to convey a character's emotions. First, you can vary your *rate of speaking*. Reading your lines quickly can show that your character is excited or in a hurry. A slow rate can indicate thoughtfulness or depression. You can pause in your delivery to create suspense, to show surprise, or to get your listeners' attention right before an important moment.

You can also vary the *pitch* of your voice to indicate what kind of character you're portraying. A low voice can help you portray an older character, while a high voice is best for portraying a child. A low voice can also show that your character is a serious person, while a high voice can suggest a nervous or excited person. Use a medium pitch for everyday conversation and for dialogue spoken by a narrator.

You can also portray a character's emotional state by varying the *volume* of your voice. Although you must always speak loud enough to be heard, you can heighten the effect of moderate changes in volume by varying the intensity of your voice. For example, the most precious secret of a dying industrial spy might be delivered at a low volume, but with great intensity.

Remember that radio actors must sometimes use their voices to let the audience know what's happened. An actor in a ghost story might actually have to say, "The walls of the room are closing in on me," because the audience could not see this happening. That same actor would have to faint with a groan and fall with a loud thump, because without these sounds the audience would have no way of knowing that the character had fainted.

Besides helping the audience understand the play, sound effects also make the action of the play seem more real. Effects like the ringing of a telephone or the slamming of a door make the radio audience feel they're actually present at the scene of the unfolding action.

Music can be used as a sound effect. For example, you would have music in the background if your characters were at a dance. However, background music unassociated with the action can be used to create a mood, and a short passage of rising and falling music often indicates the beginning or end of a scene.

Working with the Model

In the 1930s, the English author Lawrence du Garde Peach wrote many radio plays. Read this scene from his play *The "Mary Celeste,"* paying close attention to how he instructs the actors to use their voices. Also notice what sound effects he indicates for the scene.

SCENE XVI

(The voices in this scene should be hushed and suggest fear and anxiety.)

Steward: I tell you I know an unlucky ship when I see one. Wouldn't ha' sailed on her, on'y I bin out of a ship since—

Gottlieb: It iss the sea, not the ship.

Steward: You make me tired. As if the sea ain't always unlucky.

Volkerk: You're right. There was a barque sailed out of Boston—the *Aran Hill* her name was—she killed five men one voyage. I'll say she was unlucky. Fell off the main t'gallant yard, the last of 'em did, right on top o' the durned Mate. Killed him too. That was the only bit of luck the rest of the crew had the whole trip.

Steward: That's right. I've knowed o' ships like that. Say, have you ever heard of a haunted galley? Aboard the old *Falcon*—it was in San Francisco I first saw her, blast her—there was the ghost of a drowned cook used to hang round the galley half the time. Jumped her at Monterey, I did.

Volkerk: I believe you. Everyone knows as drowned sailors comes back to the ships that killed 'em. It don't matter where the ship goes. I reckon they gets along under the sea.

Steward: I've knowed men as have seed 'em. All drowned and wet, with seaweed on 'em, and no eyes.

Gottlieb: You don't have to talk like that.

Steward: What's wrong with it? It's true, I tell you. Didn't you ever hear of the old *Spindrift?* Lost, she was, with all hands off the Bank, only they raised her a'terwards. And blame me if the whole durned crew didn't come back and take her over, all drowned, her first night out. When she put back, the new crew was all raving. You mark my words, we hain't seen the last of Bos Lorenzen this trip, nor Harbens. They'll come back—drowned. They didn't go natural, neither, and that makes it worse. And if you sees one of 'em a-lookin' at you over the side, you take my tip and don't you look back.

Gottlieb: What for will they come back?

Steward: I guess they can't help it. They *gotta* come back. It ain't like being buried on land, there ain't nothing to keep 'em down. It's the sea drawin' of 'em. I've knowed ships come home a'ter a long voyage with the crew so skeart they dursn't break open the hatches for fear o' what they'd find. Every night drowned sailors used to come and jibber at 'em through the port holes or over the stern when they was at the wheel. Half eaten, some of 'em was, by fishes.

Volkerk: *(suddenly—sharply) What's that?*

Steward: Where?

Volkerk: In the fore peak!

Steward: Aw, it ain't nothin'. Quit it, can't ye?

Gottlieb: My father, he was drowned at sea, and he come and tap at our window every night for six days afterwards till they find him and bury him at Groningen.

Volkerk: *(hoarsely)* Look!

Gottlieb: Coming over the side!

Steward: It's an arm! All white! And wet! *(suddenly shouting)* Give me that axe! I'll—! *(There is a loud thud as the axe comes down on the rail.)*

Volkerk: It's gone!

Gottlieb: There's blood!

Steward: *(very frightened)* Boys, it was Harbens—climbing aboard!

Mate: *(coming up)* What's the matter? *(The three sailors begin to tell him excitedly that they have seen the drowned body of Harbens trying to climb aboard.)*

(Fade)

A. Think about how the actors should use their voices to convey action and emotion in this scene.
  1. At the beginning of the scene the sailors are swapping stories of the supernatural. What speaking rate would be appropriate for this part of the scene? What rate would be appropriate toward the end of the scene, after Volkerk says "Look!"? What change in the characters' emotions makes a change in rate appropriate?
  2. Toward the end of the scene, the playwright gives several directions on how the actors should use their voices. For example, he indicates that Volkerk should say "Look!" *"hoarsely."* What kind of pitch would you use for a hoarse voice? When the steward delivers his last line in the scene, he should sound *"very frightened."* What pitch would you use to make the steward sound "very frightened?"
  3. The playwright puts Volkerk's line "What's that?" in italics. At what volume do you think the playwright wants these lines delivered? Where in the scene does the playwright give directions on vocal volume for the actor playing the steward? What directions on volume does the playwright give at the beginning of the scene? What difference in volume should occur between the beginning and end of the scene, and why?
  4. How do the actors' lines help the audience know what's happening after Volkerk says "Look!"? What information is presented in words that would probably be presented visually if the play were on television?
B. Think about the sound effects in this scene.
  1. What sound effect does the playwright indicate?
  2. Discuss what other sound effects you might use in this scene. (For example, you might want to play a tape of waves slapping against the side of a boat throughout the scene.)
  3. The author ends the scene by having the excited conversation of the three sailors fade out. How might you have used music to end the scene? What kind of music do you think would be appropriate to begin this scene? What music would be appropriate to end it?

Guidelines

Follow these guidelines as you decide how to use voice and sound effects in a radio drama.

1. Prepare your broadcast copy as a reading copy, using the marks for interpretation explained in the last lesson of Chapter 11.
2. Remember that in a radio play you cannot rely on great changes in volume to convey excitement since high volume will cause distortion in the sound. One way to monitor the volume levels you use is to tape your lines. After listening to your tape, you can adjust your interpretation if any of your changes in volume are too great.
3. You may wish to use commercial recordings for some of your sound effects. You will probably find, however, that you can develop interesting and realistic effects yourself by experimenting with a variety of materials. Some of the most frequently used sound effects include doors opening and closing; a telephone ringing; a doorbell ringing; paper rattling; the clinking of dishes or glasses; the pouring of liquid; and the sound of a fire burning. (A book from the library on sound effects can give you many practical suggestions.)

Preparing and Presenting

Work with three or four other students. Select a scene from a novel, play, or short story to present in radio drama form. Your scene should have several characters with intense feelings and should be at least one-half dialogue. The scene should also contain some action and should take from three to five minutes to read aloud.

Make enough copies of your selection for everyone in your group. Your group should discuss the selection, identifying the action (what happens) and the emotions of each of the characters. Each group member should then choose one of the characters to portray. (Some selections may also require a narrator to give the audience necessary background information.) One group member should be responsible for music and sound effects.

Each person should then prepare a reading copy, marked to show the interpretation to be used for the character he or she will play. The group member working on sound effects and music should mark his or her reading copy to show where effects will be used and what they will be. The group should then meet to read through the play. They should make any changes needed in the actors' interpretations to make the action seem smoother or more logical. At this meeting the group should also decide whether the sound effects and music work for the scene and make any necessary changes.

During the next few days, group members should practice their parts. Someone should read through the entire scene several times with the sound effects person, so that that person can practice inserting music and sound effects at precisely the right moments.

After several days, the group should meet for a final rehearsal of the scene, including all music and sound effects. Rehearse the scene once. Then perform it a second time, and if possible, tape this second performance. If a tape recorder is not available, rehearse your scene twice.

Before the day you present your scene, make enough copies of your selection (in its original form, not the dramatic version) for everyone in the class.

Present your scene to the class by playing the tape you have made. If you did not make a tape, present your scene by performing it, complete with sound effects and music, behind a screen or from another room.

Evaluation Checklist

After each scene is performed, copies of the selection should be distributed to the class. After you have had time to read each scene, evaluate each radio drama on the basis of the following criteria. Rate each on a scale from 1 (Poor) to 5 (Excellent). Be prepared to give reasons for each rating you give. The questions in parentheses will help you do so.

Category	Rating
The group members . . . 1. Used vocal rate, pitch, and volume effectively to convey the emotions of the characters (Which of these three characteristics was used most effectively? Why?)	
2. Used their voices to help the audience grasp the action of the play (Where else in the scene should the actors have used their voices to help the audience understand the action?)	
3. Used sound effects that were appropriate and complete (Where else in the scene would you have used sound effects?)	
4. Used music in the scene for an appropriate purpose (How else do you think music could have been used in the scene?)	

Rehearsing and Presenting a Radio Drama

When your group presents a complete radio drama, you will need to use the techniques you learned in the previous lesson. They will help you decide how the actors should use their voices and what sound effects and music will work best in the play.

A complete drama, whether on the stage, on radio, or on television, will require several rehearsals. Rehearsals give the director a chance to be sure that all the elements of the play—the actors' interpretation of their characters, the narrator's delivery, the sound effects, and the music—will work effectively for a listening audience.

At the first rehearsal, the group should **decide on roles** and **distribute scripts**. The group should choose a director to keep the action coordinated and help the actors' interpretations mesh. Two or more group members should be chosen to handle sound effects and music. Then actors should be chosen for the different roles in the play. (Sometimes an actor may have to portray more than one character. When this happens, that person should develop a distinctive voice for each of the characters he or she portrays.)

The first rehearsal is also the time to provide group members with scripts. Your group may decide to present a published radio drama or may prefer to adapt a stage play or short story into a radio drama. In either case, each person should receive an identical copy of the final script. (Some groups prefer to number each line in the script, for easy reference during rehearsal.) Before the second rehearsal, each group member should **mark the script** to indicate his or her interpretation of the assigned role.

At the second rehearsal, the actors and narrator should **read the script aloud**. (If the sound effects person has any effects ready, he or she should supply these during the reading.) Words or phrases that are difficult to read should be changed at this rehearsal. If an actor's interpretation doesn't seem to fit the character, or if several actors' interpretations don't work well together, the director may want to guide the actors in changing their interpretations. At the end of the second rehearsal, the director should inform the entire group of the work to be done before the final rehearsal. The director may suggest that several actors work together to improve a particular scene. He or she may also suggest changes in sound effects or places where effects are needed.

At the final rehearsal, **final sound effects should be tested** and the **play timed**. If the play is running too long or too short, the director can adjust the actors' rate of delivery, the amount of narration, the length of music in the opening and closing scenes, or the sound effects to make the play fit the allotted time. At the final rehearsal, the sound effects person should also check to see that the microphones are functioning properly, so that the actors can work with them easily and the sound effects will come across as intended.

You should rehearse until your performance falls within fifteen to twenty seconds of the time allowed you. During the actual performance, the director can lengthen or shorten the performance time by signaling to the actors to speed up or slow down their delivery or by adjusting the length of musical interludes.

Working with the Model

Eight students have met to rehearse a radio play, their adaptation of the short story "The Open Window," by the English author Saki (H. H. Munro). Jessica is the director, and Luis is the narrator. Carl, Roger, Mona, Yvonne, Todd, and Cynthia play characters. Todd and Cynthia also double on sound effects.

At the first rehearsal, the group assigned roles and read through the script, marking their copies and discussing interpretations. By the second rehearsal, the students know their parts well, and most of the sound effects are ready. Jessica has already had the actors and narrator perform the first two pages of the script. Read this transcript of part of the rehearsal.

Jessica: Before we go on, I'd like to briefly review what we've done so far. "The Open Window" is set in England at about the turn of the century. You've all done your accents well. They're not 100 percent British, but I think they'll *suggest* the English upper classes to our listeners. The play opens with the narrator telling us about a young man with a silly name, Framton Nuttell. Framton has "bad nerves," as they used to say, and he has gone to the country to rest. His sister—that's you, Cynthia—has given him letters of introduction to several people.

Cynthia: Framton's sister has only five lines at the beginning of the play. After that, I go back over to sound effects.

Todd: Cynthia, do you think you can walk from the mike to the tape deck in time for the first sound cue?

Cynthia: Maybe not. Jess, what if Todd runs the tape of country noises—the birds, rustling leaves, and so on? Then I could do the doorbell effect that comes a few seconds later.

Jessica: Fine. That's Todd on tape, Cynthia on doorbell. Both of you mark it in your scripts.

Luis: While these effects are going on. I'm doing a voice-over. I tell how Framton is met at the door by ''a very self-possessed young lady of fifteen.''

Jessica: That ''self-possessed'' turns out to be very important, Luis, so be sure the audience hears it.

Luis: I remember: I'm to narrate everything in a clear, deadpan style.

Jessica: Yvonne, you play the girl who's named Vera.

Yvonne: *(as Vera)* ''My aunt will be down in a minute, Mr. Nuttell. In the meantime, you must try and put up with me.''

Carl: And Framton—that's me—feels very uncomfortable. This is the point where Vera starts telling him about her aunt.

Jessica: Right. Carl, don't make Framton sound *too* foolish. Remember, the audience has to identify with him if the story is going to work.

Carl: *(marking his script)* ''Embarrassed, but not too foolish.''

Jessica: Now, Yvonne, would you do Vera's big narrative speech— the one where she explains why her aunt keeps the French window open in the late afternoon?

Yvonne: *(as Vera)* ''Out through that window, three years ago to the day, her husband and her two young brothers went out for their day's shooting. They never came back.''

Jessica: Excuse me, Yvonne, but could you put a little more mystery into that last sentence?

Yvonne: *(as Vera)* "They never came back. In crossing the moor to their favorite snipe-shooting ground, they were all three engulfed in a treacherous piece of bog. Their bodies were never recovered. That was the dreadful part of it."

Jessica: Good. Lower your voice now—this has really got to grip the audience.

Yvonne: *(as Vera)* "Poor aunt always thinks they will come back some day—they and the little brown spaniel that was lost with them—and walk in at that window, just as they used to. That is why the window is kept open every evening till it is quite dusk. Poor dear aunt, she has often told me how they went out, her husband with his white waterproof coat over his arm, and Ronnie—her youngest brother—singing 'Bertie, why do you bound?' as he always did."

Jessica: Fine. Let's hear your voice tremble now.

Yvonne: *(as Vera)* "Do you know, sometimes on still, quiet evenings like this, I almost get a creepy feeling that they will all walk in through that window—"

Jessica: That's a sound cue.

(Cynthia opens door with sudden loud noise. Yvonne and Carl, as Vera and Framton, gasp.)

Jessica: Excellent!

Roger: That should knock the audience right out of their chairs.

Jessica: Now let's skip the next scene for the time being. The aunt comes in—that's you, Mona—and says hello to Framton. She tells him that her husband and brothers should be home any minute. Framton is horrified and tries to change the subject of conversation. He talks about his nerves instead, but the aunt is obviously bored and keeps looking out the window. Suddenly—Mona, will you take the speech?

Mona: *(as the aunt)* "Oh! Here they are at last! Just in time for tea—and don't they look as if they are muddy up to the eyes!"

Luis: *(as narrator)* "Framton shivered and turned toward the niece with a look of sympathy. But the girl was staring out through the open window with dazed horror in her eyes. Framton swung round in his seat and looked in the same direction. . . ."

Carl: *(as Framton)* gasps and moans of terror.

Luis: *(as narrator)* "In the deepening twilight, three figures were walking across the lawn toward the window. They all carried guns under their arms, and one of them had a white coat over his shoulder. A tired brown spaniel kept close at their heels."

Jessica: Roger, let's hear that distant voice.

Roger: *(muffling his voice)* "I said, Bertie, why do you bound?"

Carl: *(as Framton)* "No! No!"

Jessica: Sound cue!

(Todd and Cynthia make sound of furniture being knocked over. Todd runs tape of footsteps running along hall, door opening, and footsteps running away down gravel path.)

Jessica: Five seconds' silence—time it.

(Todd imitates heavy footsteps on the floor.)

Todd: *(as the aunt's husband)* "Here we are, my dear! Fairly muddy, but most of it's dry. Who was that who bolted out as we came up?"

Mona: *(as the aunt)* "A most extraordinary man . . . could only talk about his illness and dashed off without a word of apology. One would think he had seen a ghost."

Yvonne: *(as Vera)* "I expect it was the dog. He told me he had a horror of dogs. He was once hunted into a cemetery on the banks of the Ganges by a pack of pariah dogs and had to spend the night in a newly dug grave, with the creatures snarling and grinning and foaming just above him. Enough to make anyone lose their nerve."

Jessica: Okay, narrator, give us the punchline.

Luis: *(as narrator)* "Romance at short notice was her specialty."

Jessica: Great, just great. But I wonder about that word "romance."

Cynthia: Yes, some people might think it means "love story" instead of "adventure."

Luis: Why don't we change it to "drama"?

Jessica: Good. Does anyone object? All right, everybody change your scripts.

Roger: Also, I'm not sure many listeners will know what "pariah" dogs are. Shouldn't we change it to "wild"?

Jessica: I think so. Do we all agree on that? Change "pariah" to "wild" in Vera's last speech.

Mona: Todd, did I catch the sound of an automobile on your last tape?

(Todd reruns tape.)

Carl: Yes, there it is, behind the running footsteps. That doesn't belong in the English countryside of 1900.

Jessica: Todd, can you record another thirty seconds of footsteps, minus the cars?

Todd: Sure, I'll do it before the final rehearsal.

Jessica: Fine. Let's take a break now, and then we can run through the play again, without interruption.

A. Think about what the group accomplished at its *first* rehearsal.
   1. How did the students divide the work of presenting the play?
   2. What did they do with their scripts during the first rehearsal?
   3. What non-spoken part of the play was prepared between the first and second rehearsals?
B. Think about what the group accomplished during its *second* rehearsal.
   1. What does Jessica do to help the actors understand their parts?
   2. What change in responsibility is made at this rehearsal?
   3. What changes in interpretation are made at this rehearsal?
   4. What technical error is noticed at this rehearsal? When will it be corrected?
C. Think about how the students use their scripts at this rehearsal.
   1. In whose script is the change in the sound effects assignment marked?
   2. In whose script is a change in interpretation marked?
   3. What changes were made in the narration and dialogue of the scripts? Why were these changes made? In whose scripts were they made? Why are these particular changes so important?

D. Think about the work the group will have to complete during this rehearsal and the final rehearsal.
    1. What will occur at the two rehearsals?
    2. What changes in the script do you think the students might make at the final rehearsal?
    3. What changes in sound effects do you think the students might make?
    4. What kind of music, if any, do you think would be appropriate for this play? At what points in the play would you use it?
E. Read Saki's short story "The Open Window." Compare the original story with the portions of the script that were read at the rehearsal. Think about the difference between the printed story and the radio version. Think about how *you* would adapt the story for radio.

Guidelines

Follow this checklist to be sure you complete all the necessary steps when rehearsing a radio play or other drama.

First rehearsal

____ Distribution of scripts to cast and crew

____ Talk by director, explaining play and production

____ Assignment of roles to actors (including doubling, if necessary)

____ Assignment of music and sound effects to crew (who may also be actors)

____ First reading of the script, to answer questions and understand basic interpretation

Second rehearsal *(or as many intermediate rehearsals as are necessary)*

____ Performance of the script, in character and with music and sound effects, if available

____ Explanation by director of motivation, interpretation, and timing

____ Marking of scripts to indicate any changes in interpretation

____ Changing of scripts when necessary for dramatic effect

Final rehearsal

_____ Performance of script in final form, with complete music and sound effects

_____ Checking and adjustment of microphones, speakers, tape recorders, and other equipment

_____ Timing of performance to within fifteen to twenty seconds of allotted time

Preparing and Presenting

Working with four to six other students, prepare a script for a radio drama. Your script may be an expanded version of the scene you prepared in the previous lesson, or it may be an adaptation of a play, short story, or scene from a novel. The play should communicate the action through voice, narration, sound, and music. It should last about ten minutes.

Rehearse the play, following the directions given in this lesson. (If the cast is large and roles cannot be doubled, you may need to add more students to your group.) Time the play and tell the class how long you expect it to take. Present your play either by playing a tape recording or by acting it in front of a microphone in another room.

Evaluation Checklist

After copies of each original scene are distributed to the class, evaluate each radio drama on the basis of the following criteria. Rate it on a scale from 1 (Poor) to 5 (Excellent). Be prepared to give reasons for each answer you give. The questions in parentheses will help you do so.

Category	Rating
1. The cast conveyed the setting well through sound, dialogue, and narration. (How could information about the setting have been better conveyed?)	
2. The cast conveyed the action of the play well through sound and dialogue. (Did the play rely excessively on narration? How could the action have been better conveyed?)	
3. The characters in the play were well distinguished by their voices and dialogue. (How could the presentation of different characters have been improved? If some roles were doubled by the same actors, how easily could the characters be told apart?)	
4. The use of music was effective. (What music could be changed, added, or deleted to make the play more effective?)	
5. The sound effects were appropriate, clear, and convincing. (What effects could be changed, added, or deleted to make the play more effective?)	
6. The performance time was close to the announced time. (Should the performance have been paced differently? What material, if any, could have been added or deleted to bring the performance closer to the ideal length?)	

Combining Images and Sound in a Television Script

Some contemporary experts believe that words provide only part of the total message communicated in any given speaking situation. Voice tones, facial expressions, gestures, the speaker's reputation, and other factors also contribute to the speaker's message. If these factors are important in a normal speaking situation, they are even more important in television. In a speech the spoken word is the primary means of communication. The basic language of television, however, is the picture. People who create television productions often consider visual images and nonverbal sounds the foremost means of communication. Words are used to supplement and clarify pictures—not the other way around. Radio scripts include directions for sound effects in parentheses. Television scripts reflect the importance of visual images. Such scripts are usually prepared in parallel columns with the directions for those operating cameras and other equipment on the left and the narrative on the right.

Scripts for different kinds of television productions are prepared in different ways. A documentary or dramatic production may be written in full with all spoken and visual material included as in the models. A script for a commercial is likely to include a storyboard with the video images drawn in sequence down the left side of the script and the accompanying narration on the right side. Newscasts may include detailed instructions and narration for the studio crew but refer to interviews or on-site portions with coded symbols.

Advanced planning varies also. Some advocate that, because television is a visual medium, the composition of a story to be televised should begin with the gathering of pictures—using only a general outline of the story to guide the photographers. Others suggest a more structured approach, with the narrative developed along with the visuals. The popularity of song videos has encouraged many producers to approach the creation of short productions with very limited scripting in advance.

Working with the Model

In order to understand how television production works, you must first become familiar with its terminology and techniques. Many of the terms have come from or are used in other media, but the definitions below apply to television. These definitions will enable you to communicate in the language of television and prepare you for writing a television script.

Techniques	Abbreviations	Definitions
Close-up	CU TCU ECU	A close shot that allows for one individual, usually from the shoulders up; a *tight close-up* (TCU) and an *extreme close-up* (ECU) are each progressively closer to the subject.
Medium Shot	MS	Includes a figure to the waist; sometimes allows enough width to include two figures in the same picture; also known as *two-shot*.
Long Shot	LS ELS	Includes the figure or figures in relation to their surroundings; the entire figure may be shown from head to foot; an extreme long shot (ELS) is a view from a considerable distance.
Angle		Viewpoint from which the shot is taken, usually from above or below a subject; shooting from below subject causes it to look larger and is called a *low angle shot*; shots from above a subject are *high angle shots.*
Wide Angle	WA	Includes a broad horizontal view.
Reverse Angle		A view of the subject from the opposite direction from which it has just been seen; can be a 180 degree change in camera view from the preceding shot, but in television it is usually less than 180 degrees so that one camera will not show the other.
Establishing Shot	ES	A long shot used to orient the viewer to the surroundings and to establish the relationship of subject to the other elements in the scene; also known as a *cover shot*.
Point of View	POV	The position from which a shot is taken.

Over-the-Shoulder Shot	OS	Looks at one subject framed by the back of the head and shoulder of another subject in the foreground; commonly used in a pair of reverse angle shots covering a conversation between two people.
Dolly		To move the entire camera on a platform in order to follow action or achieve a change in perspective; or the wheeled platform for a television camera.
Pan		To turn the camera in a horizontal plane while it is in one place in order to follow the subject or to change the view of the subject; a *swish pan* is one that is too fast to keep the image clear.
Tilt		To move the camera up and down on a vertical plane while it is kept in one place. (The camera *pans* left and right, *tilts* up and down.)
Zoom		To use a special lens to enlarge a subject, making it appear closer without moving the camera.
Cut		An abrupt change from one scene to another; also frequently called a *take* in television.
Fade		The gradual disappearance of a scene as it ends.
Dissolve	DISS	A gradual transition between scenes by fading out one picture and fading in its replacement.
Wipe		To move one scene in as another scene moves out without overlapping; usually the scene moves in from the left and out to the right.
Videocassette Recorder	VCR	Machine used to record television programs from a receiver; can also play back programs, movies, etc.
Edit		To put together on one tape the desired production footage and any special effects in final program form.

Talent	Any person who appears in front of the camera.

The following are excerpts from a script prepared for an instructional videotape produced to teach viewers how to operate a video edit control unit.

A.

Name   J. A. Smith   Production "Using Edit"
Date   9/12/88
Page 1 of 4

Video	**Audio**
MS (Show entire control unit)	Narrator: LET US ASSUME THE IN-CUE ON THE SOURCE MACHINE HAS ALREADY BEEN SET UP, AND THE OUT-CUE HAS JUST BEEN ESTABLISHED WITH THE SEARCH CONTROLS ON THE RE-CORD MACHINE. NOW YOU ARE READY TO ACTIVATE THE EDIT MODE CONTROLS. THE PREVIEW EDIT BUTTON IS FIRST DE-PRESSED. . . .

B.

Name   J. A. Smith   Production ''Using Edit''
Date   9/13/88
Page 1 of 4

Video	**Audio**
MS (show entire machine) CUT TO:	
CU (show finger pointing to button)	Narrator: LET'S ASSUME YOU'VE SET UP YOUR IN-CUE ON THE SOURCE MACHINE HERE.
CU (Finger pointing)	AND YOU JUST FINISHED ESTAB-LISHING YOUR OUT-CUE OVER HERE ON THE RECORD MA-CHINE.
CU (Finger pointing)	NOW YOU ARE READY TO WORK HERE.
ECU (Finger pushes button)	FIRST, YOU PUSH THE PREVIEW EDIT BUTTON. . . .

A. Compare the two excerpts.
   1. Which script includes more direction in the video portion and more details in the audio portion?
   2. How do *A* and *B* scripts differ, then, in overall effectiveness?
B. Compare the language of the two scripts.
   1. Which one uses the active voice and which uses the passive voice?
   2. Which one uses contractions? Why do you suppose the author chose to use them?
   3. Script *B* uses more informal language, more common words. The author chose to speak of ''pushing'' the button rather than ''depressing'' it, for example. Do you think it was a good choice? Why?
   4. What words in the audio portion of *B* are dependent on the video portion for their clarity? Are there any words in *A* with a similar reliance on the video instructions? Which audio portion, therefore, more clearly parallels the video portion?
C. Discuss instructional videotapes and films you have watched.
   1. Describe examples of instances in which the pictures and words have worked together as in example *B*.
   2. Describe examples in which the person making the film (or tape) relied on the words and did not make good use of visual images. What images could have been used?

Guidelines

When preparing a script for a video production, keep the following suggestions in mind.

1. Use a format similar to the one in the model. Identify the specific production, your name, and the date. Include video and sound instructions in the left-hand column, language to be spoken in the right-hand column.
2. Type (or print) major directions and text in capital letters.

3. Use words to supplement and clarify pictures—not the other way around. The language of television is the picture, not the spoken word.
4. Write in the active voice. Make the subjects of your verbs the actors, not the recipients of the actions.
5. Use informal, conversational language. Use contractions, simple sentences, and common but exact words.

Preparing and Presenting

Work with a team of at least six other students. Write a six-minute script that will explain to an outsider something that is happening at your school. It might be a class-related event, a student activity, the achievement of an individual, or the accomplishment of some group of students.

Prepare a general script using the same format as in the models in this lesson. Be careful to limit your subject to something that can be adequately reported in no more than six minutes. After each group has completed its script, exchange scripts with another group and discuss the results.

Evaluation Checklist

Evaluate the other group's script on the basis of the following criteria. Rate each script on a scale from 1 (Poor) to 5 (Excellent). Be prepared to give reasons for each rating you give.

Category	Rating
The script . . . 1. Followed the basic format given in the models	
2. Used capital letters for major direction and text	
3. Used words and images that complement each other to effectively communicate the intended message	
4. Was written in the active voice	
5. Used informal, direct, conversational language	

Communicating Visual Ideas in a Shot Sheet

Once the script for a television production is finished, the director marks the script to indicate what shots will be needed, what instructions the other crew members will need, and what cues the talent will need. Usually the director will make detailed notes and instructions on the script using standard symbols and abbreviations.

After the director has marked the script, then he or she can prepare the **camera shot sheet**, the detailed instructions for the camera operators to follow during the taping. This compact sheet describes every shot that will be taken. The description includes the content of the shot, its type and length, and the sound to be included. The shot sheet also gives the movement from shot to shot and the exact sequence of shots. The shot sheet is usually small enough for the camera operators to attach to the backs of their cameras during the actual taping. Such a

precise plan requires the director to carefully visualize the script, to translate the actual words and ideas on paper into the images and sounds that would best convey meaning, action, and mood of the script.

Working with the Model

The model shot sheet below will give you an idea of how invaluable a guide the shot sheet can be. Notice that even something as simple as a few lines from a nursery rhyme can be much more complicated to break down than one would expect.

Camera Shot Sheet

Name _Karen Henderson_   Production _"Mary Had a Little Lamb" Animation_

Date _11/4/87_   Tape # _1_   Page _1_ of _1_

Length of Shot	Shot Type	Description	Audio
2.5 sec.	ES	Establish outside of Mary's house in morning	Music
3 sec.	LS	Zoom to long shot of Mary and lamb leaving side by side	Mary had a little lamb,
2 sec.	ECU	Cut to extreme close-up of lamb's face, showing white fleece, pink ribbon	its fleece was white as snow,
2 sec.	MS	Cut to panning medium shot of Mary walking down sidewalk, carrying school books	and everywhere that Mary went,
1.5 sec.	CU	Cut to close-up of lamb smiling and winking into camera	the lamb was sure to go.
1.5 sec.	MS	Cut to Mary, smiling down at lamb, from lamb's POV	Music
2 sec.	LS	Cut to long shot of Mary and lamb from behind, walking into horizon; fade to black	Music

A. Think about the model shot sheet.
   1. What is the purpose of the shot sheet?
   2. Why is the establishing shot first?
   3. Does the extreme close-up shot of the lamb seem necessary? Why or why not?
   4. Why do you think the director chose to pan on Mary walking down the sidewalk? Why might this camera movement be effective for this kind of action?
   5. Did the director plan a variety of shots, each appropriate to the audio portion?
   6. What shots might have been added or omitted? What purpose would each new shot serve?
   7. Why do you think the director chose to fade to black in the last shot? What is the effect of such a technique?

Guidelines

When you prepare a shot sheet, you are outlining and organizing the entire television shooting production. Therefore, the shot sheet must be clear, accurate, and thorough. Keep in mind the following pointers.

1. Enter the camera shots in the proper sequential order.
2. Include shots of subjects or of action that closely parallel the audio portion.
3. Include all necessary shots so that the audience can easily follow your message or story.
4. Use a variety of shots so that the audience will not become bored, but don't arbitrarily choose shots. Each camera shot should be the best one to convey that particular idea or image.
5. Include enough information about what shot is needed in the Description section so that the various members of the crew will have enough information to plan their tasks.
6. Try not to include any shots that are unnecessary or that might disorient or confuse the audience.
7. Try to estimate the length of each shot, but keep in mind that when you actually begin shooting, you may have to make adjustments.

Preparing and Presenting

In groups of three or more, prepare a Camera Shot Sheet following the one in the model. You might base it upon another nursery rhyme, an action poem, or even a short excerpt from a story. Your shot sheet need not have seven shots as in the model, but be sure to include at least four to eight shots that clearly and logically convey in images the text of the audio portion. Try to include as many of the following shots as possible to ensure variety.

1. A long shot (LS)
2. A medium shot (MS)
3. A close-up (CU)
4. An extreme close-up (ECU)
5. A pan following someone who is moving
6. A high angle shot
7. A low angle shot
8. A zoom
9. A dollying shot
10. An over-the-shoulder shot

As a way of checking and revising your shot sheet, you might consult the Evaluation Checklist below before you write your shot sheet in its final form.

Evaluation Checklist

One student from each group should read or present the shot sheet to the other members of the class. Evaluate the sheets on the basis of the following criteria. Rate them on a scale from 1 (Poor) to 5 (Excellent). Be prepared to give reasons for each rating you give.

Category	Rating
The camera shot sheet . . . 1. Includes shots that are in a logical sequence	
2. Shows action that closely parallels the audio portion	
3. Includes enough shots so that the audience could easily follow the message or story	
4. Adequately explains each shot in the Description column	
5. Includes a variety of shots so that the end product will be interesting to watch	
6. Does not include any unnecessary shots	
7. Does not include any confusing or disorienting shots	

Producing a Television Script

Television production is very much a group process. The job simply cannot be done without the cooperation and contributions of all of the crew members, from the producer and director to the grip, or stage-hand. Each person has a specific role to perform. Because so many people contribute to a complex production, each of them must clearly understand his or her roles and responsibilities.

Working with the Model

Television production requires people to perform skillfully in a variety of jobs and to use equipment to produce the sounds and images that are called for by the script. The following are the major roles in a creative production team.

Producer: The boss; provides creative control for the entire production; sets the budget, hires the director and other major crew members, and provides direction to all members of the team.

Director: Interprets the script; provides instructions to all technical and talent members of the team to carry out the script. (In a small studio, producer and director may be one person.)

Associate Director: Times program; directs background action; lays out floor plans for rehearsals; makes sure all have scripts; presets camera shots; gives cues to the director.

Camera Operator: Operates the camera; takes cues from the director and/or the camera shot sheet.

Floor Manager: Makes sure people and things are in proper places; prompts actors; maintains schedules; arranges for facilities.

Production Assistant: Does everything from making up cue cards to handling artwork; takes care of the details.

The actual televised program of course requires the coordination of other departments too, such as casting, production services, settings, art, special effects, costumes, props, music, and sound. The roles defined above, however, are the ones most closely involved with the shooting of the program.

In addition to the cameras and editing equipment, there are several other vital pieces of equipment.

Mike Boom: A microphone suspended from a long horizontal arm, usually suspended above and in front of the performer.

Lavaliere: A very small microphone that can be worn around the neck or clipped onto a piece of clothing; also called a *neck mike.*

Switcher: A mixing panel that allows scenes from more than one camera to be included on a tape without blank spaces showing on the tape. (This word can also mean the person who operates the video switches, usually the *technical director,* or TD.)

Mixer: An electronic panel that permits sound and video images to be added from different sources while maintaining even levels of sound, brightness, and focus.

Video tape recorder: VTR; a recording machine that records video, audio, and control signals on videotape.

The following steps will give you a total perspective of the way a production is put together. Usually these chronological steps are followed once an accepted draft of the script, or the final script itself, is given to the director.

1. **Preproduction planning:** Script breakdown; securing the facility and equipment; hiring the cast and crew.
2. **Rehearsal:** There are several kinds of rehearsals—*blocking,* or the planning of movement and the physical placement of talent, cameras, and production equipment; technical rehearsal; control room rehearsal; run-through; and dress rehearsal.
3. **Production:** The actual shooting of the television program.
4. **Postproduction:** Editing; mixing; inserting graphics, art, music, and pick-up shots (which take the place of a blunder), etc.

A. Think about the responsibilities of the production team.
   1. Which person usually has the most creative control of the entire production? Why do you think so?
   2. If a director has thoroughly prepared and has inspired confidence and cooperation in the entire crew, the production should run fairly smoothly. What kinds of skills and qualities do you think a good director needs?
   3. Which person times the program? Why is this an important responsibility in television?
   4. Which person has more direct contact with the actors/talent and props in most productions? Who do you think he or she is most likely in close contact with on the set?
   5. If the writer or director makes a last-minute change in the script, who might make sure that the cue cards are revised? Name another task for which this person is responsible.

B. Think about the steps of a television production.
   1. What might be some results of poor preproduction planning?
   2. If a light needs to be reset or a camera angle changed, during which step is this likely to occur? Why? If the actors have a question about the script, during which step should they ask it? Why?
   3. When shooting a television show, *continuity,* or the logical flow of images with each shot having a clear relationship to the one that precedes it and the one that follows it, is most important. How can the director better ensure that continuity exists and that the actual shooting runs smoothly?
   4. Videotape editing allows the director to shoot scenes in the most convenient order and to assemble them in their proper sequence in postproduction. What might be some reasons why scenes would be shot out of chronological order?

C. Try to visit a local television station or cable station and observe a studio rehearsal or live air show. Ask if you can borrow a marked script. If the technical director or floor manager has time, ask a few brief questions about the markings they use, the division of responsibilities, and their on-air procedures.

Guidelines

When you are taping your script, try to keep in mind the following pointers.

1. Stick to the script. Don't include any shots that aren't called for specifically by your final script unless you have a good reason to do so.
2. Carefully plan your camera shots so that you include a variety of shots in a logical order to best convey the ideas intended.
3. Make sure the audio portion is clear, distinct, and audible. Try to avoid shooting in a crowded, noisy place, such as a traffic intersection.
4. Use available light (natural light) as much as possible. When necessary tape in a very well-lit room.
5. Keep in mind the audience and what you want them to see and hear. Everything you shoot should be geared toward the overall purpose you decided upon when you wrote the script.
6. Remember that television production requires teamwork.

Preparing and Presenting

Working with the same team that wrote the television script, produce a six-minute videotape of that script. The various roles and tasks of the taping should be divided among the group. One student should take the role of producer/director. Others will have responsibility for such specific tasks as operating the camera, operating the VTR, and performing talent roles called for by the script. Rehearse carefully so that all members of the team know what is expected of them. If you have equipment available that permits editing outside of the camera, use that equipment to polish the production.

Each team should show its tape to the class. Then, if editing equipment is available, arrange all of the tapes in a single program that can be shown to a broader audience in the school.

A local television news producer may be available to help you with the process of putting the different episodes together. Watching a network show such as *60 Minutes* or a locally produced magazine show may give you some ideas for putting your tapes together.

Evaluation Checklist

Evaluate each videotape on the basis of the following criteria. Rate each on a scale from 1 (Poor) to 5 (Excellent). Be prepared to give reasons for each rating you give.

Category	Rating
1. The words and the images portrayed on the screen complement each other and led to effective communication of the intended message.	
2. The pictures show that the team understood the different kinds of camera shots and did an effective job of planning them.	
3. The team was careful to include a variety of shots, all of which were appropriately matched to the text or action.	
4. The audio was clear and audible.	
5. The scene was well lit—not too bright or too dark.	

Chapter 12 Review

Summary

Putting on an effective radio drama is an exciting challenge because performers use only sound to convey all of the elements of the play—scenery, mood, action, and character's emotions. Performers vary their vocal rate, pitch, and volume to convey the action of the story as well as their interpretation of the characters. Sound effects and music can greatly enhance the impact of a performance. They help the audience understand the play as well as make the action seem more real.

Television incorporates most of the production techniques of three older media: stage, film, and radio. Because television uses visual images as well as words, music, and sound effects, it can be an extremely powerful means of communication. However, images are far more crucial to communication in television than in most other media. The spoken language, sound effects, and music support and clarify the image, but it is the image that primarily communicates ideas in television. Writing a television script and a camera shot sheet give you practice in linking sound and images to communicate a unified message. Producing a video gives you experience in role playing the various positions on a production staff, using the equipment, and actually communicating an intended message. If you learn how television works and what it can do, you can communicate quite powerfully, whether your goal is to inform, educate, or entertain your audience.

Reviewing Vocabulary

Number your paper from 1 to 16. Next to each number , write the letter of the group of words that correctly defines the word(s).

1. radio drama
2. mike boom
3. tilt
4. close-up
5. producer
6. fade
7. production
8. POV
9. talent
10. camera shot sheet
11. director
12. wide angle
13. pan
14. zoom
15. VTR
16. dolly

a. the position from which a shot is taken
b. any person who appears in front of the camera
c. the detailed instructions for the camera operators to follow
d. the person who interprets the script and instructs the crew
e. the oral interpretation of a poem, story, or play for dramatic presentation over the radio
f. to turn the camera in a horizontal plane
g. a microphone suspended from a long horizontal arm
h. a recording machine that records video, audio, and control signals on videotape
i. a very close camera shot of the subject, usually from the shoulders up
j. the gradual disappearance of a scene as it ends

k. the actual shooting of a television program

l. the person who provides creative control for the entire production

m. to move the entire camera on a platform to follow action

n. a shot that includes a broad horizontal view

o. to use a special lens to enlarge a subject without moving the camera

p. to move the camera up and down on a vertical plane

Reviewing Facts and Ideas

1. How can varying your rate of speaking, pitch, and volume convey a character's emotions?
2. How are sound effects and music important in radio dramas?
3. Why is it important to mark your script before presenting a radio drama?
4. Who is responsible for guiding the actors' interpretations of their characters and keeping the actions of a radio drama coordinated? Why is this role important?
5. What is the primary means of communication in television? What is the relationship between spoken words and images in a television production?
6. What kind of language should you use in a television script? Why?
7. What is a camera shot sheet? Why is it important to carefully plot out camera shots before taping?
8. Who is responsible for making sure that all television crew members work together smoothly and efficiently?
9. Who makes most of the decisions regarding the technical aspects of a television show and the execution of the script?
10. What are some activities carried out in the rehearsal step? Why is this step so important to a successful production?

Discussing Facts and Ideas

1. There are many tapes of old radio dramas available. Obtain one and listen to it as a class. Discuss the way in which music and sound effects are used to convey images in this particular drama.
2. Some have suggested that television does not contribute to the development of imagination the way radio does. Decide whether you agree or disagree and give reasons for your opinion.
3. Certain television programs have been so successful that their reruns continue to receive high ratings. Discuss what qualities cause these programs to remain popular for such a long time.

Applying Your Knowledge

1. Local cable television companies usually have public access channels on which nonprofessionals can air programs. Work with a cable company in your community to produce a program. You may want to develop a show focusing on some unique program in your school. You may want to take a topic of local interest, such as a proposal for a new park, and do an interview show in which you interview a panel of local officials.
2. You may have viewed the one-minute introductions to college campuses that are aired during the broadcasts of football or basketball games. Work with a crew of students to prepare a similar promotional presentation about your school. When you are satisfied with it, see if you can get a local station or cable company to broadcast it. (Before beginning the taping, check with the stations to see what tape format you will have to use to enable them to broadcast it.)

Problem Solving

Whether as a student, as a worker, or as a member of your community, you need to be able to work with other people in order to solve problems. Often a problem will arouse strong emotions in people, and it is important that you be able to discuss it without quarreling. Here are guidelines to follow when working with others to solve a problem.

- When the group is organized, it should include people who have different interests or attitudes toward the problem. To solve a job-related problem, for example, shop or clerical workers, supervisors, salespeople, and managers might work together.
- Be sure each participant knows enough about the problem to be able to contribute ideas to the group.
- Follow the steps in the problem-solving sequence. (See pages 53–54.) Be sure to answer all the questions in each step before going on to the next step.
- Keep the group's discussion focused on the problem at hand, rather than on other problems or complaints.
- Don't let personality conflicts intrude on the discussion of the problem.

Activities

1. Work with several other students. Ask each student to identify the one or two most important problems facing the school. Select the problem that seems most complicated or that causes the greatest difference of opinion. Work with the other students to find a solution to this problem.
2. Ask several people to identify the most important problem that faces your community. Include people of different ages, occupations, and backgrounds in this group. Select one problem and meet with these people (if your teacher approves) or with other students to find a solution.

Presenting an Award

When you are asked to present an award, you will be expected to "say a few words" about the award and its recipient. The important thing to remember is to be brief and to focus attention on the receiver of the award, not yourself.

Plan to deliver your speech extemporaneously—reading a speech tends to make you seem unenthusiastic or even insincere. Tell the audience about the history and significance of the award and describe the qualifications and achievements of the recipient. Praise the recipient warmly and sincerely, but not to such lengths as to embarrass him or her. Finish by expressing your congratulations and best wishes.

Activity

1. Prepare and deliver a presentation speech for one of the following awards (or for an award of your choice).

   - a trophy for the varsity football team's most valuable player
   - a book for the winner of a short-story contest for high school students
   - a certificate for first prize in your school's science fair
   - an "Oscar" for the best performer in your school's play
   - a plaque for the student with the most creative shop project
   - an award for the student who put in the most volunteer hours at the local hospital
   - an award for the most unselfish student in the school

CHAPTER 13

Drama

After working through this chapter, you should have begun to develop proficiency in the following skills:

Lesson	Skills
Lesson 1	• improvising
Lesson 2	• developing a character
Communicating on the Job	• reading a speech or report written by someone else
Communicating as a Citizen	• role playing to understand communication problems

Improvisation

Effective dramatic performance requires an actor to react skillfully to the dramatic situation created by the author, to the other characters, and to the setting. In some respects, to paraphrase rather loosely Shakespeare's observation of several centuries ago, we are all players on the stage of life. One basic means we have of adapting to our environment is to improvise: to react on the spur of the moment with actions that respond to the changes on the stage that is our life. In drama, **improvisation** is defined as a process of presenting physical actions, including speech, without practice or rehearsal.

Improvisation developed into a dramatic form of its own in the 1950s. However, improvisation can make significant contributions to the development of basic acting skills needed by those who are interested in performing more traditional forms of drama. Effective improvisation requires actors to concentrate on a **problem**, the specific task addressed in the scene through which they reveal *who* they are, *where* they are, and *what* they are doing. When you improvise, you do not preplan what you will do in a scene. You concentrate on the problem and on reacting to the setting and the others in the setting.

Working with the Model

Consider the following examples of improvisation. In both instances the *where* for the scenes was a corner bus stop and the *who* was a young or old person. The *what* was simply that the actors were waiting for a bus. The **focus**, or point of concentration, for each actor was to represent the age of the person waiting for the bus.

Scene 1

The first actor skips on stage, chewing gum. He glances around, sees nothing, and begins to blow bubbles with his gum. He gets the gum stuck on his nose, cleans up the sticky mess with his tongue and finger, and glances down the street—still seeing nothing. He spins around, catches sight of shop windows, goes to them, and peers in, pressing his hands against the glass. He sees a passerby and asks her when the next bus is due. He moves downstage (toward the front of the stage), blowing more bubbles with his gum, and fumbles in his pocket looking for something. He cannot find it at first. A quick search in his coat pocket ends with a smile as he pulls out a yo-yo and begins to twirl it. Suddenly he looks up and sees the bus coming. Frantically he tries to control the yo-yo, return it to his pocket, and find the bus fare.

Scene 2

The second actor comes on stage with a firm, aggressive stride. Her right hand is gripping something by a handle. She glances down the street, sees nothing coming, and sits down on the bench. She puts on her lap what she has been carrying and opens it in such a way that we recognize it as a briefcase. She thumbs through a few sections of the case, pulls out a folder, extracts a page from the folder, glances at it, and frowns. She looks through the briefcase again, finds a pen, clicks the point, and makes notes on the page she had been examining. As she writes, she looks up nervously, wondering where the bus is. Impatiently she returns the paper and folder to the briefcase, closes the case, and sets it on the ground next to her. Spotting a passerby, she asks if he has a schedule so she can check when the next bus is due. She accepts the schedule he offers her with a mumbled thanks, glances at it, looks at her watch, and rather distractedly returns it to the passerby. She notices the store windows behind the bus stop, uses them to adjust her skirt and pat her hair in place. As she is doing this, she hears the bus coming. Quickly she heads for the curb, remembering at the last moment the briefcase she had left by the bench.

In order to bring the written description of these scenes alive, watch as several students enact them before the class. The students should provide not an exact replication of the scene as described but a general interpretation of the two people of different ages waiting for a bus. Use their actions and your understanding of the written descriptions above as the basis for answering these questions.

A. Think about the age each of the actors was portraying.
   1. What were the clues in the first scene that revealed age (as compared to those that revealed the person was waiting for a bus, etc.)?
   2. How old did you think the first person was? What actions would you add or delete to make the person five years older or five years younger?
   3. What was the age of the person in the second scene? What would you do to depict her as 30 years older?

B. An improvisation should follow a logical sequence.
   1. Describe the actions in the first scene that represent the beginning, the development, and the ending of the sequence.
   2. Work with another student to develop a revised version of scene two by including a different beginning action and a different ending action. Concentrate on preserving the character's age in this scene as you originally perceived it.

C. An improvisation may involve a number of different kinds of responses by an actor.
  1. Identify those actions that appeared to be responses to sensory stimulation—that is, those that demonstrated the actor's response to sight, sound, taste, feel, or smell. If the actions seem to leave out some of the senses, think about how they could have been incorporated.
  2. Identify those actions that included the use of real or imagined physical objects. The scenes could be played with real briefcases and bubble gum. How might using real objects change the actor's performance? Would those props limit or expand the ability of the actor to use imagination? Why do you think so?

Guidelines

The improvisational scenes in the model involved basically only one character. You should progress beyond such scenes to ones in which you work with other students to solve a group problem. As you do so, you will learn to (1) keep your attention on the problem and its focus, (2) relate to the others with whom you are working, and (3) work cooperatively to solve the group's problem.

As you engage in improvisation, keep the following in mind.

1. Relax and focus your body and awareness on the activity.
2. Use all five of your senses to accomplish the task.
3. Use your entire body. Facial expressions, changes in posture, hand and arm gestures, and movement all contribute.
4. When using imaginary objects, concentrate on details and exaggerate the way you deal with them so that others can understand what you are doing.
5. Think of why you are doing what you are doing and why the other persons in the scene are doing what they are doing. React to the situation and to their actions.
6. Think of the setting in which you are acting. React naturally to it. For example, if your scene occurs in a fine restaurant, react as you would in that setting. If the scene is occurring in a cafeteria, alter your actions accordingly.
7. Move the actions of an improvisation forward in a logical sequence: (a) Make the problem apparent and begin to deal with it. (b) Develop the action. (c) End the action, making it clear how you have dealt with the problem.

Preparing and Presenting

Work with four students to perform an improvisation. In order to prepare for this activity, work with your teacher and other members of the class to develop a viewing list of television programs. Include five to ten programs on your list and try to watch each program at least twice. You may decide during your planning that there are ten programs that all of you watch frequently enough that additional watching is not necessary.

Your team will be the major characters in a television program. Your teacher will have the remote control that turns on the channel on which you will be performing. For example, the teacher may tell you that the channel has just been turned to an episode of *The Cosby Show* dealing with Bill's dieting problem. Quickly you will decide which of you plays which part. Then one will begin an action that would be typical of what might be observed on that show. Others of you will react to that action. Later the teacher may change the channel so that you are doing a scene from a *Star Trek* episode featuring a loss of power on the *Enterprise*. In each case you will have to deal with the *who*, *where*, and *what* of the scene in a way that reveals you have become the members of that specific cast and are reacting as they would react.

Evaluation Checklist

Evaluate the group improvisations on the basis of the following criteria. Rate them on a scale from 1 (Poor) to 5 (Excellent). Be prepared to give reasons for each rating you give. The questions in parentheses will help you do so.

Category	Rating
The actors . . . 1. Solved the problem they presented	
2. Concentrated on the problem, their characters, the setting, and what they were doing (Did they appear to be thinking of you as an audience or of some problem other than the one presented to them?)	
3. Communicated with each other as they improvised	
4. Concentrated on "being" the characters from the television program rather than "telling" about them	
5. Were reacting to each other (Did they listen to what each other said and react to the nonverbal messages sent?)	
6. Were relaxed and enjoyed themselves	
7. Made use of all five senses	
8. Used effective bodily movement	

Characterization

Characterization is the essence of acting. It is the creative process whereby the actor grasps the fundamental personality of the role he or she is portraying and communicates it to the audience, making the audience see not the actor, but the character. A **character** is a person, or a thing with human characteristics, faced with a problem and trying to resolve it. A character is revealed to an audience by what the character does, how he or she does it, and why he or she does it. A character is also revealed by the actions, words and attitudes of other characters.

You have learned that it is important to understand the ideas and emotions that an author is trying to communicate in order to effectively interpret a piece of literature. As an oral interpreter, you perform as yourself communicating another's ideas. As a character in a play, you become immersed in the character the playwright has created, and you communicate the author's ideas and emotions as the character would be expected to communicate them.

To prepare a character, study the play so that you understand the plot and the emotional and intellectual messages intended by the play-wright. If the time and locale of the play are unfamiliar, become acquainted with them. You then need to focus on an in-depth understanding of the character you will portray. Characterization is successful when the actor is able to discern the essence of the character and communicate this essence through voice, mannerisms, and physical movement.

Working with the Model

N. Richard Nash wrote *The Rainmaker* in 1955. This scene from the play features Starbuck, a brash, self-professed traveling rainmaker, and Lizzie Curry, a shy woman who no longer dares to dream. Read the scene and note the ways in which the essence of each character is revealed. As you examine it, the conflict and the essential ideas will become evident.

From THE RAINMAKER

Claiming to be able to bring rain for a fee, Starbuck has arrived at the Curry ranch during a severe draught. On this summer evening, Lizzie goes out to the bunkhouse with bed linens for Starbuck, who is boarding with the Curry family.

Starbuck: Who's that? *(He rises tautly.)*

(Lizzie *stands in the doorway, trying not to look into the room. She is carrying the bed linens. She knocks on the door frame.)*

Lizzie: *(trying to sound calm)* It's me—Lizzie.

(An awkward moment. Then Lizzie, *without entering the room, hands the bedding across the threshold.)*

Lizzie: Here.

Starbuck: What's that?

Lizzie: Bed linens—take them.

Starbuck: Is that what you came out for?

Lizzie: *(after a painful moment)* No . . . I came out because . . . *(She finds it too difficult to continue.)*

Starbuck: *(gently)* Go on, Lizzie.

Lizzie: I came out to thank you for what you said to Noah.

Starbuck: I meant every word of it.

Lizzie: What you said about Jim—I'm sure you meant that.

Starbuck: What I said about you.

Lizzie: I don't believe you.

Starbuck: Then what are you thankin' me for? What's the matter, Lizzie? You afraid that if you stop bein' sore at me you'll like me a little?

Lizzie: No . . . *(and she starts to go.)*

Starbuck: *(stopping her)* Then stay and talk to me! *(as she hesitates)* It's lonely out here and I don't think I'll sleep much—not in a strange place.

Lizzie: Then I guess you never sleep. Running from one strange place to another.

Starbuck: *(with a smile)* Not runnin'—travelin'.

Lizzie: Well, if that's the kind of life you like . . .

Starbuck: Oh, it's not what a man likes—it's what he's got to do. Now what would a fella in my business be doin' stayin' in the same place? Rain's nice—but it ain't nice all the time.

Lizzie: *(relaxing a bit)* No, I guess not.

Starbuck: People got no use for me—except maybe once in a life-time. And when my work's done, they're glad to see me go.

Lizzie: *(caught by the loneliness in his voice)* I never thought of it that way.

Starbuck: Why would you? You never thought of me as a real rain-maker—not until just now.

Lizzie: I still don't think it!

(Now she starts to go more determinedly than before. Starbuck *stops her physically this time.)*

Starbuck: Lizzie—wait! Why don't you let yourself think of me the way you want to?

Lizzie: *(unnerved)* What do you mean?

Starbuck: Think like Lizzie, not like Noah.

Lizzie: I don't know what you're talking about.

Starbuck: What are you scared of?

Lizzie: You! I don't trust you!

Starbuck: Why? What don't you trust about me?

Lizzie: Everything! The way you talk, the way you brag—why, even your name.

Starbuck: What's wrong with my name?

Lizzie: It sounds fake! It sounds like you made it up!

Starbuck: You're . . . right! I did make it up.

Lizzie: There! Of course!

Starbuck: Why not? You know what name I was born with? Smith! Smith, for the love of Mike, *Smith!* Now what kind of handle is that for a fella like me? I needed a name that had the whole sky in it! . . . Star-buck! Now there's a name—and it's mine.

Lizzie: No, it's not. You were born Smith—and that's your name.

Starbuck: You're wrong, Lizzie. The name you choose for yourself is more your own than the name you were born with. And if I was you I'd choose another name than Lizzie.

Lizzie: Thank you—I'm very pleased with it.

Starbuck: Oh, no you ain't. You ain't pleased with anything about yourself. And I'm sure you ain't pleased with "Lizzie."

Lizzie: I don't ask *you* to be pleased with it, Starbuck. I *am.*

Starbuck: Lizzie? Why, it don't *stand* for anything.

Lizzie: It stands for me! *Me!* I'm not the Queen of Sheba—I'm not Lady Godiva—I'm not Cinderella at the Ball.

Starbuck: Would you like to be?

Lizzie: Starbuck, you're ridiculous!

Starbuck: What's ridiculous about it? Dream you're somebody—*be* somebody! But Lizzie? That's nobody! So many millions of wonderful women with wonderful names! . . . Leonora, Desdemona, Carolina, Paulina! Annabella, Florinda, Natasha, Diane! *(then, with a pathetic little lift of his shoulders)* Lizzie.

Lizzie: Good night, Starbuck!

Starbuck: *(with a sudden inspiration)* Just a minute, Lizzie—just one little half of a minute. I got the greatest name for you— the greatest name—just listen. *(then, like a love lyric)* Melisande.

Lizzie: *(flatly)* I don't like it.

Starbuck: That's because you don't know anything about her. But when I tell you who she was—lady, when I tell you who she was!

Lizzie: Who?

Starbuck: *(improvising)* She was the most beautiful . . . ! She was the beautiful wife of King Hamlet! Ever hear of him?

Lizzie: *(giving him the rope)* Go on! Go on!

Starbuck: He was the fella who sailed across the ocean and brought back the Golden Fleece! And you know why he did that? Because Melisande begged him for it! I tell you, that Melisande—she was so beautiful and her hair was so long and curly—every time he looked at her he fell right down and died. And this King Hamlet, he'd do anything for her— anything she wanted. So when she said: "Hamlet, I got a terrible hankerin' for a soft Golden Fleece," he just naturally sailed right off to find it. And when he came back—all bleedin' and torn—he went and laid that Fleece of Gold right down at her pretty white feet. And she took that fur piece and wrapped it around her pink . . . shoulders and she said: "I got the Golden Fleece—and I'll never be cold no more." . . . Melisande! What a woman! What a *name!*

Lizzie: *(quietly)* . . . You take a lot of stories—that I've read in a hundred different places—and you roll them up into one big fat ridiculous lie!

Starbuck: *(angry, hurt)* I wasn't lyin'—I was dreamin'!

Lizzie: It's the same thing!

Starbuck: *(with growing anger)* If you think it's the same thing then I take it back about your name! Lizzie—it's just right for you. I'll tell you another name that would suit you—Noah! Because you and your brother—you've got no dream.

Lizzie: *(with an outcry)* You think all dreams have to be your kind! Golden Fleece and thunder on the mountain! But there are other dreams, Starbuck! Little quiet ones that come to a woman when she's shining the silverware and putting moth flakes in the closet.

Starbuck: Like what?

Lizzie: *(crying)* . . . Like kids laughing and teasing and setting up a racket. And how it feels to say the word "Husband!" . . . There are all kinds of dreams, Mr. Starbuck. Mine are small ones—like my name—Lizzie. But they're *real* like my name—real! So you can have yours—and I'll have mine!

(Unable to control her tears, she starts to run away. This time he grabs her. . . .)

Starbuck: Lizzie . . .

Lizzie: Please . . .

Starbuck: I'm sorry, Lizzie! I'm sorry!

Lizzie: It's all right—let me go!

Starbuck: I hope your dreams come true, Lizzie—I hope they do!

Lizzie: They won't—they never will!

Starbuck: Believe in yourself and they will!

Lizzie: I've got nothing to believe in.

Starbuck: You're a woman! Believe in that!

Lizzie: How can I when nobody else will?

Starbuck: *You* gotta believe it first! *(quickly)* Let me ask you, Lizzie— are you pretty?

Lizzie: *(with a wail)* No—I'm plain!

Starbuck: There! You see? You don't know you're a woman!

Lizzie: I am a woman! A plain one!

Starbuck: There's no such thing as a plain woman! Every real woman is pretty! They're all pretty in a different way—but they're all pretty!

Lizzie: Not me! When I look in the looking glass . . .

Starbuck: Don't let Noah be your lookin' glass!

Lizzie: He's not. My looking glass is right on the wall.

Starbuck: It's in the wrong place. It's gotta be inside you.

Lizzie: No . . .

Starbuck: Don't be afraid—*look!* You'll see a pretty woman, Lizzie. Lizzie, you gotta be your own lookin' glass. And then one day the lookin' glass will be the man who loves you. It'll be his eyes, maybe. And you'll look in that mirror and you'll be more than pretty—you'll be beautiful!

Lizzie: *(crying out)* It'll never happen!

Starbuck: Make it happen! Lizzie, why don't you think "pretty" and take down your hair? *(He reaches for her hair.)*

Lizzie: *(in panic)* No!

Starbuck: Please, Lizzie! *(He is taking the pins out of her hair.)*

Lizzie: No—no . . .

Starbuck: Nobody sees you, Lizzie—nobody but me! *(taking her in his arms)* Now close your eyes, Lizzie—close them! *(as she obeys)* Now—say: "I'm pretty!"

Lizzie: *(trying)* I'm—I'm—I can't!

Starbuck: Say it! Say it, Lizzie!

Lizzie: I'm . . . pretty.

Starbuck: Say it again!

Lizzie: *(with a little cry)* Pretty!

Starbuck: Say it—mean it!

Lizzie: *(exalted)* I'm pretty! I'm pretty! I'm pretty!

A.   Consider the essential qualities of each character.
  1. How would you describe the personality of each? What voice, mannerisms, actions would be needed to reveal each character's personality?
  2. How would you describe the mood of each character at the beginning of the scene? At the end? What brings this change about? How might an actor use voice, mannerisms, or actions to reveal these moods?
  3. Why are the two characters as they are? What motivates them to behave as they do? What words from the scene help you understand the characters' motivation?

B.   Discuss your answers to the questions above with others in your class. If you have different interpretations, explore the reasons for your difference. If some of the students have seen the play produced, compare the characterizations in the performance with yours.
  1. Before class read through the scene with another person. Use the result of the class discussion to help you interpret the two characters.

2. Repeat the performance of the scene in class, adding as much physical action as needed to help communicate your interpretation of the character.

C. Use improvisation to extend the scene beyond the lines included in the excerpt.

1. Brainstorm at least five problems to extend the scene.
2. Choose one problem as the basis for an improvisation. As you improvise, remember to behave as the character established in the excerpt would. React to the behavior of the other character as your character would react.
3. Continue your improvisation. Assume that Lizzie's brother enters the scene. Have a student assume his character and continue with the interactions that might occur at that point.

Guidelines

When you are preparing a role for a play, remember the following guidelines.

1. Seek to communicate the essential characteristics of the role you are portraying. Become immersed in the character.
2. Consciously select those mannerisms and physical movements that will reveal your understanding of the character.
3. Select those elements of voice and action that will reveal your interpretation of the character's personality.
4. Your portrayal of the character needs to reflect your understanding of the entire play and the role your character fulfills in it. You need to know why your character behaves as he or she does in each interaction with others in the play. Be aware of the specific contribution(s) your character makes toward resolving the essential problem of the play.
5. At all times stay in character. That is, once a rehearsal or performance has begun, all of your actions should be those that might be expected of the character you are playing—not of your own personality or mood. If the character is sad and lonely, you must be sad and lonely, even if you have just received the happiest news of your life. This is true as you enter and leave the stage. It is also true as you are merely standing in the background while others are speaking their lines.

One thing you may find reassuring is that if you are concentrating on acting and reacting as your character would in a situation, your performance will not likely be as affected by stage fright. Real stage fright comes from worrying about what people think about you instead of concentrating on how your character should respond in a particular passage of the play.

370

Preparing and Presenting

Work with a small group of other students. Choose one of your number to be the director. Select a scene that you can present to your class. Your teacher or school librarian can help you select a scene.

Read the entire play and discuss it with your group. Select a scene that would take between five and ten minutes to present. Discuss the characters in the scene. Be sure to talk about why the characters are doing what they are doing. Analyze what actions and words of the characters tell you about them. Determine which of you will take which part and then read through the scene. Discuss how your reading brought out the essential characteristics of each part and what could be done to improve your characterizations. Memorize the part (the lines and actions) for the character you will be performing.

Rehearse the scene. The director should provide a common interpretation that reveals the ideas and emotions intended by the playwright. You may need to change your original interpretation of the voice and actions of your character in order to comply with the director's idea. Perform your scene before the class.

Evaluation Checklist

While one group is performing, the other students in the class should be preparing to answer the following questions.

1. Think about each character.
   a. What was the age of the character? How did you know?
   b. What was the basic personality of the character? How did you know?
   c. What was the mood(s) of the character? How did you know?
   d. Why did the character do and say what he or she did? How do you know?
   e. What was the main contribution of the character to the scene? Why do you think so?
2. Were the actors able to stay in character throughout their involvement in the scene? If not, when did they fall out of character? What should they have done instead?
3. Were the physical actions and voice of each character natural, simple, and appropriate for the character? Did they come in reaction to the events in the play?
4. What contributions did the actions and words of others make to the development of each character? For example, did the anger of one character help reveal the meekness of another?

Chapter 13 Review

Summary

Improvisation, or the process of presenting physical actions and speech without practice or rehearsal, can greatly improve your basic acting skills because it requires you to react spontaneously and naturally within given limitations. First, attempting to address a problem gives you a framework within which to act and react to others. In each scene you concentrate on doing a specific task and on achieving a natural flow of dramatic action centered around this task.

Second, you focus, or direct and concentrate your attention on a particular aspect of the scene. Such focus gives you a better "grip" on the scene and gives more specificity to your actions.

Being aware of your body, your senses, the other persons in the scene and their actions, and the setting will also help you react spontaneously and naturally as the character you are playing.

Characterization is the creative process whereby the actor grasps the fundamental personality of the role he or she is portraying and communicates it to the audience. Studying the words your character says, the words said about your character, the setting, how your character interacts with others, as well as the overall ideas and emotions of the play will help you understand your character. Then you can successfully convey the character to your audience through voice, mannerisms, and physical movement.

Reviewing Vocabulary

Number your paper from 1 to 5. Next to each number, write the letter of the group of words that best defines the word in dark type in the sentence.

a. a person, or a thing with human characteristics, faced with a problem and trying to resolve it
b. the point of concentration in an improvisation; the specific aspect of the scene to which a character directs his or her attention
c. the process of presenting physical actions, including speech, without practice or rehearsal
d. the specific task addressed in an improvisation
e. the creative process whereby the actor grasps the fundamental personality of the role he or she is portraying and communicates it to the audience

1. Samuel's **characterization** of the old seaman was based largely on a cracking voice and stooped posture.
2. Our thespian club has invited a local mime to come speak to us on **improvisation**.
3. The **problem** of this improvisation is to represent a man waiting to see his dentist.
4. The **focus** of this improvisation is on revealing the man's anxiety over getting a tooth pulled.
5. Mr. Simms, our dramatic coach, assigned the flamboyant, self-confident **character** to Andrea to help her overcome her shyness and self-consciousness.

Reviewing Facts and Ideas

1. In your own words, define improvisation. In what everyday situations do people improvise?

2. Define problem. How does concentrating on this problem help you improvise?
3. Define focus. How does directing your attention on this focus help you improvise?
4. Why is it important to listen to and react to others in a group improvisation?
5. The actions of an improvisation usually have a logical sequence. Describe the main purpose of each of the three parts of an improvisation: introduction, body, and conclusion.
6. What is a character? In what ways is a character revealed to an audience?
7. Bodily movement is an essential part of both improvising and creating a dramatic character. Explain how using movement, gestures, mannerisms, and facial expressions can help convey the action, emotions, and ideas of an improvisation and of a dramatic character.
8. What things should you look for in a script or scene to reveal the essence of a character? Which is most crucial in giving you information upon which to base your character? Why do you think so?
9. What is a character's motivation?
10. How might improvising new scenes for your character help you develop and communicate your interpretation of the character?

Discussing Facts and Ideas

1. Watch a televised drama. Discuss how the qualities of different characters are revealed. How do the actors let you know the what, how, and why that reveal the essential features of each character? Do they rely primarily on the words they speak or are there other things that contribute as much or more to the interpretations? If so, what other things?

2. A quarterback on a football team often has to improvise when a play he has called does not start out right. Think of other real-life situations in which people have to improvise. How can such responses help you understand the actor's task when performing on a stage?
3. Think of the most memorable character you have ever seen in a play, in a film, or on television. Make a list of the actor's specific behaviors that made the character memorable. Compare your observations with those of others in the class. Try to discover the kinds of behavior that were common among the different actors identified.

Applying Your Knowledge

1. One source indicates that the five plays most often performed in high schools between 1945 and 1984 were:

   You Can't Take it With You
   Our Town
   Arsenic and Old Lace
   Harvey
   The Curious Savage

   Obtain a copy of one of these plays and prepare a scene from it that features interaction between at least three characters. The scene should be no more than five minutes long. After you have presented it, discuss with your class why that play is likely to have been so popular over the years.
2. Make a list of famous characters from works of literature. Improvise scenes in which the characters from different works meet each other. Have the characters interact based on a problem you present them. For example, your list might include the three witches from *Macbeth* and Scarlett O'Hara from *Gone With The Wind*. Present Scarlett and the witches with the problem of all air traffic from your local airport being canceled because of heavy fog.

Reading a Speech or Report Written by Someone Else

As a worker or organization member, you may be called upon to read aloud a speech or report written by someone else. You may have time to prepare this presentation, or you may have little or no time. Follow these guidelines in each of the three cases.

1. If you have a day or more to prepare the presentation, read the speech through several times. If necessary, type or neatly print the text to make it easier to read. Ask the author to explain any passages that you do not understand or that your listeners might not understand. If possible, have the author rewrite these parts, or get permission to rewrite them yourself. Practice delivering the speech, concentrating on the meaning of the words and sentences. You should practice until you are able to look at the audience more than 50 percent of the time you are reading.

2. If you have only an hour or so in which to prepare the presentation, read the speech over as many times as you can. Mark the important passages that you will emphasize. Look up any words whose pronunciation you are unsure of. Deliver the speech in a clear, relaxed manner. Do not rush and do not speak in a monotone.

3. If you are given no time at all in which to prepare the speech, do your best to read it in a natural, relaxed manner that your audience can understand. Avoid hurrying and mumbling. Do not complain about the lack of preparation, the subject matter, or the author's style.

Activity

1. Practice reading a selection from a magazine article or speech written by someone else. Remember that you are not allowed to cut, condense, or adapt this selection. After practicing your presentation several times, deliver it before the class. Ask the other students to evaluate your presentation in terms of clarity, variety, and interest.

Role Playing to Understand Communication Problems

Role playing is a way of acting out situations or problems to understand them better. In a role-playing session, each person plays a part, such as job applicant, interviewer, customer, or store clerk. Each player acts the way he or she thinks the real person *would* act under the circumstances. Afterwards, the players often discuss what they have learned from the session. Here is an example of a role-playing session.

Rob: Can I help you, ma'am?

Etta: I need a fan belt for my Volkswagen.

Rob: Let's see, is that a 'seventy?

Etta: 'Sixty-eight!

Rob: All right, let me check. Hmm . . . we're out of 'sixty-eights.

Etta: Don't you people ever have *anything* in stock?

Rob: However, this 'seventy belt should do just fine. Would you like one of our mechanics to install it?

Etta: No! You people have enough of my money already!

Rob: I agree, it's always best to do it yourself. *(Ending the role-playing session.)* Well, Etta, how does it feel to be the customer for a change? Did you enjoy letting off steam?

Etta: Yes, and I can understand why some of them get so angry.

Rob: How would you describe the way I handled it?

Etta: No matter what I said, you were always polite.

Activity

1. Think of a problem that affects you at school, on a team, or on the job. Working with one or more other students, role-play the situation in front of the class. You may play either yourself or one of the other people involved. Discuss with the other students what the role-playing session has shown them about the problem and possible solutions.

CHAPTER 14

Listening and Responding

After working through this chapter, you should be proficient at the following skills:

Lesson	Skills
Lesson 1	• measuring the time you spend on radio and television • evaluating the effect of radio and television on your life • deciding how you can benefit the most from electronic media
Communicating on the Job	• using a microphone
Communicating as a Citizen	• listening critically to documentaries and docudramas

Evaluating Your Radio Listening and Television Viewing

Most Americans spend thousands of hours each year watching television. Many people are unaware of how much time television really takes out of their lives. They turn the set on when they arrive home from school or work and leave it on until they go to bed. If asked, they might say that they watch very little television or that they think most programs are bad. Although they may be unaware of it, the time devoted to television is time during which they are not reading, talking, thinking, walking, exercising, meeting people, or earning money.

One way to get more control over your time is to keep a **media diary**. You can find out how much time radio and television actually take out of each week. Then you can decide how much time you want to devote to radio and television.

Working with the Model

Two students, Sohalia and Craig, kept media diaries for one week. Here are the portions of their diaries for Monday, Tuesday, and Wednesday. As you read their media diaries, think about how much time you spend listening to radio or watching television on those days of the week.

MEDIA DIARY: SOHALIA

Day	Medium	6 A.M. to Noon	Noon to 6 P.M.	6 P.M. to 10 P.M.	Total
Mon.	Radio	15 min.	10 min.	——	25 min.
	TV	——	——	1 hr.	1 hr.
Tues.	Radio	5 min.	10 min.	——	15 min.
	TV	——	——	30 min.	30 min.
Wed.	Radio	10 min.	15 min.	——	25 min.
	TV	——	30 min.	1 hr.	1½ hrs.

TOTAL RADIO/TV TIME FOR 3 DAYS: 4 hrs. 5 mins.

MEDIA DIARY: CRAIG

Day	Medium	6 A.M. to Noon	Noon to 6 P.M.	6 P.M. to 10 P.M.	Total
Mon.	Radio	30 min.	1 hr.	30 min.	2 hrs.
	TV	——	30 min.	3 hrs.	3½ hrs.
Tues.	Radio	20 min.	1½ hrs.	——	1 hr. 50 mins.
	TV	——	30 min.	4 hrs.	4½ hrs.
Wed.	Radio	20 min.	1 hr.	30 min.	1 hr. 50 mins.
	TV	15 min.	1 hr.	3½ hrs.	4 hrs. 45 mins.

TOTAL RADIO/TV TIME FOR 3 DAYS: 18 hrs. 25 mins.

A. Think about Sohalia's media diary.
  1. Consider the length of time Sohalia spends listening to the radio in each part of the day. Is she more likely to be listening to specific programs or using the radio as background to some chore? Explain your answer.

2. Consider the time Sohalia spends watching television. How careful do you think she is in selecting the programs she wants to watch? Explain your answer.

B. Think about Craig's media diary.

1. Considering the amount of time Craig spends watching television, how careful do you think he is in selecting the programs he wants to watch? Explain your answer.

2. Craig's teachers estimate the following amounts of homework are required each evening for his classes.

Math	30 minutes
Spanish	30 minutes
Civics	1 to 2 hours
Speech	30 minutes to 1 hour
Chemistry	0 to 30 minutes

In view of his radio and television habits, when do you think Craig does his homework?

C. Keep a media diary of your own for one week. At the end of the week, add up the amount of time you spent on radio and television. Then list the things you had wanted to do during the week but had no time for. Include

reading books
doing homework
shopping
sports
time with friends
learning job skills

Estimate the time you would have liked to spend on these activities. Compare this time with the time you spent on radio and television. What conclusions do you come to? Report your findings to the class.

Guidelines

A media diary shows you *how much* time you spent, but not how well it was spent. A **media evaluation** records what you watched or listened to, how much you enjoyed each program, and whether or not you learned anything. You may use the following letter ratings:

A excellent
B good
C mediocre
D bad
F very bad

Here is a sample media evaluation for one evening.

MEDIA EVALUATION

Time	Program	Rating	Comment
7:00 P.M.	Network News	A −	Made me aware of current events (only one story was silly)
7:30 P.M.	Embarrassing Questions	F	Terrible—wish I'd turned it off.
8:00 P.M.	Gas 'n' 'Gators	D −	Dumb!
8:30 P.M.	Weinstein's Wombats	C +	Some funny jokes, but could have been much better
9:00 P.M.	Bullets in the Bayou	C −	Brainless violence, and pretty dull
10:00 P.M.	Great Expectations, Part 3	A	Excellent BBC series— wish it wasn't on so late!
11:00 P.M.	Local News	B	First 4 stories well done; then I fell asleep.

Record your feelings about a program immediately after watching or listening to it. You will have a record of your reactions to refer to the next time that program, or a similar one, is on the air. If you are wondering whether to watch or listen to a program, ask yourself the following questions.

- Do I have any reason to believe that this program will be worth watching or listening to?
- Have I ever enjoyed any other program in this series?
- The last time I watched or listened to this program, or a similar one, what reaction did I record?
- Will I be glad tomorrow that I watched or listened to this program? Will I be glad next week?
- Is there anything else I either should do or would like to do instead of watching or listening to this program?

Answering such questions will help you take back control over some of the time you once gave to radio and television. This practice in managing your time will become more important as you go on to college or enter the job market. Successful college students, workers, and business people have all learned how to manage their time. First, they allow ample time for the work they *must* do. Then they think about their other activities, including entertainment, very carefully. Finally, they schedule only those activities that they believe they will enjoy or learn from.

Activity

1. Write a media evaluation of the radio and television programs you listen to during a single week. Give each program a letter grade and write down your reactions to each in a few words. At the end of the week, count the number of programs you enjoyed and the number you felt were a waste of time. Add up the number of hours you spent on worthless programs. Think about the things you would rather have done during those hours. During the following week, ask yourself the questions in the Guidelines section before you turn on any program. See if you are able to reduce your radio and television time by the number of hours you felt were wasted.

Preparing and Presenting

Working with five other students, conduct an experiment to see how well you spend your radio and television time. Each student should keep a media diary and make a media evaluation for one week. At the end of the week, all six students should meet and pass out copies of their diaries and evaluations. The entire group should study and discuss each person's listening and viewing habits. (This group discussion should have a leader and should be conducted according to the guidelines in Chapter 3.) At the end of the meeting, each student should decide how, and by how much, he or she will reduce the amount of time spent on radio or television. Each student should also decide on one program that he or she feels is worth watching or listening to regularly.

During the following week, the members of the group should put their resolutions into effect by reducing their radio and television time. Then the group should present the results of its experiment to the class. The presentation should be in two parts. In the first part, the group leader should report on the success of the experiment. (It may be better not to use names. The leader can say, "Student A reduced his time by 4 hours a week," "Student B reduced her time by 2½ hours a week," and so forth.) In the second part, each student should report briefly to the class on the one program he or she believes is really worth watching or listening to. The report should include a description of the program and of the student's reaction to it.

Evaluation Checklist

Evaluate the presentations on the basis of the following criteria. Rate each presentation on a scale from 1 (Poor) to 5 (Excellent). Be prepared to give reasons for each rating you give.

Category	Rating
The student . . . 1. Controlled the time he or she spent on radio and television well	
2. Watched few worthless programs or programs he or she did not enjoy or learn from	
3. Successfully reduced the time spent on radio and television according to his or her goal	
4. Watched or listened to the program that he or she decided was worth watching or listening to regularly	

Chapter 14 Review

Summary

Many Americans devote more time to radio listening and television viewing than they would like to admit. One way to discover how much time you spend on radio and television is to keep a media diary. This diary also might help you discover how unselective you are in choosing radio and television programs as well as how much time you could have spent doing more fruitful things.

A media evaluation shows what you listened to and watched, how much you enjoyed each program, and whether or not you learned anything. Both a media diary and a media evaluation can help give you greater control over your time.

Reviewing Facts and Ideas

1. What is a media diary? What is the purpose of keeping one?
2. What is a media evaluation? How can keeping one help you to better control the time you spend on radio and television?
3. One of the basic criteria of a media evaluation is whether you feel the time you spent listening to or watching the program was wasted or worthwhile. What two factors help you determine whether the time was wasted or worthwhile? Which one is more important to you? Why?
4. According to your media evaluation, what kind of programs do you tend to listen to or view the most? What kinds of programs would you prefer to listen to or view on a more regular basis? Why?

5. How much of your time do you spend listening to the radio or watching television while doing other things? Is this practice distracting? Why or why not?

Discussing Facts and Ideas

1. Watch a television broadcast of a current event and discuss the following.
   a. Was the program entertainment or reporting?
   b. Did the reporter understand the subject?
   c. Did the broadcast distinguish fact from opinion?

2. There is much concern about the potential adverse effects of television violence. Some claim that the violence is so great that children watching television lose sight of reality and don't understand, for example, the finality of death. Others say that similar complaints have been made in the past about comic books and radio and that people shouldn't be too concerned about television violence. Discuss this problem in your class. Invite one of your school counselors to share his or her views on this issue.

Applying Your Knowledge

1. Select a television program that you think was presented in a biased manner. Write a letter to the manager of the station that aired the program, explaining your objections to the program's biased point of view.
2. Interview a group of children on their television viewing habits. Prepare a report on the results of your interview and share it with the PTA of the children's school.

Using a Microphone

If you know how to use it, a microphone or public address system can help you communicate with a large audience. Before using such a system, however, you must be prepared. Remember these rules.

1. Test the microphone setup before you begin speaking, preferably before any listeners have arrived. Have another person in the room or auditorium tell you if the level of your voice is appropriate and if you are speaking clearly.
2. Because most microphone systems do not reproduce sound with high fidelity, you must speak *more slowly and more distinctly* than usual in order to be understood.
3. Find the proper distance from your mouth to the microphone, and stay at that distance. If you move too close, your voice will be distorted. If you turn your head away from the microphone, you will be inaudible.
4. Speak at approximately the same voice level. The system has been adjusted for a specific level. Any sound much louder will be painful for your listeners, and any sound much softer will not be heard.
5. Do not touch the microphone with your mouth or fingers, blow into the microphone, or hold the microphone stand.
6. Remember that coughs, rattling papers, muttering under your breath, and other sounds will all be audible to your listeners.
7. If you are using a "body mike" (for a televised interview, for example), be aware of where the microphone is attached to your clothing and where the cord is. Do not touch or disconnect the microphone or pull or trip over the cord.

Activity

1. Working with other students, take turns reading the same passage over a microphone system in a large room or auditorium. Have a panel of four to six other students evaluate each reader in terms of articulation, clarity, and proper use of the microphone. After studying your evaluation, practice ways to improve your use of the microphone.

Listening Critically to Documentaries and Docudramas

A television **documentary** is a program about a historic event or a current issue. It uses authentic films, recordings, and interviews to inform the audience about an event or issue that cannot be covered on a brief news broadcast. Many documentaries are informative and fair, but some are one-sided. When watching a documentary, ask yourself:

- Does this program present all sides of an issue?
- Is it consistent with what I already know about the issue?
- Does it distinguish between fact, opinion, and conjecture?
- Are films, interviews, and other materials presented in a complete, undistorted form?
- Do the reporters appear to understand the issue, and do they present it objectively?

A **docudrama** is a fictional drama based on real events. It uses actors to portray famous people and is intended primarily as entertainment. (*The Missiles of October, Franklin and Eleanor*, and *Backstairs at the White House* are examples.) As you watch a docudrama, ask yourself:

- Does this program show events that are a matter of public record, or are the authors inventing scenes and events?
- Have the authors tried to make the program more entertaining by presenting people as either heroes or villains?
- Have the authors had to suppress events or characters in order to avoid lawsuits from people who are still alive?

Activity

1. Watch a documentary or docudrama about a current or historical event. Then do independent research on that event. Compare scenes from the documentary or docudrama with the facts you learn. Decide whether the program was essentially accurate or whether it distorted facts in order to be more entertaining or persuasive. Report on your findings to the class and learn how students who did not research the program reacted to it.

Contest Speaking

How to Use the Handbook of Contest Speaking

Speech and debate contests will provide you with opportunities to develop your speaking skills. You will obtain expert opinions about your performance and have the chance to compete with students representing other schools.

This handbook will introduce you to the major activities included in speech tournaments. Colleges, high schools, and other institutions sponsor competitive speaking events. The host of each tournament establishes rules and procedures related to the specific activities. Therefore, you will want to become thoroughly familiar with the specific requirements before competing.

In addition to tournaments, you may have an opportunity to participate in specialized speaking contests. Businesses and service organizations offer scholarships and other prizes for the students who win their contests.

The general elements of speech communication discussed throughout this text apply to all contest speaking. You will be most successful if you demonstrate original thought, clear expression, good choice of words, positive attitude, and effective use of voice and gestures.

The National Forensic League provides information and an organizational framework for high school students interested in competitive speaking. Your state probably has its own organization with its own rules. Your speech teacher can help you locate materials that will supplement this handbook and help prepare you to participate in contests.

Contest Debating

Contest debates are conducted according to strict time limits and on an assigned proposition. The proposition is always worded in positive language and proposes a change in current policy. (For more about the nature of debate, see Chapter 9.) Each debater works with a partner. One or more judges listen to each round and select the winning team.

Guidelines

1. The most common format for competitive debating is the cross-examination model. Affirmative speakers are cross-examined by negative speakers and vice-versa. The time limits vary with different

tournaments. The following times are most common on the national level.

First Affirmative Constructive	8 minutes
Cross-Examination	3 minutes
First Negative Constructive	8 minutes
Cross-Examination	3 minutes
Second Affirmative Constructive	8 minutes
Cross-Examination	3 minutes
Second Negative Constructive	8 minutes
Cross-Examination	3 minutes
First Negative Rebuttal	4 minutes
First Affirmative Rebuttal	4 minutes
Second Negative Rebuttal	4 minutes
Second Affirmative Rebuttal	4 minutes

2. The affirmative team has the burden of analyzing a current problem and defending the plan for solving it which is expressed in the debate proposition. The debate proposition is usually a national topic debated throughout the country during a specific year.
3. Teams may be allowed preparation time during the debate. This is usually a period of 2 minutes between constructive and rebuttal speeches. Some tournaments establish other rules for preparation time throughout a debate.
4. The purpose of the cross-examination period is to clarify points made by the opposition and to expose weaknesses in their arguments or evidence. Both the questioner and the witness should speak concisely and to the point. They should avoid showing off or exhibiting personal hostilities.
5. Teams are judged on the basis of analysis, reasoning, evidence, refutation, delivery, and cross-examination skills. Usually, each speaker is rated. The teams are given ratings ranging from *poor* to *superior*, and the winner of each round is identified.
6. Debaters generally participate in several rounds of debate during a tournament. Rounds are scheduled so that the strongest teams eventually face each other, and the entire contest has one winning team.

Preparing for Competition

1. Debate speaking involves the same skills as an expository speech based on analysis (see Chapter 5) and a persuasive speech appealing to logic (see Chapter 6). The first step is to analyze the problem and the proposition thoroughly, understanding your opponents' position as well as your own.

2. Research the topic, making sure that your evidence is accurate, complete, and up-to-date. Several publishers and debate associations offer yearly handbooks on the national topic, but a debate handbook is no substitute for doing your own research and background reading.
3. Prepare a brief, outlining your analysis of the problem, the arguments on both sides, and the evidence you will use (see Chapter 9).
4. Although preparation is vital to good debating, only the first affirmative speech can be fully prepared in advance. All other speeches will be influenced, both in argument and choice of evidence, by what has been said in other speeches. Debaters must have good listening skills (see Chapters 4, 7, and 11). They must be able to think on their feet and to select and organize evidence while their opponents are speaking.
5. Remember, judges usually vote for the team that gave the most persuasive arguments rather than one that simply collected the greater amount of evidence.
6. At every stage of the debate, be courteous to your opponents, your partner, and the judges.

Activities

1. Invite a pair of students who have participated in an interscholastic debate to speak to your class. Ask them to present an abridged version of the debate. After the debate, ask the students to explain the strategies and techniques they have found most useful in debating.
2. The National Forensic League makes available recordings of championship debates. If your school has these recordings, listen to several of the debates. Compare the various ways in which different affirmative and negative teams approached the topic.

Impromptu Speaking

Impromptu speeches must be delivered with a minimum of preparation. This competition tests the student's ability to rapidly organize an effective speech and to deliver it smoothly and confidently.

Guidelines

1. The speaker does not enter the room until it is his or her turn to speak.

2. The speaker is given a choice of three topics. Topics may be single words or brief phrases, or they may be cartoons or excerpts from editorials. Frequently, the topic will fall into a broad area that has been announced in advance (for example, national events during the first half of the year).
3. The speaker is given 2 or 3 minutes to prepare.
4. The speaker speaks on the topic for 5 or 6 minutes. Time signals are given to help the speaker stay within the limit.

Preparing for Competition

1. Read widely to stay informed about current events. If a topic area is announced, follow developments in newspapers, news magazines, news broadcasts, and public affairs programs. You may find it helpful to keep notecards on current events, although notes will not be permitted during your preparation or speech.
2. Prepare anecdotes, examples, and statistics that you may be able to use in your speech. Don't hesitate to use personal experiences, if they are relevant.
3. Organize your speech into a clear *introduction, body*, and *conclusion*. In the introduction, use an anecdote or idea you have prepared in advance to get the audience's attention.
4. Tell your audience what you will say and why, say it, and then summarize what you have said. Stick closely to the topic and keep your speech simple and concise. Make no more than three points. Concentrate on proving or illustrating those points with specific examples.
5. Try to be original in your approach to the topic. Remember, the judge has to listen to many similar presentations.
6. No matter how nervous you may be, try for a smooth, relaxed, self-confident delivery.

Activities

1. With the other members of your class, conduct two rounds of impromptu speaking. For the first round, have the speakers draw quotations from famous authors on such topics as friendship, pride, patriotism, or peace. For the second round, have them draw editorial cartoons on national issues. Evaluate the impromptu speeches on the basis of adherence to the topic, knowledge of the topic, originality, persuasiveness, organization, gestures, and voice.
2. The best preparation for impromptu speaking is to practice it several times a week for at least a month before the contest. Your class can select a general topic area, and each student can draw a different specific topic each time he or she speaks.

Extemporaneous Speaking

An extemporaneous speech, like an impromptu speech, cannot be prepared in advance. The extemporaneous speaker, however, has been given a more specific topic area beforehand. He or she can do detailed background research and has a longer preparation time in which to organize the speech. Judges listen for persuasive, factual examples as well as for organization and delivery.

Guidelines

1. On the day of the contest, the speaker draws three specific topics from a large number of topics. The speaker chooses one of the three and is given 30 to 60 minutes in which to prepare a speech.
2. While preparing, the speaker can usually consult research files and other materials he or she has brought.
3. The speaker may be permitted to use one or two notecards while speaking. In some contests, however, notes are prohibited.
4. The speaker delivers a 5- to 7-minute speech on the topic. Time signals are usually given.
5. In some contests, the judges may question the contestants after all the speeches have been delivered. Sometimes contestants must question each other.

Preparing for Competition

1. Extemporaneous speaking requires a thorough, up-to-date knowledge of current events. Generally, the topic area is announced in advance (for example, international events related to energy problems). You will have several months in which to do systematic research. This should include reading and taking notes on major newspapers, news magazines, and recent books; watching newscasts and current affairs shows; and interviewing teachers, public officials, and other experts on current problems and issues. Try to find sources of information that the other speakers will probably not use.
2. Keep your notes on cards or in a loose-leaf notebook, and bring them up to date frequently. Have a separate entry and bibliography on each subtopic and keep a copy of the most informative article or articles on each subtopic. Take these notes and articles with you to the contest.
3. When you draw your three topics, pick the one on which you are best informed, can make the most effective speech, and are best prepared to answer questions. Briefly review your notes and arti-

cles on this topic and analyze the topic. Decide how you can best answer the question or provide the information that is needed.

4. Organize your speech around a single purpose: either to inform or to persuade. Be sure this is the purpose implied in the topic you have chosen. Outline an introduction, a body, and a conclusion for your speech. Keep the parts of your speech clear and distinct. In the introduction, capture your audience's attention by using a personal anecdote, an unusual fact, or an arresting opinion. In the body, follow a clear organizational plan: problem-to-solution, parts-to-whole, chronological, or thesis-proof-proof. In your conclusion, remind your audience of what you have said and summarize your arguments.

5. Your delivery should be confident and relaxed. Your language should not be too formal. If you use a prepared anecdote or example in your speech, be sure that it does not stand out from the rest of your speech.

6. Answer any questions directly and concisely. Take a few seconds to organize your answer before you speak. Treat the questioner politely, even if you find the question irrelevant or annoying.

Activities

1. Conduct an extemporaneous speaking contest with the other students in your speech class. Decide on a general topic area. Each student should have a week in which to do research. On the day of the contest, each speaker should draw a topic and take 10 minutes to prepare. (If your teacher arranges to hold the contest after school or on the weekend, the speakers can have the usual 30 to 60 minutes of preparation.) Each person should speak for 5 to 8 minutes on a topic of national importance. Evaluate the speakers on the basis of adherence to the topic, preparation, use of facts and statistics, originality, persuasiveness, organization, gestures, and voice.

2. Conduct an extemporaneous speaking contest in which every member of the class does research on the speaking topic. After the speeches, the students should question each speaker for 2 to 3 minutes. When evaluating the speeches, take into account how well each speaker was able to answer the questions.

Original Oratory

An oration is a speech that has been carefully written out and memorized. In an original oratory contest, you will be expected to deliver a persuasive speech from memory. You will be judged on the originality, organization, and persuasiveness of the speech, as well as on the quality of your delivery.

Guidelines

1. An original oration must be your own work. You must certify that it is original, and you will usually not be permitted to quote more than a certain amount (for example, 100 words) from other sources. The length of the oration may be defined by the total number of words (1,200, for example) or the time limit (8 to 10 minutes).
2. You will usually submit a copy of the oration to the judge or judges, who will follow it as you speak.
3. The oration is usually a persuasive speech on a national or international issue. It may offer a solution to a problem, warn of a national danger, or urge the audience to support a particular cause. The speech should be well organized, take a clear position on issues, and be expressed in precise, understandable language.
4. Your words may vary slightly from the prepared text, if you feel the change sounds more natural. Clarity and smooth delivery are more important than absolute accuracy.

Preparing for Competition

1. Select your topic carefully. It should be a contemporary issue that interests you and on which you have strong feelings. It should also interest your audience. As you research the topic and outline your speech, think of the precise thesis that you will be proving in the oration. You need not state this thesis in so many words, but you should keep it in mind as you write. Use specific facts and vivid examples to inform and persuade your listeners. (See Chapter 5 and Chapter 6 for further guidelines.) Prepare a strong opening and closing for your oration.
2. Take several months to write and rewrite your oration. When you have completed the first draft, read it to as many different listeners as you can. Use their reactions and comments to improve the clarity and persuasiveness of the speech.
3. Do not memorize the oration word by word or sentence by sentence. Instead, practice reading the entire speech aloud over and over. Gradually, you will find that you no longer need to look at the manuscript, except as an occasional reminder. The final step is to discard the manuscript. If you keep the purpose and shape of the entire speech clearly in your mind, you will probably not lose your place or "freeze up." Even if you forget the exact words, your

knowledge of the subject and of your thesis should enable you to keep speaking.

4. Your delivery should sound natural, confident, and spontaneous, not like a recitation. Practice your delivery many times in front of different audiences. Change any sentence in your speech that you cannot say easily and comfortably.

Activities

1. Practice original oratory with the other students in your class. Each speaker should prepare a 4- to 5-minute oration on one aspect of a national or international issue. As the student delivers the speech from memory, the other members of the class should follow copies of the speech. Evaluate the speakers on the basis of organization, persuasiveness, use of facts and examples, clarity, quality of memorization, and quality of delivery.

2. In a collection of speeches, find an oration by a famous orator of the past. Memorize and practice a portion of this speech and deliver it before the class. Have the other students follow a copy of the speech. Ask them to evaluate the quality of your memorization and delivery. Also discuss with them why this oration was effective and how you think the speaker may have originally delivered it.

Oral Interpretation of Prose or Poetry

In an oral interpretation contest, each speaker prepares a program of several prose passages or poems that are tied together by a common theme. The speaker interprets each selection, reading it so that its meaning is made vividly clear to the audience. Speakers are judged on their understanding of the selections as well as on preparation and delivery.

Guidelines

1. The selections should conform to the rules of the contest. For example, there may be a prescribed theme, or certain materials (for example, humorous selections) may be prohibited.

2. You should prepare a spoken introduction to each selection, announcing the author and title and preparing the audience by giving them any necessary information. You should also prepare transitional remarks to bridge selections.

3. Prepare a manuscript of the entire presentation. Often, you will have to submit this manuscript to the judges.

4. Costumes, props, and makeup are not used in interpretive speaking. The purpose is to *suggest* characters and situations by means of your voice rather than to act them out.
5. The time limit for the event is usually 7 to 10 minutes. Afterwards, the judge may give a spoken critique of your performance.

Preparing for Competition

1. Choose your selections very carefully. They should be of high literary merit and understandable to a general audience. (Many great works of literature are not suited to reading aloud.) Avoid selections that have been used frequently in speaking contests. Also avoid language or situations that might offend members of your audience.
2. Be sure that you understand each selection thoroughly and that you can pronounce all the words and suggest each of the characters. Remember, you are trying to make the author's emotions and ideas clear to the audience rather than imposing your interpretation on the author's work.
3. Prose selections will probably have to be cut to fit within the time limit. When you cut, be sure that the essential scenes and actions remain and that the emotional climax of the selection is still effective.
4. When reading poetry, be sure you understand the meter (rhythm) and rhyme scheme. Your delivery, however, should be flexible. Do not read line by line or with a mechanical rhythm.
5. Your delivery should be clear, confident, accurate, and effective. (For more guidelines on oral interpretation, see Chapter 11.)

Activities

1. Practice oral interpretation with members of your class. Each student should prepare a brief program (not over 5 minutes) of prose or poetry selections on a given theme. Other students may follow the speaker on their own copies of the selection. Evaluate the oral interpretations on the basis of selection, presentation, understanding of the material, gestures, and vocal delivery.
2. With one or more other students, listen to recordings of prose or poetry as read by professional actors. Discuss the actors' interpretation of each selection and evaluate it in terms of understanding of the material and effectiveness of interpretation and delivery. Discuss the ways in which your own interpretation would be similar or different.

Dramatic Interpretation

In serious dramatic interpretation, the speaker presents a scene from a play (or sometimes from a work of prose fiction), representing the different characters by means of his or her voice. The presentation is judged on the basis of adaptation, understanding, delineation of characters, and clarity and effectiveness of delivery.

Guidelines

1. Depending on the rules, the selections may be limited to adaptations ("cuttings") from published plays, or they may include dramatic passages from novels or short stories. Some contests permit speakers to read their selections. Others require that they speak from memory. Humorous scenes are usually excluded.
2. Props, costumes, and makeup are not used. The speaker is interpreting the scene to the audience, not acting it out for them. You should use your voice to *suggest*, rather than impersonate, the different characters.
3. You should prepare an introduction announcing the author and title and setting the scene. You may need to deliver further remarks during the course of the scene in order to clarify the stage directions or dramatic situation.
4. The time limit for this event is usually 10 minutes. Afterwards, the judge may give a spoken critique of your performance.

Preparing for Competition

1. Choose the scene carefully. You may use a "cutting" made especially for speaking contests, or you may prepare your own. Be sure that your adaptation can be clearly understood and does not distort the author's intentions. Avoid language or situations that might offend your audience.
2. Be sure you understand the characters and situation thoroughly. Create a different voice characterization for each person (two or three is the best number), but do not do imitations. Practice your presentation in front of different audiences to be sure it is effective. Tape-record the scene as well and listen carefully to be sure that the characters and conflicts come across distinctly.
3. As you speak, try to create and sustain a dramatic mood. Do not allow your gestures or delivery to break that mood or to distract your listeners. Try to let the mood linger for a few moments after you have completed your presentation.

Activities

1. Prepare a dramatic scene from a play, story, or novel and present it before the class. Use your voice and a few gestures to distinguish the characters and to interpret the action for your listeners. The presentation should last about 3 to 5 minutes. Afterwards, ask the members of your class to evaluate your presentation in terms of your understanding of the scene, the clarity of your presentation, the distinctness of the characters, and the effectiveness of your delivery.
2. Listen to a recording of a professional actor reading dramatic scenes from novels or short stories. Notice how the actor is able to suggest distinct characters by very slight alterations in his or her voice and delivery. Record your own reading of the selection and compare it with the professional's.

Humorous Interpretation

Like prose interpretation and dramatic interpretation, humorous interpretation is the presentation of a selection adapted from a published work. Besides interpreting the actions, emotions, and characters, the speaker must also make the audience laugh. Speakers are judged on timing and comic ability, as well as on understanding, preparation, and delivery.

Guidelines

1. The rules are similar to those for other oral interpretation events. The speaker may read the selection or may be required to recite from memory. The material may be limited to selections from published plays, or it may be chosen from any written source.
2. As in other oral interpretation, the speaker must prepare an introduction and transitions. The different characters are suggested rather than acted out.
3. The time limit for this event is generally 10 minutes. The judge usually gives a critique of the performance afterwards.

Preparing for Competition

1. Choose and adapt your selection (or "cutting") with the same care you would give to serious material (see "Oral Interpretation of Prose or Poetry" and "Dramatic Interpretation," above). Be sure the selection is suited to you and to your audience and is genuinely

funny. Avoid humor that is cruel, offensive, or aimed at racial or religious groups.

2. Prepare your interpretation with the aim of conveying the author's meaning to your listeners (see Chapter 11). Pay close attention to the humor in the material and how you can make it most effective. Practice your timing—that is, the rate at which you speak, the way you deliver funny lines, and the length of time you allow for audience laughter.

3. Practice your selection in front of as many different audiences as you can. Notice where and why they laugh and change your material or your interpretation to produce the response you want. (For a professional viewpoint, read Woody Allen's description on pages 63–64 of the way he tries out jokes.

4. Pace your performance so that it builds toward a humorous climax. Don't defuse the laughter by mugging, exaggerating, or overemphasizing minor jokes at the expense of the total effect.

Activities

1. Prepare a 3- to 5-minute presentation of one of your favorite humorous stories, anecdotes, or speeches. Practice your interpretation before friends or members of your family and then deliver it before the class. Observe the places where the audience laughed—or failed to laugh—and change your interpretation accordingly.

2. Listen to a recording of an actor or a comedian telling a humorous anecdote. Observe the way this person paces the performance and times the jokes. Practice delivering the same material and see if you can duplicate or improve on the professional's delivery.

Specialized Events

The following specialized events are found in speaking contests at various local and state levels.

Expository Speaking

In the expository speaking event, the student delivers a prepared speech explaining an institution, concept, or process. The rules may permit or prohibit notes. Speakers select their own topics from general categories that have been announced in advance. The time limit is usually 8 minutes. (See Chapter 5 for guidelines on expository speaking.)

Radio and Television Speaking

In the most common format, students in the radio and television speaking event are given 10 to 15 minutes' worth of teletype news copy. Each student has 30 minutes in which to edit this copy down to 4 minutes' delivery time, check the accuracy of the copy, and practice delivery. Carefully timed practice sessions are essential. In some broadcast speaking events, students read editorials they have written on assigned topics. (For guidelines on radio speaking, see Chapter 12.)

Readers' Theater

Readers' theater is oral interpretation, by a small group of readers, of adapted prose or drama selections. Two to six performers (generally) sit or stand on the stage. Lighting effects and backdrops may be permitted. The time limit is usually 30 to 40 minutes. Performances are judged on suitability, adaptation, understanding, gestures, and delivery. An imaginative director and many rehearsals give a performance the smoothness and unity needed to win.

Combination Events

A combination event requires a speaker to take part in a series of different speaking competitions; for example, one round of impromptu speaking, one round of extemporaneous speaking, and one round of original oratory. (These events are described in detail above.) Besides careful preparation and practice for all of the events, the contestant must pay close attention to the different rules of each.

Discussion

In a group discussion event, students participate either as members or as leaders of a problem-solving group. Participants are judged on preparation and on the quality of their contributions. Some events include panel discussions on topics of national importance, with each participant offering a different perspective or opinion. (For guidelines on group discussions, see Chapter 3.)

Student Congress

The National Forensic League sponsors regional and national student congresses. These events give students an opportunity to learn about legislative procedures and to develop their skills in parliamentary procedure as well as in speaking.

Guidelines

1. The participants may form a unicameral congress (with a single house), or a bicameral congress (with two houses: a senate and a house of representatives). The National Forensic League recommends a membership of 20 to 45 participants in each house.
2. The following officials are needed for each student congress session:
   - a *general director*, who makes practical arrangements for the congress
   - an *official scorer*, who awards merit points for each speech and who nominates two congress members for honors
   - a *parliamentarian*, who makes sure that the appropriate rules of parliamentary procedure are followed and who nominates two congress members for honors
   - a *page*, who carries messages between student congress participants
   - a *timekeeper*, who makes sure that no speaker exceeds the official time limits.

3. The members of each session of the student congress elect a presiding officer, whose main responsibility is to provide strong, thoughtful leadership for the congress.
4. All bills and resolutions are submitted to congress members before the student congress convenes.
5. Parliamentary procedure is used in conducting all congressional debate.
6. The National Forensic League requires that each legislative day consist of at least four hours, not counting the time spent in elections. The N.F.L. suggests the following order of business:
   - call to order
   - roll call of members
   - consideration of the calendar
   - election of presiding officer
   - committee meetings (optional)
   - calendar; debate of bills and resolutions
   - selection of superior congressman or congresswoman
   - awarding of congress gavel to presiding officer
   - fixing time for next meeting
   - adjournment

7. Before the end of each session, the scorer and the parliamentarian each nominate two students for the title of Most Outstanding Representative. The three students who received the highest scores are also nominated (if they have not already been). Then all the students vote for the most outstanding member of the congress.

Preparing for Competition

1. Prepare for a student congress by studying the bills and resolutions carefully. Do careful research on the topic of each bill and resolution, gathering arguments and evidence on both sides. Take notes during your research. Then organize your notes (either on cards or in a loose-leaf notebook) so that you will be able to refer to them during the congress.
2. If you submit a bill or resolution for a student congress, carefully plan the speech in which you will introduce that bill or resolution. Prepare to give a well-organized persuasive speech developed with appeals to logic (see Chapter 6).
3. Before the congress begins, be sure you are familiar with the use of parliamentary procedure (see Chapter 8).
4. Always show your respect both for the congress and for the other participants.

Activities

1. Attend a student congress sponsored by the National Forensic League. Write a short essay in response to one of the following questions:

   - Select one bill. How was that bill introduced, debated, and voted upon during the congress? In what ways could the participants have improved the process of dealing with that bill?
   - Who was chosen the outstanding member of the student congress? What particular qualities made that student outstanding? In what ways might other students have improved their contributions to the student congress?

2. With the other members of your class, form and conduct a practice student congress. You may debate specific issues that you have studied in a civics, history, or government class. If you conduct the congress at the level of the entire school, you may invite local government officials or community leaders to testify during the sessions.

Historical Speeches

"The Gettysburg Address"
Abraham Lincoln

From "The Greatness of Lincoln"
Richard S. Emrich

"Join Hands, Hearts, and Minds"
Rosalyn S. Yalow

The Nobel Prize Acceptance Speech
William Faulkner

"Blood, Toil, Tears, and Sweat"
Sir Winston Churchill

From "A Glory Has Departed"
Jawaharlal Nehru

The Gettysburg Address

Abraham Lincoln

Abraham Lincoln delivered the following speech on November 19, 1863 at the dedication of the National Soldiers' Cemetery at Gettysburg, Pennsylvania. In this address he eloquently dedicates the Civil War cemetery to the "honored dead" and to the principles for which they nobly gave their lives.

Fourscore and seven years ago our fathers brought forth on this continent a new nation, conceived in liberty, and dedicated to the proposition that all men are created equal.

Now we are engaged in a great civil war, testing whether that nation, or any nation so conceived and so dedicated, can long endure. We are met on a great battlefield of that war. We have come to dedicate a portion of that field as a final resting-place for those who here gave their lives that that nation might live. It is altogether fitting and proper that we should do this.

But, in a larger sense, we cannot dedicate—we cannot consecrate—we cannot hallow—this ground. The brave men, living and dead, who struggled here, have consecrated it far above our poor power to add or detract. The world will little note nor long remember what we say here, but it can never forget what they did here. It is for us, the living, rather, to be dedicated here to the unfinished work which they who fought here have thus far so nobly advanced. It is rather for us to be here dedicated to the great task remaining before us—that from these honored dead we take increased devotion to that cause for which they gave the last full measure of devotion; that we here highly resolve that these dead shall not have died in vain; that this nation, under God, shall have a new birth of freedom; and that government of the people, by the people, for the people, shall not perish from the earth.

From "The Greatness of Lincoln"

Richard S. Emrich

The following speech was delivered to Congress by Richard S. Emrich in 1959.

It is common knowledge that when one stands too close to a mountain range, one cannot see which mountain is the highest and towers above the rest. It is only at a distance that a true perspective is gained and the great peak can be distinguished from the foothills. So it was that some who lived close to Lincoln could not see his greatness and failed to see which speech was great at Gettysburg. So it is that we, 150 years after his birth, are able to see that no American is greater; that he was "the grandest figure on the crowded canvas of the nineteenth century"; that he represents the America we love as does no other man; that he abides and grows greater with the years; that there was in his simple figure an Olympian quality, a nobility and a grandeur; that he was of God . . . and that all of this greatness is revealed in the mood approaching religious awe which we feel when we visit his Memorial. One hundred fifty years since his birth, and the outline of his figure towering above his contemporaries, becomes clearer with the distance. . . .

There are, of course, some aspects of his figure which we will never understand, and at which we can only wonder. Trying to understand his strange combination of sorrow and jest, of loneliness and wit, is like gazing into a great forest; you can see so far, and then there is hidden mystery. Or how was it, to take another example, that in the midst of an age in which histrionic and florid oratory was the style, a man arose—with one year of formal schooling, poor, self-taught—who used language as the clean, chaste, and simple expression of his thought? From what mysterious spring did he drink that he would not, could not, fit into the oratorical pattern of his day? And how was it that he did not strive for beauty yet achieved it? We can never comprehend him, grasp him, wrap him up in a neat package; but we can from his writings see the broad outline of his greatness. . . .

. . . there was something truly remarkable about his method of reasoning. We all know that this self-educated man went deeper than most men, and that after a century much of what he said is still strangely fresh. Why is it, as Richard Weaver says, that he is more quoted than the more intellectual Jefferson or the academic Wilson? What can we learn about his method of reasoning?

Well, he was not corrupted by the modern advertising assumption that the average mental age is twelve years, or by a trust in promotional tricks that make all things trivial. He respected the people, and, as

Herndon said, would not think of cheating a man out of his vote any more than he would cheat him out of his money. For his own sake and for his hearers he liked to boil a matter down to a terse statement. "I could not sleep, although I tried to, when I got on such a hunt for an idea until I had caught it; and when I thought I had got it, I was not satisfied until I had repeated it over and over again until I had put it in plain language enough, as I thought, for any boy I knew to comprehend. . . . This was a kind of passion with me." Herndon says that his opponents were afraid of his condensation. This means that Lincoln never threw a battery of arguments at people, like a scattering shotgun. He went to the essence of the matter; or, as he said, he liked to come at a question like a surveyor, from the north, south, east, and west until he focused it. And then this essence was passed on to the people. "We won't break up the Union, and you shan't"; ". . . of the people, by the people, and for the people"; ". . . to do the right as God gives us to see the right." "Slavery is a violation of eternal right. We have temporized with it from the necessities of our condition; but as sure as God reigns and school children read, that black foul lie can never be consecrated into God's hallowed truth." These essences of a clear mind soaked down into the public consciousness until he was able to carry the people with him. . . .

Join Hands, Hearts, and Minds

Rosalyn S. Yalow

The second woman to receive the Nobel Prize in physiology or medicine, Dr. Yalow delivered the following acceptance speech in Stockholm, Sweden in 1977.

Your Majesties, Your Royal Highnesses, Ladies, Gentlemen, and you, the Students, who are the carriers of our hopes for the survival of the world and our dreams for its future. Tradition has ordained that one of the laureates represent all of us in responding to your tribute. The choice of one among the several deemed truly and equally distinguished must indeed be difficult. Perhaps I have been selected for this privilege because there is certainly one way in which I am distinguishable from the others. This difference permits me to address myself first to a very special problem.

Among you students of Stockholm and among other students, at least in the Western world, women are represented in reasonable proportion to their numbers in the community; yet among the scientists, scholars, and leaders of our world they are not. No objective testing has revealed such substantial differences in talent as to account for this discrepancy. The failure of women to have reached positions of leadership has been due in large part to social and professional discrimination. In the past, few women have tried and even fewer have succeeded. We still live in a world in which a significant fraction of people, including women, believe that a woman belongs and wants to belong exclusively in the home; that a woman should not aspire to achieve more than her male counterparts and particularly not more than her husband. Even now women with exceptional qualities for leadership sense from their parents, teachers, and peers that they must be harder-working, accomplish more and yet are less likely to receive appropriate rewards than are men. These are real problems which may never disappear or, at best, will change very slowly.

We cannot expect in the immediate future that all women who seek it will achieve full equality of opportunity. But if women are to start moving towards that goal, we must believe in ourselves or no one else will believe in us; we must match our aspirations with the competence, courage, and determination to succeed; and we must feel a personal responsibility to ease the path for those who come afterwards. The world cannot afford the loss of the talents of half its people if we are to solve the many problems which beset us.

If we are to have faith that mankind will survive and thrive on the face of the earth, we must believe that each succeeding generation will be wiser than its progenitors. We transmit to you, the next generation, the total sum of our knowledge. Yours is the responsibility to use it, add to it, and transmit it to your children.

A decade ago during the period of worldwide student uprisings there was deep concern that too many of our young people were so disillusioned as to feel that the world must be destroyed before it could be rebuilt. Even now, it is all too easy to be pessimistic if we consider our multiple problems: the possible depletion of resources faster than science can generate replacements or substitutes; hostilities between nations and between groups within nations which appear not to be resolvable; unemployment and vast inequalities among different races and different lands. Even as we envision and solve scientific problems—and put men on the moon—we appear ill-equipped to provide solutions for the social ills that beset us.

We bequeath to you, the next generation, our knowledge but also our problems. While we still live, let us join hands, hearts, and minds to work together for their solution so that your world will be better than ours and the world of your children even better.

The Nobel Prize Acceptance Speech

William Faulkner

The celebrated American novelist William Faulkner delivered the following speech in Stockholm, Sweden to accept the 1949 Nobel Prize for literature. In it he dedicates his literary acclaim to those writers after him and urges them to realize their moral obligation to write about the universal truths of the human condition.

I feel that this award was not made to me as a man, but to my work—a life's work in the agony and sweat of the human spirit, not for glory and least of all for profit, but to create out of the materials of the human spirit something which did not exist before. So this award is only mine in trust. It will not be difficult to find a dedication for the money part of it commensurate with the purpose and significance of its origin. But I would like to do the same with the acclaim too, by using this moment as a pinnacle from which I might be listened to by the young men and women already dedicated to the same anguish and travail, among whom is already that one who will someday stand here where I am standing.

Our tragedy today is a general and universal physical fear so long sustained by now that we can even bear it. There are no longer problems of the spirit. There is only the question: When will I be blown up? Because of this, the young man or woman writing today has forgotten the problems of the human heart in conflict with itself which alone can make good writing because only that is worth writing about, worth the agony and the sweat.

He must learn them again. He must teach himself that the basest of all things is to be afraid; and, teaching himself that, forget it forever, leaving no room in this workshop for anything but the old verities and truths of the heart, the old universal truths lacking which any story is ephemeral and doomed—love and honor and pity and pride and compassion and sacrifice. Until he does so, he labors under a curse. He writes not of love but of lust, of defeats in which nobody loses anything of value, of victories without hope, and, worst of all, without pity or compassion. His griefs grieve on no universal bones, leaving no scars. He writes not of the heart but of the glands.

Until he relearns these things, he will write as though he stood among and watched the end of man. I decline to accept the end of man. It is easy enough to say that man is immortal simply because he will endure; that when the last ding-dong of doom has clanged and faded from the last worthless rock hanging tideless in the last red and dying evening, that even then there will still be one more sound: that of his puny inexhaustible voice, still talking. I refuse to accept this. I believe that man will not merely endure: he will prevail. He is immortal, not because he alone among creatures has an inexhaustible voice, but because he has a soul, a spirit capable of compassion and sacrifice and endurance. The poet's, the writer's, duty is to write about these things. It is his privilege to help man endure by lifting his heart, by reminding him of the courage and honor and hope and pride and compassion and pity and sacrifice which have been the glory of his past. The poet's voice need not merely be the record of man; it can be one of the props, the pillars, to help him endure and prevail.

Blood, Toil, Tears, and Sweat

Sir Winston Churchill

The following speech was delivered by Sir Winston Churchill to the House of Commons on May 13, 1940 shortly after he became Prime Minister. One of the most crucial speeches in modern history, it assured England that the new administration could confidently handle the war and assured the rest of the world that England would fight to the end. Note that the style of capitalization, although inappropriate for modern American writing, was standard in Churchill's speeches.

I beg to move,

> That this House welcomes the formation of a Government representing the united and inflexible resolve of the nation to prosecute the war with Germany to a victorious conclusion.

On Friday evening last I received His Majesty's Commission to form a new Administration. It was the evident wish and will of Parliament and the nation that this should be conceived on the broadest possible basis and that it should include all parties, both those who supported the late Government and also the parties of the Opposition. I have completed the most important part of this task. A War Cabinet has been formed of five Members, representing, with the Opposition Liberals, the unity of the nation. The three party Leaders have agreed to serve, either in the War Cabinet or in high executive office. The three Fighting Services have been filled. It was necessary that this should be done in one single day, on account of the extreme urgency and rigour of events. A number of other positions, key positions, were filled yesterday, and I am submitting a further list to His Majesty tonight. I hope to complete the appointment of the principal Ministers during tomorrow. The appointment of the other Ministers usually takes a little longer, but I trust that, when Parliament meets again, this part of my task will be completed, and that the administration will be complete in all aspects.

I considered it in the public interest to suggest that the House should be summoned to meet today. Mr. Speaker agreed, and took the necessary steps, in accordance with the powers conferred upon him by the Resolution of the House. At the end of the proceedings today, the Adjournment of the House will be proposed until Tuesday, 21st May, with, of course, provision for earlier meeting, if need be. The business to be considered during that week will be notified to Members at the earliest opportunity. I now invite the House, by the Motion which stands in my name, to record its approval of the steps taken and to declare its confidence in the new Government.

To form an Administration of this scale and complexity is a serious undertaking in itself, but it must be remembered that we are in the preliminary stage of one of the greatest battles in history, that we are in action at many other points in Norway and in Holland, that we have to be prepared in the Mediterranean, that the air battle is continuous and that many preparations, such as have been indicated by my hon. Friend below the Gangway, have to be made here at home. In this crisis I hope I may be pardoned if I do not address the House at any length today. I hope that any of my friends and colleagues, or former colleagues, who are affected by the political reconstruction, will make allowance, all allowance, for any lack of ceremony with which it has been necessary to act. I would say to the House, as I said to those who have joined this Government: "I have nothing to offer but blood, toil, tears, and sweat."

We have before us an ordeal of the most grievous kind. We have before us many, many long months of struggle and of suffering. You ask, what is our policy? I can say: It is to wage war, by sea, land, and air, with all our might and with all the strength that God can give us; to wage war against a monstrous tyranny, never surpassed in the dark, lamentable catalogue of human crime. That is our policy. You ask, what is our aim? I can answer in one word: It is victory, victory at all costs, victory in spite of all terror, victory, however long and hard the road may be; for without victory, there is no survival. Let that be realised; no survival for the British Empire, no survival for all that the British Empire has stood for, no survival for the urge and impulse of the ages, that mankind will move forward towards its goals. But I take up my task with buoyancy and hope. I feel sure that our cause will not be suffered to fail among men. At this time I feel entitled to claim the aid of all, and I say, "Come then, let us go forward together with our united strength."

From "A Glory Has Departed"
Jawaharlal Nehru

A *eulogy* is a formal speech in high praise of something or some-one, usually a deceased person. The following is an excerpt from the 1948 eulogy, "A Glory Has Departed" by Jawaharlal Nehru. The subject is the assassinated Mahatma Gandhi, whose death was mourned by millions in India and throughout the world.

A glory has departed and the sun that warmed and brightened our lives has set, and we shiver in the cold and dark. Yet he would not have us feel this way. After all, that glory that we saw for all these years, that man with the divine fire, changed us also—and such as we are we have been moulded by him during these years; and, out of that divine fire many of us also took a small spark which strengthened and made us work to some extent on the lines that he fashioned. And so if we praise him, our words seem rather small, and if we praise him to some extent we also praise ourselves. Great men and eminent men have monuments in bronze and marble set up for them, but this man of divine fire managed in his lifetime to become enshrined in millions and millions of hearts so that all of us become somewhat of the stuff that he was made of, though to an infinitely lesser degree. He spread out this way all over India, not in palaces only, or in secret places or in assemblies, but in every hamlet and hut of the lonely and those who suffer. He lives in the hearts of millions and he will live for immemorial ages.

Contest Speeches

From the 1986 Championship Team Debate

Brian Kramer
Robert Unikel
Holly Bartling
Steve Dvorske

1985 Final Round U.S. Extemporaneous Speech

Cortney Sylvester

1985 Final Round Original Oratory

Andy Thornton

From the 1986 Championship Team Debate

Brian Kramer, Robert Unikel, Holly Bartling, Steve Dvorske

Below are the first constructive affirmative and the first constructive negative speeches of a 1986 National Forensic League cross-examination debate. This is a verbatim transcript of the actual debate, including any mistakes that might have been made. As in most competitive debates, each speech is followed by a brief cross-examination by an opposing team member. The affirmative team, Brian Kramer and Robert Unikel, won the debate. You will note that this contest debate uses certain formalities, such as referring to the headings of the debate outline, that make each presentation read more like a brief than a speech.

First Constructive Affirmative, by Brian Kramer of Glenbrook North High School, Northbrook, Illinois

We are appalled at the tragic and needless death of thousands of Americans each year as a result of unsafe drinking water. Unfortunately, the action needed to save these innocent human beings has lagged behind available but unused technologies. With a firm commitment to ending this maniacal slaughter, we ask you to consider the following contention. Granually activated carbon filters carcinogenic impurities. GAC filters carcinogenic impurities.

An unfortunate aspect of our water situation is noted in subpoint A: Water impurities kill thousands of Americans. Water impurities kill. The connection between low water quality and cancer has been proven by a preponderance of available studies. Dr. Upton, Director of the National Cancer Institute, reported in 1979, ''Nine of ten studies showed a number of statistically significant associations between water quality and cancer.'' Contaminants in drinking water are known to cause bladder and gastrointestinal cancer. Jacqueline Warren of the National Resource Defense Council reviewed the data in May of 1984: ''To date, there is strong suggestive evidence of such a link in more than 20 epidemiological studies that have demonstrated a statistically significant association between bladder and gastrointestinal cancer in the consumption of chemically contaminated drinking water.'' The harms of cancer from drinking water were quantified by Page, Harris, and Bruser of the Environmental Protection Agency and the Environmental Defense Fund in 1981: ''Gastrointestinal and urinary tract cancer, to which organic drinking water contaminants have been most consistently linked, constitute about 30 percent of all cancer illness and death, or about 200,000 new cancer cases and 115,000 deaths each year.'' It is certainly ironic that the fluid which is considered to sustain life is tainted so as to threaten life itself.

414

Our advanced society has the technology to deal with this situation, but unfortunately, subpoint B: The present system refuses to act. The system is not acting. In examining issues of water quality protection, it is important to deal with two major areas: general water quality protection and specific technological achievements. Realize subpoint one: The Federal government has failed to act. The Federal government is not acting. Although the Federal government has the authority to deal with water contamination, the Environmental Protection Agency has consistently ignored water quality problems. Senator Durenberger explained in the *Congressional Record* on January 3, 1985: "To date, there are still only a handful of standards for drinking water. The Environmental Protection Agency has done virtually nothing to use the authority granted to it by Congress and the Safe Drinking Water Act to protect the public health." Not only has an inaction been the norm, but specific technological advances have been prevented as well.

Subpoint two: Granually activated carbon has been resisted. GAC has been resisted. Recently proposed legislation fails to require the use of granually activated carbon. As reported in *Engineering News Record*, May 29, 1986, page 7: "Although granually activated carbon is designated as an effective method of removing synthetic organic chemicals, communities under development are not required to use GAC." Water utility companies, under the misconception that granually activated carbon, or GAC systems, are expensive, have acted to prevent GAC from being implemented. Harvard Professor Peter Rogers explained in the July 1983 issue of *Atlantic Monthly* on page 84: "In 1978 the EPA proposed carbon filters as the optional choice for the control of hazardous chemicals in water. Soon after, a group of 90 investor-owned water utilities, the Coalition for Safe Drinking Water, was formed to resist an EPA requirement on the score. Although the coalition expressed doubts about how well the filters would work, their underlying complaint was cost." These concerns are clearly unwarranted, as we see in subpoint C. The affirmative builds a constructive solution to an unfortunate but genuine problem. The affirmative will solve.

Note subpoint one: Granually activated carbon solves for cancer death. GAC solves for cancer death. The granually activated carbon system filters the impurities from the water and thereby eliminates the cancer risk. Page, Harris, and Bruser explain the effectiveness of this process in their 1981 work, "The Scientific Basis of Health and Safety Regulation": "Removal of organic chemical contaminants from drinking water is associated with the prevention of cancer deaths, non-fatal cancer illnesses, immunogenic and teratogenic effects, the reduction of anxiety caused by knowing that drinking water poses health risks, and the improvement of the case in order of tap water." Peter Rogers discussed the process more specifically in 1983. "Flushing water that has been disinfected with chlorine through a carbon filter at the end of the treatment cycle can effectively remove trihalomethanes and any other hazardous organic chemicals present.'' According to a report released in 1980 by the National Academy of Sciences, this process is highly effective, as Page, Harris, and Bruser revealed in 1981. Granually activated carbon will reduce cancer risk from drinking water by 90 percent.

Please realize subpoint two: Granually activated carbon is feasible and economical. It is feasible and economical. GAC systems have proven successful in Europe, where they're used extensively. The *Federal Register* reported on November 29, 1979: ''GAC is used to remove organical chemical contaminants from potable water in 21 cities in Europe. It had been operating for up to ten years.'' Most of these plants had been operating without any adverse effects or undue difficulties. The GAC process is economically feasible. Martin Shoencamp, Director of the Zurich Waterworks, discussed the feasibility in November of 1979: ''GAC filtration is indispensable and at a cost of one-eighth of the total treatment cost, its use is economically feasible.'' The GAC technology should certainly no longer be ignored. Ron Tunnelly of the *National Civic Review* announced in June of 1975: ''The most promising technique for dealing with organic chemicals is the use of activated carbon. It is remarkably efficient in trapping and removing organic chemical contaminants.''

In light of the overwhelming evidence in favor of granually activated carbon technology, we ask you to consider the following plan: Section 1—Legislation: The federal government will establish the Water Quality Purification Act. Water utilities must utilize granually activated carbon filtration systems in compliance with the Safe Drinking Water Act. Utilities must keep those systems in proper working order to insure that the maximum number of carcinogenic contaminants be filtered from the water. Granually activated carbon shall be implemented. Section 2—Logistics A: The cost of GAC implementation shall be funded through all normal governmental means, including, if necessary, the establishment of a national lottery. B: The plan shall be enforced through fine and imprisonment. Normal judicial means shall be used. C: Affirmative speech is so served to aide interpretation of legislative intent. On behalf of those individuals who could have been saved, who can be saved, and who will be saved with granually activated carbon filtration, we ask you to vote affirmative in today's debate.

Cross-Examination   (A: Affirmative, N: Negative)

N: A lot of people are dying because of our water quality. Is that what you contend?

A: Yes, that's what our evidence contends. . . .

N: It says nine out of ten studies show an association, right?

A: . . . Yes, the evidence indicates that nine of ten studies do show an association between the drinking water and cancer.

N: One study doesn't, right?

A: One out of every ten studies might not indicate this correlation, correct.

N: And nine only show an association, right?

A: Well, nine indicate a link between it, and we give the quantification of 115,000 lives later on.

N: Let's go to that Page, Harris, Bruser card in '81 where it says 115,000 deaths. . . . Where do these people live?

A: Well, they live throughout the entire nation. They're people who drink the water when it's contaminated because the purification systems are not proper.

N: So they live anywhere, right?

A: Well, most people, yes, throughout the entire nation people are dying because of this, yes.

N: Okay. Then you talk about in the Warren card right above that in '84, it says "suggestive evidence in epidemiological studies," right?

A: It says twenty studies have concluded with the affirmative, that's what the evidence indicates.

N: But it's just "suggestive evidence."

A: Well, no, it says twenty studies have correlated.

N: But it says "suggestive" too.

A: Well, that's what that means. The studies—the twenty of them— have clearly concluded affirmative.

N: Now, is the EPA specifically saying to all these water utility companies, "Hey, don't put GAC in?"

A: Well, the EPA is not acting right now. The EPA has the authority—

N: Does that stop the water utility from saying, "I like GAC, I'm going to put it in?"

A: Well, . . . yes, there are people inside the industries who do not want to implement it. That's what our lobbyist evidence indicates, and the fact that the EPA does not want to have GAC implemented means that these plants aren't going just to all of a sudden say, "Hey, let's install GAC." Because they fear the misconception of cost, for example.

N: These lobbyists are very effective, aren't they?

A: Yes, they are effective in stopping the actual GAC implementation-free path, not—

N: Does your plan ban lobbyists?

A: No, our plan does not necessarily—does not ban lobbyists but it enforces our regulations so that it ensures the lobbyists, for example, have to begin implementing—

N: GAC solves, Page, Harris, and Bruser, again in '81. Removal of contamination is "associated" with decrease of cancer. Right? Only associated.

A: No, it says that it will indeed link—

N: No, I wrote the card down. I think it says only "associated."

A: No, it says that empirically in Europe it has been proven to get rid of cancer, that it's the only way to solve the problem.

N: No, that's not the card I'm talking about. I'm talking about the first one under little one.

A: Well, that card says that removal would be the best possible way.

N: Are you sure?

A: That's what the card says, it says that it would prevent "cancer deaths, non-fatal cancer illnesses, immunogenic and teratogenic effects. . . ."

N: Okay, read that card, read that word.

A: Right, it's "associated with the prevention," but that's where the link is, association—

N: Ninety percent of the risk, not 90 percent of the cancer.

A: No, it says it will solve from 90 percent of the cancer deaths.

N: Oh, read that card, too.

A: Sure. "Granually activated carbon will reduce cancer risk from drinking water by 90 percent," but that's the direct—the risk is what's—

N: I already know. . . .

First Constructive Negative, by Holly Bartling of Shawnee Mission-West High School, Overland Park, Kansas

I'd like to start out first with an overview, and that's on technology lock. Realize A, the affirmative mandates one specific technology, and that's GAC. B: Realize the present system doesn't just use chlorine, as the affirmative would like to have you think. There are multiple technologies in the status quo—specifically, ozone. It is successful, and it works. From *Business Week*, May 7, 1984, page 118: "Ozonation, in fact, is the fastest growing sector of the U.S. water purification business." And also from A.C. Anderson, *American Journal of Public Health*, page 1291, in 1982: "Ozone is a strong oxidizing agent and reacts with a wide variety of organic compounds. Ozone can oxidize trihalomethanes in the presence of ultraviolet light, does not form trihalomethanes in water, and can also remove trihalomethane precursors." In the present system, there's better technology. Realize subpoint C: You have an advantage with the status quo. And that's the fact that there's increased innovation and better technology in the present system, not just one technology—that is, GAC.

Go to contention one. They tell you, A, that water impurity kills. Four responses here. One: Chlorine does not cause cancer. From Young and Canerecks in 1983: "Causal interpretations of this modest association between colon cancer death and chlorinated water are unjustified in view of the indirect ascertainment of water exposures and incomplete information on potential confounding factors." But two: The harm isn't proven. From Joseph A. Cortruvo, *Environmental Science Technology*, March 1981, quoting: "From an NAS review commissioned by the EPA, the results suggest that higher concentrations of THMs in drinking water may be associated with an increased frequency of cancer of the bladder. The results do not establish causality, and the quantitative estimates of increased or decreased risks are extremely crude." But in three: Realize that the findings are inconsistent. From Moriso S. Gotlieb, *Environmental Health Perspective*, 1982, page 46: "Association between chlorination and other sites of cancer are often heavily dependent on the matching variables of race, sex, age, and year of death. And the effects observed were not found to be consistent in any way, which would suggest a true drinking water effect." But argue four: The risk is small. From Claire Stewart, *Science*, June 5, 1985, page 1086: "Unless a very large increase in cancer has been overlooked or unless the usual assumption of linear dose-effect relationship is seriously in error, the number of excess cancers from chloroform in water must be zero for the most probable case."

But he gives you a '79 Upton card. I'll have four responses here. One: The card is incredibly generic. It's not specific to any kind of water pollution. It just says, "there's hazardous waste in the water." That could be from pesticide run-off. But two: Argue a threshold press here. How many THMs have to be in the water before the cancer occurs? Make them give you that threshold and make them prove they can reduce the level of THMs in the water past that. Or they have no solvency. Three: Prove that GAC can solve for the hazardous chemicals they claim are causing the cancer. The evidence on GAC solvency only deals with organics. And four: Prove that there are no harms from the well water, because that's where the majority of the harms come from. From "Environmental Progress, Intelligence, and EPA Perspective," EPA, June 1984: "More than 50,000 small drinking water systems serve

11.4 percent of the U.S. population relying on community water supply systems. These systems typically have the greatest problems with microbial contamination. Similar problems can often occur in the over 160,000 private wells and systems that serve seasonal facilities and the traveling public.'' Realize that these wells have absolutely no kind of mandates on how much to be cleaning up, so don't let them claim no harm from the smaller wells because they can't solve for them.

Go to the '84 card on 20 studies. Argue one: That card is incredibly generic, too. It just says that there are chemicals in the water. It doesn't say anything about GAC can solve for them. Two: The card only says correlation, and you cannot extrapolate causality from correlation. From Joseph A. Cortruvo, *Environmental Science and Technology*, March 1981, page 273: ''The epidemiological evidence is thus incomplete and preliminary. A causal relationship cannot be established by the correlational studies.'' But thirdly, realize that they give no threshold as to how much cancer is caused just by the chemical toxins. They don't give a threshold as to how many toxins cause the cancer.

Go to the Page, Harris, and Bruser card. Argue one: The card just says that 30 percent of all illnesses are gastrointestinal, but what they don't prove is that all of the cancers that occur are coming from the drinking water. But two: It actually won't equal colon cancer. From Joseph A. Cortruvo, *Environmental Science and Technology*, March 1981. Quoting an NAS review commissioned by the EPA: ''The positive association found for bladder cancer was small and had a large margin for error—not only statistical, but much more because of the very nature of the studies.'' So realize that the studies are actually bad.

But go down finally to subpoint B where he tells you the status quo can't act. Specifically, that government is not acting. Group the Durenberger card, and I'll have five responses. One, in 1986, prove that EPA's ignoring the standards. They just give you a 1985 card. There's been SDWA reauthorizations in 1986. But two: That's absolutely no inherent barrier. They have to prove that the industries are the ones that are not complying because that's where the harms would occur if the drinking water facility clean-up places are the ones that aren't complying. But three: There's absolutely no structural barrier here unless they prove that the EPA is going out and forcing industry to not comply to the standards. Four: Industries can get GAC in the present system. That's no inherent barrier. And five: Ignorance to GAC is no barrier. We can go out and educate the people if GAC is such a good proposal. Secondly, he tells you GAC's resisted. Argue one: No analysis here. Why would EPA be resisting their own recommendations? That doesn't make sense. But two: If EPA's the problem, they're using status quo mechanisms of operation, so that won't take it out.

Subpoint C: The affirmative solves. Specifically, they tell you that GAC solves. Argue one: The card only says ''association.'' Cross-apply the correlation card I read you above that says, ''correlation cannot be linked to causality.'' Two: They don't take out the cancer that's claimed in the harms. The harm cancer deals with toxic substances, and this deals with organics. Three: They don't stop the deaths. The card says they just decrease the risk. Argue threshold here big time. Make them prove they decrease the risk and not just stop having the cancers occur. Go to the '83 card unremoved THMs. Argue one: They have to reduce past the threshold. Then two: The card only deals with taking out organics and THMs. It says nothing about the chemical substances claimed as harms on case side. On the Page, Harris, and Bruser card on decreased risk, argue one: The card only says it removes 90 percent of the risk. There's still a 10 percent risk in getting cancer and also it doesn't say that it removes 90 percent of the toxins that cause cancer. There's still a 10 percent risk. Make them prove that this 10 percent risk won't throw the people over the threshold and still give them cancer. But two: The deaths come from the chemical substances, and they don't prove that GAC can take that out.

Go to little two where they tell you it's feasible. They give you a Europe card. Argue one: Europe's systems are very different. They use ozone in Europe. From *Industrial Water Engineering*, March-April 1982: ''Ozone has been used for more than 60 years in the drinking water treatment on the European continent.'' Or ''more than 1,000 municipal water treatment plants use ozone as part of their chemical treatment.'' So don't let them claim this empirical solvency because it's very different. Two: Make them give an empirical U.S. study where it solved. And three: Realize that GAC can solve. From *American Waterworks Association's Journal*, 1985, page 17: ''If there would be an appreciable reduction in the risk of cancer or other disease, we would spend whatever necessary. However, we feel that given the evidence, there just isn't any measurable improvement with GAC treatments.'' But finally, go down to the '79 card, where he tells you it costs one-eighth of the total cost. This is really important. The card doesn't say it costs one-eighth of how much perhaps chlorine would cost, it says it costs one-eighth of all the treatment in the—costs for all the treatment facility, and I'll contend that's a lot of money. Go to the '75 card where they tell you there's promising tech. Argue one: They don't prove it can solve in the long term. But two: That was eleven years ago. Come on, there's going to be a lot better technology in 1986.

I'll finally have an underview, and that's on justification. Argument one: You can solve with home GACs in the present system. Little one: If they're good, you can get them now. Little two: They're cheap. From Rogers in 1983: ''*Consumer Reports* review 14 of them in the February 1983 issue and rate five either good or excellent. The three best were Culligan at $175, Sears at $23, and AMF Cuno at $67.'' Subpoint B: Negative is superior. Little one: You get more individual rights if you vote for the present system because they can go out and get their home GACs. But two: You get more superior solvency because those that have the well waters can go get the GAC. Because of the fact that the present system is better, I ask you to vote negative.

Cross-Examination

A: You indicate that right now we're not like Europe because we're not using ozone, right?

N: Yes.

A: But wasn't your first observation dealing with the fact that we're using ozone in solving?

N: Okay, now that evidence deals with the fact that that status quo has many technologies and that ozone is an option.

A: Doesn't the evidence specifically say ozone?

N: Yes, but what you must prove—see, what I'm contending here is that there are many options. There are still people in the present system using chlorine, and so you can't prove solvency on that.

A: Do you disprove that right now that the GAC systems are working right now in Europe, in the twenty-one cities where it's implemented?

N: What I said is you can't imply this is empirical evidence because in Europe they're only using ozone, and it doesn't take any kind of knowledge to use these GACs because the ozone dissipates.

A: Okay. Calm down. Now, you indicate that on case side we can't find a causality between the studies. That our studies are foreign, right?

N: No. The card specifically said you can't link colon cancer, I believe.

A: Well, it says that there's all kinds of factors, like smoking et cetera?

N: Do you want to hear the body of the card?

A: I just asked you a question. Isn't that what it says, like smoking, and stuff like that?

N: No.

A: Well, what is the evidence saying then?

N: Do you want the body of the card?

A: Well, that third subpoint says the findings are inconsistent.

N: Oh, that card.

A: Right, right.

N: Okay. I thought you said the correlation card.

A: Okay, that evidence indicates that—

N: That there's variables and that—

A: Right. Why do your studies, for example, that well waters cause cancer not use these variables?

N: No, well what this card here specifically says is that there are so many inconsistent findings affirmative that you don't know that there's a harm.

A: It doesn't specify affirmative, does it? It's either way.

N: It says there's no way which would suggest a true drinking water affect.

A: Well, how would accurate studies be conducted on wells, therefore, if there's no variables at all?

N: On wells.

A: Yeah, you indicate that wells are extracausal factors, correct?

N: No. The well card that I read to you says that about 50 percent of the people are reliant on well water and not community facilities.

A: Okay.

N: That's from a different card.

A: Okay, fine. Now, you indicate that now, there's no inherent barrier, et cetera. Do you read any evidence that we're implementing GAC?

N: No, we don't have to be implementing GAC. I said there's nothing that's stopping anyone from going and getting it.

A: Okay, but—

N: Just because no one gets it doesn't mean that it's a barrier.

A: Do you ever prove that we're getting it? I mean should we assume that we're getting it? I mean, should the judge automatically assume since you assert that that we have GAC right now?

N: What I say here is that you have no barrier to prevent people from going out and getting GAC. That's all I have to show is the mechanism.

A: What do you mean a barrier to going out and getting it? Buying it for well water? Do you mean buying it so you can put it on the side of your faucet, right?

N: Well, I don't know what you're arguing on. Are you arguing the home ones or yours?

A: Okay, below you're arguing that we have a PMN amount because of the well water, right?

N: Right.

A: Okay, but why, if the well water, if they can go and they can still buy these things to put on their home faucets, why should we effect this at all?

N: Because I'm saying that you're not solving for all. Now, you're implementing that—

A: Now, wait a second, do we have to solve for every one? I mean, we're saving for 115,000 lives.

N: Well, Steve will deal with that.

A: Okay, that's fine. Now, you indicate we do not prove that it's going to solve for the long term.

N: Yeah, the card just says that it's going to be feasible.

A: No, doesn't the evidence indicate that it would be indispensible and it would cost less?

N: Yeah, but it doesn't say in the long term it can be used.

A: Why . . . where are you getting . . . why does it say long term? It says it could be implemented, it's feasible. Why would that assume only today?

N: Well, that doesn't necessarily mean that it's long term. The card never said it.

A: Okay, thank you.

1985 Final Round U.S. Extemporaneous Speech

Cortney Sylvester

Cortney Sylvester of Barnesville High School in Barnesville, Minnesota, won second place in the U.S. Extemporaneous category of the 1985 National Forensic League Tournament. His topic was "What would be the ramifications of a United States trade balance with Japan?"

A banker, an electrician, and a politician were taking an IQ test. One of the questions on this test read, "What term would be used to describe the problem resulting when outflow exceeds inflow?" Well, the banker, considering his financial institution, said, "Overdraft." The electrician, considering his circuitry, said, "Overload." The politician, on the other hand, stared dumbly into space and asked, "What problem?" Certainly, in this day and age the politicians of the United States are having no trouble whatsoever recognizing perhaps the most important inflow-outflow imbalance we are experiencing—specifically, the inability of the United States to export the same amount it imports. Because of the potential economic upheaval that our trade deficit holds, it is important that the United States strike at this imbalance at its greatest point of origin. In other words, we should increasingly be asking ourselves, "What would be the ramifications of a United States trade balance with Japan?" In order to answer this question, it is necessary to look at two things. We first of all have to examine the causes of the deficit in order to gain an understanding of the problem. And then second, we must turn our attention to the impact of balancing our trade with the people of Japan.

Now, initially, of course, we have to examine precisely why we have a problem at this time. According to the *Wall Street Journal* in April, the United States currently imports some $37 billion more in goods than it exports to Japan. For this reason, we must examine precisely why the United States is unable to export what it imports. And there are three basic causes of the problem. Now the first is that the United States is experiencing a high growth rate relative to Japan. According to the April 8th issue of *U.S. News and World Report*, the United States is experiencing an expansion. We came out of our recession essentially faster than did Japan. Now, this makes the United States an extremely attractive market for Japanese goods in comparison to the Japanese market for American goods because in the United States the impact of growth is a surge in demand while capital flow is at its high point. In other words, we have the money to buy, and we have the willingness to do so. Now, in Japan, on the other hand, both slower rates of growth hold down demand, hold down the availability of capital, and hold down the ability of the people to buy our goods.

A second cause of the imbalance with Japan, however, is the way the Japanese protect their domestic industries. Now, George Will, writing in the April 22nd issue of *Newsweek* magazine, explained that although the Japanese are inviting American goods through the rhetoric of their government, they have been unable to overcome their basic fear of strangers. Their attitude toward outsiders to their society has fostered a trade policy that makes it extremely difficult for American and other foreign goods to enter the marketplace whatsoever. Not only are the Japanese increasingly unable to buy American goods, they are increasingly unable to find them in the marketplace whatsoever because their industry is so protected.

Finally, though, and perhaps most importantly, is the fact that comparing the American dollar to the Japanese yen is something like comparing a sumo wrestler to Wayne Gretzky. The high value of the American dollar in comparison to that yen holds an impact on the trade deficit because a large dollar value means that in Japan the same amount of yen buy a smaller amount of value in American goods. Now, at the same time in the United States, the same amount of dollar expenditure brings in a larger amount of yen value. Now, for this reason

American goods look deceptively expensive overseas, and foreign goods look extremely attractive here. Now, that means that the United States cannot market its goods overseas as effectively as can Japanese firms market their goods here. Data Resources, Incorporated of Lexington, Massachusetts estimates that the dollar's impact on the trade deficit has been the cause of some two-thirds of the total imbalance.

Increasingly, it is becoming apparent that the United States is unable to compete on a worldwide basis with the Japanese in terms of marketing our goods and in terms of inviting the United States' participation abroad. In balancing the inflow and outflow of American products, it is vital that we examine what impact that would have upon the economies of both the United States and the world, and that is why it is now important to turn our attention to the second area of analysis and examine what ramifications this would hold.

Now, initially, of course, the fact that the United States does not market its own goods in the United States as effectively as do the Japanese means that the United States would benefit in terms of its domestic economy from reducing this trade imbalance. Irwin Teller, an economist with Manufacturers' Hanover Trust in New York, estimates that since 1980, growth has been held from one-third lower than it should be, and some two million jobs have been lost because of cheap import competition. Obviously, if we can bring our trade balance with Japan specifically into line, it would be a major step by the United States toward improving the performance of its own economy and removing the competition that our industry now faces.

At the same time, however, the importance for the United States is magnified when we examine the worldwide impact of reaching an agreement of Japan over the balance of trade. According to Arthur Dunkel, the director of the General Agreement on Tariffs and Trade Organization, if we can reduce our trade imbalance, this would reduce the fervor of the talk of protectionism in this country. This is important to the world for a number of reasons, the most important of which being, as Dunkel explains, the enactment of protectionist legislation in the United States would bring about a concommitant retaliation by other nations. As a matter of fact, the reaction of Japan's Prime Minister Yasuhiro Nakasone points to this very effect. Even though Nakasone lobbies fervently for the purchase of American goods in Japan, he has still stated publicly that if the United States enacts any more protectionist legislation, he will only increase the protection of his domestic markets.

Obviously, according to Dunkel, what the world does not need at this time is an increase in the number of barriers to free exercise of trade. The United States' economy simply cannot handle any more barriers, and neither can the rest of the world. For this reason, it is overwhelmingly clear that the United States has an obligation to itself and to the other nations to reduce the imbalance of trade from which it now suffers. Of course, reducing our imbalance of trade with Japan is only part of the problem. The *New York Times* reported in May that we still experience some $123.3 billion of trade shortfall with the other nations of the world. But it is clear that taking a step toward reducing the shortfall with Japan would help to bring the inflow and outflow of American goods more into line. We cannot allow our goods to trickle forth at such a small pace, for this allows the outflow of American goods to become the slow trickle of our economic life blood.

1985 Final Round Original Oratory

Andrew Thornton

Andrew Thornton of Churchill High School in San Antonio, Texas, won fourth place in the original oratory category of the 1985 National Forensic League Tournament.

A Better Looking Dog

American playwright David Rabe suggests in his play *Hurly Burly* that at some point in the 1950s the United States must have jackknifed because most of the nuts rolled to California. The rest ended up in Washington, D.C. Well, last summer while I was walking down Washington's Wisconsin Avenue, I met living proof of at least part of his theory. A young man dressed in blue boots, green satin pants, and a satin shirt studded with rhinestones walked up to me and asked, "Do you like yourself?" Then he handed me a leaflet. Well, I was so busy looking at his blue-tipped mohawk and his silver earring and necklace that I didn't pay much attention to his question. Since then, though, as I have shared the experience with others, I've begun to think about the question, "Do you like yourself?" Do you, no, I mean, do you really like yourself? When you look into a mirror, are you really satisfied with the reflection? When you're home by yourself, do you enjoy the company?

According to a study by Dr. J. L. Byer, Columbia University, most of us don't like ourselves. Oh, we don't necessarily hate ourselves, though some of us even do that. But he estimates that over 80 percent of us are dissatisfied with the person we carry inside our bodies. Maybe we're too fat or too thin. Perhaps we're not as intelligent as we would like to be or we lack talent in some area. There are hundreds of traits to criticize, and most of us find more than enough to keep us occupied, and that's good. Being dissatisfied with ourselves makes us work to be better. To an extent, yes. But as James Reed points out in his article, "The Misery Factor," much of the time we dwell on our shortcomings, allowing them to stifle our potential. Somehow we learn to thrive on anxiety, paranoia, and self-criticism. We tend to become infatuated, not with the good in ourselves but with the bad. The result is usually a self-imposed depression as we view ourselves as second rate. Psychologist A. M. Greeley conducted a study involving employees and executives at three major corporations, students and faculty at four universities, and enlisted men and officers at two military installations. Only 18 percent said that they were truly happy with themselves. Why is that? Greeley argues one reason is that it's fashionable. People mistake self-criticism for humility.

Another reason, though, is what he calls "the merchandising of perfection." In other words, society bombards us with images of "the perfect person." The beautiful face, the perfect body, the perfect specimen. Well, it's always the gorgeous girl who drinks diet Coke in our advertisements. The magnificent hunk who gets the girl because he uses Close-Up. The homely housewife always ends up with "the Tidy Bowl man." I mean, have you ever seen a cover girl with bags under her eyes and buck teeth? True, the advertisements don't tell the whole story, but the message is clear: It's important to be one of the beautiful people. If we're not, we feel relegated to the bottom rung on the social ladder.

The third reason has to do with ability assessment. No longer is it better off just to do something. The current attitude is that if we don't do it better than everyone around us, we're not worth very much. We can't just participate. We have to excel. We have to win. To be adequate is to be inferior, and since there's no place for an average person in a competitive society, we often judge ourselves unworthy. All right, so maybe I don't have as much muscle tone as the guys who show off at the beach, but that doesn't mean I should sit at home staring at ads about "how Max became a man" to depress myself. Maybe Max can't play the piano. I can. You know, many people can't stand up in front of a group and give a speech. You can. In fact, everyone in this room has special abilities that are unique. But instead of building on them towards self-fulfillment, we allow our shortcomings to push us towards self-rejection. We become the person who says, "Yeah, so I've been walking under blue skies. They're probably full of invisible toxic pollution. And even if people do like me, they shouldn't. I'm just a useless blob of protoplasm." The martyr complex comes very easily. It's our way of punishing ourselves because we don't like who we are. But as Eric Fromm states in *The Art of Loving*, we must love ourselves to be happy. Now that doesn't mean we shouldn't want to improve ourselves or that we can't be disappointed when we fail to meet our own expectations.

What it means is that we have to accept ourselves. As we are, for what we are. Imperfect . . . yes, different . . . certainly. But nonetheless, valuable.

So, how do we arrive at self-acceptance? Phase one was acknowledgment of self-worth. In his civil war epic, *John Brown's Body*, Steven Vincent Benét creates a living portrait of Abraham Lincoln—certainly not one of the beautiful people. Had he lived today, he probably couldn't win the Republican primary, much less the presidency. He had the wrong image. In the poem, though, Benét states that "honest Abe" would have been happy anyway. At one point, Lincoln says, "It's up to me to whittle what I can with what I've got. I'm ready to admit you can make the better looking dog out of the same raw material, but what I am, I am. So this will just have to do." Historical accounts echo that same self-acceptance. Lincoln believed in what he had to offer. You and I need that same kind of belief. We have to look beyond our exterior flaws and take hold of what we are at the very core. Everyone of us can be a good person. Kind, compassionate, and empathetic. These are the qualities of the heart, from which true self-worth stems. Oh, I wouldn't mind being taller, smarter, more athletic. It might even be fun to radiate a little appeal. But I've got to whittle what I can with what I've got. And I've got something worth having.

Once I accept that, then the second phase is to let go of undeserved self-criticisms. In other words, I can't play the self-pity game. If there's something about me that I want to change, and can change, then it's up to me to do something about it. But what I won't change, or can't change, can't be pitied away. Psychologist Sidney Jourard shares the story of Amy. At age 18 she was 5'5" and weighed 168 pounds. She tried the "Scarsdale diet," the "banana diet," every other diet she could find, and over a 7-year period, lost 391 pounds. Over that same time period she gained 394 pounds. So, at age 25, she was 5'5" and weighed 171 pounds. She hated herself and continually punished herself because she was fat. Finally, with the help of her doctor she said, "I admitted the fact that I'd never look good in a bikini." At that point she quit dwelling on her physical self and began concentrating on other parts of her life—specifically, working with handicapped children. As she began emphasizing something she could do, and do well, she quit dwelling on her misery and began to believe in herself as a person. You and I could find that same contentment in our value as human beings. And once we do, and we can, we won't have to feel inferior because we are imperfect. Our value will be based on internal qualities rather than external show.

Then the final phase is to cushion ourselves against what T.S. Eliot once called "the acid cruelty of the world"—the unkindness of others. For as long as we live, there will always be those who tell us where we fall short. Oh, I admit, some of the criticism may be given in good faith. Much of it, however, is due to the pecking order of society. Others want to escape their insecurities by pointing out how they're better than someone else. We are all victims of such attacks. Therefore, it's important to remember that the problem is with the critic, not with us. "Man, you're stupid!" "What a loser!" We're all vulnerable to these remarks every minute of the day, and if we let them pile up and get to us, they shake our confidence. In *The Dignity of Self*, Gerald Sykes says that the best approach is to forgive the unjust judgments, however hard that may be, because they play on our emotions and not on our true sense of well-being. Then we must reaffirm our acceptance, remembering that our difficulties and our limitations are all part of our humanity.

Much of the time it's not easy to accept ourselves because in our minds we want to measure up to some kind of ideal image. Everyone wants to be liked. Most of us want to be admired. Unfortunately, we usually think we have to be something other than what we are to achieve that status. But the only thing that makes us truly worthy is being ourselves the best way that we can. Last summer when that guy walked up to me in his weird outfit, I made a quick judgment. Oh, I didn't say anything. But I thought it, never realizing maybe he was happy with himself. That's the only judgment that really mattered. In the same way, what you and I think of ourselves is what matters most in our own lives. Your value as a human being is based on what you do. So do what you can with what you have. Maybe someone could make a better looking dog out of the same raw material, but no one can make you better or more worthy than you can make yourself.

accent ('ak-ˌsent) Speech habits typical of a particular group of people in a city, state, or region.

affirmative (ə-'fər-mət-iv) The side of the debate that argues for the change advocated in the proposition; presents arguments and evidence to support the proposition.

after/because fallacy Assuming that if something happened *after* something else, it happened *because* of that something else.

agenda (ə-'jen-də) A list or outline of things to be done during a meeting.

amendment The process of changing the wording or the intent of a motion.

analogy (ə-'nal-ə-jē) An extended comparison based on the resemblance in some ways between two things ordinarily considered unlike.

analytical expository speech A speech in which one analyzes a speech, poem, novel, advertisements, song, short story, etc., helping the audience to understand its meaning and appreciate its value.

anecdote ('an-ik-ˌdōt) A brief story; often used by speakers to illustrate a point or to sway listeners.

angle The viewpoint from which the subject is videotaped or filmed, usually from above or below a subject.

appeal to emotion The method of persuasion based on appeals to three basic needs: physical needs, psychological needs, and social needs; an appeal to feeling as opposed to logic.

argument The statement of an objective reason that directly supports the position of either the affirmative side or the negative side of a debate.

articulation (är-ˌtik-yə-'lā-shən) The manner of forming sounds; good articulation is characterized by crisp, clear consonants and distinct vowels so that every sound is easy to understand.

associate director The person who times the program, directs background action, lays out floor plans for rehearsals, makes sure all have scripts, presets camera shots, and gives cues to the director.

atmosphere ('at-mə-ˌsfir) The overall emotional effect or appeal of a work of art or literature.

audience The person or group of listeners to whom one's speech, voice, gestures, and movements should be geared.

bandwagon A movement, faction, or cause that propagandists urge audiences to support or "jump on" simply because everyone else is.

begging the question Stating a position that needs to be proved as though it had already been proved.

bias ('bī-əs) A prejudice either for or against certain people, institutions, or ideas.

the "big lie" An outright, often outrageous, falsehood repeated loudly and frequently in order to slander an opponent, cause, race, religion, or party.

bodily movement Actions that help clarify a speaker's meaning as well as provide emphasis and feedback.

body The part of a speech in which the main ideas are supported and developed with illustrations, statistics, etc.

body of knowledge The information, experiences, and understandings of a group of people; the extent to which speaker and listener share a common body of knowledge determines the nature of the communication process.

brief A complete debate outline of all the necessary definitions, arguments, and evidence on both sides of a proposition.

camera operator The person who operates the camera.

camera shot sheet The detailed instructions for a camera operator to follow during a taping.

captioned   Furnished with printed subtitles that can be seen by viewers.

chairperson   The person in charge of conducting a meeting.

character   A person, or a thing with human characteristics, faced with a problem and trying to resolve it.

characterization   The creative process whereby the actor grasps the fundamental personality of the role he or she is portraying and communicates it to the audience.

chronological pattern   (ˌkrän-əl-ˈäj-i-kəl ˈpat-ərn)   A pattern of organization arranged according to the order of time, sequence of events.

cliché   (klē-ˈshā)   A trite phrase or expression; overly familiar or commonplace.

close captioned   Furnished with printed subtitles that must be decoded by special machines.

close-up   A very close camera shot that includes one individual, usually from the shoulders up.

coloration   (ˌkəl-ə-ˈrā-shən)   The individual quality of a person's voice that distinguishes it from any other person's voice; determined by the shape of one's nasal cavity and pharynx.

conclusion   The last part of a speech in which the main ideas are summarized and/or reemphasized.

connotation   (ˌkän-ə-ˈtā-shən)   The implied or suggested meaning of a word; the emotional message a word suggests because of its favorable or unfavorable associations.

consensus   (kən-ˈsen-səs)   General agreement; group solidarity in sentiment and belief.

consonant   (ˈkän-sə-nənt)   A kind of speech sound produced by touching, or nearly touching, one's tongue and other parts of the mouth together.

constructive speech   The first speech given by each debater; presents the arguments in support of the proposition.

credible   (ˈkred-ə-bəl)   Believable; capable of being trusted as a speaker.

criteria   (krī-ˈtir-ē-ə)   Standards by which something is judged.

cross-examination   In debate, the questioning of the opposing side after each constructive speech.

cut   To make an abrupt change from one scene to another.

debate   A competition between persuasive speakers.

deduction   (di-ˈdək-shən)   A process of reasoning whereby one derives a specific conclusion based upon a universal premise or a general rule; conclusion arrived at by deduction.

definition   The action or process of explaining, describing a concept.

denotation   (ˌdē-nō-ˈtā-shən)   The dictionary definition of a word; the literal meaning of a word.

dialect   (ˈdī-ə-ˌlekt)   A regional variety of language distinguished by differing distinctively from the standard in vocabulary, grammar, and pronunciation.

diaphragm   (ˈdī-ə-fram)   A powerful curved muscle separating the chest and the abdominal cavity; control of it is instrumental for good breath control.

diphthong   (ˈdip-ˌthöŋ, ˈdif-)   A gliding monosyllabic speech sound combining two vowels.

director   The person who interprets and adjusts the script as well as provides instructions to all technical and talent members of a team to carry out the script.

dissolve   A gradual transition between scenes by fading out one picture and fading in its replacement.

distortion   A propaganda tactic involving the misuse of facts or figures to belittle opponents or to support an argument.

docudrama   A fictional drama based on real events.

documentary   A program whose main purpose is to inform the audience about a historic event or a current issue.

dolly   To move the entire camera on a platform in order to follow action or achieve a change in perspective; the wheeled platform for a television or film camera.

edit   To put together on one tape the desired production footage and any special effects in final program form.

establishing shot   A shot used to orient the viewer to the surroundings; also known as a *cover shot.*

evidence   Facts, statistics, expert testimony, etc. used to support a logical argument.

expository speech   (ik-'späz-ə-,tōr-ē 'spēch) A speech whose main purpose is to explain something or convey information.

expression   Facial aspect or vocal intonation that clarifies meaning, displays feelings, or provides emphasis.

extemporaneous   (ek-,stem-pə-'rā-nē-əs) Performed or spoken at the spur of the moment without notes or text, or with very few notes.

eye contact   Direct visual contact; looking at members of one's audience in their eyes to keep their attention and to get feedback.

fade   The gradual disappearance of a scene as it ends.

false analogy   ('föls ə-'nal-ə-jē)   A misleading figure of speech making a comparison and then reasoning from the comparison as though it were a fact.

feedback   ('fēd-,bak)   Response from listeners that lets the speaker know whether he or she has been understood.

figure of speech   A form of expression that makes ideas more vivid by comparing them to things people have seen, touched, or felt.

floor manager   The person who makes sure people and things are in proper places, prompts actors, maintains schedules, and arranges for facilities.

focus   The point of concentration in an improvisation; the specific aspect of the scene to which a character directs his or her attention.

gesture   ('jes-chər)   The use of hands, face, body, and voice to enhance one's speech.

glittering generalization   A conclusion based almost entirely on prejudice.

group discussion   A method of solving a problem or arriving at a decision whereby members of a group share ideas and build on each other's contributions; see *problem-solving process.*

hasty generalization   A conclusion based on too little evidence.

identification   Thinking of the speaker as a person much like oneself, as a person who can be trusted and believed; encouraging identification in the audience builds credibility and goodwill.

improvisation   Process of presenting physical actions, including speech, without practice or rehearsal.

incremental   (in-krə-'mənt-ᵊl)   An approach to decision making involving taking a small step toward a decision, seeing if that is successful, taking another small step, etc., until a decision is reached.

induction   (in-'dək-shən)   A process of reasoning whereby one arrives at a generalized conclusion on the basis of particular instances, specific examples; conclusion arrived at by induction.

infer   (in-'fər)   To derive a conclusion or generalization from facts or premises.

inference   ('in-f[ə]-rən[t]s)   A conclusion or generalization arrived at on the basis of facts or premises.

informal outline   An outline for speakers using not letters and numbers (as in a formal outline) but simply listing main topics and subtopics.

innuendo   (,in-yə-'wen-dō)   An attack on a person by implication or association; insinuation casting disapproval on another's character or reputation.

interference   Anything that interrupts or alters the message between a speaker and listener.

introduction   The beginning of a speech in which the speaker gets the audience's attention, states the topic and purpose of the speech, and sometimes previews the main ideas.

language The means by which people communicate ideas and feelings; a common language is an essential element of the communication process.

larynx ('lar-iŋ[k]s) Voice box or Adam's apple, located at the top of the trachea, containing the vocal cords.

lavaliere (ˌlav-ə-'li[ər]) A very small microphone that can be worn around the neck or clipped onto a piece of clothing; also called a *neck mike*.

Lincoln-Douglas debate A format for a debate featuring one-on-one exchanges between two speakers debating a proposition of value rather than of policy.

lip reading A method used by the hearing-impaired to communicate with others.

listener One to whom a speaker speaks; an essential element in the communication process.

loaded words Words charged with positive or negative associations or hidden implications; words producing an instantaneous, unthinking reaction in an audience; "buzz words."

logical argument An objective reason used to support one's position.

long shot A shot in which the figure or figures included are shown in relation to their surroundings; the figure may be shown from head to foot.

loudness The volume of a sound.

manual alphabet A method of communication used by the hearing-impaired; involves using the fingers to represent each letter of the alphabet.

manual communication Methods of communication used by the hearing-impaired to communicate with others; one is the manual alphabet and the other is sign language.

media diary A record of how much time radio listening and television viewing actually take out of each week.

media evaluation A record of what programs a person listens to or watches as well as how much he or she enjoyed them and whether or not he or she learned anything.

mediator ('mēd-ē-ˌāt-ər) A person who resolves a conflict between two parties, promoting settlement or compromise; one who encourages two sides to communicate their ideas, emotions, and interests toward a resolution.

medium shot A shot that includes a figure to the waist.

message What a speaker conveys to a listener; an essential element of the communication process.

metaphor ('met-ə-fȯ[ə]r) A figure of speech that makes a comparison by stating or implying one thing is another.

microphone An instrument by which sound is transmitted or recorded.

misleading statistics Statistics that sound factual but that are actually unreliable and do not prove what the debater wants them to.

mixer The person who balances and controls dialogue, music, sound effects, and video images to be added from different sources while maintaining even levels.

mood The predominant state of mind or emotion evoked by a piece of art or literature.

motions Formal suggestions or proposals made by members who have been recognized by the chairperson of a meeting.

name calling Attaching a label with negative connotations to a person; using offensive names to win an argument.

narrative A story or anecdote meant to inform and/or to entertain.

narrative speaking The art of telling a story.

nasal cavity The area through which air echoes before leaving the mouth.

negative The side of the debate that argues against the change advocated in the proposition; presents arguments and evidence to oppose the proposition.

nominating speech A speech in which one explains why a particular candidate is qualified for a particular office and attempts to make the audience feel enthusiastic about the candidate.

oral interpretation   The art of reading aloud a story, poem, or speech.

oversimplify   To simplify the issue to such an extent that distortion, misunderstanding, or error result.

over-the-shoulder shot   A shot that looks at one subject framed by the back of the head and shoulders of another subject in the foreground.

pan   To turn the camera in a horizontal plane while it is in one place in order to follow the subject or to change the view of the subject.

parliamentary   (ˌpär-lə-'ment-ə-rē) Of or pertaining to rules and procedures governing the proceedings of deliberative assemblies, meetings, or organizations.

personification   (per-ˌsän-ə-fə-'kā-shən) A type of metaphor in which an object is given the qualities of a human being.

persuasive speech   (pər-'swā-sive 'spēch) A speech that attempts to change the listeners' minds on a particular issue, to make them feel a certain way, or to make them take some action by appealing to logic, their emotions, and/or their identification with the speaker, or a combination of the three.

pharynx   ('far-iŋ[k]s) The part of the alimentary canal between the cavity of the mouth and the esophagus in which air echoes, giving one's voice a specific coloration.

physical needs   A set of basic needs upon which the emotional appeals of a persuasive speech are sometimes based; those that involve the life and health of an individual's body, such as the need for food and the need to avoid physical pain.

pitch   ('pich) Highness or lowness of sound determined by frequency of vocal waves; a means of creating variety and conveying emotion in oral communication.

point of view (POV)   The position from which a shot is taken.

position   The specific purpose of a persuasive speech; what you want your listener to think or do.

post hoc (ergo propter hoc)   (See *after/ because fallacy.*)

postproduction   The final step in television production in which the editing and mixing are done; the insertion of graphics, art, music, and pick-up shots also takes place here.

posture   ('päs-chər) The position or bearing of the body.

prejudice   ('prej-əd-əs) A preconceived judgment or opinion about a particular individual, group, or race, or their supposed characteristics.

premise   ('prem-əs) An assumption; proposition upon which an inference or a conclusion is based.

preproduction planning   The step in television production during which the script is broken down, the cast and crew hired, and the equipment and facilities secured.

problem   The specific task addressed in an improvisation through which the actors reveal *who* they are, *where* they are, and *what* they are doing.

problem-solving process   The process that a group discussion follows involving defining the problem, identifying the criteria by which possible solutions will be judged, identifying and defining all possible solutions, and then selecting the best possible solution.

process speech   Speech explaining how to do something.

producer   The person who provides direction to all members of a television or film team; person who supervises a television production.

production   The actual shooting of a television program.

production assistant   A person who does everything from making up cue cards to handling art work; takes care of details.

pronunciation   (prə-ˌnən[t]-sē-'ā-shən) The manner of producing speech sounds; good pronunciation is speaking so that every word is spoken correctly and in a manner the audience will easily understand.

propaganda (ˌpräp-ə-ˈgan-də) A one-sided argument attempting to win people over to a cause primarily through an appeal to emotions; uses distorted facts, loaded words, name calling, and faulty reasoning.

proposition (ˌpräp-ə-ˈzish-ən) The formal statement of the issue to be debated.

psychological needs A set of basic needs upon which the emotional appeals of a persuasive speech are sometimes based; those that involve an individual's inner life, such as the need for love and the need for self-respect.

radio drama A kind of oral interpretation of a story, poem, or play using voice, music, and sound effects prepared for dramatic presentation over the radio.

rate Number of syllables one speaks per minute; a means of creating variety and conveying emotion in oral communication.

rational (ˈrash-ən-ᵊl) An approach to decision making involving analyzing all facts and problems logically, based on the premises and inferences that can be made from them.

reasoning backward Assuming that because members of a particular group have a characteristic in common, anyone with that characteristic must belong to the group.

rebuttal speech (ri-ˈbət-ᵊl ˈspēch) A speech, half as long as the constructive speech, in which refutation is the primary activity.

refutation (ˌref-yu̇-ˈtā-shən) An effort by speakers to answer or disprove arguments presented by the other side in a debate.

rehearsal The step of television production during which the cast and crew plan and rehearse movement and the physical placement of talent, cameras, and production equipment.

resonate (ˈrez-ᵊn-āt) To echo; to produce resonance by vibration in the nasal cavity and pharynx.

reverse angle A shot that represents a 180-degree change in camera view from the shot just before it.

Robert's Rules of Order The most commonly accepted authority on parliamentary procedure.

role playing Acting out situations or problems to understand them better.

scanning (ˈskan-iŋ) An approach to decision making involving identifying all possible solutions point by point, rejecting the unworkable ones, and then testing other possible ones in the same way.

sensory images Words and phrases appealing to one or more of the five senses—sight, hearing, touch, taste, and smell—rendering description more vivid.

setting The background or environment in which speech communication takes place; an essential element in the communication process in that it affects the nature of the communication.

sign language A method of communication used by the hearing-impaired; involves using gestures of the hands and arms to represent words and ideas.

signposts (ˈsīn-ˌpōsts) Words or phrases the speaker uses to tell the audience what part of the speech they are hearing or to emphasize important ideas.

simile (ˈsim-ə-lē) A figure of speech comparing two unlike things by the use of *like* or *as*.

slander (ˈslan-dər) To utter false charges or misrepresentations against a person; to defame; malign.

social needs A set of basic needs upon which the emotional appeals of a persuasive speech are sometimes based; those that involve an individual's relation to a group, such as the need for freedom and the need for acceptance.

spatial pattern (ˈspā-shəl ˈpat-ərn) The pattern of organization in terms of spatial arrangement.

speaker One who communicates a message; an essential element of the communication process.

speech communication process   The sending and receiving of oral messages in order to share meaning.

stereotype   ('ster-ē-ə-ˌtīp)   An oversimplified opinion, attitude, or judgment; a preconceived, standardized mental picture.

suppression   (sə-'presh-ən)   A withholding of facts in an argument or debate in order to mislead or falsify.

switcher   A piece of equipment that allows scenes from more than one camera to be included on a tape without blank spaces showing on the tape; the person, usually the technical director, or TD, who operates the video switches.

symbol   ('sim-bəl)   Something that stands for or suggests something else.

talent   Any person who appears in front of the camera.

testimonial   (ˌtes-tə-'mō-nē-əl)   An endorsement of a person, cause, argument, or campaign by a celebrity.

tilt   To move the camera up and down on a vertical plane while it is kept in one place.

topical pattern   A pattern of organization arranged according to subdivisions of the subject.

trachea   ('trā-kē-ə)   Windpipe; passage through which air passes to and from the lungs.

transference   (tran[t]s-'fər-ən[t]s)   A propaganda tactic involving the redirection of positive associations (feeling and responses) from one person, cause, or source toward another person, cause, or source that does not deserve them.

transitions   (tranz-'ish-əns)   Words or phrases that connect ideas in a sentence or paragraph with ideas in the next sentence or paragraph.

trial-and-error   An approach to decision making involving trying a likely solution to a problem and, if it doesn't work, trying alternative solutions until a solution is reached.

variety   Variation in pitch and rate that makes speech more attractive and interesting.

VCR   Videocassette recorder; machine used to record television programs from a receiver; can also play back programs, movies, etc.

visual aids   Supplemental devices, such as models, maps, charts, graphs, etc., appealing to the sight and used for illustration, demonstration, or clarification.

vocal cords   The pair of muscular folds across the center of the larynx which tighten and vibrate as air flows past them to produce sound.

volume   Loudness of sound; means of conveying emotion in oral communication.

vowel   ('vaü[ə]l)   A kind of speech sound produced by simply changing the shape of one's mouth.

VTR   Video tape recorder; a recording machine that records video, audio, and control signals on videotape.

wide angle   A shot that includes a broad horizontal view.

wipe   To move one scene in as another scene moves out without overlapping.

zoom   To use a special lens to enlarge a subject, making it appear closer without moving the camera.

Index

Acknowledgments

Broomheads & Neals: From *The "Mary Celeste"* by L. du Garde Peach. From *Radio Plays*. Used by permission of Reed International and Broomheads & Neals.

Curtis Brown, Ltd.: "Don't Cry, Darling, It's Blood All Right" from *Verses from 1929 On* by Ogden Nash. Reprinted by permission of Curtis Brown, Ltd. Copyright ©1934 by Saturday Evening Post/Copyright © renewed 1962 by Ogden Nash.

Chelsea House Publishers: From *Winston S. Churchill: His Complete Speeches 1897–1963*, Edited by Robert Rhodes James. Copyright ©1974 by Chelsea House Publishers (A Division of Chelsea House Educational Communications, Inc.). Used by permission.

City News Publishing Co., Inc.: From "The Absurdity of Eternal Peace," by Benito Mussolini. From *Vital Speeches of the Day*. Used by permission of City News Publishing Co., Inc.

Congressional Record: From "The Greatness of Lincoln" by Richard S. Emrich. Congressional Record 105:A, February 2, 1959.

Joan Daves: Reprinted by permission of Joan Daves. Copyright ©1963 by Martin Luther King, Jr. Excerpted from "I Have a Dream" by Martin Luther King, Jr.

Executors of L. du Garde Peach Royalties Trust: From *The "Mary Celeste"* by L. du Garde Peach. From *Radio Plays*. Used by permission of IPC Magazines and the Executors of L. du Garde Peach Royalties Trust.

Harcourt Brace Jovanovich, Inc.: "Four Preludes on Playthings of the Wind" by Carl Sandburg. From *Smoke and Steel* by Carl Sandburg, copyright 1920 by Harcourt Brace Jovanovich, Inc.; renewed 1948 by Carl Sandburg. Reprinted by permission of the publisher.

Harper & Row, Publishers, Inc.: From "A Glory Has Departed" by Jawaharlal Nehru, 1948. Reprinted from *Great Speeches*, William D. Boutwell, Wesley P. Callender Jr., and Robert E. Graber, editors, Scholastic Book Services, 1965. Reprinted by Permission of Harper & Row, Publishers, Inc.

Harper & Row, Publishers, Inc.: "My Grandmother Would Rock Quietly and Hum" (excluding one stanza), by Leonard Adamé in *From the Barrio: A Chicano Anthology* by Luis Omar Salinas and Lillian Faderman. Copyright ©1973 by Luis Omar Salinas and Lillian Faderman. Reprinted by permission of Harper & Row, Publishers, Inc.

Olwyn Hughes Literary Agency: For "Mushrooms." From *The Colossus and Other Poems* by Sylvia Plath. Published by Faber & Faber, London. ©1967 by Ted Hughes. Used by permission of Olwyn Hughes Literary Agency.

Jefferson Communications, Inc.: From *Shoe*. Reprinted by permission of Jefferson Communications, Inc., Reston, Virginia.